A Handbook for Stud
in Higher Education

Drawing on scholarship as well as established practice, *A Handbook for Student Engagement in Higher Education* is a sector-leading volume that unpacks the concept of student engagement. It provides ideas and examples alongside compelling theory- and research-based evidence to offer a thorough and innovative exploration of how students and staff can work together to genuinely transform the higher education learning experience.

Providing readers with evidence from successfully embedded schemes, the book uses case studies and practical, workable examples from a variety of international institutions. With the insight of world-leading contributors, it showcases what good practice looks like in higher education institutions across the globe. Simultaneously collating a wealth of contemporary research, this book creates vivid connections between theories and student engagement in higher education, with chapter topics including:

- Creating relationships between students, staff and universities
- Offering non-traditional students extracurricular opportunities
- Taking a students-as-partners approach
- Critically reflecting on identities, particularities and relationships
- The future of student engagement

In a fast-developing and significantly shifting area, this book is essential reading for higher education managers and those working directly in the field of student engagement.

Tom Lowe is the Centre for Student Engagement Manager at the University of Winchester, UK.

Yassein El Hakim is Co-Founder and CEO at VerifyEd, UK.

The Staff and Educational Development Series

Series Editor: James Wisdom

Written by experienced and well-known practitioners and published in association with the Staff and Educational Development Association (SEDA), each book in the series contributes to the development of learning, teaching and training and assists in the professional development of staff. The books present new ideas for learning development and facilitate the exchange of information and good practice.

Titles in the series:

For more information about this series, please visit:
www.routledge.com/SEDA-Series/book-series/SE0747

A Handbook for Student Engagement in Higher Education

Theory into Practice

Edited by Tom Lowe and Yassein El Hakim

Routledge
Taylor & Francis Group

LONDON AND NEW YORK

First published 2020
by Routledge
2 Park Square, Milton Park, Abingdon, Oxon OX14 4RN

and by Routledge
52 Vanderbilt Avenue, New York, NY 10017

Routledge is an imprint of the Taylor and Francis Group, an informa business

British Library Cataloguing-in-Publication Data
A catalogue record for this book is available from the British Library

Library of Congress Cataloging-in-Publication Data
A catalog record has been requested for this book

ISBN: 978-0-367-08543-8 (hbk)
ISBN: 978-0-367-08549-0 (pbk)
ISBN: 978-0-429-02303-3 (ebk)

Typeset in Galliard
by Newgen Publishing UK

With thanks from Tom to his inspirational wife Cassie for her support and guidance throughout the creation of this edited collection.

With thanks from Yaz to his amazing wife Hazel and three constantly curious kids, Imogen, Leonardo and Florence.

Contents

Figures

Tables

Abbreviations

BAME	Black Asian and Minority Ethnic
CAN	Change Agent Network
FE	Further Education
HE	Higher Education
HEA	UK Higher Education Academy
HEFCE	Higher Education Funding Council for England
HEI	Higher Education Institution
ISaPI	International Students as Partners Institute
NSS	National Student Survey (UK)
NUS	National Union of Students (UK)
OfS	UK Office for Students
PASS	Peer Assisted Study Sessions [or] Peer-Assisted Student Success
QAA	UK Quality Assurance Agency for Higher Education
RAISE	Researching, Advancing and Inspiring Student Engagement
SA	Student Ambassador
SaLT	Student as Learners and Teachers
SaP	Students as Partners
SE	Student Engagement
SoTL	Scholarship of Teaching and Learning
SSLCs	Staff–student Liaison Committees
TEL	Technology Enhanced Learning
VLE	Virtual Learning Environment
WIL	Work-Integrated Learning

Contributors

James Anderson is a Professor of Mathematics and the Associate Dean (Education) for the Faculty of Social Sciences at the University of Southampton (UK).

Liz Austen is a Senior Lecturer in Research, Evaluation and Student Engagement at Sheffield Hallam University (UK). Her role includes externally funded research within higher education and institutional research and evaluation which is focused on improving student outcomes.

Christine Black has a Masters in Speech Language Pathology from McMaster University (Canada) and is a graduate of McMaster's Arts and Science Program. She was a student scholar at the MacPherson Institute from 2015 to 2018.

Douglas Blackstock is Chief Executive of the Quality Assurance Agency for Higher Education (QAA), leading QAA's contribution to the policy, regulatory and quality landscape across the UK. He has championed student engagement in quality assurance throughout his career.

Alex Bols is Deputy Chief Executive, GuildHE, and is currently completing his doctorate in Education at UCL's Institute of Education (UK) exploring perceptions of the effectiveness of student representation. He has previously worked at NUS, Universities UK and the European Students' Union.

Catherine Bovill is Senior Lecturer in Student Engagement at the Institute for Academic Development, University of Edinburgh, Visiting Fellow at the University of Winchester, Fulbright Scholar (2019–20) and PFHEA. She publishes and presents internationally on co-created curriculum.

Colin Bryson is Director of the Combined Honours Centre at Newcastle University (UK). He co-founded RAISE and was awarded a National Teaching Fellowship in 2009. He has published widely on student engagement and working with students as partners.

Jac Cattaneo is a lecturer in Creative and Contextual Studies at the Brighton Film School and a Senior Fellow of the Higher Education Academy (both in the UK). Jac's research explores the intersection of the visual and verbal in education and scholarship.

Alison Cook-Sather is Mary Katharine Woodworth Professor of Education at Bryn Mawr College and Director of the Teaching and Learning Institute at Bryn Mawr and Haverford Colleges in Pennsylvania (USA). She has published widely on student–faculty pedagogical partnership.

Gary Donaldson is a masters student at Edinburgh Napier University where he leads the student-led ESTABLISH programme alongside his studies in marketing. Gary is also a Student Committee Member for Researching Advancing and Inspiring Student Engagement.

Yassein El Hakim has worked internationally across higher education in the UK as a consultant, speaker and author. Leading in the areas of Assessment and Feedback, Student Engagement and Educational Technology, he held the positions of Director Learning and Teaching and Student Engagement at the University of Winchester and Co-Chair of SEDA (UK). He is Co-Founder and CEO at VerifyEd.

Peter Felten is executive director of the Center for Engaged Learning, assistant provost for teaching and learning, and professor of history at Elon University (USA). His books include *The Undergraduate Experience* (2016) and *Engaging Students as Partners in Learning and Teaching* (2014).

Adam Fletcher is a consultant, writer and speaker based in the United States and focused on engaging people throughout society. He is president of the Freechild Institute for Youth Engagement and founding director of SoundOut, an international programme focused on advocating and sustaining student engagement.

Rebecca Freeman is Dean of Students at the University of Warwick (UK) where she is also Director of Student Experience in the School of Life Sciences. She provides strategic leadership for the provision of academic pastoral support for students and development of student engagement.

Allan Goody has been an academic for more than 36 years, working primarily in Australia as an academic developer focusing on the preparation of academics to teach in higher education. He is the President of the International Consortium for Educational Development.

Rachel Guitman is a recent graduate of McMaster University's Arts and Science Program (Canada). Throughout her undergraduate career, she was a student scholar at the MacPherson Institute, where she was involved in various projects focused on student–faculty partnership.

Fiona Harvey is the Director of Student Community for the University College of Estate Management (UK). She is a member of the board of trustees for The e-Assessment Association and undertaking her PhD in E-Research and Technology Enhanced Learning with Lancaster University.

Mick Healey is a Higher Education Consultant and an Emeritus Professor at the University of Gloucestershire (UK). He is the inaugural senior editor for the International Journal for Students as Partners and the Co-Leader of the International Students as Partners Institute.

Camille Kandiko Howson is Associate Professor of Education in the Centre for Higher Education Research and Scholarship at Imperial College London (UK) where she focuses on student engagement, learning gain, diversity and inclusion, and prestige and academic work.

Clare Killen works for Jisc (UK) as part of the student experience, building digital capability and digital experience insights teams. She has supported Jisc's work on student–staff partnerships for many years and is actively involved in Jisc's change agents' network.

Sarah Knight is Head of Change: Student Experience at Jisc (UK) and manages the digital experience insights service, researching staff and students' expectations and experiences of technology and the building digital capability service to support the development of staff and student digital capabilities.

Jenny Lawrence is the Head of the Teaching Excellence Academy at the University of Hull (UK). She has driven inclusion/student-partnership focused initiatives in HEIs across the UK. Her research interests include staff/student wellbeing, academic and programme leadership

John Lea is the Research Director for the Scholarship Project, a UK-wide project aimed at enhancing higher education in colleges. He has written widely on this subject, including co-authored publications commissioned by the Higher Education Academy and the Quality Assurance Agency (UK).

Rhonda Lobb is currently the REF Impact Officer at Lancaster University (UK) where she is supporting academics with REF Impact Cases. Prior to this, Rhonda worked in FE for over twenty years as a Lecturer in Business and Teacher Education.

Cassie Lowe is the Learning and Teaching Enhancement Officer at the University of Winchester (UK), where she researches and leads on a range of projects. Alongside this, she is also an hourly paid lecturer in English Literature and is completing a PhD in literature and psychoanalysis.

Tom Lowe is the Centre for Student Engagement Manager at the University of Winchester (UK) where he is the Programme Leader for the postgraduate courses in Student Engagement in Higher Education and oversees strategic projects relating to engagement, belonging and employability.

Wilko Luebsen currently administers the PASS Scheme and evaluates the Upward Bound programme at London Metropolitan University (UK). Previously, he has been involved in the REACT project as a researcher and development consultant to promote student engagement across the HE sector.

Jenny Marie is Head of Quality Enhancement at the University of Greenwich (UK). She previously led University College London's flagship student engagement scheme, UCL ChangeMakers (2015–2018). She has facilitated for the International Students as Partners Institute and consulted on partnership schemes internationally.

Elizabeth Marquis is an Assistant Professor in the Arts and Science Program and School of the Arts at McMaster University (Canada). She was formerly Associate Director (Research) at the MacPherson Institute, where she co-developed and oversaw McMaster's Student Partners Program.

Madeleine Pownall is a PhD student and Postgraduate Teaching Assistant in Social Psychology at the University of Leeds (UK), having recently graduated from the University of Lincoln (UK). Madeleine is a student member of the Researching, Advancing, and Inspiring Student Engagement (RAISE) committee.

Susan Rowland is Deputy Associate Dean Academic (Future Students and Employability) in the Faculty of Science at the University of Queensland (Australia). She leads and manages the student experience, leadership, and mentoring programme that serves the almost 9,000 students enrolled through the Faculty.

Stuart Sims is a Senior Lecturer in Higher Education at the University of Portsmouth (UK). He leads on embedding curriculum co-design approaches cross-institutionally and teaches on Portsmouth's Academic Professional Apprenticeship. At the time of writing, Stuart was a Senior Educational Developer at the University of Winchester (UK).

Kiu Sum is a PhD nutrition student at the University of Westminster (UK) and also a Registered Associate Nutritionist with the Association for Nutrition. In addition to her academic study, she has an interest in educational pedagogy and collaborates with others on student engagement projects in Higher Education.

Digby Warren is Professor and the Head of the Centre for the Enhancement of Learning and Teaching at London Metropolitan University (UK). His chief area of expertise is curriculum development and associated teaching, learning and assessment processes, alongside co-founding the London Metropolitan PASS Scheme.

Cherie Woolmer is a Postdoctoral Fellow at the MacPherson Institute at McMaster University (Canada) and Editorial Manager of the *International Journal for Students as Partners*. She supports McMaster's Student Partners Program and conducts research with students on pedagogical partnerships.

Foreword

Student engagement is hard work, but quality takes time

Douglas Blackstock, Chief Executive,
Quality Assurance Agency for Higher Education (QAA) (UK)

This book marks an important point in understanding how far student engagement policy and practice, and the research into its purpose, benefits and impact,
have come in the last three decades. As asked by the editors, I reflect on this in
a sketch of my own journey, offering an indication of the trajectory of student
engagement in the culture of higher education in the UK in particular.

My first attempts to engage students in the quality of their learning and
teaching started in 1984 when, having got involved in the Students' Association
at Glasgow College of Technology (now Caledonian University, UK), I was
tasked with recruiting course representatives. It was not easy, especially reaching
part-time, postgraduate and mature students. It also became apparent I would
have to go through the same process from scratch the following year, the one
after and the one after that.

Our reps also came back with familiar stories: not taken seriously, the challenge
of participating in meetings with academic staff, and assertions that they weren't
truly representative of all students.

I later became President and a member of both the Governing Body and the
Academic Board. I felt ill-equipped to participate in either. There was no support
available, including for the Vice President who led on preparing our student
submission to an external review by the Council for National Academic Awards.

Roll forward into the 1990s and the need to better support student
representatives was becoming more evident. There had been big growth in student numbers, with lots of issues arising from rapid growth and greater complexity within institutions. Complicating matters, new (and competing) forms of
external scrutiny were beginning to be applied to universities.

As manager at the Students' Union at Greenwich (1992–96), I helped prepare
students for an audit by the Higher Education Quality Council (HEQC, UK).
As a sign of progress to come, when the HEQC *Guidelines on Quality Assurance*
were updated in 1996, they included a section on Student Communication and
Representation for the first time.

When interviewed at the Quality Assurance Agency for Higher Education
(QAA, UK) in 2001, I was clear that my priority would be to support students.
What I didn't realise until after I arrived was that in the noble cause of making

peace, a cap was put on the number of sections to be included in the new QAA Code of Practice. Two of the sections to be sacrificed were student representation and international students.

That didn't deter us and, in developing Institutional Audit in 2002, we reintroduced the Student Written Submission. It ushered in a new era in the student focus of QAA. We provided support for Students' Unions, and, working in partnership with the National Union of Students, Universities UK and (GuildHE predecessor) the Standing Conference of Principals, developed regular events for students. Their branding, *Quality Takes Time,* is as true now as it was back then.

But it was our team in QAA Scotland who were able to go much further and, in partnership with the sector, included students on review teams and established a national support initiative, SPARQS (Student Partnerships in Quality Scotland). It operates to this day and is widely seen as a beacon for good practice across Europe and beyond.

The success of QAA Scotland prompted heated debate within QAA. A clear determination followed from our Board that we needed to apply Scotland's practice across the UK. Given my background and commitment to the change, I was asked to develop a new student engagement strategy for QAA. I also had the task of persuading the sector, including funding bodies, that students should play their full part in reviews

I recruited Derfel Owen, now Director of Academic Services at University College London, to help put this into action. It wasn't easy. Not all in the sector – or QAA for that matter – wanted to come on this journey. We pushed on: engaging support, analysing practice of student involvement in internal reviews and running a pilot with six students as observers on audit teams. This campaign culminated in our student representatives taking the stage at a sector conference. They were so impressive that many hearts and minds were won.

We moved quickly to students being full members across all QAA review teams. Another former colleague at QAA, Maureen McLaughlin, recruited and trained hundreds of students and establishing a broader support team, mainly ex-student officers. In 2009, we argued, with the support of Board members, for student engagement to be at the heart of QAA's work. How could we credibly ask universities and colleges to do more to engage their students while not heeding our own advice?

In time, two student places were reserved on the Board, a Student Advisory Board was established, plans for a new student engagement chapter of the UK Quality Code were laid, and an organisational culture changed.

Writing in Association of University Administrators Perspectives in 2014, three Australian academics, in an article entitled *Partners or opponents: the engagement of students in compliance driven quality assessment,* stated that in: "the UK, the engagement of students in external review is extraordinary".

When we started this work, it was unusual to have a student on the Board of a sector body. It is now unusual not to have one.

So why tell this story? In my view student engagement is a defining feature of UK higher education. It sets us apart from others, including our main competitor nations.

But it is not a given that everyone sees it that way, as evidenced by the discussions surrounding the recent reform of the UK Quality Code. It is hard work, because you get new cohorts every year and staff have many competing demands on their time.

That's why this book matters. It evidences the challenges, the opportunity and the value for students, staff and their institutions. It also looks to the future and adds to the evidence that student engagement matters and makes a difference.

Part I

Introduction to student engagement in higher education

Chapter 1

An introduction to student engagement in higher education

Tom Lowe and Yassein El Hakim

Higher education institutions (HEIs) in the twenty-first century are hurtling towards a full marketisation of the sector, with growing pressure from numerous governments globally to produce measurable student outcomes, enhance learning and evidence an investment worthy of the taxpayer and tuition fees from students. HEIs, facing such imminent marketisation, competition and accountability, find themselves with two possible options in how to approach their relationship with their students (see Figure 1.1):

(1) A 'Students as Customers' approach. With this, for students to engage with the development of their education, they are limited to complaints, end-of-course feedback forms, campus demonstrations and outbursts on social media.
(2) A 'Student Engagement' approach. With this, universities/colleges involve students actively in decision-making and students work with staff in partnership in order to enhance education, sharing responsibility for mutual support as a community of members.

This edited collection will showcase practice in HEIs from across the globe, offering theory-influenced and truly transformative educational-development projects, schemes and research activity – commonly termed 'student engagement' and carried out by students and staff in partnership – to enhance students' experiences at their institutions. Because universities, colleges and students' unions have opened up their organisations and processes to involve students in decision-making, both students and staff have stepped into new spaces to enhance their higher education (HE) experience; students are empowered as partners and peers to participate in educational development. Currently, such student engagement initiatives are proliferating in HEIs throughout the world, extending well beyond a few HEI 'champions' and establishing a sector-wide core of practice. Student engagement and/or partnership discussions, projects and approaches are steadily breaking down traditional hierarchical power structures between staff and students, since both parties are meeting halfway in critically appraising HE delivery and amending it for the benefit of all stakeholders. From the very

Students as customers approach
- Students as paying customers for higher education
- University providing marketised services
- Students left to engage only via end-of-course experience feedback surveys, complaints, social media & student protests.

Student engagement approach
- Emphasis on a community of learners, where students are partners/members
- Students are engaged in decision-making, enhancement, quality processes etc.
- Students are empowered to meet staff about educational developments
- Staff are empowered to meet staff about educational developments

Figure 1.1 Choice in higher education direction when approaching students

one-sided '*this is the way we have always run education*', HEIs have moved to collaborative conversations about '*how we can develop education together*'. This chapter offers an introduction to these contemporary ways of working, drawing out the major areas of activity and research and identifying the challenges student engagement practices face. In the context of worldwide sector change, this handbook recognises how varied perspectives – of students, academics, educational developers, strategic leaders, policy makers and student service-providers – are influencing student success and learning through engagement. The book offers an up-to-date and comprehensive collection of sector-leading, theory-influenced best practice by colleagues and students with years of reflection upon and experience in student engagement. We hope that colleagues will find the publication thought-provoking and that it will enable them to grasp the implications of the enhancement practices outlined here and empower them to take back to their own institutions both the practices and the lessons already learned by others in implementing them.

Student engagement

It is important to mention that studies and ideas relating to contemporary student engagement do not constitute a solely modern phenomenon. As early as 1906, Dewey outlined his theory of a 'Democratic Education', in which all parties – and, notably, the students – have the right to have a say in how they are educated (Dewey, 1916). Often, these discussions about educational development emanated from sociological educational theorists who viewed democratising, emancipatory and widened access to education as integral to reformed education systems. Taking a student-centred approach has been seen as one possible means of breaking down the barriers that exist globally and prevent social mobility, identified by thinkers such as Pierre Bourdieu (Zanten, 2005, p.671) and Paolo Freire as structures that continue to oppress those not in power (Freire, 1973). Involving students in the process of developing education brings learners into the conversation, enabling them to contribute to the process of making education more accessible, its practices more inclusive and the learning more engaging. Studies relating to pupil and student voice have been extensively researched in primary and secondary education: they outline the benefits to learning and engagement (Czerniawski and Kidd, 2011; Fielding, 2004) and inspire wider studies in HE as part of exploring 'good undergraduate education', as discerned by Chickering and Gamson, with their core principle of encouraging 'student–faculty contact' (Chickering and Gamson, 1987). Students having a say in their education was even emphasised in 2011 by the United Nations, which declared that all students (pre-18) have a right to have a say in their education (Lansdown, 2011).

The term 'student engagement' (and also disengagement) in the HE sense was conceptualised in the 1980s as a means of understanding and reducing student boredom, alienation and dropping out (Finn and Zimmer, 2012). At a time in the United States when there was low student progression into the second year of HE and shifts in funding allowed HEIs to profit from students' staying on into Sophomore and Senior years, scholars such as Astin, Pascarella and Terenzini began to use the term in relation to the prevention of college drop-out. They argued that students who are engaged in education-related activities are more likely to progress through HE (Tchibozo, 2008; Tinto, 2006; Astin, 1984). Soon, beyond the US, there were parallels to be seen in HE across the world, where governments began to change how they focused on universities, putting a greater emphasis on learning and student development. This also led to the growth, internationally, of 'educational development' networks to enhance post-secondary teaching and research in the scholarship of teaching and learning (See SEDA est. 1993; ISSOTL est. 2004; RAISE est. 2009). Further parallels could also be seen in the UK, with the publication of the 2011 HE White Paper *Students at the heart of the system* (BIS, 2011), in Australia, with the publication of the *Higher Education Reform Package* (Australian Government, 2017), and in Europe, with movements towards engaging students as partners in quality assurance (ENQA, 2005). New activities were beginning to be formed in HE, leading to the creation of learning and teaching teams and the appointment of educational developers. Students' union priorities were also beginning to emerge within new spaces where colleagues and students alike would begin to consider how HE could be enhanced. This catalysed development from didactic knowledge exchanges to student production of knowledge, journeys and experiences (Neary and Winn, 2009).

Further research into the field of student engagement has led to the posing of critical questions about HE more broadly, such as reviewing students' transition (Gale and Parker, 2014), investigating students' sense of belonging (Thomas, 2012) and exploring the alienation of students from non-traditional backgrounds and of first-generation students in HE (Shaw, Humphrey, Atvars and Sims, 2017; Mann, 2001). As HEIs in certain nations – such as Australia, the USA, Canada and UK – increase their capacity (and, with it, their student numbers), the proportion of young people attending university has grown exponentially (e.g., in the UK, 12 per cent participation in the 1950s to almost 50 per cent in 2017). Alongside this increase, positive steps towards increasing the diversity of the student body entering HE have been taken. The motivations of students attending

HE have shifted and there is now more emphasis on the outcomes of learning, often noted as a key component of student choice and often linked by government, students and parents to notions of the employability gain from HE (Department for Education, 2017; Moore and Morton, 2017; UUK, 2017; Unite 2017). The drive towards inclusivity in HE pushes universities to evolve their practice and review their accessibility and this is why student engagement research and practices have often been adopted as a means of exploring development. Mann comments that engagement is the opposite of alienation and allows students to become full members of the HE community (Mann, 2001). Ensuring that students not only remain in HE, but are also able to access the support services they require, engage within and beyond the curriculum and succeed, has been, and continues to be, a priority for HEIs and educational development (ENQA, 2005; Office for Students, 2019a; Office for Students, 2019b; Hunter, Tobolowsky, and Gardner, 2010).

Since the 1990s, there has been a dramatic growth of research in the development area of student engagement in the scholarship in teaching and learning. A significant development for HE globally was Professor George Kuh's definition of student engagement as representing both the time and energy students invest in educationally purposeful activities and the effort institutions devote to using effective educational practices (Kuh and Hu, 2001). Following Kuh's and other colleagues' work, the creation and inception of one of the most notable surveys of student engagement in contemporary HE, the National Student Survey of Student Engagement (NSSE), which provided a tool for institutional measures of student engagement and, further, the means of gauging areas in need of focused enhancement (NSSE, 2019). This survey introduced a comparative measure for students' collective engagement in their studies, at both course and institution levels, inspiring countless institutional surveys and several national surveys worldwide, such as the UK Engagement Survey (UKES), the Australian Survey of Student Engagement (ASSE) and the Irish Survey of Student Engagement (ISSE). Section 5 of the NSSE, in particular, engages the wider campus/HEI community by asking specific questions about '*the Supportive Campus Environment*', which was drawing in new stakeholders of interest to conversations about student engagement such as professional student service providers, careers coaches and counsellors. As these surveys began to feed into unique selling points (USPs) and, latterly, league tables for universities and colleges worldwide, university managers/administrators inevitably followed suit, though with differing motivations for enhancing student engagement and thus placing emphasis on producing 'satisfied students' to ensure a competitive and reputational standing in an ever-marketised sector. Certainly a measurable account of students' engagements with their university experience holds value, but this book is not about student engagement in the HE curriculum directly, or HE surveys, although these are certainly types of student engagement in their own right and have stimulated large research studies in related areas (Bunce, Baird and Jones, 2017; Senior, Moores and Burgess, 2017; Kandiko and Mawer, 2013).

The contextual factors mentioned earlier – predominantly focused in Western HE – catalysed the emphasis on student engagement, which included what we shall refer to as 'push' and 'pull' factors. Push factors include the previously outlined marketisation of HE, which featured the introduction of tuition fees, increased student numbers, more providers and greater diversity of students (Lea, 2015). Other push factors include greater accountability of HE to students, the growth in students' unions and their interest in HEI governance, government, tax payers and the media, which all placed more emphasis on learning, students' value for money/investment and such outcomes of the HE experience as employable graduates (Office for Students, 2018; Frankham, 2017; Dunne, 2017). Finally, the stronger push factors include measures of HEI accountability, such as national surveys, league tables, measures of HEI success and new experimental measures such as the UK Teaching Excellence and Student Outcomes Framework (Office for Students, 2019). Pull factors, as outlined throughout this chapter and this collection, include an increased emphasis on ensuring that HE is accessible to students and that they can thrive during their time at university and feel that they belong there. HEIs, pulled towards student engagement initiatives as a means of ensuring that students succeed and have had a transformative experience, work with students to enhance their own institutional operations and ensure that courses facilitate learning in an accessible way for diverse audiences. Notably, the students themselves are also agents of student engagement (a fact which, it could be argued, represents both push and pull factors), with student agency, activism, lobbying and campaigning on a local course or institutional level by students' unions (Shaw and Atvars, 2018; Bols, 2017; Brooks, Byford and Sela, 2015). The growth and professionalisation of students' unions, taking them into such previously inaccessible university spaces as quality assurance, student representation and sabbatical officers on university committees, put great pressure on HEIs to develop themselves and led to new insights into enhancement. The above push and pull factors related to student engagement practices brought different stakeholders together around the table, where many of the practices discussed in this collection were created.

As student engagement gained traction through research studies in the USA and the NSSE, more papers began to be published asking '*What does student engagement mean?*', '*What is and what is not student engagement?*' and '*Who owns student engagement?*' Owing to the growth in popularity of student engagement as a discourse, the UK Higher Education Academy funded, in 2010, a literature review of it; in that year, Trowler conducted her literature review of the term to date, outlining three major areas of student engagement, including: (a) behavioural engagement, (b) cognitive engagement and (c) emotional engagement, all of which follow the trend of student engagement in HE up until this point and focus on learning in the HE environment (Trowler, 2010). Subsequent emphasis on engaging students in educational developments, enhancement or change has been apparent. Buckley, in 2014, outlined that student engagement can be either in the curriculum or in policy, defining a split between curriculum-based engagement and decision-making student engagement (Buckley, 2014). Bryson, also in 2014, argued that student engagement can be split by (1) *'Students Engaging'* and (2) *'Engaging Students'* (Bryson, 2014b). Many quality assurance bodies in Europe define student engagement as involvement in the quality and development processes, such as sitting on review panels, student representation and other forms of participatory engagement (Morris, 2018; UKSCQA and QAA, 2018; ENQA, 2005). Asked for their view of what student engagement means, students defined it as linked to *'belonging'*, *'being'* and *'transformation'* in their studies, outlining more emotional definitions of student engagement rather than seeing it as 'measurable' or 'participatory' (Solomonides and Reid, 2009).

It was during this rise in popularity of the area of student engagement that the first major complexity in its study, discourse and practice emerged: its ambiguity. Student engagement has multiple definitions in the HE sector and in HEIs locally, being interpreted in endless ways by many scholars and individuals (Dunne, 2016; Bryson, 2014). Conversations, studies, definitions and practice relating to student engagement can be as down-to-earth as talking about enhancing students' physical or emotional engagement with the curriculum, or can be as complex as student ownership, participation and involvement in university-wide policy or enhancement schemes: 'We could define student engagement in any way we want' (Finn and Zimmer, 2012, p.137). This offers flexibility as a great strength when talking about students' experiences in HE, but the lack of definitive boundaries can cause student and staff confusion across an institution. There is a danger that the buzzword could become a 'fuzzword' (Vuori, 2013, p.509) and that, at both institutional and sector level, lack of conceptual clarity before beginning projects or studies could carry a number of risks. For example, Buckley states: 'if we are not clear about what student engagement is, then our ability to improve, increase, support and encourage it through well-designed interventions will be severely diminished' (Buckley, 2014, p.2). Zepke also notes that it 'is up to teachers and institutions to interpret and shape such ideas for specific and unique contexts, subjects and, most importantly, learners' (Zepke, 2013, p1). It is therefore crucial at the start of any study, project or discussion relating to student engagement that clear definitions are outlined of what type of student engagement is being discussed, so all involved are clear which area of student engagement is being explored before you start.

Students as partners

At this point, it is important to draw on the wealth of students-as-partners or working-in-partnership initiatives that are occurring within the student engagement wave of practice and on which many of the chapters of this book will focus. Working with students as partners – and/or moving towards institutional partnership with students (and students' unions) – is a goal shared by many HEIs; it is associated with joint decision-making at a strategic level and co-design of curriculum and services at a local level (Bovill, Cook-Sather, Felten, Millard and Moore-Cherry, 2016; Cook-Sather, Bovill and Felten, 2014). Partnership can also be defined as a way of working in all HE business that should be embodied by all (Healey, Flint and Harrington, 2014; NUS, 2012). Healey, Flint and Harrington's seminal work on partnership commissioned by the UK Higher Education Academy – now AdvanceHE – outlined eight principles of partnership that are at the core of partnership work or partnership schemes globally: '*authenticity, inclusivity, reciprocity, empowerment, trust, challenge, community and responsibility*' (Healey, Flint and Harrington, *op.cit.*, pp.14–15). Partnership is often the goal aspired to by student engagement practices, with the decision-making, value of contributions and sometimes even workload being completely equal between staff and students, whether on a small learning and teaching research project or a cross-institutional project run in partnership by the students' union and HEI (for examples, see Chapters 8, 14 and 16). However, there are also considerations to be made in relation to the practicalities and inclusivity of these partnership projects, which culminate in tensions discussed in the later chapters of this book: for example, scalability, accessibility, logistics and measuring impact. Nevertheless, the sheer momentum of 'students working as partners' within the literature has seen almost more growth than 'student engagement' in recent years, with a students-as-partners global movement transforming HE from the micro to the macro level (Mercer-Mapstone, 2019; Matthews, Cook-Sather and Healey, 2018; Bryson, 2015).

Student engagement theory into practice

This book will focus on student engagement with regard to the initiatives, projects and discussions run by HEIs and students' unions to create dialogue, reflection, enhancements and projects in the realm of educational development. Student engagement, also referred to as the movement towards student–staff 'partnership' or 'students as partners' internationally, has received great investment and attention. This book will note several best practices in the area of staff/student participation at HEIs. As discussed above, student engagement as a term and an area of study began with a specific focus on engagement within the curriculum or classroom (Finn and Zimmer, 2012), in an attempt to measure it through such schemes as the NSSE to inform enhancements (NSSE, 2019). The term 'student engagement', especially in a UK or wider Western HE context, has more recently been incorporated to label the processes whereby students and staff work together, discussing and researching to inform enhancement in educational developments and quality processes (Gravett, Kinchin and Winstone, 2019; Stalmeijer, Whittingham, de Grave and Dolmans, 2016; TSEP, 2014; QAA, 2012). It is this use of the term 'student engagement' that this collection will cover, referencing practices known to many institutions – student representation, students as partners and student peer coaches – and more contemporary roles such as students as panel members in quality assurance, student digital champions and student fellows (Lowe and Dunne, 2017; Dunne, 2016; Bryson, 2014a).

Student engagement in educational developments

Notable scholars such as Feldman and Newcomb (1969) as well as Chickering and Gamson (1987) began inspiring educators and strategic leaders to ask colleagues to reflect on their teaching practices, and managers on their strategies, and to begin asking students why and how we teach in HE, through reflection on the whole university/college experience (Feldman and Newcomb, 1969; Chickering and Gamson, 1987). This move towards asking questions and suggesting the previously considered impossible triggered new conversations about the Scholarship of Teaching and Learning (SOTL) to enhance pedagogy at HEIs; this in turn opened the field to engaging students in these conversations and to work with them to enhance education (Gravett, Kinchin and Winstone, 2019; Fletcher, 2017). The power of students as partners created a discourse about notions of empowering student agency through partnership, noting significant student developmental opportunities through which students would experience success of real-world projects in an organisational setting – their own HEI (Sum, 2018, Callaghan, 2016, and Horsley, 2016, offer student accounts). As with previous SEDA Edited Collections, there have emerged areas of focus within the Scholarship of Teaching and Learning (SOTL) and/or such educational developments as, to name a few: 'Researching Learning' (Cousin, 2009), 'Intercultural Practice' (Killick, 2017), 'Technology-Enhanced Learning' (Branch, Bartholomew and Nygaard, 2015) and enhancements in 'Assessment and Feedback' (Winstone and Carless, 2019). Though these developments all include an emphasis on student engagement, this collection will focus on those activities deemed 'student engagement practices' or 'research areas' that have created networks and movements such as *RAISE (Researching, Advancing and Inspiring Student Engagement)*; peer-reviewed journals such as the *International Journal of Students as Partners* (IJSaP), the *Journal of Educational Innovation, Partnership and Change* (JEIPC) and *Student Engagement in Higher Education Journal* (SEHEJ); and government-funded projects such as *The Student Engagement Partnership* (TSEP, 2014), *Realising Engagement through Active Culture Transformation* (REACT, 2019) and the *National Student Engagement Programme* in the Republic of Ireland (NStEP, 2019).

Emphases on learning, belonging, progression to additional academic years and retaining students in HE study are all motivations that have also drawn many to student engagement practices. The considerable work put in place for the 'First-Year Experience' and transitions to HE (Pascarella and Terenzini, 2005) and subsequent focus on the 'Helping Sophomores Succeed' has drawn in not just educational developers but wider student-facing roles such as faculty members, instructors/teaching colleagues and professional student-facing services (Hunter, Tobolowsky and Gardner, 2010; Felten, Gardner, Schroeder, Lambert and Barefoot, 2016). This area of focus looks beyond the curriculum and at the entire student experience, including the social, support and extra-curricular side of students' HE journeys, often referred to as 'the student journey' or 'the student experience'. However, both these terms can be viewed critically, because they suggest there is a single path that all students follow and experience, which is not the case at any HEI because students are not a homogenous group. When these studies go beyond staff studying students and move towards students working with staff to develop educational and institutional services, the opportunities offered via student engagement collaborations are transformational in grounding projects and co-creating authentic, often student-led, outcomes. Institutions have begun to engage students in all of their business, not just the curriculum, with students on committees related to student affairs, students on interview panels for new staff, students attending strategy days and students involved in such core areas for development in HE as sustainable development, campus re-design and mental health (Teslenko, 2019; Student Minds, 2019; Lees and Adams, 2017).

Student engagement practice

As student engagement activities, or practices, blossomed from 2010 onwards, Bryson has further defined these activities as either *'engaging students'* or *'students engaging'* (Bryson, 2014b, pp.18–19). Bryson's seminal chapter in *Understanding and Developing Student Engagement* recommended the HE community to think of student engagement in these two ways, with recommendations and considerations for enhancements for wider, deeper and more inclusive engagements being different for possible 'types' or 'pathways' of engagement (Bryson, 2014b). More recently, Bryson has defined student engagement practices that are run as schemes cross-institutionally: as Type A – 'exclusive' opportunities, where a single or select group of students has engaged; or Type B – 'inclusive/democratic' opportunities, like student representation (Bryson, 2017). These activities were inspired by such sector-leading practices in student engagement as Bryn Mawr College's 'Students Ambassadors in Learning and Teaching' (SALTS) (USA) (Cooke-Sather, 2013), Birmingham City University's 'Students as Partners' (UK) (Freeman, Millard, Brand and Chapman, 2014) and, notably, the University of Exeter's 'Students as Change Agents' scheme (UK) (Dunne and Zandstra, 2011). Many of these practices will be summarised below with further comprehensive case studies throughout this collection. Dunne, in 2016, noted the expansion of countless student engagement roles, stating that they all meant slightly different things, but all worked towards the same means of developing education with staff (Dunne, 2016, p.3):

Students as Partners	*Student Fellows*
Student Partnerships	*Student Colleagues*
Student–staff Partnerships	*Students as Champions*
Students as Researchers	*Students as Producers*
Students as Co-Researchers	*Students as Change Makers*
Students as Learners and Teachers	*Students as Co-Producers*
Students as Change Agents	*Students as Co-creators*
Students as Co-constructers	

Student voice

Ensuring students have the opportunity to voice their experiences in education is not a new idea, with scholars of pre-tertiary education for many decades studying pupil voice, student voice and the learner voice, from nursery/kindergarten age through to secondary education (Carey, 2012; Czerniawski and Kidd, 2011; Fielding, 2004). Student voice can be defined in two ways: either as feedback via any forum (face-to-face, surveys or other feedback-gathering means, such as an online platform) or conversations about education between a staff member and a student. Therefore, student voice can be seen to be the foundation of any higher participatory student engagement in educational development; Fletcher outlines key principles to ensure that staff are accessible to students through honest discourse about education without a division between them (Fletcher, 2017). Surveys have also seen a dramatic growth both nationally and locally at HEIs, with student engagement and/or satisfaction surveys prominent in many nations – e.g. the Australian Survey of Student Engagement, National Survey of Student Engagement, National Student Survey (UK) – as well as a large number of internal surveys (Library Survey, First Year Survey etc.) and course-level academic evaluations. Surveys offer an incredibly efficient means of gaining mass student feedback, but they have been highly criticised for their limited reliability, numerous research limitations and over-use (Muijs, 2012; Porter, Whitcomb and Weitzer, 2004). Too many surveys have been reported as creating survey fatigue in some education systems, leading HEIs and students' unions to take more creative approaches to student voice, such as 'Student Voice Forums', 'Student Feedback Exhibitions', satisfaction apps and anonymous idea logs, which offer additional accessible opportunities for students to express their views and are often shorter, more engaging and inspire conversations.

Student representation

To embed student voice practice at a HEI, many institutions and even national HE associations have advocated and embedded student representation at programme and wider institutional levels to ensure that it can feature formally in wider HE business (Bols, 2017; Carey, 2012). This is an area of student engagement practice which is a given in some nations like New Zealand and the UK, but, in others, this is still an area of development sought after by such projects as the Student Voice Project: Australia (Student Voice Project: Australia, 2019). The UK Quality Assurance Agency for Higher Education places heavy emphasis on student representation in HE committees and decision-making, asking HEIs to show evidence of where students are engaged in core university and academic business during external reviews (UKSCQA, 2018; QAA, 2012). The UK take-up of student representation sees typically two student representatives – per year group and per academic course – sitting on three or four course-level committees a year (e.g. 'Student–Staff Liaison Committees'), alongside additional informal duties as representatives of their cohorts and training for their students' union. The students' union often manages these schemes, offering institutional-wide iden-tity for a student engagement activity – and therefore engaging every academic discipline (often backed by university policy) – and then sending elected faculty and/or institutional officers (such as an elected students' union president) to sit on higher university committees. This has led the student voice to professionalise, or upskill with training, so that students feel both sufficiently proficient to enter these often new settings with their complex jargon-filled business and ready to engage with the opportunities for educational development. Staff, too, have had to adapt, opening up their own practice for potentially unwelcome feedback and more liberal conversations about education with their students. As this practice of student engagement becomes the norm, institutional culture will develop to such a point that a student will be expected at every meeting. This area of activity has seen particular energy in the UK (further explained by Bols' chapter in this book) as it was made a legal requirement for students' unions to be registered along-side any HE provider in the UK in the 1994 Education Act (Department for Education, 1994). Student representation is a tangible example of how students and staff strive to engage in new spaces beyond informal conversations along-side academic study or services. This is outlined in Figure 1.2 alongside other approaches where students or staff engage in discourse concerning education.

Students taking responsibility

Student engagement practices have also included students' participation in schemes which place them in positions of responsibility, either in formal positions as part of university business or as part of the student–student support functions

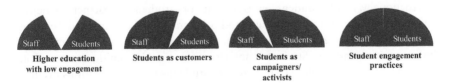

| Higher education with low engagement | Students as customers | Students as campaigners/ activists | Student engagement practices |

Figure 1.2 Balance of student–staff relationships in higher education

of a university. Students now find themselves as equal members on national, local and course level quality-assurance panels across Europe: the national quality associations – such as the European Association for Quality Assurance (ENQA, 2005) – and quality-assurance bodies are paving the way for the HEIs' training and enabling students to be part of HEI review (QAA, 2018). These bodies expect institutions to comply and so ensure a successful uptake of 'Student Reviewers' who, as full and equal panel members, act as quality reviewers of documentation and courses at a local level (Owen, 2013). Students have also taken other formal roles – such as sitting on interview panels for new staff at the Universities of Lincoln and Chester – and conducting teaching observations – at Lingnan University, Hong Kong, and University College London (UK) (Marie and Azuma, 2018; Hoh, 2017; Crawford, 2012). In addition to taking on roles as part of formal university processes, students have also taken on responsibilities in supporting other students by means of peer mentoring, peer coaching and peer support. Student engagement roles in which students take an element of responsibility – for others or for processes – are often referred to as 'Active Student Participation' or even 'Student Agency' (Keenan, 2014). University-wide schemes commonly referred to as 'Peer-Assisted Learning' (PAL) are often supported by one or two staff members, yet engage as many as 150 student peer coaches/leaders, who run development sessions and offer one-to-one advice across an HEI, engaging hundreds of students in their academic skills-development transition to HE study (Warren and Luebsen, 2017; Green, 2011; Hill, Liuzzi and Giles, 2010; Capstick, Fleming and Hurne, 2004).

Students as partners in educational developments

In the UK, North America, Australia (and now, also, increasingly across Europe), educational development teams support opportunities for students to take up student-partnership roles, such as 'Change Makers' (Marie, Arif and Joshi, 2016), 'Students as Partners' (Marquis, Puri, Wan, Ahmad, Goff, Knorr, Vassileva and Woo, 2016) and 'Student Fellows' (Sims, King, Lowe and El Hakim, 2016). These activities, which may be either individual research student-partnership projects or large HE-wide schemes, see students actively contributing to enhancing university processes, curriculum and the wider student experience (Healey et al., 2014). These practices and activities have become a priority for UK universities for the purposes of enhancing students' educational experience as well as fulfilling policy requirements (QAA, 2012, NUS, 2012). Practice has expanded internationally, with student engagement or students-as-partners schemes adopted as an area for enhancement and Scholarship of Learning and Teaching (SOTL) (Matthews, 2016). Such student activities now make a significant contribution to our campuses. Students' capabilities are at last becoming apparent from what they do in such roles. That dozens of student–staff collaborations occur in one academic year confirms that enhancement through student engagement is becoming widespread in the sector (Sims, King, Lowe and El Hakim, 2016).

More broadly, student engagement in co-creation – championed and described by colleagues such as Cook-Sather, Felten and Bovill – recognises that the student role in change projects cannot always be equally split in a 50/50 partnership between staff and students (Cook-Sather, Felten and Bovill, 2014, p.28). Examples in the UK include students' reviewing student transition and creating a buddy scheme on the Fashion, Media and Marketing Programme at the University of Winchester (UK) (Sims, King, Lowe and El Hakim, 2016), enhancing technology in learning in the classroom at the University of Exeter (Dunne and Zandstra 2011) and re-designing the English Literature curriculum at the University of Reading (UK) (Becker, Collier and Setter, 2018). Partnership – as part of the empowerment of students through student engagement opportunities – offers '*a valuable alternative to the rhetoric of consumerism*' (NUS, 2012) and gives students ownership in their HE community by making them agents of change. In the area of student engagement, on which many of the chapters in this book will focus, student–staff partnership (or students-as-partners) has certainly received the highest number of publications in the last decade, where SOTL colleagues have shared practice, conducted research into the benefits and constraints of partnership and, more recently, written critical reflections on the notion of partnership within educational developments (Bryson and Furlonger, 2018; Healey and Healey, 2018; Matthews, Dwyer, Hine and Turner, 2018).

Critically reflecting on student engagement

Embarking on working with students through many of the practices outlined in this collection is not easy, but, if students and institutions persist, the benefits to campus and course communities can be incredibly rewarding. Of course, all student engagement practice has its difficulties, just like any area of university business. Projects, initiatives or even conversations are never without boundaries, and such conversations can often be uncomfortable for one or both parties. To work towards mitigating these potential reservations to student engagement, both parties need (a) to travel some distance in order to meet on common ground and gain empathy with each other's position and (b) to be patient and reflective in assessing these difficult conversations before working towards a shared goal. Reflecting on student engagement (and partnership) approaches has led to a recent wave of critical reflection in the literature, all worthy of an edited collection in their own right (Krčmář, 2019, Kahu and Nelson, 2018 and O'Shea, 2018 are illustrative of the range). The majority of these research papers, reflections and critiques do not aim to eradicate student engagement from institutional practice, but rather to appraise our practices critically in order to make them more robust, accessible, true to our initial values and more meaningful for those involved.

The various pull and push factors on the agenda may, from a values' standpoint, enhance learning for altruistic or emancipatory means or, for strategic purposes, boost student satisfaction or the reputation of the HEI. Whether or not certain motivations towards student engagement are right or wrong, there has been a shift in the weighting of contemporary HE, putting greater emphasis on 'excellence' in education and on attempts to measure it; this has inevitably focused institutional attention on prioritising students' experiences. Students, too, can vary in motivation and opportunities to work with staff may draw particular students on the basis of the attributes and accessibility of those roles. For example, is the role to be paid or unpaid? A paid role will certainly attract students with a financial motivation or those who cannot afford to miss a paid opportunity beyond their studies. If an opportunity is about asking questions, critiquing or challenging university/college business, some students may be attracted for activist reasons, whereas less vocal students may deem the opportunity not suited to their qualities or skillset. Considering the opportunity itself, the time commitment and expected level of expertise it demands, together with its accessibility, are crucial considerations in initiating student engagement practices: the opportunities must be accessible to diverse students – and not only those students with the privilege of free time, financial comfort, the demographic characteristics of the majority and no other commitments such as part-time work or caring responsibilities. Every new intake of students and the turnover of staff and students' union officers will bring new challenges and new possibilities (Shaw and Atvars, 2018). Consistent levels of support, resource and commitment will be required, as well as the ability to be flexible and open to new ideas (NUS, 2012, p.11). It is important to build partnerships robust enough to cope with constant criticism and re-evaluation of student engagement in the light of new evidence about it (NUS, 2012), as, despite the fact that HE is moving in this direction, vocal critiques of student engagement practice are still evident, both locally and in the literature (Zepke, 2018; Macfarlane and Tomlinson, 2017).

Recent attempts to 'measure' student engagement have emerged through data analysis schemes which quantify students' interactions with HE, in terms, say, of attendance, time spent on the Virtual Learning Environment and interactions with staff (Lowe, 2018). As outlined in Trowler's literature review and Bryson's book, student engagement is about more than just attendance (Bryson, 2014b; Trowler, 2010); it is linked to '*belonging*', '*being*' and '*transformation*' (Solomonides and Reid, 2009; Barnett, 2009; Bryson and Hand, 2007). This has led to adverse criticism of the term 'student engagement' in relation to educational development, for appropriation, reporting, structuralising and becoming too much as part of HE business (Freeman, 2016). HE scholars – your own HEI may be no exception – therefore criticise student engagement for becoming too focused on practice and policy and insufficiently on learning or the curriculum (Macfarlane and Tomlinson, 2017), to the extent that it has been referred to as the product of a marketised, neoliberal system which seeks to appropriate the student voice and move away from traditional student representation (student voice) schemes.

When confronting this type of criticism of student engagement in educational development, it is important to recognise the views of others and emphatically to meet those critics with such reassurances as '*Yes, your definition of student engagement is also correct.*' Student engagement cannot be defined as one measurable action or a single feeling or emotion. Student engagements, or interactions, or conversations, or projects or feelings are not type 1, 2 or 3; they are A–Z. The minimum engagement a student can have with a HEI is to click on its website or visit the campus; the maximum is to co-design/mark/teach a whole degree programme in partnership or redesign a major part of a university service. It is up to the students and staff, at the start of meetings, projects or discussions, to define what type of student engagement they are focusing on. Conversations related to learning, teaching, service delivery, representation, accessibility, change and participation are all so much more meaningful when students are engaged throughout the process. Following our example laid out in this chapter, it is important that each individual student engagement project outlines the focus of student engagement in its own context before it begins.

Going forward

At the start this book, the editors recognised that they had to take a stance, one from which chapters of practice, inspired by theory, could follow, for, increasingly in HE, we have to navigate new spaces, language, structures and priorities. Members of HE communities must remember why we are here in the first place. It must be about changing together, via engaging conversations. Furthermore, if HE is changing, a path of conversation which brings all stakeholders around the table to discuss education developments must also adapt if it is to ensure that universities become an accessible space for all – not providers and customers, but communities of learners who seek to develop HE in partnership. Though staff engagement is absolutely key to success in student engagement approaches, there is no set practice or methodology to deploy in an individual HEI, or even local departmental practices. Rachel Wenstone outlined that, as either a positive or negative, student engagement is a flexible enough (or even vague enough) concept to be appropriated by a whole range of interests (NUS, 2012).

When considering embarking on a student engagement project, study or discussion, here are seven considerations to be thinking about:

1. Start with the why

What are you trying to do? To improve learning and to help students to succeed or staff to innovate? To enhance service delivery or to decolonise the curriculum?

2. What are your values?

Write out your projects' values. Are they student-centred, inclusive, aiming to engage diverse students and staff? Are they empowering?

3. Get reading

Read this book, the journals noted above, websites and all of the great work that is out there so your project can stand on the shoulders of other HEIs' lessons learned.

4. Be flexible

Your project or scheme will not run exactly the same as UCL's, London Metropolitan's or Winchester's. It will be become individual, mould itself into your HE culture and take its own shape. No one model fits all, so do not be frustrated when it does not work perfectly the first time.

5. Evaluate with caution

Evaluating student engagement initiatives is messy. Testing the impact of an intervention in any individual student's experience of HE is incredibly difficult, owing to the number of unknown variables that cannot be controlled. Do not be disheartened if you do not see an 'impact', because often you simply know it did great things. Pursue and gather mixed, experimental data and tell the personal stories of the students and staff involved.

6. Continuously reflect

Reflective practice tells us a great deal about improving how we work in many professions – and the same is true of student engagement. Reflect on who you are engaging and how you are engaging; ask if your practices and approaches are accessible to the diverse student body; reflect on your values and aims, to see if you are still doing what you set out to do.

7. Try again

Nothing works as you expect when trying it for the first time. It is important to reflect and try the initiative, forum or study again, for small changes can have a large impact. Keep trying, stay persistent and have conversations with students, asking why they thought the project went the way it did.

We hope that readers, whether experienced in or new to student engagement, will join us in welcoming this publication, following six years of renewed activity in student engagement during which practices, projects, reflections and research have led to a plethora of positive work. Together in our ever-changing HE sector, students are now at the table, not as recipients of education but as partners in the conversations – and we hope this book inspires more practice in this growing area within educational development.

Our thanks to SEDA for the opportunity to create this publication.

References

Astin, A.W., 1984. Student Involvement: A Developmental Theory for Higher Education, *Journal of College Student Development*, 5, pp.518–529.

Australian Government, 2017. The Higher Education Reform Package. Retrieved from: https://docs.education.gov.au/system/files/doc/other/ed17-0138_-_he_-_glossy_budget_report_acc.pdf

Barnett, R., 2009. Knowing and becoming in the higher education curriculum. *Studies in higher education*, 34(4), pp.429–440. Retrieved from: https://doi.org/10.1080/03075070902771978

Becker, L., Collier, J. and Setter, J., 2018. Students as change partners in the School of Literature and Languages at the University of Reading. *Journal of Educational Innovation, Partnership and Change*, 4(1). Retrieved from: http://dx.doi.org/10.21100/jeipc.v4i1.712

Bols, A.T.G., 2017. Enhancing student representation. *Journal of Educational Innovation, Partnership and Change*, 3(1), pp.81–89.

Bovill, C., Cook-Sather, A., Felten, P., Millard, L. and Moore-Cherry, N., 2016. Addressing potential challenges in co-creating learning and teaching: overcoming resistance, navigating institutional norms and ensuring inclusivity in student–staff partnerships. *Higher Education*, 71(2) pp.195–208. Retrieved from: https://doi.org/10.1007/s10734-015-9896-4

Branch, J., Bartholomew, P. and Nygaard, C., 2015. *Technology enhanced learning in higher education*. Farringdon: Libri Publishing

Brooks, R., Byford, K. and Sela, K., 2015. The changing role of students' unions within contemporary higher education. *Journal of Education Policy*, 30(2), pp.165–181. Retrieved from: https://doi.org/10.1080/02680939.2014.924562

Bryson, C. and Furlonger, R., 2018. A shared reflection on risk in trying to work with students in partnership. *Teaching and Learning Together in Higher Education*, 1(24), p.8. Retrieved from: https://repository.brynmawr.edu/tlthe/vol1/iss24/8/

Bryson, C. and Albert, F., 2017. *Authentic partnership – what, how and why?* Keynote presentation at the Change Agents Network (CAN) Conference, April 20–21, University of Exeter.

Bryson, C., 2015. Researching, Advancing and Inspiring Student Engagement (RAISE) IN: Lea, J. ed., 2015. *Enhancing learning and teaching in higher education: Engaging with the dimensions of practice*. Milton Keynes: Open University Press.

Bryson, C. (ed.) 2014a. *Understanding and developing student engagement* (SEDA Series). London: Routledge.

Bryson, C., 2014b. Clarifying the concept of student engagement. In: *Understanding and developing student engagement* (pp.21–42). London: Routledge.

Bryson, C. and Hand, L., 2007. The role of engagement in inspiring teaching and learning. *Innovations in education and teaching international*, 44(4), pp.349–362. Retrieved from: https://doi.org/10.1080/14703290701602748

Buckley, A., 2014. How radical is student engagement? (And what is it for?). *Student Engagement and Experience Journal*, 3(2), pp.1–23. Retrieved from: https://doi.org/10.7190/seej.v3i2.95

Bunce, L., Baird, A. and Jones, S.E., 2017. The student-as-consumer approach in higher education and its effects on academic performance. *Studies in Higher*

Education, 42(11), pp.1958–1978. Retrieved from: https://doi.org/10.1080/03075079.2015.1127908

Callaghan, L., 2016. From disengaged to super engaged: my student journey. *Student Engagement in Higher Education Journal*, 1(1).

Capstick, S., Fleming, H. and Hurne, J., 2004. January. Implementing Peer Assisted Learning in Higher Education: The experience of a new university and a model for the achievement of a mainstream programme. *Peer Assisted learning conference*, 6.

Carey, P., 2012. Student Engagement: Stakeholder Perspectives on Course Representation in University Governance. *Studies in Higher Education*, 38(9), pp.1290–1304. Retrieved from: https://doi.org/10.1080/03075079.2011.621022

Chickering, A.W. and Gamson, Z.F., 1987. Seven principles for good practice in undergraduate education. *AAHE Bulletin*, 3, p.7. Retrieved from: https://doi.org/10.1016/0307-4412(89)90094-0

Cook-Sather, A., 2013. Catalyzing multiple forms of engagement through student–faculty partnerships exploring teaching and learning. In E. Dunne and D. Owen (eds.), *The Student Engagement Handbook: Practice in Higher Education*. Bingley: Emerald Publishing Group.

Cook-Sather, A., Bovill, C., and Felten, P., 2014. *Engaging students as partners in learning and teaching: A guide for faculty*. San Francisco, CA: Jossey-Bass.

Cousin, G., 2009. *Researching learning in higher education: An introduction to contemporary methods and approaches*. London: Routledge.

Crawford, K. 2012. Rethinking the student/teacher nexus: Students as consultants on teaching in higher education. *Towards teaching in public: Reshaping the modern university*, pp. 52–67.

Czerniawski, G. and Kidd, W. (eds.) 2011. *Student voice handbook: Bridging the academic/practitioner divide*. Bingley: Emerald Group Publishing.

Department of Business, Innovation and Skills (BIS), 2011. *Students at the Heart of the System*. The Stationery Office. Retrieved from: www.gov.uk/government/uploads/system/uploads/attachment_data/file/31384/11-944-higher-education-students-at-heart-of-system.pdf

Department for Education, 2017. Higher Education and Research Act 2017. Retrieved from: www.legislation.gov.uk/ukpga/2017/29/contents/enacted

Department for Education. 1994. Education Act. Retrieved from: www.legislation.gov.uk/ukpga/1994/30/contents

Dunne, E., 2016. Design Thinking: A framework for student engagement? A personal view. *Journal of Educational Innovation, Partnership and Change*, 2(1). Retrieved from: http://dx.doi.org/10.21100/jeipc.v2i1.317

Dunne, E. and Zandstra, R., 2011. Students as Change Agents-New ways of engaging with learning and teaching in Higher Education. *Higher Education Academy Subject Centre for Education*. Retrieved from: https://dera.ioe.ac.uk/14767/

Dunne, J., 2017. Working placement reflective assessments and employability enhanced through highlighting graduate attributes. *Journal of Teaching and Learning for Graduate Employability*, 8(1), pp.40–59. Retrieved from: https://doi.org/10.21153/jtlge2017vol8no1art616

European Association for Quality Assurance (ENQA), 2005. Standards and guidelines for quality assurance in the European Higher Education Area. *Report, European Association for Quality Assurance in the European Higher Education*. Retrieved from: https://enqa.eu/wp-content/uploads/2015/11/ESG_2015.pdf

Feldman, K.A. and Newcomb, T.M., 1969. *The impact of college on students*. New Jersey: Transaction Publishers.

Felten, P., Gardner, J.N., Schroeder, C.C., Lambert, L.M. and Barefoot, B.O., 2016. *The undergraduate experience: Focusing institutions on what matters most*. San Francisco, CA: Jossey Bass.

Fielding, M., 2004. Transformative approaches to student voice: Theoretical underpinnings, recalcitrant realities. *British Educational Research Journal*, 30(2), pp.295–311. Retrieved from: https://doi.org/10.1080/0141192042000195236

Finn, J. D and Zimmer, K. S., 2012. Student Engagement: What is it? Why does it Matter? In Christenson, S. L., Reschly, A., L. and Wylie, C. (eds.), *Handbook of research on student engagement*. Berlin: Springer Science + Business Media.

Fletcher, A. F., 2017. *Student voice revolution: The meaningful student involvement handbook*. CommonAction Publishing.

Frankham, J., 2017. Employability and higher education: The follies of the 'Productivity Challenge' in the Teaching Excellence Framework. *Journal of Education Policy*, 32(5), pp.628–641. Retrieved from: https://doi.org/10.1080/02680939.2016.1268271

Freeman, R., 2016. Is student voice necessarily empowering? Problematising student voice as a form of higher education governance. *Higher Education Research and Development*, 35(4), pp.859–862. Retrieved from: https://doi.org/10.1080/07294360.2016.1172764

Freeman, R., Millard, L., Brand, S. and Chapman, P., 2014. Student academic partners: student employment for collaborative learning and teaching development. *Innovations in Education and Teaching International*, 51(3), pp.233–243. Retrieved from: https://doi.org/10.1080/14703297.2013.778064

Freire, P., 1973. *Education for critical consciousness*, 1. London: Bloomsbury Publishing.

Gale, T. and Parker, S., 2014. Navigating change: a typology of student transition in higher education. *Studies in Higher Education*, 39(5), pp.734–753. Retrieved from: https://doi.org/10.1080/03075079.2012.721351

Gravett, K., Kinchin, I.M. and Winstone, N.E., 2019. 'More than customers': conceptions of students as partners held by students, staff, and institutional leaders. *Studies in Higher Education*, pp.1–14. Retrieved from: https://doi.org/10.1080/03075079.2019.1623769

Green, P., 2011. A literature review of peer assisted learning (PAL). *National HE STEM*.

Healey, M. and Healey, R., 2018. 'It depends': Exploring the context-dependent nature of students as partners' practices and policies. *International Journal for Students as Partners*, 2(1), pp.1–10. Retrieved from: https://doi.org/10.15173/ijsap.v2i1.3472

Healey, M., Flint, A. and Harrington, K., 2014. *Engagement through partnership: students as partners in learning and teaching in higher education*. York: Higher Education Academy. Retrieved from: www.heacademy.ac.uk/system/files/resources/engagement_through_partnership.pdf

Hill, E., Liuzzi, F. and Giles, J., 2010. Peer-assisted learning from three perspectives: student, tutor and co-ordinator. *The clinical teacher*, 7(4), pp.244–246. Retrieved from: https://doi.org/10.1111/j.1743-498x.2010.00399.x

Ho, E., 2017. Small steps toward an ethos of partnership in a Hong Kong university: lessons from a focus group on 'homework'. *International Journal for Students as Partners*, 1(2). Retrieved from: https://doi.org/10.15173/ijsap.v1i2.3198

Horsley, G., 2016. From fresher to fresh perspective. *Student Engagement in Higher Education Journal*, 1(1).

Hunter, M., Tobolowsky, B. and Gardner, J., 2010. *Helping sophomores succeed: Understanding and improving the second year experience*. Chichester: John Wiley and Sons.

International Society for the Scholarship of Teaching and Learning (ISSOTL), 2019. Retrieved from: www.issotl.com/ (accessed 31 July 2019).

Kahu, E.R. and Nelson, K., 2018. Student engagement in the educational interface: understanding the mechanisms of student success. *Higher Education Research and Development*, 37(1), pp.58–71. Retrieved from: https://doi.org/10.1080/07294360.2017.1344197

Kandiko, C. B. and Mawer, M. 2013. *Student expectations and perceptions of higher education*. London: King's Learning Institute.

Keenan, C., 2014. Mapping student-led peer learning in the UK. Higher Education Academy. Retrieved from: www.heacademy.ac.uk/knowledge-hub/mapping-student-led-peer-learning-uk (accessed 19 July 2019).

Killick, D., 2017. *Developing intercultural practice: Academic development in a multicultural and globalizing World*. London: Routledge.

Krčmář, K. (ed.) 2019. *The Inclusivity Gap. Inspired by Learning*. Available for purchase here: www.inspiredbylearning.eu/book/10 (accessed 19 July 2019).

Kuh, G.D. and Hu, S., 2001. The effects of student–faculty interaction in the 1990s. *Review of Higher Education* 24(3) pp.309–332. Retrieved from: https://doi.org/10.1353/rhe.2001.0005

Lansdown, G., 2011. *Every child's right to be heard. A resource guide on the UN committee on the rights of the child general comment*, 12. Retrieved from: www.unicef.org/french/adolescence/files/Every_Childs_Right_to_be_Heard.pdf

Lea, J. (ed.) 2015. *Enhancing learning and teaching in higher education: Engaging with the dimensions of practice*. Milton Keynes: Open University Press.

Lees, B. and Adams, A., 2017. Students as recruiters. Paper given at Change Agent Conference 2017, Exeter, 21 April. Retrieved from: https://can.jiscinvolve.org/wp/files/2017/04/Becky-Lees-Uo-Chester.pdf

Lowe, T., 2018. Data analytics: a critique of the appropriation of a new measure of 'student engagement'. *Student Engagement in Higher Education Journal*, 2(1), pp.2–6.

Lowe, T. and Dunne, E., 2017. Setting the scene for the REACT programme: aims, challenges and the way ahead. *Journal of Educational Innovation, Partnership and Change*, 3(1), pp.24–39. Retrieved from: http://dx.doi.org/10.21100/jeipc.v3i1.678

Macfarlane, B., and Tomlinson, M., 2017. Critiques of student engagement. *Higher Education Policy*, 30(1), pp.5–21. Retrieved from: https://doi.org/10.1057/s41307-016-0027-3

Mann, S., 2001. Alternative perspectives on the student experience: alienation and engagement. *Studies in Higher Education*, 26(1) pp.7–19. Retrieved from: https://doi.org/10.1080/03075070123178

Marie, J. and Azuma, F., 2018. Partnership support for departments with low student satisfaction. *Student Engagement in Higher Education Journal*, 2(1), pp.70–77.

Marie, J., Arif, M. and Joshi, T., 2016. UCL ChangeMakers projects: Supporting staff/student partnership on educational enhancement projects. *Student Engagement in Higher Education Journal*, 1(1).

Marquis, E., Puri, V., Wan, S., Ahmad, A., Goff, L., Knorr, K., Vassileva, I. and Woo, J., 2016. Navigating the threshold of student–staff partnerships: A case study from an Ontario teaching and learning institute. *International Journal for Academic Development*, 21(1), pp.4–15. Retrieved from: https://doi.org/10.1080/1360144x.2015.1113538

Matthews, K. E., 2016. Students as partners as the future of student engagement. Student Engagement in Higher Education Journal, 1(1).

Matthews, K. E., Cook-Sather, A. and Healey, M., 2018. *Connecting learning, teaching, and research through student–staff partnerships: Toward universities as egalitarian learning communities*. Retrieved from: https://espace.library.uq.edu.au/view/UQ:722373

Matthews, K.E., Dwyer, A., Hine, L. and Turner, J., 2018. Conceptions of students as partners. *Higher Education*, 76(6), pp.957–971. Retrieved from: https://doi.org/10.1007/s10734-018-0257-y

Mercer-Mapstone, L., 2019. The student–staff partnership movement: striving for inclusion as we push sectorial change. *International Journal for Academic Development*, pp.1–13. Retrieved from: https://doi.org/10.1080/1360144x.2019.1631171

Moore, T. and Morton, J., 2017. The myth of job readiness? Written communication, employability, and the 'skills gap' in higher education. *Studies in Higher Education*, 42(3), pp.591–609. Retrieved from: https://doi.org/10.1080/03075079.2015.1067602

Morris, D., 2018. Beyond student satisfaction: student voice, student engagement, and quality learning in Ellis, R. and Hogard, E. (eds.), *Handbook of Quality Assurance for University Teaching*. London: Routledge.

Muijs, D., 2012, Surveys and sampling, in Briggs, A.R., Morrison, M. and Coleman, M. (eds.), *Research methods in educational leadership and management*. London: Sage Publications.

National Student Engagement Programme (NStEP), 2019. *National Student Engagement Programme*. Retrieved from: https://studentengagement.ie/home/ (accessed 6 August 2019).

National Survey of Student Engagement (NSSE), 2019. University of Indiana. Retrieved from: http://nsse.indiana.edu/ (accessed 30 July 2019).

National Union of Students (NUS), 2012. A manifesto for partnership. Retrieved from: www.nusconnect.org.uk/resources/a-manifesto-for-partnership/ (accessed 13 August 2019).

Neary, M and Winn, J., 2009. Student as producer: reinventing the undergraduate curriculum, pp.192–210. In: M. Neary, H. Stevenson and L. Bell (eds.), *The future of higher education: policy, pedagogy and the student experience*. London: Continuum.

Office for Students, 2018. *Securing student success: Regulatory framework for higher education in England*. Retrieved from: www.officeforstudents.org.uk/publications/securing-student-success-regulatory-framework-for-higher-education-in-england/v

Office for Students, 2019a. *Teaching excellence and student outcomes framework, 2019*. Retrieved from: www.officeforstudents.org.uk/advice-and-guidance/teaching/what-is-the-tef/ (accessed 19 July 2019).

Office for Students, 2019b. *Understanding and overcoming the challenges of targeting students from under-represented and disadvantaged ethnic backgrounds*. Retrieved from: www.officeforstudents.org.uk/media/d21cb263-526d-401c-bc74-299c748e9ecd/ethnicity-targeting-research-report.pdf

O'Shea, S., 2018. Equity and students as partners: The importance of inclusive relationships. *International Journal for Students as Partners*, 2(2), pp.16–20. Retrieved from: https://doi.org/10.15173/ijsap.v2i2.3628

Owen, D., 2013. Students engaged in academic subject review. In: Dunne, E. and Owen, D. (eds.), *Student engagement handbook: practice in higher education*. Bingley: Emerald Group Publishing.

Pascarella, E.T. and Terenzini, P.T., 2005. *How college affects students*, 2. San Francisco, CA: Jossey-Bass.

Porter, S.R., Whitcomb, M.E. and Weitzer, W.H., 2004. Multiple surveys of students and survey fatigue. *New Directions for Institutional Research*, 121, pp.63–73. Retrieved from: https://doi.org/10.1002/ir.101

Quality Assurance Agency (QAA), 2012. Quality Code Section B5: Student Engagement. Retrieved from: www.qaa.ac.uk/en/Publications/Pages/Quality-Code-Chapter-B5.aspx#.VSEBn4hXerU

REACT, 2019. *Realising Engagement through Active Culture Transformation*. Retrieved from: www.studentengagement.ac.uk (accessed 19 July 2019).

Researching, Advancing and Inspiring Student Engagement (RAISE), 2019. Retrieved from: www.raise-network.com/home/ (accessed 31 July 2019).

Senior, C., Moores, E. and Burgess, A.P., 2017. 'I can't get no satisfaction': measuring student satisfaction in the age of a consumerist higher education. *Frontiers in Psychology*, 8, pp.980. Retrieved from: https://doi.org/10.3389/fpsyg.2017.00980

Shaw, C. and Atvars, T., 2018. Two sides of the same coin: a university and student union perspective on partnership and risk. *Teaching and Learning Together in Higher Education*, 1(24), p.6. Retrieved from: https://repository.brynmawr.edu/tlthe/vol1/iss24/6/

Shaw, C., Humphrey, O., Atvars, T. and Sims, S., 2017. Who they are and how to engage them: A summary of the REACT systematic literature review of the 'hard to reach' in higher education. *Journal of Educational Innovation, Partnership and Change*, 3(1), pp.51–64. Retrieved from: http://dx.doi.org/10.21100/jeipc.v3i1.685

Sims, S., King, S., Lowe, T. and El Hakim, Y., 2016. Evaluating partnership and impact in the first year of the Student Fellows Scheme, *Journal of Educational Innovation, Partnership and Change*, 2(1). Retrieved from: http://dx.doi.org/10.21100/jeipc.v2i1.257

Solomonides, I. and Reid, A., 2009, July. Understanding the relationships between student identity and engagement with studies. In: *The student experience: Proceedings of the 32nd HERDSA Annual Conference*.

Stalmeijer, R., Whittingham, J., de Grave, W. and Dolmans, D., 2016. Strengthening internal quality assurance processes: facilitating student evaluation committees to contribute. *Assessment and Evaluation in Higher Education*, 41(1), pp.53–66.

Staff Education Development Network (SEDA), 2019. Retrieved from: www.seda.ac.uk/ (accessed 31 July 2019).

Student Minds, 2019. *Co-producing mental health strategies with students: A guide for the higher education sector*. Retrieved from: www.studentminds.org.uk/co-productionguide.html

Student Voice Project: Australia, 2019. *Aims of the Student Voice Project: Australia*. Retrieved from: http://studentvoiceaustralia.com/aims/ (accessed 31 July 2019).

Sum, K., 2018. Growing from a Seed. *Student Engagement in Higher Education Journal*, 2(1), pp.7–11.

Tchibozo, G., 2008. Extra-curricular activity and the transition from higher education to work: A survey of graduates in the United Kingdom. In: *Higher Education Quarterly*. 61(1), pp.33–56. Retrieved from: https://doi.org/10.1111/j.1468-2273.2006.00337.x

Teslenko, T., 2019. Engaging Students and Campus Community in Sustainability Activities in a Major Canadian University, pp.3–20. In: Leal Filho, W. and Bardi, U. (eds.), *Sustainability on University Campuses: Learning, Skills Building and Best Practices*. New York: Springer.

The Student Engagement Partnership, 2014. *The Principles of Student Engagement: The Student Engagement Conversation*. London: TSEP. Retrieved from: http://tsep.org.uk/the-principles/

Thomas, L., 2012. *Building student engagement and belonging in higher education at a time of change: final report from the What Works? Student Retention and Success programme*. London: Paul Hamlyn Foundation. Retrieved from: www.heacademy.ac.uk/knowledge-hub/building-student engagement-and-belonging-higher-education-time-change-final-report

Tinto, V., 2006. Research and practice of student retention: what next? *College Student Retention*, 8(1), pp.1–20. Retrieved from: https://doi.org/10.2190/c0c4-eft9-eg7w-pwp4

Tomlinson, M., 2016. The impact of market-driven higher education on student-university relations: Investing, consuming and competing. *Higher Education Policy*, 29(2), pp.149–166. Retrieved from: https://doi.org/10.1057/hep.2015.17

Trowler, V., 2010. Student engagement literature review. Higher Education Academy. Retrieved from: www.heacademy.ac.uk/system/files/studentengagementliteraturereview_1.pdf

UKSCQA and QAA, 2018. Student Engagement Advice and Guidance Theme, *UK Quality Code for Higher Education*. United Kingdom Standing Committee for Quality Assessment and Quality Assurance Agency for Higher Education. Retrieved from: www.qaa.ac.uk/quality-code (accessed 8 August 2019).

Unite, 2017. *Student Resilience: Unite Students Insight Report*. Retrieved from: www.unite-group.co.uk/sites/default/files/2017-03/student-insight-report-2016.pdf

Universities United Kingdom (UUK), 2017. *Education, consumer rights and maintaining trust: what students want from their university*. Retrieved from: www.universitiesuk.ac.uk/policy-and-analysis/reports/Pages/what-students-want-from-their-university.aspx

Vuori, J., 2013. Student Engagement: Buzzword of Fuzzword?, *Journal of Higher Education Policy and Management*, 36(5) pp.509–519. Retrieved from: https://doi.org/10.1080/1360080x.2014.936094

Wait, R. and Bols, A., 2015. *Making Student Engagement a Reality: Turning Theory into Practice*. London: Guild HE. Retrieved from: www.guildhe.ac.uk/wp-content/uploads/2015/11/6472-Guild-HE-Student-Engagement-Report-36pp.pdf

Warren, D. and Luebsen, W., 2017. 'Getting into the flow of university': a coaching approach to student peer support. *Journal of Educational Innovation, Partnership and Change*, 3(1), pp.262–269. Retrieved from: http://dx.doi.org/10.21100/jeipc.v3i1.599

Winstone, N. and Carless, D., 2019. *Designing effective feedback processes in higher education: A learning-focused approach.* London: Routledge.

Zanten, A.V., 2005. Bourdieu as education policy analyst and expert: A rich but ambiguous legacy. *Journal of Education Policy,* 20(6), pp.671–686. Retrieved from: https://doi.org/10.1080/02680930500238887

Zepke, N., 2013. Student engagement: A complex business supporting the first year experience in tertiary education. *International Journal of the First Year in Higher Education,* 4(2). Retrieved from: https://doi.org/10.5204/intjfyhe.v4i2.183

Zepke, N., 2018. Student engagement in neoliberal times: what is missing? *Higher Education Research and Development,* 37(2), pp.433–446. Retrieved from: https://doi.org/10.1080/07294360.2017.1370440

Creating relationships between students, staff and universities for student engagement in educational developments

Yassein El Hakim, Camille Kandiko Howson and Rebecca Freeman

Introduction

There has been a clear shift nationally in the UK over the past ten years and within universities concerning the perceived role, agency and hierarchical position of students within the educational system. Internationally, there is broad acceptance of student engagement as an indicator of positive learning experiences and outcomes. Pascarella, Seifert and Blaich (2010) stated that their findings suggested: 'that increases on institutional [National Survey of Student Engagement] NSSE scores can be considered as reasonable proxies for student growth and learning across a range of important educational outcomes.

A key consideration is how institutions respond to and engage with metrics such as the National Survey of Student Engagement or its international variants such as the UK Engagement Survey (UKES) and those in Ireland, Australia and China (see Coates and McCormick, 2014). Such data can aid and enhance other educational outcomes like progression, learning gains, retention and satisfaction, but are most effective when incorporated into wider development strategies. International pressure on universities to perform in league tables is further increasing the importance of some of these metrics to institutions and their leaders.

There are multitudes of ways that institutions now view their students. Many of these perceptions are influenced by cultural and historical traditions. For example, a popularized view reported through the media in England is that students have become consumers of knowledge and subsequently their degrees. This is a view that has been challenged across the UK HE sector by multiple governmental and membership bodies, such as: the National Union of Students, the Higher Education Academy and Leadership Foundation for HE (both now merged with the Equality Challenge Unit to form Advance HE), Jisc, the Quality Assurance Agency and the Staff and Educational Development Association.

There is a danger of a self-fulfilling prophecy occurring if the perception of students as customers is gradually adopted by society, so that students themselves then begin acting more as consumers than learners. There are, of course, transactional elements of a student's experience, e.g. a student pays rent to their university for a room, and there are rightly expectations inherent within that agreement. However, regarding the learning process and its interactions, such expectations or a notion of entitlement can be problematic and may create divisions between students, academics and their institutions. These may well result in the disempowerment of students and a reduction in opportunities for constructive dialogue between students and staff about academic and educational enhancement and development. The 'customer' rhetoric increases the likelihood of creating an environment where it is harder for students to work closely with staff to enhance their learning experiences. In England, this perception has been fuelled by the tripling of student fees twice within a ten-year period, but it is also evident in the US and Australia in response to increases in tuition fees and changes in funding arrangements. This aligns with the '3P model' (Biggs, 1993), which discusses: presage, process and product. The first, 'presage', points to variables such as funding or resources, which fund the system. Biggs (1993) and Astin (1977) both focus on presage which feeds into the creation of an 'Input-Environment-Output' model of education.

Students' engagement and relationship with their programmes and universities have clearly shifted as a consequence. This has provided challenges for those working with students and academics, as we negotiate strong political and institutional imperatives for engagement with students, whilst considering how to best develop education at a time of changing identities and roles within complex contexts.

In some respects, the view that students have multiple roles and identities is appropriate, and in fact one of these roles is, appropriately, that of consumer. This is particularly promoted by student services departments and offices within institutions, such as library services, dining and accommodation (Temple, Callender, Grove and Kersh, 2014). However, given the high fees paid and other financial contributions that many students make towards their education, there is a blurring between the role of students as customers in some contexts and as learners in others. The main omission in the media is the responsibility of the student within the learning process. Nicol (2009) suggests there are responsibilities for both staff and students in ensuring that learning is optimized, starting from the first day of a student's educational programme. In this chapter we go one step further to posit that students, staff and institutions have a shared responsibility to collaboratively enhance the educational experience through the acknowledgement and deeper understanding of the learning process and reflections on the current learning environment and experience from all three perspectives.

This chapter will consider some international cases which illustrate alternative ways of creating and supporting roles for students to work collaboratively with staff to enhance academic and educational development. Moving beyond ideas of students as customers, these examples offer approaches of working *with* students, which focus primarily on the purpose of engagement in a particular context and shape relationships in ways that develop and enhance the teaching and learning environment within an institution. We identify several principles for student engagement drawn from the literature and the cases presented that can potentially shape relationships between students and staff to develop productive cultures of engagement towards academic development.

Background

We use a broad, yet inclusive, definition of 'Student Engagement'. Trowler (2010) states that:

> *Student engagement is concerned with the interaction between the time, effort and other relevant resources invested by both students and their institutions intended to optimize the student experience and enhance the learning outcomes and development of students and the performance, and reputation of the institution.*
>
> (p.3)

This definition encompasses a wide range of student engagement activity that has developed around the world in response to different drivers, imperatives and political and cultural contexts. In the US, Australia, New Zealand and Ireland, students' engagement with their own studies has been the central tenet, in part, reflected by surveys of student engagement similar to that of the NSSE (National Survey of Student Engagement, 2004, 2005).

Drawing on a historical politicization of student engagement in representation, student engagement in the UK seems to be adopting a broader, more political interpretation, which focuses on how students are engaged by and with their institutions in enhancing their educational experience and related decision-making. This is in contrast to, but not incompatible with, the large-scale comparative data offered through NSSE. Whilst the more political interpretation focuses on students' direct involvement in committees and policy-making, data-gathering has been central to a shift in how universities in the US create learning environments for their first year students whose multiple benefits aid retention – and, in particular, improve the learning experience of students in their first year (Kuh, Kinzie, Schuh and Whitt, 2005). This difference in approach highlights the flexibility in the concept of student engagement to capture diverse modes, attitudes and approaches of bringing students into development and enhancement activities within institutions.

National surveys of student engagement provide useful policy data and help to influence national conversations about how students learn, effective educational practices and student outcomes. However, the use of engagement data within institutions is dependent on embedding it within enhancement, governance and decision-making processes. This further emphasizes how educational development policies and practices influence student behaviours and activities inside and outside of the classroom, the interaction between academics and students, and the environment in which students learn.

While there has been a clear emphasis on student engagement over the last ten years in higher education, particularly since the introduction and subsequent increase in tuition fees in England, the imperatives behind particular approaches to engagement are often unclear to the students and staff involved. Recent research (Freeman, 2013; Freeman, 2016) has demonstrated that students, academics and senior management at times see quite distinct imperatives behind student engagement in their own institutions. These range from an understanding of students as paying customers and of a requirement by government and other agencies for accountability, to a desire for greater democracy between students and staff, or an understanding of higher education as a joint political project.

Roles, position and power

Student engagement has been defined as relating to the extent of a student's active involvement in (learning) activities (Wellborn, 1991). Although narrow and relatively simplistic, a similar view of engagement can be applied to educational development where engagement can be seen as the active involvement in contexts that allow students to enhance their own educational experience and the experiences of others, individually or collaboratively with others (staff, students, community, senior management teams, etc.). Although student engagement could be perceived simply as active involvement in an activity, it has been acknowledged as having many defined and interrelated aspects.

Reeve (2012) described four related forms of engagement: Behavioural, Emotional, Cognitive and Agentic. Behavioural engagement is focused on the level of persistence, effort and attention/concentration on task. This is largely what surveys of student engagement focus on. Emotional engagement is determined by encouraging task-facilitating emotions (e.g. curiosity) and reducing task-withdrawing emotions such as anxiety, frustration and fear. This type of engagement is often the focus of teaching-focused interventions and student-support initiatives. Cognitive engagement centres on deep and sophisticated learning strategies for individuals, seeking conceptual understanding rather than memorization and self-regulatory strategies. Cognitive engagement is measured by engagement surveys, as well as learning-focused activities and related curricular and co-curricular enhancements. Most dominant in the UK context is what Reeve (2012) describes as Agentic Change: *'the proactive, intentional and constructive contribution [of the student] into the flow of the learning activity (e.g. offering input, making suggestions)... Enriching the learning activity, rather than passively receiving it as a given'* (p.151). This distinction clearly furthers the work of Wellborn (1991) and aligns more clearly with the contemporary culture growing across higher education (particularly in the UK).

The premise of agentic change is of importance to this chapter as it captures the intersection between student engagement, academic development and educational change. Following the processes Reeve ascribes to agentic change, there is an increasing trend across the higher education sector for the enhancement of the learning and teaching experience of students to be achieved by students and with students. Students' involvement and engagement in learning activities affords them opportunities for greater depth and breadth of understanding, both of learning and the learning environment. This is true of academic development too, where the students' involvement can create empathetic and informed positions of the current context, but can also offer suggestions for its enhancement. Reeve's notion of agentic engagement during a learning activity also offers an opportunity to consider the relationships between staff and students for academic development. He states that agentic engagement involves proactive and constructive contribution, offering input and making suggestions.

In considering the benefits and challenges of different approaches to both students and staff in development activities, there needs to be attention to how such approaches might inform their understanding of the purpose of higher education as well as their roles within their institutions. In the enhancement of academic practice the role and impact of the student voice, student input and student activity or agency in changing practice has been well documented (Dunne and Owen, 2013). The results of this are discussed here in relation to Self-Determination Theory (SDT) (Ryan and Deci, 2000). The theory describes three 'basic' motivational human needs as key indicators of intrinsic motivation: autonomy, relatedness and competence. The higher a person's perception of their competence at something, their relatedness to it and their perception of control or choice within the context, the higher their intrinsic or self-regulated extrinsic motivation (Mageau and Vallerand, 2003). Reeve (2012) describes the three basic needs in relation to student engagement as: '*the source of students' inherent and proactive intrinsically motivated tendency to seek out novelty, pursue optimal challenge, exercise and extend their capabilities, explore, and learn.*'

This theory could be utilized to deepen our understanding of how future relationships between students, academic developers, academics, senior management teams and national higher education sector communities further enhance academic development as a process across a broader, more transparent and inclusive community. In this respect, there is a clear opportunity to further investigate the perceptions of autonomy, relatedness and control in students and various staff within universities globally to identify and evaluate cultural and context-specific differences and impacts (Krause, North and Davidson, 2019).

Change within organizations is often initiated by top-level decisions in response to external contexts, funding or governmental policies. If such relationships between students, staff and academic developers are nurtured and empowered, a strong foundation for academic and educational development activities and research impact could occur, thus creating change within institutions at programme, department or faculty/school level. Finn (1989) discusses engagement as a learned behaviour, and Lawson and Lawson (2013) develop this in describing the need for conditions of engagement that would 'nurture' such a learned behaviour, or even initiate the behaviour. This aligns with the NUS *Student Experience Report* (NUS, 2008), concerning involvement and feedback, where 92% reported that they had the opportunity to give feedback on their learning, but only 51% said they felt they were listened to. The course structure was often modular and many students submitted their feedback on a module at the end, thus not seeing any changes in response to their comments. Universities have subsequently shifted their practice as a result of this research to include mid-module evaluations or other mechanisms so that students see the responses to their feedback in each module.

Where students have not been permitted roles or responsibilities that give significant autonomy or 'choice within boundaries' over their learning and/or wider educational experience, they can develop a perceived or real lack of control or impact, following their feedback. Consequently, students could perceive some learning environments as the domain solely of academics and universities and may feel that education is done 'to' rather than 'with' them. Such a perception could be accompanied by a feeling of learned helplessness and that would not be helpful in driving intrinsic motivation according to Self Determination Theory (SDT).

If given opportunities to enter into partnerships with staff through reflective and evidence-informed activities, students could, in line with SDT, perceive higher levels of autonomy and relatedness, whilst enhancing the learning experiences of their peers, breaking perceptions of learned helplessness and generating a culture of partnerships and relationships. This in turn could encourage peers to engage in academic and educational development activities to benefit their degree programmes, institutions or the national/global HE sector. The following cases illustrate examples of educational development projects where education is evolving into something far more engaging, authentic, challenging, impactful, democratic and holistic.

Student engagement in educational development

Several cases included here depict the varied practice across the sector in regard to students' engagement with educational development. Simultaneously, across the sector a growing selection of universities have begun to systematically structure and sustain programmes, whereby students can actively participate within Educational and Academic Development. Notably, one of the highest profile examples is the University of Exeter's (UK) initiative. The Students as Change Agents initiative engaged students as partners in the shaping and leading of their own educational experiences. Exeter gained profile for championing a scheme that offered students the opportunity to volunteer to work with staff across the university in order to enhance aspects of the learning experience and environment. Birmingham City University (UK) has also gained recognition for the number of students that they worked in partnership with across the institution through a range of opportunities and the embedded nature of the Student Academic Partners scheme, with impressive statements of employment both during their degree and once they graduated.

The University of Winchester (UK) launched the Student Fellows Scheme following the successful leadership of two national projects: a Jisc-funded project called Fastech (Feedback and Assessment for Students with Technology) in 2010–13; and a HEA-funded project called TESTA (Transforming the Experience of Students Through Assessment) in 2009–12. The Fastech project sought to identify ways in which technology could enhance the students' experience of assessment and feedback. It was decided that bursaries would be offered for second year undergraduate students to become Fastech Fellows. The roles were structured so that the students would immerse themselves in one specific aspect of the assessment and feedback process within their programmes and identify with an academic partner any potential enhancements that could be possible. The Fastech Fellows scheme was a huge success, seeing over 90% of fellows completing projects and several receiving notable mentions nationally.

Subsequent to the fellows' impacts on Fastech, an institutional proposal to fund and support 60 Student Fellows across the institution was both supported by the Senior Management Team and the Student Union equally. Following six years of the scheme being funded, students have been responsible for: over 400 projects, six publications in peer reviewed journals, numerous presentations at dozens of conferences nationally, as well as significant impacts on students' experiences across the University of Winchester (and other institutions who are initiating similar schemes). The Fellows' projects have included: researching the commuter student experience at Winchester leading to commuter student facilities being commissioned; technology enhanced learning projects to embed digital skills in the curriculum; co-designing international accredited modules; and communicating student extra-curricular activities at Winchester leading to a new opportunity directory called Get Involved, which launched in 2017. The Fellows Scheme resulted in 60 students engaging in a process of educational development with a staff partner and vastly increased the number of staff and students who engaged with the Learning and Teaching Development Unit from across the university over the duration of the scheme.

At the University of Warwick (UK), Student Technology Champions (Freeman et al., 2014) led the development of technology in relation to learning and teaching in Life Sciences, designing interactive tutorials and developing videos both for prospective students and to enable the focus of lab assessment to be on refining lab skills. This project was then rolled out across the institution as part of the inaugural activity of Warwick International Higher Education Academy (WIHEA) which provides a collective institutional voice on learning and teaching. An initial WIHEA project round funded student champions to work with departments to develop and embed technology in departments (WIHEA,

2017). Since 2016, collaborative partnership between students and staff is a requirement of all WIHEA-funded projects with 24 projects being undertaken under the broader strategic priorities of: student research; internationalization; interdisciplinary studies; student engagement; assessment and feedback; and group work (WIHEA, 2018). WIHEA also has a number of student WIHEA Fellows who are committed to the development of learning and teaching as part of WIHEA and work on a range of projects and policy to inform Warwick's strategic development of learning and teaching.

Student engagement in research

The University of Western Australia launched the Undergraduate Learning and Teaching Research Internship Scheme (ULTRIS) in 2009. It offered internship opportunities to a selection of students, providing valuable practical research experience. The research experience centred on enhancing the awareness of the scholarship of teaching and learning, and collecting and analysing data and 'context-relevant information' that informs the teaching and learning community at UWA. A stipend of $3000 is made available for those selected in order to reduce their need to seek externally paid work, and so be able to focus on the research project identified. The project is only available to second and third year students. ULTRIS was still recruiting in 2015 with the theme of 'Transformative Teaching and Learning'. The scheme also gained further internal recognition when it won UWA's own Award for Excellence in Teaching.

At King's College London (UK), student interns were engaged in the data analysis and development of recommendations from data collected in a local survey named the King's Experience Survey, part of a national student engagement survey pilot that informed the creation of the UK Engagement Survey (UKES). Teams of four undergraduate student interns, drawn from different disciplines and campuses across the institution, were provided with qualitative research methods training. The student interns were asked to analyse anonymized qualitative comments from each department. Students were provided with the quantitative findings from the survey to contextualize their analysis. They drew out major themes from the different departments and captured relevant quotes to highlight major issues for students. The student interns then worked collaboratively with academic development staff to write up their analysis and to provide student-led recommendations based on the data. Customized reports for each department were presented at relevant School/Departmental Education Meetings. Students greatly appreciated the opportunity to engage with 'real' research, particularly that which could lead to the enhancement of their own educational experience. Academic development staff found the students extremely helpful in transforming the analysis into recommendations that could directly enhance the learning environment for students. Student engagement in the analysis also helped to gain buy-in from academic staff and senior management.

Student engagement driving institutional/national change or innovation

When students are engaged to lead changes with guidance and support, there can be transformative learning experiences for both the students and leaders of institutions/organizations. Jisc's Summer of Student Innovation was a national initiative that aimed to generate innovative ideas from students within UK higher and further education. The ideas were submitted to a website, voted on by individuals from at least ten different eligible institutions/organizations. The premise behind the voting system was that students and staff from other universities would identify the importance of such projects. Projects have included: apps, video platforms, self-help resources, games, democratic voting spaces and student life planning tools. Students who received the highest votes were awarded a £5000 grant from Jisc to grow their ideas into tools which can be used by fellow students and staff across the sector. In 2014, there were dozens of entries from further education and higher education students and 8400 votes. One of the most significant aspects of the Jisc scheme is the wide-ranging partnerships formed across the sector. Many of the projects have received further funding following continued success and adoption across the sector, which validates the scheme and benefits the sector.

At the University of Lincoln (UK), the Student as Producer initiative emphasizes students as collaborators in the production of knowledge. Student as Producer is a development of the institution's policy of research-engaged teaching. As part of the initiative, undergraduate students partner with academic staff in the design and delivery of their teaching and learning programmes, and in the production of work of academic content and value. This whole-institution initiative engages students both individually and collectively in enhancement of the overall teaching and learning environment. It was led from the Centre for Educational Research and Development, highlighting the key role for educational developers in driving institutional change and enhancement activities.

Activities are supported by professional staff and student services departments, with funding for specific projects being made available to both staff and students. Associated activities and outputs have included: students engaged as consultants for enhancing academic teaching and as a support for other students, co-developing open access resources for institutional development; undergraduate student research opportunities; funding for staff to develop their curriculum along the lines of research-engaged teaching; and collaborative conferences engaging students, academic staff and senior management celebrating research-engaged teaching and extra-curricular activities. Student engagement has become embedded in institutional decision-making through collaboration with the Students' Union. Students report feeling empowered and an acknowledged part of the university community. Educational development has been enhanced through having an underlying set of values and it has taken a greater role in institutional governance through quality assurance processes and senior management roles.

In summary, when considering working with students within institutional roles, partnerships or educationally developmental relationships:

1. Context is all-important – even if schemes can be adopted or adapted, the context into which they are being applied will be different and deserves significant acknowledgement.
2. Terminology matters – how the schemes are titled can impact the perception of partnership, e.g. the phrase 'Students as...' inherently generates assumptions of acting, pretending or impersonating. This is not, however, a reflection of the actual partnerships and beliefs of those who lead them.
3. Funding the opportunities divides opinion and adds complexity – where opportunities are funded in order to be inclusive they can create management relationships as opposed to partnerships. Bursaries seem more autonomous but can result in less predictable outcomes.
4. Meeting high expectations – where high expectations are set, students can regularly meet/exceed them and in doing so, they can dispel myths of 'students insufficient capabilities/development' in order to understand complex contexts and concepts or to impact intransigent areas of an institution.
5. Developing collaborations between students and staff can be complex but the richness and relevance of the outcomes and process ensure stronger educational development.

Leadership of academic development

Student engagement in academic development can lead to unforeseen positive results. There will be a variety of conclusions to draw from the conceptual and theoretical underpinnings, the three sub-categories and variety of cases drawn upon. However, one of the most significant reflections from these examples is regarding the leadership of educational development and change: how does meaningful change get led and by whom?

Northouse (2007) defines leadership as 'a process whereby an individual influences a group of individuals to achieve a common goal' (p.3). In defining leadership as a process, he implies that: a leader affects and is affected by followers, leadership is not linear but interactive and dynamic, leadership involves influence, leadership occurs in groups and creates attention to goals. Middlehurst (1993) and Deem (2001) describe 'a deep-seated desire' within academic communities for collegiality and academic freedom, where leaders and changes occur through a consultative process. Bolden, Petrov and Gosling (2009) offered further evidence of how leadership exists in HE by stating:

> Like the rest of the education sector the majority of research on leadership and management in HE concludes that leadership in universities is widely distributed (Middlehurst, 1993; Knight and Trowler, 2001) or should be distributed across the institution.

Gronn (2000, 2002) suggests the distributed leadership model of 'collective' over 'leader-centric' creates collaborative work that is greater than the sum of the parts. In schemes such as those described earlier, success is more likely when a project is led by the person who created it, or at least has a strong supporter, often within the senior management. Spillane, Halverson and Diamond (2004) suggest that leadership (within a distributed model) is generated from the interactions of people within a context, instead of an individual leader's actions. Bennett, Wise, Woods and Harvey (2003) outline that distributed leadership has three assertions where: leadership is emergent from interacting individuals; there is an openness to the boundaries of leadership; and varieties of expertise are distributed across the many, not the few. The last point is of particular interest in relation to leadership of academic development, where not only expertise but experience can often draw from varying departments and students across an institution. The value to HEIs in creating more opportunities for such expertise to be shared through working groups or task forces is clear.

Kotter (1990) identifies a distinction between management and leadership, whereby management produces order and consistency, while leadership produces change and movement. Kotter's contention that leadership produces change and movement through activities such as establishing direction, aligning people, motivating and inspiring and empowering followers might not regard students as leaders of their learning environment and experiences. However, from the observed cases and other research (Soriano, Mann and Friesen, 2019), it is clear that students who are 'empowered' at a variety of levels to fully engage with staff, programme teams, departments and universities are, in many cases, the right people to co-lead and motivate phenomenal changes in higher education.

It has been stated that, in order to improve the quality of our programmes, educational development has to focus on 'normalizing quality activities, with an emphasis on improving rather than proving quality; and enhancement rather than merely on compliance' (Radloff, 2005, p.78). This aligns with the QAA's stance on student engagement, where Student Reviewers help in the governance of HE institutions. The QAA website clearly supports this assertion by stating, 'Students are partners in their learning experiences so each review team has a student as a full member.'

Somekh (1998) spoke of five key concepts central to successful innovation:

1. messiness, the acceptance of situational complexities, and the recognition that different motivations prevailing from different points of view within an organization;
2. the power of individuals to make a positive contribution to bring about change;
3. partnership and creating a critical mass of shared meanings and understanding;
4. professional development is central to the process of planning and implementing change;
5. and the need for the integration of theory and practice, for example, by the use of action learning approaches.

The cases drawn on herein create powerful partnerships and opportunities for such concepts and features to intersect and grow within some innovative relationships. Martin (2007, 2009) also identified congruencies across a number of themes such as self-efficacy, attributions, valuing, control, self-determination, goal orientation and self-worth and integrated these themes into a multi-dimensional framework. The identification of congruencies throughout this chapter suggests that the intersection of SDT, learned helplessness, empowerment and leadership (specifically, distributed leadership) cumulatively provide a strong rationale for why such schemes succeed in creating educational changes that are relevant, impactful and evidence-informed. Inclusive teams of academics, students and academic developers within an autonomous and empowered context of distributed leadership, provide a powerful approach for leading educational development.

References

Astin, A., 1977. *Four critical years*. San Francisco, CA: Jossey-Bass.

Bennett, N., Wise, C., Woods, P. A. and Harvey, J. A., 2003. *Distributed leadership: a review of literature*. National College for School Leadership.

Biggs, J., 1993. From theory to practice: a cognitive systems approach. *Higher Education Research and Development*, 12(1), 73–85. Retrieved from: https://doi.org/10.1080/0729436930120107

Bolden, R., Petrov, G. and Gosling J., 2009. Distributed leadership in higher education: rhetoric and reality. *Educational Management Administration and Leadership*, 37(2), 257–277. Retrieved from: https://doi.org/10.1177/1741143208100301

Coates, H., and McCormick, A. (eds.), 2014. *Engaging University Students: International Insights from System-Wide Studies*. Dordrecht: Springer.

Deem, R., 2001. Globalisation, new managerialism, academic capitalism and entrepreneurialism in universities: is the local dimension still important? *Comparative Education*, 37(1), 7–20.

Dunne, E. and Owen, D. (eds.), 2013. *Student Engagement Handbook: Practice in Higher Education*. Bingley: Emerald Group Publishing.

Finn, J., 1989. Withdrawing from school. *Review of Educational Research*, 59(2), 117–142.

Freeman, R., 2013. Student engagement in practice: ideologies and power dynamics in course representation systems. Student engagement handbook: practice in higher education (eds.) Dunne, E. and Owen, D., 2013, 145–162. Bingley: Emerald.

Freeman, R., Griffiths, M., Harvey, J., Lee, L., Moffat, K., Williams, L., 2014. Student technology champions: collaborative enhancement of learning and teaching technology in the life sciences. *Society of Experimental Biology, Teaching and Communicating Science in the Digital Age – a symposium*. London.

Freeman, R., 2016. Is student voice necessarily empowering? Problematising student voice as a form of higher education governance. *Higher Education Research and Development* 35(4), 859–862. Retrieved from: https://doi.org/10.1080/07294360.2016.1172764

Gronn, P., 2000. Distributed properties: a new architecture for leadership, *Educational Management Administration and Leadership* 28(3), 317–38. Retrieved from: https://doi.org/10.1016/s1048-9843(02)00120-0

Gronn, P., 2002. Distributed leadership as a unit of analysis, *Leadership Quarterly* 13, 423–51. Retrieved from: https://doi.org/10.1016/s1048-9843(02)00120-0

Knight, P. and Trowler, P., 2001. *Departmental Leadership in Higher Education: new directions for communities of practice*. Buckingham: Open University Press/SRHE.

Kotter, J. P., 1990. A force for change how leadership differs from management. New York: Free Press.

Krause, A. E., North, A. C. and Davidson, J. W., 2019. Using self-determination theory to examine musical participation and well-being. Frontiers in Psychology, 10, 405. Retrieved from: https://doi.org/10.3389/fpsyg.2019.00405

Kuh, G. D., Kinzie, J., Schuh, J. H. and Whitt, E. J., 2005. *Student success in college: Creating conditions that matter*. San Francisco, CA: Jossey-Bass.

Lawson, M. A., and Lawson, H. A., 2013. New conceptual frameworks for student engagement research, policy, and practice. *Review of Educational Research*, 83, 432–479. Retrieved from: https://doi.org/10.3102/0034654313480891

Mageau, G.A. and Vallerand, R.J., 2003. The coach–athlete relationship: a motivational model. *Journal of Sports Sciences*, 21, 883–904. Retrieved from: https://doi.org/10.1080/0264041031000140374

Middlehurst, R., 1993. *Leading Academics*. Buckingham: SRHE and OU Press. Cited in Bolden, R., Petrov, G. and Gosling J., 2009. Distributed Leadership in Higher Education: Rhetoric and Reality. Educational Management Administration and Leadership, 37(2), 257–277. Retrieved from: https://doi.org/10.1177/1741143208100301

Martin, A. J., 2007. Examining a multidimensional model of student motivation and engagement using a construct validation approach. *British Journal of Educational Psychology*, 77, 413–440. Retrieved from: https://doi.org/10.1348/000709906x118036

Martin, A. J., 2009. Motivation and engagement across the academic lifespan: A developmental construct validity study of elementary school, high school and university/college students. *Educational and Psychological Measurement*, 69, 794–824. Retrieved from: https://doi.org/10.1177/0013164409332214

Middlehurst, R., 1993. *Leading Academics*. Buckingham: SRHE and OU Press. Cited in Bolden, R., Petrov, G. and Gosling J., 2009. Distributed Leadership in Higher Education: Rhetoric and Reality. Educational Management Administration and Leadership, 37(2), 257–277. Retrieved from: https://doi.org/10.1177/1741143208100301

National Union of Students (NUS), 2008. *Student Experience Report*. National Union of Students.

Nicol, D., 2009. Quality Enhancement Themes: The First Year Experience. The Quality Assurance Agency for Higher Education. Retrieved from: www.enhancementthemes.ac.uk/docs/ethemes/the-first-year/transforming-assessment-and-feedback.pdf?sfvrsn=c62f981_12

Northouse, P.G., 2007. *Leadership theory and practice* (4th ed.). Thousand Oaks, CA: Sage Publications.

Pascarella, E.T., Seifert, T.A. and Blaich, C., 2010. How effective are the NSSE benchmarks in predicting important educational outcomes? *Change*, 42(1), 16–22. Retrieved from: https://doi.org/10.1080/00091380903449060

Radloff, A., 2005. Supporting student learning in the 21st century university: What's the job and whose job is it? In G. Grigg and C. Bond (eds.), Supporting learning in the 21st century: Refereed proceedings of the 2005 Annual International Conference of the Association of Tertiary Learning Advisors Aotearoa/New Zealand (ATLAANZ), 2–17. Dunedin: Higher Education Development Centre, University of Otago.

Reeve, J., 2012. A self-determination theory perspective on student engagement. In S. L. Christenson, A. L. Reschly and C. Wylie (eds.), Handbook of research on student engagement (pp.149–172). Boston, MA: Springer US.

Ryan, R. M., and Deci, E. L., 2000. Self-determination theory and the facilitation of intrinsic motivation, social development, and well-being. American Psychologist, 55, pp.68–78.

Somekh, B., 1998. Supporting information and communication technology innovations in higher education. *Journal of Information Technology for Teacher Education*, 7(1), 11–32. Retrieved from: https://doi.org/10.1080/14759399800200028

Soriano, L., Mann, D. and Friesen, M.R., 2019. Enhancement of Student Learning through Self- Reflection. Proceedings from Canadian Engineering Education Association (CEEA-ACEG19) Conference. Retrieved from: www.academia.edu/39591889/Enhancement_of_Student_Learning_Through_Self-reflection

Spillane, J.P., Halverson, R. and Diamond, J.B., 2004. Towards a Theory of Leadership Practice: A Distributed Perspective, *Journal of Curriculum Studies* 36(1), 3–34. Retrieved from: https://doi.org/10.1080/0022027032000106726

Temple, P., Callender, C., Grove, L. and Kersh, N., 2014. Managing the student experience in a shifting higher education landscape. Higher Education Academy. Retrieved from: https://s3.eu-west-2.amazonaws.com/assets.creode.advancehe-document-manager/documents/hea/private/resources/managing_the_student_experience_1568037252.pdf

Trowler, V., 2010. Student Engagement Literature Review. Higher Education Academy. Retrieved from: https://s3.eu-west-2.amazonaws.com/assets.creode.advancehe-document-manager/documents/hea/private/studentengagementliteraturereview_1_1568037028.pdf

Wellborn, J. G., 1991. Engaged and disaffected action: The conceptualization and measurement of motivation in the academic domain. Unpublished doctoral dissertation, University of Rochester, New York.

WIHEA, 2017. 2015–16 Funded Projects. Retrieved from: https://warwick.ac.uk/fac/cross_fac/academy/funding/projectfunding/ (accessed 22 August 2019).

WIHEA, 2018. 2017–19 Funded Projects. Retrieved from: https://warwick.ac.uk/fac/cross_fac/academy/funding/2016-17fundedprojects/ (accessed 22 August 2019).

Chapter 3

"I am a part of the university"

Why universities offering non-traditional students extracurricular opportunities leads to higher levels of student engagement: a mature student's perspective

Gary Donaldson

Along the student journey, student engagement approaches, roles and projects offer the opportunities for non-traditional students to join the conversation, become part of educational development and work with staff as partners. This chapter will explore what student engagement in practice means to those in the thick of it, the mature students themselves. This was a position I was recently in myself and, in this chapter, I shall discuss and reflect upon how student engagement – and everything that goes along with that term – has influenced my higher education (HE) journey throughout both my undergraduate and postgraduate studies; most notably, how my role as a Student Ambassador (SA) for my university has fostered engagement that has benefited both my overall experience and my university. I shall also discuss the viewpoints of and first-hand accounts by other mature students who worked as SAs, in order to understand what student engagement means for them as individuals and how it has shaped their own HE journeys. This includes stories and reflections that the students feel show their personal experience of engagement in practice, through working as SAs. I shall argue that engaging mature students in extracurricular opportunities such as SA roles can benefit everyone involved, and propose that there is no such thing as a 'fixed notion of student engagement'; I shall explain why it almost certainly should be considered a dynamic and highly individualistic concept – especially in relation to non-traditional students.

If you had asked me at the start of my journey into either further or higher education what was meant by the term 'student engagement' I should have fumbled for an answer, as the concept was not something that I had thought about before. I'd likely have answered that student engagement meant a student who showed up to class, spoke in seminars, took notes and handed in assessments on time. During my interviews with other mature students, there was universal agreement that student engagement was not a common term for any of us initially. I suppose that I wasn't wrong, with the answer I'd have given, as those four points may go some way to facilitate a student becoming engaged in her/his student journey, yet throughout the past several years I have certainly learnt that 'student engagement' as a concept is far more comprehensive than that and can mean different things to different individuals – to different students, if you will. It is therefore not easy to define.

Student engagement has been hard for me to define; it has also for some time been a contentious issue amongst academic practitioners. Krause (2005, p.3) describes it as *"the time, energy and resources students devote to activities designed to enhance learning at university"*. Krause also suggests that those students whose experience demonstrated that they were actively involved in university life showed greater student engagement, higher levels of perceived satisfaction with their studies and higher levels of academic success; they were far more motivated to continue with their studies throughout their academic careers (*op. cit.*, 2005). Although there has been a cultural shift in recent years, when student engagement was discussed in the past it was often defined in relation to the academic side of being a student. What is interesting is that, as both an undergraduate and postgraduate student, if I were to be measured against many of the criteria for the archetypal 'engaged student', according to many HE practitioners, I believe I should be considered very much an *unengaged* student. Contrarily, I believe that I was anything but unengaged and, throughout the rest of this chapter, I – as an engaged and empowered student who is part of the 'University Community' – detail why that was the case.

An individual is considered a mature student if s/he enters post-secondary education at age 21 or above (UCAS, 2019). I entered full-time post-secondary education, after several false starts throughout my late teens and early 20s, at the age of 28. I'd left school at 16: at the earliest opportunity, I'd had my form signed by all of my secondary school teachers and left the building. I'd always had a mixed experience of secondary education. On the one hand, when I put the effort in, I received very good grades. However, on the other, I was growing up as a gay teen in the late 1990s and early 2000s with all of the emotional turmoil and distraction this created. It was a time very different from now and, looking back, I can see that gaining a formal education was not a priority – my priority was finding my tribe and living the life that I had read about in magazines and guidebooks and that I had watched on television. The ground-breaking television series 'Queer as Folk' was a revelation to me. So it could be said that I was educating myself on what being gay meant and I was keen to learn – it just didn't often translate to my classes during secondary school which to me were an inconvenience and something I could not wait to escape. I was not at all engaged in my formal education at this point.

I worked in a variety of jobs until my mid-to-late 20s, but throughout this period I knew that I wanted more for my life and I could not shake off the feeling that I had somehow 'missed out' on going to university. My sister put it in perspective when we were out for a meal one evening; she commented that, if I went back to study for a degree (I was 27 at the time), I'd probably still have around 40 years of employment once I had graduated... and was it not better to be working in something that I enjoyed? The wheels had been set in motion. I enrolled and studied for an HNC in Advertising and Public Relations at a further education (FE) college before applying – and receiving an offer – for university; I entered HE as a direct entrant into the second year. I completed my BA in Marketing Management with Consumer Studies in summer 2018 and my MSc in Intercultural Business Communication with Teaching English to Speakers of Other Languages (TESOL) in autumn 2019, at the age of thirty-three.

In the early months of my return to education, I had the goal of being what I considered the perfect student and tried valiantly to attend all classes, take notes in all classes and hand in all my assessments on time (perfect student engagement, right?). But in my reality – and I believe it was the reality of many mature students in the 2010s – life (together with trying to build a body of work that would be attractive to future employers) got in the way: I often did not attend class in person. I did not always have the mind-space to take coherent notes and, on more than one occasion, I handed in coursework past the official deadline. My striving for 'student perfection' was always doomed to fail and, during my first year at university, it led to many moments of 'Is studying right for me?' I compared myself to other younger students who seemed to be becoming, to my mind, 'pillars of student engagement' and felt inadequate by comparison.

As a self-funding mature student, I had to work. The members of my family were fantastically supportive, yet I did not want to rely on them fully. As a mature student, I also had – already in place when I re-entered education – a lifestyle that I did not want to lose and I had to work to afford to maintain this. It is well documented that students often have to combine studying with part-time work, owing to the mismatch between current student funding and the realistic cost of living (Devlin et al., 2008). However, although much of the literature on the topic suggests that a student's working alongside her/his studies can have a negative impact on engagement, I got to thinking – could there also be positives to be gained from working alongside my studies? From my own experience, I'd argue that there are.

What set off my interest in student engagement – and in hindsight ensured that I was indeed an engaged student (albeit in my own way) and did not drop out of university – was applying for and beginning my role as a Student Ambassador (SA) within my university. Many higher education institutions (HEIs) have student ambassador schemes or similar. An SA at my institution is a paid role within the university on a zero-hour contract. Once appointed, a student is added to the email pool of ambassadors and various departments within the university will email the ambassador pool when they have *ad hoc* paid work available. This role was very varied and could consist of a few hours working at an open day, working for multiple weeks on student card production and the much sought-after, recurring and regular work in a department as its dedicated 'Student Assistant'. Zero-hour contracts are a contentious issue, but, in this context, they were right for me – I worked often when my studies were quieter and worked less when my studies were more demanding. The flexibility of such a role was favourable.

I remember vividly that, just before finding out that I'd received the role, I called my family and told them that because university simply was not for me (that old chestnut!) and because I was struggling with the coursework, I was considering leaving and returning to the world of work. However, it would not be an exaggeration to say that being offered the SA role changed everything for me. Very quickly, I got to know the university staff and realised that we had more in common than not and that my input counted. An interesting point is that I thought that the scheme was probably more suited to more traditional (i.e. younger) students but I applied regardless.

From personal experience, and from talking to other mature students, it can be difficult (yet not impossible) to make friends as a mature student in university. We often do not stay in student accommodation and lectures are far too big and anonymous to meet anyone. In many HEIs within the United Kingdom (UK), there is limited face-to-face class time and students are ushered in and out of over-subscribed classrooms – hardly conducive for meeting new people and fostering relationship-building. This, in recent years, has been frequently the state of play for many institutions. It was therefore often during tutorials that I – and many mature students – would try to meet other students. I am a sociable person, but, for many mature students, doing this can be terrifying. I think that, early on during the tutorial, we tend to look for someone who, being around our age, seems the kind of person towards whom we could gravitate. If the whole tutorial group appears much younger, it can feel very isolating. Becoming an SA gave me another opportunity to meet others within the university – not just other mature students who had been drawn to a working role within the institution, but also staff members – who ultimately became good friends. Having these relationships made me feel a part of the university and made it far less of an intimidating place. The perceived barriers between me and the institution had been broken down and I felt that my experience and what I had to offer mattered.

The role of SA, and more specifically the regular paid role that I was now being offered, allowed me to discontinue external part-time work that constantly pulled me away from the university. I think that this allowed me to become far more engaged in university life. I now was not just arriving on campus for class, but I was within the university most days working on various ambassadorial roles. Because I was engaged with several departments, I felt more involved in what was going on from day-to-day in the university and I'd often attend daily events with other ambassadors or staff members. Had I done this before the ambassador role, it would have made me feel even more isolated and lonely, as I'd not have known anyone there. There is truth in the saying that you can feel the loneliest in the busiest room. Being an SA, who through ambassador responsibilities was on campus more often, made me feel connected as a student to other people as never before.

My role as an SA also made me feel far more connected to the university than I ever had been. I worked at a variety of events conducted by the university, including open days, public lectures and charity events. Both members of staff and students began to recognise my face and we'd often chat at more than one event. This was transformative for me, as I no longer felt like just a number within the huge student body. I felt vital and this led to a sense of belonging within the university that would go some way to ensuring that I completed my studies. It started to feel more like home – a comfortable space. As a mature student during my first few months at university, I'd felt like a small fish in a big sea – a feeling I'd not had for a long time and one really difficult to alleviate. However, working as an SA helped with this greatly and my engagement levels soared. Bianca, a mature student who also worked as an SA, agrees; she commented, "*I would have not, as a mature student, been that engaged if it wasn't for the student ambassador scheme. The scheme kept me engaged and I developed a lot from it – mostly confidence in my abilities that has translated to my academic work*".

I was asked by a member of the Student Recruitment Team to travel with her to Ireland to promote the university at an event for potential students. I'd eventually take this trip a number of times through my time at the university and it really defined my place as a student. I remember that, the first time I presented at the event, I was very nervous and really researched the university so that I could present the facts confidently. Throughout the years, I grew more and more confident and, during my final trip to Ireland in this capacity, I could, when discussing all the opportunities (such as the travel that I'd enjoyed throughout my studies and grabbed with both hands), clearly see how far I had come as a student and how engaged I really had become. By presenting what opportunities were available to potential students at my institution, I realised the extent of my own engagement – although it had not been so much with the more traditional aspects of what university life represents. I owe a lot to this staff member who saw something in me early on and gave me this opportunity to develop.

I have no doubt that the SA role and my subsequent feeling a part of the university in that way are why I did not leave the university during several tough times, both connected to my studies and personal. I knew the staff because I had worked for them and didn't want to let them, or myself, down. In fact, working as an SA allowed me the opportunity to meet a great variety of members of staff – including members of the academic skills team, who, because barriers had been broken down, ultimately helped me improve my written coursework grades. I met staff who coached me on presenting skills, since many of my earlier roles, as I have mentioned, involved presenting at various events. This coaching in presentation also led me to feel far more comfortable when presenting during modules, which in turn led to higher grades for this type of assessment. Stewart, a mature student who also worked as a Student Ambassador, agrees that this type of speaking opportunity can benefit a mature student. Stewart commented that "*through an opportunity to speak at Murrayfield Stadium to prospective students who were also veterans about my return to education, I was able to increase my confidence in public speaking which had a marked effect on my presentation grades at university and ultimately my engagement level*".

Towards the final year of my undergraduate programme, and of my role as an SA, I was offered the opportunity to step across into a more regular role as a Widening Participation Ambassador (WPA) for the Widening Participation Team

(WPT) within the university; in particular, to work on a specific digital transition and engagement project for incoming students, which would ultimately become known as the Establish project (Edinburgh Napier University, 2019). I wanted to feel as prepared as possible, as I knew there was a level of responsibility involved in this type of role, and I therefore began to research student engagement in depth, as it was a dominant term in the sector and within my university. Doing so allowed me to see how far I had come since those early days of wanting to leave university quietly and without trace. My research confirmed my feeling that, just because I was not engaging in many of the traditional aspects of student engagement – being a part of a society, being involved in the student union or socialising with course mates – I was in fact a very engaged student, but in a different way from the norm.

The project that I worked on for the WPT was a success and I continued to build the programme throughout my postgraduate studies. Ultimately, alongside the team, I developed Establish into a fixture of the university's Widening Participation strategy and nurtured a sub-team of five other WPAs to continue the work, as the need for such a sub-team had grown. I am very proud of the Establish project and feel again that being involved in such an extracurricular initiative, albeit still within the university, led to greater engagement for me in relation to my postgraduate degree. I also continued to invite the Establish student team to student engagement events and conferences and it felt rewarding to hear their interest in student engagement grow – in particular, one student, who commented that learning about why student engagement is important had led her to focus on being more engaged in her own journey. That I also wrote an evaluative study of the Establish project for my MSc dissertation really does go to show how my part-time engagement and employment within the university shaped my academic work.

What has been described as evidence of an engaged student also now applied to me: I was feeling far more comfortable within the university, my grades were improving and I was feeling much more motivated to continue with my education. My new role with the WPT also opened many new doors for me, including being introduced to the Researching, Advancing and Inspiring Student Engagement (RAISE) Network, which furthered my knowledge about student engagement practice. I am now a Student Committee Member and am actively involved with the network on a continuing basis. I also felt that, by working consistently and having university staff members comment that my past work experience was an asset to both the institution and my academic work, I had been able to retain some semblance of my life as it had been before I returned to education. It made the journey far more comfortable, relatable and enjoyable.

In conclusion, I think my story, along with the input from other mature students, is a perfect example of why one size does not fit all when it comes to student engagement. I was a very engaged student, but not in the traditional way, and I should not have fitted what conventional opinion sees as an engaged student, especially in the view of some in the university community who focus heavily on the academic side of the university experience. However, university to me was never about getting the best grades. It was about social mobility and opening up my horizons to new perspectives and experiences. Being engaged in university developments had the same outcome as many other opportunities often cited as purposeful, such as those relating to student voice and partnership. I think universities should be creating many more opportunities for non-traditional students to join projects within their walls – projects that do not necessarily relate to their course – and I'm sure that funding bodies should be supporting this with adequate funding.

I think my experience shows that being engaged as an SA as a mature student allowed me and the other students interviewed for this chapter an opportunity to deploy skills that we brought into the university to foster for ourselves a greater sense of belonging and ultimately improve engagement for us as individuals. This type of opportunity can benefit both the student and the institution and was a main factor in my not leaving university before I had completed both of my degrees.

By building a community that embraces student involvement in shaping the university experience for others, an HEI will create fertile ground for a diversely engaged student body. We are individuals within this body and this community, and our sense of engagement is individualistic; being able to access the potential benefits – for staff in educational developments and for students in being able to thrive – therefore depends on having a range of options for engagement that will suit everyone.

This paper has discussed and argued for one approach, borne out by personal experience, to engage non-traditional students such as mature students during their HE journey, but the possibilities are potentially endless. How do we ensure that non-traditional students are considered when planning student engagement strategy? I argue that we need to ask them, work with them and be inspired by them to facilitate positive engagement for all.

References

Devlin, M., James, R. and Grigg, G., 2008. Studying and Working: A national study of student finances and student engagement. *Tertiary Education and Management*, 14(2). Retrieved from: https://doi.org/10.1080/13583880802053044

Edinburgh Napier University, 2019. *ESTABLISH: Who better to talk to about being a student than an actual current student?* Retrieved from: www.napier.ac.uk/study-with-us/widening-participation/students-helping-students (accessed 8 July 2019).

Krause, K., 2005. *Understanding and promoting student engagement in university learning communities.* Melbourne: Centre for the Study of Higher Education, University of Melbourne. Retrieved from: www.liberty.edu/media/3425/teaching_resources/Stud_eng.pdf

UCAS, 2019. *Mature Students' Guide.* Retrieved from: www.ucas.com/file/35436/download?token=2Q6wiw-L (accessed 8 July 2019).

Chapter 4

Theory and principles underpinning 'students engaged in educational developments'

SEEDs for the future

Yassein El Hakim and Tom Lowe

Introduction

At the inception of this book, we toiled over having a specific chapter focused on establishing a theoretical underpinning across the broad, diverse and rapidly growing subject of 'student engagement'. The concern was naive and unwarranted. Every author in this collection has drawn on theory in some way and applied it, either explicitly, implicitly or indirectly. This meant that our focus could be on several theories that bridged many of the chapters and spoke to core principles, which can unpack and support the most common reasons that the number of students engaged in educational developments is growing so rapidly in higher education institutions, internationally. Distilled to its essence, student engagement for educational development appears to build upon: empowerment, transparency, trust, openness and action. These features will be explored further in this chapter.

The beauty of theories, and the application or evidence of them within society, is that many individuals will already recognise them within their own contexts. Common definitions, constructs and standardised terminology allow others globally 'to stand on the shoulders of giants' to quote Isaac Newton (1675, cited in Merton, 1965). Theories often develop by individuals or groups defining key terms, creating hypotheses, researching and testing them, discussing findings, critiquing methodologies or variables, establishing a body of evidence or data that increasingly support or refute a theoretical position. Crucially these common definitions, terms and practices, create a sort of 'interoperability' and shared understanding across a global community. For example, Cognitive Evaluation Theory (Deci and Ryan, 1980) proposed that awarding external rewards to individuals for completing tasks that were previously completed for no reward led to a reduction of intrinsic motivation. Individuals subsequently sought external rewards for completing the task and were less intrinsically motivated by it. Many parents, teachers and coaches will now be thinking of scenarios where this theory is evident in their lives. Respectively, these may include examples such as children wanting sweets or money for chores, students only doing learning tasks when exam marks are involved or athletes only playing when paid or able to 'win'. That has always been the power of a theory: it creates awareness and clarity of thought in the minds of the many who engage with it, ponder it, research it, test it, question it, debate it, present on it or write about it. At their crux, theories, including how they are created, developed, researched and applied, advance our social construction of knowledge across society (Vygotsky, 1978).

Student engagement: improving learning outcomes and educational development

The literature concerning student engagement is impressively wide, critical and deeply researched. Trowler (2010) has drawn together an in-depth literature review that articulates the wide variety of student engagement literature. Trowler also goes some way towards explaining the difficulty in gaining consensus in this subject area by stating:

> *Many articles, conference papers and chapters on student engagement do not contain explicit definitions of engagement, making the (erroneous) assumption that their understanding is a shared, universal one. In addition, studies tend to measure that which is measurable, leading to a diversity of unstated proxies for engagement recurring in the literature, and a wide range of exactly what is being engaged with under the mantle of 'student engagement'.*
>
> (2010, 17)

Through the review, three foci of student engagement were identified with examples from the literature:

1. **Improving individual student learning and learning outcomes** (Kuh, 2005 and Kuh, 2009)
   - Student attention in learning
   - Student interest in learning
   - Student involvement in learning
   - Student 'active' participation in learning
   - 'Student-centredness' – student involvement in the design, delivery and assessment of their learning
2. **Improving structure and process** (Magolda, 2005)
   - 'Representation as consultation', such as tokenistic student membership of committees or panels to obviate the need for formal consultation with students
   - Students in an observer roles on committees
   - Students as representatives on committees (delegate role)
   - Students as full members of committees ('trustee' role)
   - Integrated and articulated student representation at course, department, faculty, SRC/SU or NUS level

3. **Identity development** (Kezar, 2005)
   - Engagement towards individual student 'belonging'
   - Identity attached to representation
   - Engagement of groups such as 'non-traditional' students

However, even though the review states that there are a wide variety of different dimensions, types and levels of student engagement, there appears to be little theoretically that purports to underpin students' involvement in educational development schemes, initiatives or opportunities. Student engagement in these areas has resulted in substantial impacts for the individuals, programmes or institutions, which many have witnessed when working either individually or collectively in schemes evidenced in this book and elsewhere (See Chapters 9, 12, 13, 17 and 18 for examples).

Student engagement as a subject has historically been observed and researched from the angle of students engaging with their studies, in order to better their achievement of learning outcomes. Indeed, the National Survey of Student Engagement (Kuh, 2001; 2005) has contributed to a large body of research that clearly iterates many benefits for students who engage more with their studies, including, but not limited to, performing better academically than those who report less engagement. This area is clearly very important and impactful for individual students, but there has been a greater potential observed in the last decade regarding student engagement – a 'greater good' or 'a new way of working', if you will.

The potential of student engagement to improve the learning experience of students on a module, course, programme, learning pathway within faculties and institutions around the world has been emphasised by many (Cook-Sather, 2020). The concept has grown of 'Students Engaged in Educational Developments', where students have the capability to engage and work with professional, teaching, senior management staff, etc. on a level playing field. Such roles and engagement are becoming acknowledged as both expected but also highly valuable to cohorts, communities, institutions and the education sector through new approaches, projects, roles and responsibilities taken up by students with the university/college/students' union. This view was captured articulately by Magolda:

> the University of Kansas expects students to have a voice in campus governance. Indeed, the University requires that all policy committees (with the exception of personnel committees) have a minimum of twenty percent of their members be students. As one student senate officer commented, 'Students are on an equal playing field with faculty and others in terms of governance.
>
> (2005, 2; cited in Trowler, 2010)

The impacts and value can be transformative far more than just through governance, for instance, through improving specific learning aspects (Rush and Balamoutsou, 2006) and learning design (Coates, 2007; Rust, Price and O'Donovan, 2003).

The importance and positive impact of student engagement in the realms of academic performance and educational developments appears compelling (Astin, 1984; Kuh, 2001, 2003; Chickering and Gamson, 1987; Pascarella and Terenzini, 1991). The view that 'students engaged in educational developments' (SEEDs) are transformative for the students, the educational development community, educational institutions, communities and society more broadly, has been less well researched. As such, this chapter will (1) illustrate the power and potential impact of engaging students in educational developments, (2) identify seven underlying principles of good practice in student engagement that build on theory and research and (3) emphasise the importance of context in this movement spreading across educational institutions and education, globally.

(1) Students engaged in educational developments: an unrealised potential

There was one Student Fellow project at the University of Winchester (UK) that perfectly encapsulates the power of students engaged in educational developments. The University had founded a scheme, co-funded by the university senior management team and the students' union, whereby it offered a £600 bursary to 60 students annually who then carried out projects in partnership with a staff member. Two particular students studying law decided to share one bursary and agreed to work with the head of department for law. They had been proactive in taking the initiative and spoke with their cohort of peers to understand if their experiences were shared. Having validated a few potential projects, they established consensus as a trio (two Student Fellows, one staff member). They selected one project whose simplicity and impact were unimaginable at the beginning. The students spoke of an unknown, mysterious assessment – a moot (a form of authentic assessment within a mock courtroom). They had little understanding of the standard expected given the novelty of this assessment mode. Assessment variety, including encountering novel assessment types, was something that the TESTA methodology (Jessop, El Hakim and Gibbs, 2014), also founded at the University of Winchester, had repeatedly shown internationally within modular programmes. Having also completed the TESTA process, the Law Department provided the data to build on. According to TESTA's findings, the variety of assessments experienced across many degree programmes in the UK ranged between 16 and 32 distinct types, with an average of 48 summative assessments across a degree. Many students at different universities had reported a feeling of apprehension around new types of assessment, where no practice at the assessment type had been experienced previously – another unintended consequence of siloed modules within disconnected programmes.

The two Student Fellows working collaboratively with a supportive head of law proposed that the third year students, when undertaking their moots simply filmed their assessment and agreed to play them back to the first years. The simplicity was beautiful and yielded incredibly high engagement with the observation replay. It was the impact that astonished, but in line with findings by Rust et al. (2003), grades for first year moots jumped almost 10% year on year, with many students attributing this to the 'vicarious experience' (Bandura, 1977) as a key learning point in advance of the assessment. Simple, affordable, evidenced-informed and well executed, the process was so successful that both staff and students continued the practice in future years, funding additional Student Fellow roles out of their own departmental budgets.

Any practising educational developer will stress the importance of reflection following such a change and would also acknowledge many different variables, too. Here are three from this scheme:

1. Projects often saw students empowered within authentic working relationships with staff, in order to be successful in the Student Fellow role.
2. Development of ideas that engaged with student and staff perspectives allowed empathy with both perspectives to be strengthened, and mutually beneficial solutions sought to problems.
3. Creation of such opportunities can often increase the confidence, motivation and impact of students across the wider institutional context.

(2) Seven principles of good practice in student engagement

There are now a great number of theories, too great to concisely underpin student engagement fully for this introductory chapter. However, through our reading and engagement in the sector over the last ten years, from founding the Student Fellows Scheme, to nationally funded research, to speaking/consulting across the sector, there does seem to be some convergence of complementary and aligning theoretical underpinnings.

Self-Determination Theory (Deci and Ryan, 1985; Ryan and Deci, 2000), Social Learning Theory (Bandura, 1973), Growth Mindset (Dweck, 2006), Social Constructivism (Vygotsky, 1978) and Student Centred Learning (Lee and Hannafin, 2016) all afford powerful antecedents and constructs for creating principles of good practice. These theoretical frameworks have been interpreted and drawn upon to create the 'Seven Principles of Good Practice in Student Engagement', inspired by the timeless principles articulated in Chickering and Gamson (1987). The seven principles of good practice in student engagement that follow draw on some of the most powerful literature and theories and are associated with a substantial weight of research supporting their key constructs.

Seven principles of good practice in student engagement

1. Good practice encourages proactive ownership (Covey, 1989);
2. Good practice creates autonomy-supportive contexts (Mageau and Vallerand, 2003);
3. Good practice encourages a growth mindset (Dweck, 2006);
4. Good practice breeds belonging (Deci and Ryan, 1985; Thomas 2012);

5. Good practice supports with scaffolding (Lee and Hannafin, 2016);
6. Good practice encourages courageous vulnerability (Brown, 2012);
7. Good practice encourages student-centred learning (Lee and Hannafin, 2016).

GOOD PRACTICE ENCOURAGES PROACTIVE OWNERSHIP

"Our basic nature is to act and not be acted upon" – so wrote Covey in 1989. This is as much a reflection on today's society as it is a principle of good practice when creating student engagement. Think of the many times every day we may perceive ourselves as being acted upon: advertising thrust upon us online, becoming indebted (through student loans, property loans, payday loans), cars pulling out in front of us. When empathising with the learner, one can see that a similar experience may exist: content assigned to read, assessments assigned to complete, students in a group forced to work and present together. This quote is regarding the first of 'the seven habits of highly effective people', which is *being proactive*.

Covey (1989) defines proactivity as "*having the initiative and the responsibility to make things happen*" (p.71). The central tenets of the habit of proactivity are the ability to respond and the freedom to choose (see Figure 4.1). When looking at proactive people Covey says that the locus of control is within, not without; as such, those individuals would not blame circumstances, conditions or conditioning for their behaviour. The freedom to choose means one can reject becoming reactive (where one can be affected by the weather or other externally controlling forces). Proactivity, freedom and agency are all characteristics of the sector-inspiring, student engagement practice of the 'Students as Change Agents' scheme at the University of Exeter (UK), pioneering an approach where students were supported to go out, evidence-change and enhance learning and teaching individually or as small teams (Dunne and Zandstra, 2011). This practice, pioneered by Elisabeth Dunne and colleagues, is often cited as one of the first student engagement practices globally.

Being proactive rather than reactive will mean a different language too. Here are some examples of the way two different people can interpret and reflect on situations.

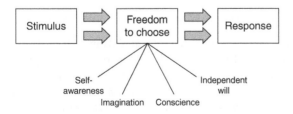

Figure 4.1 Illustration of choice between stimulus and response
Source: Covey, 1989

Reactive language would include statements like:

There's nothing I can do.
I have to do that.
I can't.

Whereas a proactive version would sound like:

Let's look at our alternatives.
I will choose an appropriate response.
I choose.

Brown (2012) references shaming as an example of the power of language; Dweck (2006) notes the malleability of intelligence when observing a different mindset. It also complements aspects of learned helplessness – the inability to change the outcome given a repeating stimulus (Seligman and Maier, 1967); autonomy – the perception of control within boundaries (Ryan and Deci, 2000). Language is a vital component of education and learning experiences as many will attest. However, Brown (2012) references and cites where the power of language is used in 'shaming' students within educational contexts. This can be compounded depending on the mindset of the student. Dweck (2006) notes that perceived malleability of intelligence exists where individuals have a growth mindset. However, a fixed mindset paired with academics who wish to demonstrate their academic prowess can increase learned helplessness – the inability to change the outcome given a repeating stimulus (Seligman and Maier, 1967) resulting in the altogether too often stated phrase 'I can't ...' By providing some level of autonomy – the perception of control within boundaries (Ryan and Deci, 2000) the intrinsic motivation of students can be increased and aligned with a greater focus on mastery in line with a growth mindset and more persistent resilience.

When considering students engaging in educational development there is a clear need for a proactivity where the students can be responsible and show initiative as in the example cited above. However, it is important to stress the efficiency in taking the initiative would be significantly enhanced by engaging the academics first.

GOOD PRACTICE CREATES AUTONOMY-SUPPORTIVE CONTEXTS

The impact that Self-Determination Theory (Deci and Ryan, 1985; Ryan and Deci, 2000; Ryan and Deci, 2017) has had on education is both significant and growing. The theory, at its heart, values centrally the power and impact of intrinsic motivation. Intrinsic motivation is defined as *"an inherent propensity to actively develop skills, engage challenges, and take an interest in new activities even in the absence of external prompts or rewards"* (Ryan and Deci, 2007). Initially developed within the realm of sport (Frederick and Ryan, 1993), the impact of the theory and its associated research findings are compelling. SDT has grown out of research findings that provide a contrast to the ideas proposed by behaviourists, regarding behaviour being controlled or motivated by reinforcements (Skinner, 1953; Hull, 1943).

In understanding the focus on active human nature, a deeper understanding of intrinsic motivation is needed. White (1959) suggested that psychological satisfactions, instead of biological needs, could stimulate intrinsically motivated actions. Specifically, the psychological satisfactions are feelings of *competence* or *effectance*, with deCharms (1968, cited in Ryan and Deci, 2007) later adding the importance of feeling that "one is the initiator of one's own action" (p.3). This is a crucial element of the student engagement and partnership movement, creating not just active learners in our higher education communities, but active partners who have a role to play in developing their educational setting and community. For example, see the work of the Combined Honours Centre at Newcastle University where students and staff have run a plethora of activities to enhance student transition through a buddying scheme, a sense of belonging through a course society and course co-ownership through a student–staff partnership committee (Furlonger, Johnson and Parker, 2014).

Cognitive Evaluation Theory (Deci and Ryan, 1980) a sub theory of SDT, stated that environmental conditions which diminish feelings of competence or autonomy can reduce intrinsic motivation. However, SDT (Deci and Ryan, 1985; Ryan and Deci, 2000) articulated the three basic psychological needs building on these sub-theories:

- Competence is the need to be effective in efforts and actions;
- Autonomy is the need to feel that one's pursuits are self-governed and self-endorsed;
- Relatedness refers to being connected socially and a sense of 'belonging' (and the subsequent impacts of satisfying these needs).

The impact of the learning environment created by coaches, teachers, parents and leaders is significant and has become a central focus based on supporting these needs. Mageau and Vallerand (2003) identified the need for coaches and teachers to create learning environments that encourage 'autonomy-support' to allow intrinsic motivations to be sustained and grow. Environments that are structured like this are called 'autonomy-supportive' and this is the thinking underpinning many current student-engaged educational development schemes.

GOOD PRACTICE ENCOURAGES A GROWTH MINDSET

Carol Dweck sums up the Growth Mindset beautifully, using the words of political theorist Benjamin Barber: "I don't divide the world into the weak and the strong, or the successes and the failures... I divide the world into the learners and non-learners" (Barber, quoted in Dweck, 2012, p.16). It is a mindset that has been observed often within student engagement activities, evidence and exemplars. Dweck (2012) outlines that individuals who have a growth mindset believe that the brain is a muscle like any other in the body and is malleable. The power of a growth mindset also relates to one's resilience to failures or rather (due to the perception of what a failure is)... learning!

Students who have engaged in educational developments are (or grow to be) keen to engage, persistent in the face of failure, developmental in their approach and hungry to learn about contexts, knowledge, evidence, processes or activities. A learner who believes they can learn more and their intelligence is not a fixed entity will continue throughout their lives to be voracious learners. By observing the fixed and growth mindsets in many different contexts it is surprising, given the context of higher education, to find any fixed mindsets among academics or students. Work by Dweck (2006; 2012) and Lawson and Lawson (2013) has demonstrated the impacts of associated mindsets, perceived benefits and subsequent behaviours, building into 'conditions for engagement'. This may lead to an intersection with Self-Determination Theory and lead to what might be classified as 'Self-Determined Learning': a concept where an individual or group of individuals with a growth mindset, within an autonomy-supportive environment, could lead their own learning and even tutor others within the community.

Growth mindsets are built into an array of Peer Mentoring-related activities embedded within courses and across entire universities/colleges/schools. For example, the Changing Mindsets project at the University of Portsmouth (UK) trains and enables student mentors to run growth mindset projects to increase their peers' motivation, agency and confidence in order to raise student attainment and rates of retention. The project has been built on by a HEFCE funded project, Changing Mindsets (2017) focused on closing the attainment gap of BME and working class students. Changing Mindsets is a student and staff workshop-based intervention that builds a growth mindset and is a collaboration with the University of the Arts London (UK); the University of Brighton (UK); Canterbury Christ Church University (UK) and the University of Winchester (UK) to "*close the attainment gap in student experience, retention, progression, academic attainment and employability by changing mindsets and eroding stereotype threat and implicit bias as barriers to learning*".

GOOD PRACTICE BREEDS BELONGING

Having observed an alignment between student engagement and Self Determination Theory (Ryan and Deci, 2000) for many years, the impact of relatedness between these two approaches in education is key. The basic human need of relatedness is described within Self Determination Theory. It aligns closely to student engagement, with a growing student need to be identified as an individual (not a number), being an active member of a community and learning to approach learning 'academically' through their work and activities. These learning environments create opportunities for close contact with academics, academic networks, postgraduates and peers (Chickering and Gamson, 1987; Gibbs, 2010). At a time when many jobs are facing rapid automation, such engagement and desire to engage beyond the compulsory needs of a degree will often generate beneficial experiences and knowledge. These in turn can create positive perceptions in the individuals involved that perpetuate the seeking of more opportunities to become even more engaged (Lawson and Lawson, 2013). At the University of Winchester (UK), by running an array of educational development and students' union-related student engagement opportunities (which included experimental feedback workshops involving hundreds of students and student–staff partnership projects (Student Fellows) from 2013–2019), we noted that students' pride in their institution increased when they were members of that community, not merely subjects to learning, but partners in the institution's development (Lowe, Shaw, Sims, King, and Paddison, 2017; Humphrey and Lowe, 2017).

Many others have identified the key importance of creating, encouraging and nurturing a sense of belonging and relatedness in higher education students' experiences (Cook-Sather, 2018; Masika and Jones, 2016). Thomas (2012) actually went on to illustrate the impact on retention, satisfaction and academic performance of students who were meaningfully engaged in their higher education settings.

GOOD PRACTICE SUPPORTS WITH SCAFFOLDING

This is possibly the simplest to set up yet most difficult to do well. Many understand the term scaffolding, mostly due to the constant visibility of its structure covering buildings, like clothes on humans. The structure is a solid one, enabling builders to create taller buildings than they could from the ground; floor by floor the building is created. Every building has a strong and deep foundation to reflect the height it will one day grow to be – the taller the building, the more significant the foundation. The analogy is perfect for learning and student engagement too.

Hannafin, Hill, Land and Lee (2014), understanding that student-centred learning is a complex process, suggested that students should be scaffolded through the process from owning the project, researching for the project and sharing the project outcomes. The research that supported the proposal was compelling and could also usefully be applied to students engaged in educational development. In particular the evidence drawn on included: scaffolding that allows competence to be demonstrated, at which point the scaffolding is withdrawn, promoting independence (Vygotsky, 1978); metacognitive scaffolding to guide goal setting, planning, monitoring and self-evaluation, leading to better assignments exhibiting more self-directed behaviours (Wolf, Brush and Saye, 2003) and peer feedback driven revisions and iterations (Kim and Ryu, 2013).

Most important for many student engagement schemes internationally is the audience. Authentic audiences or real world learning have repeatedly shown that motivation, autonomy and ownership increase (Wigfield and Eccles, 2000; Kearney and Schuck, 2006). This is something that has been observed many times in the Student Fellows Scheme at the University of Winchester and countless others where we have consulted. When a project, task or assessment is authentic and the audience is real, the outputs and outcomes are often far better. The standards have been surprising for many who have now seen an undergraduate student presenting at a conference, publishing a paper with an academic, forming a member of bid teams – the list goes on. Many more such examples of student involvement will continue to happen as one of the largest, un-actualised potentials (Maslow, 1943) in higher education is further empowered and activated.

Finally, while the shift to becoming more self-directed is the ambition of HE, Kandiko and Mawer (2013) described how it can cause considerable anxiety for first year students making this transition. Hence scaffolding can facilitate a positive experience and transition which some may find challenging (Lea, Lobb, Cattaneo and Lawrence, in this volume, Chapter 19). This is where the opportunity to develop research skills during induction can be vital in shaping the new identity of HE students.

GOOD PRACTICE ENCOURAGES COURAGEOUS VULNERABILITY

In addition to scaffolding and empowering student-engaged roles, institutional leaders need to engender a safe space within which to speak openly, collaborate equally, suggest freely, critique constructively and share generously. It is clear from observations and secondary evidence, however, that staff or students who challenge the status quo can face ridicule, name-calling, blaming or social isolation. These are all signs that shame and vulnerability have permeated the institutional culture (Brown, 2012). Vulnerability is interwoven in daily life with constant elements of uncertainty, risk and emotional exposure and shame. However, when your role involves proposing changes to established practices, processes or policy – as many student partners do – the ability to evidence risky developments needs to be supported by the environment. Brown (2012) describes the need for educational institutions to reignite creativity, innovation, and learning in order to rehumanise education and work. Going on to describe a process of "disruptive engagement", Brown repeats a defining and all-too-familiar quote (many will have heard a version of this) to illustrate the need:

> There are times when you can ask questions or challenge ideas, but if you've got a teacher that doesn't like that or the kids in the class make fun of people who do that, it's bad. I think most of us learn that it's best to just keep your head down, your mouth shut, and your grades high.

(p.187)

Organisations are often compared to machines, as Sir Ken Robinson does here: "People have values and feelings, perceptions, opinions, motivations, and biographies, whereas cogs and sprockets do not. An organisation is not the physical facilities within which it operates; it is the networks of people in it" (Robinson, 2011, p.188).

By empowering students as agents, partners or representatives, such roles and initiatives offer authority and identity for students engaged in educational development. Many student voice/representation programmes are widely adopted in higher education. They are often provided with substantial training and support for students to represent their cohorts on student–staff liaison committees where they reflect their peers' views and voices on the programme. Students' unions are also there to support the student representatives in difficult times or when they feel a wider campaign or conversation is required. Branding, training, support structures and identity are all key to ensure students feel motivated and empowered and are enabled to thrive in our student engagement opportunities.

GOOD PRACTICE ENCOURAGES STUDENT-CENTRED LEARNING

Lee and Hannafin identified an intersection building on support for autonomy, social constructivism and scaffolding that has resulted in the development of a theory of student-centred learning. Student-centred learning (SCL), they say, "identifies students as the owners of the learning (Lee and Hannafin, 2016, p.707).It has many aspects relevant to student engagement in educational development. Also, it is worth noting that the process of student-centred learning could equally apply to traditional views of student engagement, i.e. with one's own studies or more innovative applications of students' engagement such as student-engaged educational development.

In the technology sector there is a phrase called 'user-experience testing' or 'user-research'. It means to scientifically test the user experience or to research the user experience (which varies given the stage of product development) in order to design the best possible experience. In education, the phrase 'learner-experience' is central to any learning pathway or course designed and/or developed by an institution, organisation, company or individual. Looking at how student engagement could increase the focus on learner experience will transform the impact of learning for students around the world. Think what a difference it would make, if students were given equal power themselves to engage in educational developments beyond mere student representation.

Sharing best practice is key in any area of education development. As colleagues embark on new projects, initiatives and schemes, valuable opportunities to network and stand on the shoulders of other great practice internationally include: taking the time to read published literature cited in this collection; visiting other institutions' websites or campuses; and attending networking events such as RAISE,[1] SEDA,[2] the Students as Partners Round Table (AUS),[3] or the McMaster University Students as Partners Summer Institute (CAN).[4]

(3) Culture, leadership and language

Within the concept of leadership being reflected through an organisation, significant acknowledgement will need to be paid to literature on organisational cultures as they are the Petri dish for Reflected Leadership to grow or die. Cultures can be defined in many ways and at several levels, although for the purpose of this paper, we will use the commonly accepted definition from Kluckhohn (1951): *"culture is an acquired and transmitted pattern of shared meaning, feeling, and behaviour that constitutes a distinctive human group"* (cited in Ayman and Korabik, 2010, p.158).

Schein (2010) also described cultures existing across multiple levels which he defines as: Macrocultures, Organisational cultures, Subcultures and Microcultures. Macrocultures are described at the level of nations, religious groups and global occupations, whereas organisational cultures are more focused on the cultures in existence within organisations (e.g. private, public, non-profit, etc.). Subcultures can exist as small groups inside organisations and microcultures are identified as a unit within the organisation which cuts across the institution thus creating a microsystem. However, all four share a key underpinning principle, that a culture is a dynamic phenomenon which influences individuals in many ways. Schein (2010) stated that *"culture can be thought of as the foundation of the social order that we live in and of the rules we abide by"* (p.3). This speaks to our inherent need for structures within which we can operate and the fact that these exist at different levels begs the question of whether individuals conform to differing cultures depending on the one they are in.

Bandura (1973) demonstrated 'Social Learning Theory' when children watched adults commit violent acts to a 'bobo doll'. The children who observed the violent acts subsequently performed those acts more than children who were not so exposed. This reaction was emphasised when positive reinforcement for the aggressive act by the child occurred. This could easily be described in line with behaviourist perspectives – for example, thinkers like Skinner and Pavlov who would state that with conditioning, such behaviours could be exhibited by most living organisms. Certainly the use of reward and punishment is strongly utilised within human societies and also within the other levels of culture that Schein (2010) defined.

Cultures have been described as stable, where language exists within cultures to have shared understandings, role clarity and socialisation. Language provides the meaning of everything within our day-to-day lives. This is fascinating, as the rate of change in the English language which is being both spoken and written, largely due to the exponential utilisation of electronic communication and mass media, is currently faster than any other time in history.

Conclusions

Within a context of student engagement there are two overarching aspects within the environment that can impact the success of schemes from our experience: that of *culture* and of *language*. To ensure student engagement schemes or initiatives are successful, participants in them need to perceive them as if they *are authentically inclusive, transparent, trusting and empowering*. When student engagement opportunities are created for students to have close contact with a member of staff, be it as a student, research assistant, pedagogic partner or to support them in a project, it is often positively received by the student. But this perception can be enhanced or tarnished by the language and culture the role exists within. If we want students to take the opportunity to demonstrate their autonomy, courage and competence, the opportunities must be presented in such a way as to scaffold and support the student in what may be a novel role to allow them to exceed expectations.

Where this is not established, negative experiences await. One Student Fellow at the University of Winchester stated, "The project has not been that great an experience. The staff member told me that they need to 'use' me to accelerate their research and the proposal submitted was just a means to an end!"

Reflecting on this, our team created reflection points with staff and student partnerships to ensure such practice never recurred. However, the attitudes of some staff towards students are revealed in their language. Phrases noted from consulting and researching internationally over the last decade have included: *separating the wheat from the chaff, bums on seats,* and *this cohort is the worst yet.* There have been many other, similar, phrases. It is important to note these comments were from a few academics, not the majority, and the frequency has reduced dramatically over the past decade as students have become more equal partners in the learning experiences and environments created at institutions, by engaging beyond the core involvement with their studies.

A better way of working has been created by bringing diverse stakeholders together to acknowledge and address strengths and weaknesses, respectfully, openly and transparently, so shifting the language used. Feedback from students through the TESTA process has been effective, whether directly changing a programme team's established practice, altering the pedagogic approach of the programme, improving the staff experience of assessment, or impacting positively the learning outcomes and NSS scores (simultaneously in some instances). We have seen that student engagement approaches creating a culture and language that encapsulates *authentic inclusivity, transparency, trust and empowerment* aligned with specific application of the 'Seven Principles of Good Practice in Student Engagement' can create a powerful way to embed and grow an array of student engagement opportunities that support student learning and educational development partnerships.

Notes

1 RAISE (Researching, Advancing and Inspiring Student Engagement) Available at: www.raise-network.com/home/ (accessed 31 August 2019).
2 SEDA (Staff Educational Development Association (UK) Available at: www.seda.ac.uk/ (accessed 31 August 2019).

3   Students as Partners Round Table (AUS) Available at: www.ncsehe.edu.au/ event/national-students-partners-roundtable/ (accessed 31 August 2019).
4   McMaster University Students as Partners Summer Institute (CAN) Available at: https://macblog.mcmaster.ca/summer-institute/ (accessed 31 August 2019).

References

Astin, A., 1984. Student involvement: a developmental theory for higher education. Journal of College Student Development. 25, 297–308.

Ayman, R. and Korabik, K., 2010. Leadership: Why gender and culture matter. *American Psychologist*, 65(3), 157–170. Retrieved from: https://doi.org/ 10.1037/a0018806

Bandura, A., 1973. *Aggression: a social learning analysis.* Englewood Cliffs, NJ: Prentice-Hall.

Bandura, A., 1977. Self-efficacy: Toward a unifying theory of behavioral change. Psychological Review, 84(2), 191–215. Retrieved from: https://doi.org/ 10.1037/0033-295X.84.2.191

Brown, B., 2012: *Daring greatly: how the courage to be vulnerable transforms the way we live, love, parent, and lead.* New York: Gotham.

Chickering, A. W. and Gamson, Z. F., 1987. Seven principles for good practice in undergraduate education. AAHE Bulletin, 3–7.

Coates, H., 2007 A model of online and general campus-based student engagement. *Assessment and Evaluation in Higher Education*, 32(2), 121–141.

Cook-Sather, A., 2018. Listening to equity-seeking perspectives: how students' experiences of pedagogical partnership can inform wider discussions of student success. *Higher Education Research and Development*, 37(5), 923–936, DOI:10.1080/07294360.2018.1457629

Cook-Sather, A., 2020. Student engagement through classroom-focused pedagogical partnership: a model and outcomes from the United States. In this volume.

Covey, S., 1989. *The 7 Habits of Highly Effective People.* New York: Free Press.

deCharms, R. C., 1968. *Personal causation: The internal affective determinants of behavior.* New York: Academic Press.

Deci, E. L., and Ryan, R. M., 1980. The empirical exploration of intrinsic motivational processes. In L. Berkowitz (ed.), *Advances in experimental social psychology*, 13, 39–80. New York: Academic Press.

Deci, E. L., and Ryan, R. M., 1985. *Intrinsic motivation and self-determination in human behavior.* New York: Plenum.

Deci, E. L., and Ryan, R. M., 2000. The 'what' and 'why' of goal pursuits: Human needs and the self-determination of behavior. *Psychological Inquiry*, 11, 227–268.

Dunne, E and Zandstra, R., 2011. *Students as Change Agents. New ways of engaging with learning and teaching in higher education.* Bristol: ESCalate. Retrieved from: http://escalate.ac.uk/downloads/8247.pdf

Dweck, C.S., 2000. *Self-theories: Their role in motivation, personality, and development.* Psychology Press.

Dweck, C.S., 2006. *Mindset: The new psychology of success.* London: Random House.

Dweck, C.S., 2012. *Mindset. How you can fulfil your potential.* London: Constable and Robinson.

Frederick, C. M. and Ryan, R. M., 1993. Differences in motivation for sport and exercise and their relations with participation and mental health. *Journal of Sport Behavior,* 16(3), 124–146.

Furlonger, R., Johnson, S. and Parker, B., 2014. Experiences of engagement: The successes and issues from a student perspective.' In Bryson C. (ed.) *Understanding and developing student engagement* (pp79–90). London: Routledge.

Gibbs, G., 2010. *Dimensions of Quality.* Higher Education Academy.

Hannafin, M. J., Hill, J. R., Land, S. M. and Lee, E., 2014. Student-centered, open learning environments: Research, theory, and practice. In *Handbook of Research on Educational Communications and Technology: Fourth Edition* (pp. 641–651). New York: Springer. Retrieved from: https://doi.org/10.1007/978-1-4614-3185-5_51

Hull, C. L., 1943. *Principles of behavior: an introduction to behavior theory.* Appleton-Century.

Humphrey, O. and Lowe, T., 2017. Exploring how a sense of belonging is facilitated at different stages of the student journey in higher education. *Journal of Educational Innovation, Partnership and Change,* 3(1), 172–188. Retrieved from: http://dx.doi.org/10.21100/jeipc.v3i1.583

Jessop, T., El Hakim, Y. and Gibbs, G., 2014. The whole is greater than the sum of its parts: a large-scale study of students' learning in response to different programme assessment patterns. *Assessment and Evaluation in Higher Education,* 39(1), 73–88. Retrieved from: doi:10.1080/02602938.2013.792108

Kandiko, C. B. and Mawer, M., 2013. *Student Expectations and Perceptions of Higher Education.* London: King's Learning Institute.

Kearney, M. and Schuck, S., 2006. Spotlight on authentic learning: Student developed digital video projects. *Australasian Journal of Educational Technology,* 22, 189–208.

Kezar, A., 2005. Promoting student success: The importance of shared leadership and collaboration. Occasional Paper No. 4. Bloomington, IN: National Survey of Student Engagement.

Kim, M. and Ryu, J., 2013. The development and implementation of a web-based formative peer assessment system for enhancing students' metacognitive awareness and performance in ill-structured tasks. *Educational Technology Research and Development,* 61(4), 549–561. doi:10.1007/s11423-012-9266-1

Kluckhohn, C., 1951. *Values and value-orientations in the theory of action: an exploration in definition and classification.* Cited in Ayman, R. and Korabik, K., 2010. Leadership: Why gender and culture matter. *American Psychologist,* 65(3), 157–170.

Kuh, G. D., 2001. Assessing what really matters to student learning: inside the national survey of student engagement. *Change.* 33(3), 10–17.

Kuh, G. D., 2003. What we're learning about student engagement from NSSE. Change, 35(2), 24–32.

Kuh, G. D., 2005. *Promoting student success: what campus leaders can do.* Bloomington, IN: National Survey of Student Engagement.

Kuh, G. D., 2009. What student affairs professionals need to know about student engagement. *Journal of College Student Development.* 50(6), 683–706.

Kuh, G. D., Kinzie, J., Schuh, J. H. and Whitt, E. J., 2005. *Student success in college: Creating conditions that matter.* San Francisco, CA: Jossey-Bass.

Lawson, M. A., and Lawson, H. A., 2013. New conceptual frameworks for student engagement research, policy, and practice. *Review of Educational Research,* 83, 432–479. Retrieved from: https://doi.org/10.3102/0034654313480891

Lea, J., Lobb, R., Cattaneo, J. and Lawrence, J. Scholarship as student engagement in college higher education. In this volume.

Lee, E. and Hannafin, M. J., 2016. A design framework for enhancing engagement in student-centered learning: own it, learn it, and share it. *Education Technology Research and Development,* 64, 707. Retrieved from: https://doi.org/10.1007/s11423-015-9422-5

Lowe, T., Shaw, C., Sims, S., King, S., and Paddison, A., 2017. The Development of Contemporary Student Engagement Practices at the University of Winchester and Winchester Student Union, *International Journal for Students as Partners,* 1(1). Retrieved from: https://doi.org/10.15173/ijsap.v1i1.3082

Mageau, G. A. and Vallerand, R. J., 2003. The coach–athlete relationship: a motivational model. *Journal of Sports Sciences,* 21, 883–904. Retrieved from: https://doi.org/10.1080/0264041031000140374

Magolda, P., 2005. *Promoting student success: what student leaders can do.* Bloomington, IN: National Survey of Student Engagement.

Masika, R. and Jones, J. (2016). Building student belonging and engagement: insights into higher education students' experiences of participating and learning together. *Teaching in Higher Education,* 21(2), 138–150. Retrieved from: https://doi.org/10.1080/13562517.2015.1122585

Maslow, A. H., 1943. A theory of human motivation. *Psychological Review,* 50(4), 370–396

Newton, I., 1675. Personal Letter to Robert Hooke. In Merton, R. K., 1965. *On the shoulders of giants: A Shandean postscript.* Chicago, IL: University of Chicago Press.

Pascarella, E. T., and Terenzini, P.T., 1991. *How college affects students: findings and insights from twenty years of research.* San Francisco, CA: Jossey-Bass.

Pavlov, I. P., 1902. *The work of the digestive glands.* London: Griffin.

Robinson, K., 2011. *Out of our minds: learning to be creative.* Oxford: Capstone. Cited in Brown, B., 2012. Daring greatly: how the courage to be vulnerable transforms the way we live, love, parent, and lead. New York: Gotham

Rush, L. and Balamoutsou, S., 2006. Dominant voices, silent voices and the use of action learning groups in HE: a social constructionist perspective. Paper presented at the British Educational Research Association Annual Conference, University of Warwick, 6–9 September.

Rust, C., Price, M and O'Donovan, B., 2003. 'Improving students' learning by developing their understanding of assessment criteria and processes', *Assessment and Evaluation in Higher Education,* 28(2), 147–164. Retrieved from: https://doi.org/10.1080/02602930301671

Ryan, R. M. and Deci, E. L., 2000. Self-Determination Theory and the Facilitation of Intrinsic Motivation, Social Development, and Well-Being. *American Psychologist,* 55, 68–78. Retrieved from: https://doi.org/10.1037//0003-066x.55.1.68

Ryan, R. M. and Deci, E. L., 2007. Active human nature: Self-determination theory and the promotion and maintenance of sport, exercise, and health. In M. S. Hagger and N. L. D. Chatzisarantis (eds.), *Intrinsic motivation and self-determination in exercise and sport* (pp.1–19). Champaign, IL: Human Kinetics.

Ryan, R. M. and Deci, E. L., 2017. *Self-determination theory: Basic psychological needs in motivation, development, and wellness.* New York: Guilford Press.

Schein, E.H., 2010. *Organizational culture and leadership,* 2. London: John Wiley and Sons.

Seligman, M. and Maier, S., 1967. Failure to escape traumatic shock. *Journal of Experimental Psychology,* 74: 1–9. Retrieved from: https://doi.org/10.1037/h0024514

Skinner, B. F., 1953. *Science and human behavior.* New York: Macmillan.

Thomas, L., 2012. *Building student engagement and belonging at a time of change in higher education.* London: Paul Hamlyn Foundation.

Trowler, V., 2010. Student *engagement literature review.* Higher Education Academy.

Vygotsky, L. S., 1978. *Mind in society: The development of higher psychological processes.* Cambridge, MA: Harvard University Press.

White R., 1959. Motivation reconsidered: The concept of competence. *Psychological Review,* 66, 297–333.

Wigfield, A. and Eccles, J. S., 2000. Expectancy–value theory of achievement motivation. *Contemporary Educational Psychology,* 25(1), 68–81.

Wolf, S.E., Brush, T. and Saye, J., 2003. Using an information problem-solving model as a metacognitive scaffold for multimedia-supported information-based problems. *Journal of Research on Technology in Education,* 35(3), 321–341. DOI:10.1080/15391523.2003.10782389

Chapter 5

The changing nature and importance of student representation

Alex Bols

Introduction

I was first elected as a student representative in 1994 when I became a course representative for Modern History and Politics at the University of Southampton in the UK. This was also the same year as the Education Act[1] entered the Statute book, this Act focused on the role of students' unions and provided a legislative framework for their activity.

For the purposes of this chapter, student representation refers to the wider roles and activities of representing the views of students, which can include activities beyond academic representation and is often undertaken by institutional, national or international student representatives. Student representation is part of the broader field of student engagement which covers involvement, feedback, representation and other activities (Trowler, 2010). Student academic representation is just one dimension of student representation and encompasses course, class, faculty and school representatives. The 1994 Education Act resulted from a speech by the then British Prime Minister, John Major, at the 1992 Conservative Party Conference where he spoke about blowing "*the whistle on one of the last bastions of the closed shop – student unions. The days in which they march and demonstrate at the taxpayer's expense are numbered.*"[2] Whilst the final version of the 1994 Act looked quite different from what was originally proposed, the legislation, however, clearly arose out of a concern about the role of students' union and a level of distrust in student representation.

In the almost quarter century since then much has changed both in terms of the representative activity of students' unions and also the way in which universities and the wider national policy landscape seek to engage the student voice. Over this period I have been a course, faculty, institutional, national and European student representative as well as working with students' unions to improve their representation systems whilst working at the National Union of Students. I have also worked with senior university leaders across several organisations where enhancing student engagement and representation has been a key theme. Many of the changes over this period have applied to the whole UK. However, for the purposes of this chapter I will focus on the changes in England due to the particular context arising from the introduction of student tuition fees. This chapter will give an overview of the key developments relating to enhancing student academic representation over the past 25 years, where we are now – drawing on results from my own research into the effectiveness of student academic representation – and finally making some suggestions about how student academic representation might be improved in the future.

Overview of key developments

Over the past 25 years there have a significant number of policy developments affecting student engagement in England. Figure 5.1 picks out just a few of the key changes. The 1994 Act was followed by the introduction of student fees in 1998 in England for full-time undergraduates, and then their subsequent increases following legislation in 2004 and 2010. This increasing student contribution to the cost of their course has been linked by many to the rise in the idea of students as customers (McMillan and Cheney, 1996; Palfreyman and Warner, 1998; Streeting and Wise, 2009). This student consumer discourse has been accompanied by the introduction of various market mechanisms to track and respond to student views in England. This has included the establishment of the National Student Survey (NSS)[3] to systematically gather student views, the Office of the Independent Adjudicator (OIA)[4] to have a transparent complaints ombudsman, as well as transparency tools such as enhanced student information through Unistats[5] and Key Information Sets which aimed to support students to navigate the increasingly complex higher education system; more recently the Competition and Markets Authority (CMA)[6] have also taken an interest in protecting "*consumer rights*".

In addition to these government policy drivers, there has been much focus on improving the collective voice of students at a local level, not least an increased emphasis on student academic representation amongst students' unions. From 2002 there was an expectation on students' unions being able to provide a comprehensive, evidence-based Student Written Submission (SWS) of the views of all students at their institution for QAA (Quality Assurance Agency) Institutional Audit Reviews in England. Whilst the early SWSs were of varying quality across students' unions, there were rapid improvements over the next cycle of reviews resulting from significant investment in research and staff to support this gathering of student opinion.

In 2010 the Charity Commission expected all students' unions with an income of over £100,000 to register with them. This covered all but the smallest students' unions and as part of the registration process they had to define their core purpose, for which the "*educational charity*" definition was the best fit. This required students' unions to demonstrate that they met the criteria which included showing that their priorities and resource investment matched their objectives. This contributed to a renewal of investment and recognition of the importance of representation as the key activity of students' unions. This also came against a backdrop of a 46% decrease[7] in commercial revenue in students'

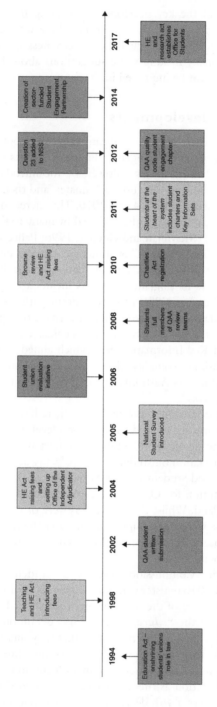

Figure 5.1 Key dates impacting on student engagement in England higher education

unions in the ten years up to 2007. This meant that whereas by the late 1990s many students' unions invested significant resources into their events, bars, travel centres and other commercial services as a way of generating income, by the late 2000s many students' unions were increasingly reliant on their institutional 'block grant' and with that came greater scrutiny from universities on how that money was being spent. All of these factors combined to create a real drive in students' unions to focus on enhancing their student representation structures.

It is also worth noting that this students' union focus did not happen in isolation. Since the 1994 Education Act there had been increasing emphasis in the public sector on accountability and transparency on how public funding was being spent, referred to as "*new public management*" discourse (Hood, 1995). The resulting quality assurance culture expected universities to demonstrate that they were listening to student/consumer voices. This was supported by a better understanding of student views, now gathered systematically by means of the National Student Survey, which also put the pressure on student representatives and students' unions not simply to repeat this data but also to help interpret it and prioritise student expectations.

Political background

There has also been a political shift over this period. I have done a quick analysis looking at the context within which all the references to the word "*student*" are made in the four UK Government White Papers' over the past 15 years – 2003, 2009, 2011 and 2016 – and grouping these references into themes, see Figure 5.2. Over these four White Papers there have been huge fluctuations in references to student support and funding depending on whether there were reforms of student finance planned, but a stability in references to widening participation.

Across these four White Papers there was a spike in references to students' union and student voice in 2011 in the *Students at the Heart of the System* White Paper (BIS, 2011), which dropped back significantly in the most recent White Paper in 2016, *Higher Education: Success as a knowledge economy* (BIS, 2016). It would be interesting to consider whether this was based on a view that student voice has been embedded across universities and so did not need prioritizing, or whether it resulted from a downgrading of the importance of student engagement in the minds of politicians and that interest in it has now passed its peak. Most striking in the data is the growth in references to students relating to information and choice – key elements in supporting students being able to navigate their way through the increasingly complicated marketplace. This would suggest a real growth – at least in the minds of politicians – of the role of the market in higher education and the position of students as customers, able to both navigate the market and also exert pressure on institutions.

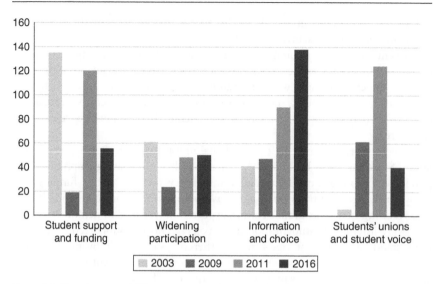

Figure 5.2 Key themes in UK government White Papers (2003–16)

Office for Students – governance criteria

This brings us to where we are now. The establishment of the Office for Students (OfS) as a market regulator in England is in stark contrast to its predecessor body,[8] the Higher Education Funding Council for England (HEFCE), which was often described as a buffer body working with both the sector and government. In the context of a market regulator, the OfS sees its role not to tell institutions what they should and should not be doing – this would be the role of the market – but rather their role is to monitor the baseline expectations of registered providers.

The OfS regulatory framework[9] included the publication of a set of new Public Interest governance principles which included a new principle on student engagement in governance. This principle seeks to ensure that "*all students have opportunities to engage with the governance of the provider*". However, this principle does not go as far as calling for all governing bodies to have students sitting on the governing body. This is something that is regulated differently across different education providers depending on their corporate form. For example, Higher Education Corporations, as many post-1992 universities are, and Further Education corporations have to have student representation, whereas other higher education providers such as those with Royal Charter or that are private companies, do not have the same legal expectation.

Having a student representative on the Board can add an important additional voice on a Board of Governors, having someone considering board decisions from a student perspective. It should, however, be noted that simply having one, or even a couple of, student board members will not ensure effective student engagement in governance, not least given the challenges of being able to adequately reflect the full range and diversity of views from the whole student body. Nonetheless, the wording of the OfS principle refers to "*all students being able to engage with the governance of the institution*", and providers will need to consider how they meet this expectation which could result in some interesting innovations in those institutions that want to make a feature of student engagement.

Individual and collective student engagement

The OfS has a number of conditions of registration including one relating to the "*support that the provider gives to students so that they can succeed in, and benefit from, higher education.*" They list a number of a number of behaviours that may indicate compliance, such as: "*The provider actively engages students, individually and collectively, in the quality of their educational experience.*" This wording is mirrored in the revised Quality Code[10] that the QAA published on behalf of the UK Standing Committee on Quality Assessment, and so institutions will be monitored against this.

The wording around individual and collective engagement is key. In many ways it reflects the different traditions of student engagement between the US and the UK. The US with its National Survey on Student Engagement (NSSE) has traditionally focused on the individual and how they are supported to be better engaged with their own learning. They consider "*student engagement to represent both the time and energy students invest in educationally purposeful activities and the effort institutions devote to using effective educational practices*" (Hu and Kuh, 2001). Whereas the UK – where there has traditionally been a much stronger student representative system – has been more likely to define student engagement as how students are able to feed back their views on a collective basis (QAA, 2012), in particular the participation of students in quality enhancement and quality assurance processes which result in the improvement of the educational experience.

When thinking about engaging students with decision-making processes, this should happen at all levels and could be expressed as a spectrum of student engagement as in Figure 5.3 above. It would then be possible to consider each of the levels of the spectrum in turn and reflect on how the ways in which students engage with each of these could be enhanced. This could then be mapped against the arrow of engagement that National Union of Students (NUS) and the Higher Education Academy (HEA) produced as part of their student engagement project back in 2010.[11] This arrow, moving towards meaningful engagement, progressed from a passive process of simply consulting students, through to involving students and ensuring their participation, and then to considering students as partners in their education. Mapping the spectrum of student engagement against the arrow of engagement could be developed into a chart considering the different levels of engagement at each decision-making level (see Table 5.1).

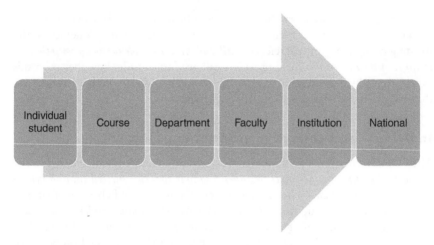

Figure 5.3 Spectrum of student engagement

Table 5.1 Spectrum of student engagement indicators

	Consultative engagement	*Involvement*	*Participation*	*Partnership*
Individual student **Course** **Department** **Faculty** **Institution** **National** **International**	Opportunities are provided for students to express individual opinions, perspectives, experiences, ideas and concerns	Opportunities are provided for students as individuals to take a more active role	Decisions are taken by students to take part or take a more active role in a defined activity	There is a collaboration between an institution/ faculty/ department/ student, involving joint ownership and decision-making over both the process and outcome

New National Student Survey questions

In 2017 for the first time there were new questions relating to student engagement added to the National Student Survey (NSS). These questions looked at individual student engagement, considering both the learning opportunities and learning community, key issues identified in Dimensions of Quality (Gibbs, 2010) relating to student success. There were also new questions looking at collective student engagement and student voice, including the extent to which students had been given the opportunities to provide feedback on their course and whether this was valued and acted upon.

Table 5.2 National Student Survey Results 2017 and 2018

UK		
Level of satisfaction related to:	*2017 (%)*	*2018 (%)*
The teaching on my course (Q1–4)	85	84
Learning opportunities (Q5–7)	84	83
Assessment and feedback (Q8–11)	73	73
Academic support (Q12–14)	80	80
Organisation and management (Q15–17)	75	75
Learning resources (Q18–20)	85	85
Learning community (Q21–22)	77	77
Student voice (Q23–25)	73	73
Students' union (Q26)	57	56
Overall satisfaction (Q27)	84	83

Following the publication of the 2018 NSS results[12] we now have two-years of data. As you will see from Table 5.2, whilst the data relating to learning opportunities, at 83%, is in line with overall student satisfaction, for questions relating to other dimensions of student engagement the results drop, with learning community (77%) and student voice (73%) below many of the other sections. Institutions would be well placed to consider how they enhance these aspects with the Government's repeated desire for new metrics for the Teaching Excellence Framework likely to home in on this new data.

Role of technology

Thinking more broadly about individual student engagement, there have been rapid developments in technology, and particularly in relation to learner analytics and the way in which these can be used. This is particularly striking in the context of being able to track student engagement in their learning and using various proxies for this. Higher education has the potential to lead the way in how it gathers, analyses and uses this kind of data. One good example is Nottingham Trent University (UK) who are using learner analytics to track student engagement.[13] They have developed a Student Dashboard which measures students' engagement with their course, calculated from a range of activities including accessing the VLE, library usage, card swipes and assignment submissions. Nottingham Trent has found these engagement measures to be a stronger predictor of success than background characteristics. They have used these scores to prompt tutors to contact students when their engagement drops off, something that staff find a valuable resource.

Collective student engagement

Having discussed the way that individual students are engaged with their learning, the other dimension highlighted in the OfS regulatory framework is the notion of collective student engagement. This considers the way in which students as a group are able to shape their academic experience. Collective student engagement happens in many ways, from student academic representative structures such as course, school and faculty representatives or representatives on university committees through to the rise in recent years of various student-led engagement projects. The projects can engage students to research student views and develop solutions – this has been seen through Student Fellow Schemes,[14] Students as Change Agents,[15] Students as Producers,[16] Student Academic Partners[17] and a range of other projects (Kay, Owen and Dunne, 2012).

There has been considerable focus on student academic representation and the processes on collective student engagement over the past decade. This has considered enhancing both the practice of the individuals that are engaged in representation as well as enhancing the actual processes of representation. This question of enhancing the effectiveness of student representation has been the focus of my own research, which has included a national survey of representatives from students' unions and institutions in English higher education institutions with degree-awarding powers, with a 46% response rate from students' unions and 47% from institutional representatives. I also conducted 11 interviews with representatives from students' unions, academic and professional services staff at three institutions – a large-multi-faculty research-intensive university, a smaller teaching-focused university and a small, specialist private provider – to provide a more in-depth perspective of student representation, as well as a couple of interviews with national student representatives. I will draw on the results of this research throughout the remainder of this chapter.

Diversity of the student body

One of the key challenges of collective student engagement is the increasing diversity of the student body. When I think back to my time as a course representative it was a much smaller and less diverse higher education sector. I was able to speak to a few people on my course and get a pretty representative view of what most students on my course thought. That is clearly much harder nowadays.

The student body as a whole has become both larger and more diverse – and so a course representative for a single module will struggle to gather a representative view without a more sophisticated approach. The way in which courses are delivered has also changed, from traditional three-year full-time models to accelerated two-year degrees and degree apprenticeships with students spending much of their time in the workplace, and a range of other modes of study. This diversity of the student body and provision places an onus on both the individual student representative and also on the student representative processes themselves to adapt to this diversity. It should also be recognised that there are relatively small numbers of opportunities for students to actually be involved in collective engagement, with only a few able to become student academic representatives. This makes it even more important to ensure that student academic representatives are able to speak on behalf of the whole student cohort.

This all becomes even more challenging as the representatives progress along the spectrum of student engagement to a higher level, whether school, faculty or institution-wide representative. There are, however, now tools available to help overcome this. The institution-wide surveys and National Student Survey can be helpful tools to identify the key issues affecting students, and opportunities provided by social media can help student representatives develop a much better understanding of what students think. The need to draw on wider student views is usually a key theme in student representative training.

This theme of using and analysing social media came out in many of the interviews I conducted, with one interviewee describing the ease of being able to access the views of 'grassroots' students. Several of the quality managers also described keeping an eye on student Facebook groups and other social media as a way of tracking issues that students were raising, and if appropriate channelling it through the relevant feedback mechanism. Some of the student representatives also described the ease with which social media enabled them to access student views but warned that this is still an area of further development, in particular to be able to ensure that comments are widely and deeply felt.

Student representative behaviours

This ability of student representatives to advocate on behalf of the wider student cohort also led to discussions with interviewees about the ideal student representative. Having been involved in student representation for many years, I have heard many complaints from institutional staff that even if they manage to get the students to elect a course representative, the representative often does not turn up, or they have not read the papers or are only able to speak from their own experiences. In the research this gave rise to the idea that there could be a certain set of behaviours that could be common to all student representatives. If this was developed further, it could be a tool to help people considering becoming representatives, to develop training to enhance these skills as well as to support existing representatives in reflecting on their own role.

One of the themes that came through in the research was the perceived importance of course representatives being democratically elected. There was a view from the students' union representatives that representatives have more of a mandate through being more formally elected: "*there is a leadership role with that, so it's not purely an advocacy role.*" Indeed, there was a perception that being elected gave the representatives more legitimacy and helped to mitigate the power imbalance that can arise between student representatives and institutional staff.

A number of key behaviours emerged from the research, with the idea that ideal student representatives should be chameleonic, good communicators, policy actors, and represent an internal externality.

- *Chameleonic* is the idea that representatives need to be able to speak the 'university management speak' so that they will be listened to more by the institution, but also be able to switch back and relate to ordinary students and speak about education in an engaging way. It was suggested that this might also help mitigate against the feeling that the representative has been co-opted or 'gone native'.
- Student representatives will need to be able to speak in different ways to different audiences and so good *communication skills* are key to the role, in particular ensuring that students know what the representative is doing, and also, given the privileged position of the representative having more information about what is going on the in the department, they can act as a conduit of information from the institution when appropriate.
- Student representatives are not simply there to be vessels of other people's views. It is not their role to simply re-present data and views of students, but rather to digest this information and use it to identify priorities, with one interviewee saying they are not simply "*ventriloquists*".
- Student representatives are a useful source of feedback for the institution, acting as a critical friend, able to give helpful advice and on occasion to say the uncomfortable thing that an institution may not wish to hear/say out loud.

These themes begin to point to some possible characteristics that could form the basis of a set of behaviours for student representatives.

Enhancing the processes of student representation

In addition to focusing on how the representatives can become more professional and effective in their role, there was also the recognition that the processes themselves had to be better. This has resulted in a focus on enhancing student representation systems over the last decade, in particular the course representative system benchmarking toolkit that was developed by NUS with the Association of Managers of Students' Unions, having looked at various dimensions of student academic representative systems and how to improve them.[18] The benchmarking toolkit considers the various different elements of student academic representative systems including: selecting representatives, contacting and training them, supporting and providing guidance, the impact of representatives, ensuring their representativity, feeding back to students, ownership of systems, measuring the effectiveness of systems, as well as recognising and rewarding representatives.

As part of my research I looked at perceptions of the effectiveness of student representation through a national survey drawing on responses of those within students' unions and institutions responsible for liaising with student academic representative systems. Table 5.3 looks at perceptions of the effectiveness of student representation on faculty/departmental committees and compares this with the perceptions articulated in the research conducted by the Centre for Higher Education Research and Information (CHERI) (Little et al., 2009).

There are two key factors that strike me.

Table 5.3 Perceptions of effectiveness of student representation on faculty/departmental committees

	Very effective (%)	Reasonably effective (%)	Not very effective (%)	Not applicable (%)	Don't know (%)
HEI 2018	13.6	59.3	20.3	1.7	5.1
Students' union 2018	15.5	56.9	19	0	8.6
Combined 2018	14.5	58.1	19.7	0.9	6.8

Source: Online survey – HEIs, n=60; students' unions, n=58

	Very effective	Reasonably effective	Not very effective	Not applicable	Don't know
HEI 2009	16	71	9	4	0
Students' union 2009	13	39	37	0	11

Source: Online survey – HEIs, n=80; students' unions, n=39

Firstly, in 2009 there was much greater divergence between how effective students' union respondents considered student representation to be at this level compared to institutional respondents. In 2009 only 52% of respondents from students' unions believed student representation to be "*very*" or "*reasonably*" effective, compared to 87% of respondents from institutions. However, by 2018 72.4% of students' union respondents agreed that student representation on faculty/departmental committee was "*very*" or "*reasonably*" effective with almost exactly the same proportion of respondents from institutions agreeing, 72.9%. This convergence of the perceptions of students' unions and institutions suggests much greater agreement about the effectiveness of student representation, perhaps reflecting a better shared understanding of the purpose of representation.

Secondly, the data show a significant rise in the perceptions of the effectiveness of student representation amongst students' unions, rising from 52% in 2009 to 72.4% in 2018, whilst at the same time there is a drop amongst institutional respondents from 87% to 72.9%. Whilst not clear, this might reflect both a recognition from the students' union respondents of the support and investment in student academic representation systems over the last decade and perhaps a more realistic view amongst institutional staff, but this could be explored further in future research.

Wider barriers to collective student engagement

Staff engagement

Over the last decade there has been much focus on the efficiency of student representation structures and enhancing the professionalism of the student

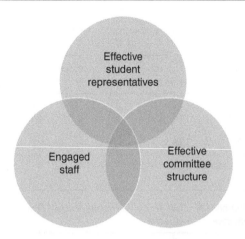

Figure 5.4 Enhancing student representation
Source: Bols, 2017

representatives themselves. However, there has been less focus on considering this effectiveness within the wider context of the institution as a whole. Whilst there is clearly more that can be done to improve student representation per se there are also other barriers to consider which I have considered as a Venn diagram (Figure 5.4).

During the research a number of staff – both professional services staff and also academics – were interviewed and there were two key aspects that kept on emerging. Firstly, the extent to which the staff of the institution were supported to get the most out of student input and, secondly, the way in the which the institutional processes – such as the committee structures themselves – are set up to deliver good decision-making.

Over many years NUS supported students' union staff to look at improving the development of student representatives through training and other activities, and yet there are not many institutions that build into academic staff development and training reflection on how they might better gather the student view and recognise the benefits of this. In my survey, 44.8% of institutional respondents did not believe that there was any training for academic staff in engaging students, with a further 17.2% believing it only happened in some departments and 15.5% replying that they did not know.

This training and development could also provide an opportunity to reflect on issues like the power differential between staff and students (both in a conscious way but also through unintended consequences) and how this might be mitigated. In one of the interviews, for example, a student representative described a departmental board meeting, where student representatives were attending. However, because there were not enough chairs in the room and the student representatives often turned up late, they ended up having to sit at the back of the room. In this particular instance it was identified as a problem and they changed the lay-out of the room to a circle to help mitigate against this, but such issues are not always identified.

Another question that staff might be supported to reflect on is the various tensions between the student voice and academic autonomy. One interviewee described having to be mindful that, whilst students on a particular academic's course were not happy with the teaching and content, this was something that the academic had spent a lot of time developing – and so the interviewee was conscious of the need to critique it in a constructive way. This was something that she had seen done less well by other student representatives, resulting in both upset staff and frustrated students. This will always depend to a certain extent on the way in which the student representative approaches this, and also if the academic is both open and receptive to suggestions about how the course can be improved it is likely to be a better discussion.

Committee structure

Another theme that emerged from the interviews was that the university committee structure itself was not always the best way of making decisions. It was suggested that even if you have excellent student representatives and staff that are actively engaged in getting the most from student feedback, even in this scenario you would only be able to go so far, as the university committee structure itself can often be a barrier to engagement and proactive decision-making.

There are some institutions that have moved to streamline their committee structures so that the full committee is only used when necessary, instead setting up task-and-finish groups for other issues. Whatever the approach your institution takes it is important to reflect on the effectiveness of these structures.

Conclusion

In conclusion, over the last quarter century student representation has received significant resource increases from both students' unions and institutions and been the focus of significant attention in the national policy agenda. The latter has considered both elements of student representation and engagement from the way individuals engage with their learning to the wider collective engagement in decision-making related to enhancing teaching and learning. The new governance principle in the Office for Students conditions of registration, along with developments surrounding technology and data, provide real opportunities to continue the trajectory of the past 25 years into the future and enhance student engagement and ownership of their learning.

Ultimately, we must remember that the aim is not just to get students engaged in their learning or involved in representation just for the sake of it – it is to improve their experience and support their development, or as the then President of NUS, Digby Jacks, said in 1972:

Representation must never be seen, except in strategic and practical terms, as an end in itself. Too many student representatives see it as a question of communication and merely sitting on the appropriate committee. The purpose of representation is to secure educational and social change.[19]

(NUS, 2011)

Notes

1 Education Act, 1994. Available at: www.legislation.gov.uk/ukpga/1994/30/contents
2 Sir John Major KG CH, 2019. Available at: www.johnmajor.co.uk/page1208.html
3 The National Student Survey, 2019. Available at: www.thestudentsurvey.com/
4 Office of the Independent Adjudicator (OIA). Available at: www.oiahe.org.uk/
5 Unistats, 2019. The official website for comparing UK higher education course data. Available at: https://unistats.ac.uk/
6 Competition and Markets Authority, 2019. Available at: www.gov.uk/government/organisations/competition-and-markets-authority
7 Times Higher Education, 2014. Off the booze: students' unions shift from serving to service. Times Higher Education, 17 April. Available at: www.timeshighereducation.com/features/off-the-booze-students-unions-shift-from-serving-to-service/2012658.article
8 Evans, G. 2018. Passing the regulatory baton from HEFCE to OfS. WonkHE, 12 March. Available at: https://wonkhe.com/blogs/passing-the-regulatory-baton-from-hefce-to-ofs/
9 Office for Students, 2018. Securing student success: Regulatory framework for higher education in England Available at: www.officeforstudents.org.uk/publications/securing-student-success-regulatory-framework-for-higher-education-in-england/
10 UK Standing Committee for Quality Assessment, 2008. UK Standing Committee for Quality Assessment publishes new Quality Code Expectations and practices. Available at: https://ukscqa.org.uk/2018/03/27/uk-standing-committee-quality-assessment-publishes-new-quality-code-expectations-practices/
11 National Union of Students (NUS) and Higher Education Academy (HEA), 2010. NUS-HEA Student engagement project – tools for effective partnership. Available at: www.sparqs.ac.uk/upfiles/1.1%20Student%20engagement%20toolkit.pdf
12 Office for Students, 2019. National Student Survey – NSS. Available at: www.officeforstudents.org.uk/advice-and-guidance/student-information-and-data/national-student-survey-nss/get-the-nss-data/

13 Jisc, 2019. Predictive analytics at Nottingham Trent University. Available at: https://analytics.jiscinvolve.org/wp/files/2016/04/CASE-STUDY-I-Nottingham-Trent-University.pdf

14 REACT, 2019. The Winchester Student Fellows Scheme. Available at: www.studentengagement.ac.uk/newsite/index.php/reactprojects/the-university-of-winchester/student-fellows-scheme

15 University of Exeter, 2019. Students as Change Agents. Available at: www.exeter.ac.uk/academic-skills-engagement-team/student-engagement/change/

16 AdvanceHE, 2019. Student as producer: research engaged teaching and learning - an institutional strategy. Available at: www.heacademy.ac.uk/knowledge-hub/student-producer-research-engaged-teaching-and-learning-institutional-strategy

17 Birmingham City University, 2019. Student Academic Partnerships. Available at: www.bcu.ac.uk/business-school/student-experience-and-employability/earn-while-you-learn/student-academic-partnerships

18 National Union of Students (NUS), 2019. Course Rep Systems Benchmarking Tool. Available at: http://s3-eu-west-1.amazonaws.com/nusdigital/document/documents/18588/dcced21f036bb553d0d9e4bef5267c0f/CourseRep-Benchmarking-Systems.pdf

19 National Union of Students (NUS), 2011. Remembering Digby Jacks - NUS President 1971–73 Available at: www.nusconnect.org.uk/articles/remembering-digby-jacks-nus-president-1971–73

References

Bols, A.T.G., 2017. Enhancing student representation. *Journal of Educational Innovation, Partnership and Change*, 3(1), pp.81–89.

Department for Education and Science, 2003. *The future of higher education*. DfES. Stationery Office. Retrieved from: http://webarchive.nationalarchives.gov.uk/20040117001247/http://dfes.gov.uk/highereducation/hestrategy/pdfs/DfES-HigherEducation.pdf (accessed 5 July 2016).

Department of Business, Innovation and Skills (BIS), 2011. *Students at the heart of the system*. Stationery Office. Retrieved from: www.gov.uk/government/uploads/system/uploads/attachment_data/file/31384/11-944-higher-education-students-at-heart-of-system.pdf

Department of Business, Innovation and Skills (BIS), 2016. *Higher education: success as a knowledge economy*. Stationery Office. Retrieved from: www.gov.uk/government/uploads/system/uploads/attachment_data/file/523396/bis-16-265-success-as-a-knowledge-economy.pdf

Gibbs, G., 2010. Dimensions of quality. York: Higher Education Academy.

Hood, C., 1995. The "new public management" in the 1980s: Variations on a theme. *Accounting, Organizations and Society*, 20(2–3), pp.93–109. Available at: https://doi.org/10.1016/0361-3682(93)E0001-W (accessed 24 October 2017).

Hu, S. and Kuh, G. D., 2001. Being (dis)engaged in educationally purposeful activities: The influences of student and institutional characteristics. Paper presented at the American Educational Research Association Annual Conference. Seattle, WA, 10–14 April.

Kay, J. Owen, D. and Dunne, E., 2012. Students as change agents: student engagement with quality enhancement of learning and teaching. In Solomonides, I and Petocz, P. (eds.), *Engaging with learning in higher education.* Farringdon: Libri Publishing.

Little, B. Locke, W. Scesa, A. and Williams, R., 2009. *Report to HEFCE on student engagement.* Bristol: HEFCE.

McMillan, J. and Cheney, G., 1996. The student as consumer: The implications and limitations of a metaphor. *Communication Education*, 45(1), pp.1–15. Retrieved from: www.tandfonline.com/doi/abs/10.1080/03634529609379028#. V3uz2dIrK2w (accessed 5 July 2016).

NUS (National Union of Students), 2011. Remembering Digby Jacks – NUS President 1971–73. Retrieved from: www.nusconnect.org.uk/articles/remembering-digby-jacks-nus-president-1971-73.

Palfreyman, D. and Warner, D., 1998. *Higher education and the law: A guide for managers.* Buckingham: Open University Press.

Quality Assurance Agency (QAA) 2012. Quality Code Section B5: Student Engagement. Gloucester. Retrieved from: www.qaa.ac.uk/en/Publications/Pages/Quality-Code-Chapter-B5.aspx#.VSEBn4hXerU

Streeting, W. and Wise, G., 2009. Rethinking the values of higher education – consumption, partnership, community? Gloucester, MA: Quality Assurance Agency for Higher Education. Retrieved from: www.sparqs.ac.uk/ch/F2%20Rethinking%20the%20Values%20of%20Higher%20Education.pdf

Trowler, V., 2010. *Student Engagement Literature Review.* Higher Education Academy. Retrieved from: www.heacademy.ac.uk/system/files/studentengagementliteraturereview_1.pdf (accessed 21 October 2018).

Chapter 6

Student engagement in evaluation

Expanding perspectives and ownership

Catherine Bovill and Cherie Woolmer

Introduction

Increasingly, scholars and practitioners are exploring the benefits of deeper student engagement and of students working in partnership with staff (Cook-Sather, Bovill and Felten, 2014; Mercer-Mapstone, Dvorakova, Matthews, Abbot, Cheng, Felten, Knorr, Marquis, Shammas and Swaim, 2017). Despite current expansion of interest and activity around student–staff partnership and engagement, one area of practice that has received relatively less attention is student engagement in evaluation – whether evaluating learning and teaching, the wider student experience or student engagement initiatives.

Many authors agree that defining student engagement is challenging and terminology is often loosely applied (Bryson, 2014; Wolf-Wendel 2009). The variety of work that comes under the banner of student engagement in higher education is vast and trying to make comparisons and connections between this diverse array of work can be confusing. Kuh (2009, p.683) argues that student engagement is composed of two key parts: "*the time and effort students devote to activities that are empirically linked to desired outcomes of college and what institutions do to induce students to participate in these activities*".

Bryson (2014, p.18) describes these two sides of student engagement as "*students engaging*" (what the student does) and "*engaging students*" (what the institution does). In seeking to understand student engagement another useful distinction is that between student engagement in governance (student representation, contributing to university committees and larger-scale quality assurance and enhancement) and student engagement in pedagogy (focusing on learning, teaching, assessment and curriculum enhancement and often referring to engagement in class or online). Finally, a third distinction can be made between small-scale initiatives involving a selected few students being engaged, and whole cohort or class approaches to engaging an entire group of students.

The complexity of what we explore in this chapter can be summarised using the different and intersecting dimensions of student engagement outlined above: (1) what the student does; (2) what the institution does/staff do; (3) focus on governance and representation; (4) focus on pedagogy; (5) involvement of selected or elected small numbers of students; and (6) involvement of a whole group of students. These dimensions highlight a wide range of possibilities when we examine student engagement in evaluation. The purpose of evaluation and one's approach to it is determined by the ways in which these various dimensions of student engagement interact. In this chapter we will focus on engaging students as partners in evaluation of learning and teaching, drawing predominantly on categories (1) and (4), but illustrating the variety of approaches that involve both (5) and (6). We aim to demonstrate how pursuing authentic and meaningful student engagement within the evaluation process can enhance student interest and motivation, increase our understanding of student engagement and enrich evaluation processes and outcomes.

Our call to involve students meaningfully in evaluation is predicated on the desire to engage in more "collaborative and dialogic" evaluative processes, as advocated by Cook-Sather, Bovill and Felten (2014: 188). One small example which illustrates the importance of student–staff dialogue in evaluation comes from academic staff in the Law faculty at Liverpool Hope University (UK). Brooman, Darwent and Pimor (2015) describe how they designed and evaluated a course only to find that the students reviewed it poorly and performed poorly in assessments. The staff realised the impact of missing student perspectives from the design process and subsequently held student focus groups and carried out further evaluation of the course before redesigning the course again. Informed by student perspectives, the outcomes from the second redesign were far more positive.

If we want to be consistent with the values of student engagement, we need to practice what we preach and engage students in evaluation processes. Furthermore, by doing so, this potentially increases the legitimacy of evaluation outcomes by including student voices and through developing student ownership of evaluation. We begin by outlining what we mean by evaluation and then move to discussing rationales for involving students in evaluation. We then present a range of examples which modify established evaluation practices to include students. These examples demonstrate the importance of shifting from 'evaluation *on* students' to 'evaluation *with* students', highlighting the added value gained from students becoming more meaningfully engaged in evaluation. Finally, we outline implications for practice that include some important considerations for engaging students in evaluation, which we believe are adaptable to different areas of evaluation, including evaluating work focused on student engagement.

What do we mean by evaluation?

Before looking at why and how we can involve students in evaluation, it is important to consider what we mean by evaluation. We adopt the UK use of the term evaluation, to refer to a way of judging the quality, impact and value of teaching and learning, often through eliciting student feedback on courses and programmes. Cook-Sather et al. define evaluation as:

a process of stepping back from and analyzing progress in any educational endeavor… either in a formative way (during the process with the goal of using what is gathered to revise the approaches we are using) or in a summative way (with the goal of evaluating what has been learned, taught, or accomplished after the process is completed).

(2014, p.187)

Cousin (2009, p.227) states that "*evaluation research allows worth to be assigned to programmes and initiatives, adding to the case for their continuing support and/or pointing to areas that need change*". Cousin also adds to the formative/ improvement-oriented evaluation, summative/judgment-oriented evaluation typology outlined by Cook-Sather et al. (2014) and suggests that evaluation can also be for the purpose of enhancing knowledge and understanding. Ahmad, Fenton and Graystone, Acai, Matthews, Chalmers (2018) suggest that mean-ingful evaluation practices should be explicitly underpinned by a number of principles, including: identifying the best timing for evaluation activity; inte-grating evaluation into practice to enable collection of process as well as output measures; prioritising what evidence is important to collect and what is possible to collect; choosing the appropriate method for the purpose and timing of evalu-ation; taking an ethical and transparent approach; engaging stakeholders; and drawing upon, where possible, qualitative and quantitative data.

In a recent critique of student engagement work, MacFarlane and Tomlinson (2017) argued that much student engagement work is undertheorised and the existing evidence base is mixed. We agree with this to a point, but the danger here is that some of the existing, excellent theorisation of student engagement will be overlooked and, whilst there is a need for more robust and systematic evaluation of student engagement, what is perhaps more starkly absent from this critique is the lack of the student voice in much research and evaluation of prac-tice. Whatever the specific focus of the evaluation, whether within or outside the curriculum, there are some important factors to consider. Several authors have drawn attention to the dangers of pursuing very formal, quantitative and posi-tivist evaluations, where the context of the higher education sector and the focus on learning and teaching involves complexity, the unpredictable, and where there is a need to respond to a wide range of stakeholders (Cousin, 2009; Pawson and Tilley, 1997). Instead Cousin proposes dialogic inquiry is required for respon-siveness and "*for a revision of the evaluator stance as an objective outsider in favour of more facilitative and formative evaluation practices*" (Cousin 2009, p.229). This has led to increasing calls for students to be active participants in evaluation and enquiry, or co-evaluators, particularly where they are directly affected, such as in learning and teaching and in student engagement work. Alongside this, there are calls for more attention to be paid to the processes of evaluation as well as outcomes (Cook-Sather et al., 2014).

We identify evaluation as a form of enquiry that overlaps with research and scholarship. Saunders (2000) describes how evaluation can be used for planning, learning, managing, developing and accountability purposes. There is an implication and expectation that data gathered through evaluation will be used to inform decision making on future activity; so it might contribute to knowledge, but it will also help to prioritise a course of action. Evaluation often involves several stages including: (i) commission and design, (ii) data collection, (iii) analysis, (iv) reporting, and (v) deciding on the course/s of action. Most forms of evaluation in higher education tend to involve students in the data collection phase (with students being respondents rather than evaluators). However, there are examples of students being involved in the commissioning of evaluation work and deciding on the course of action once results are shared. This is largely achieved through student representation on academic committees ((3) in our student engagement dimensions), involving only a (s)elected (and not always representative) group of the student body ((5) in our student engagement dimensions). We argue that student participation in any or all of the above stages is possible, sometimes involving only incremental shifts in how individuals conceptualise evaluation.

Existing approaches to evaluation

Across higher education, student engagement takes place within and outside the formal curriculum at the level of the individual student, in groups and at institutional and national levels. This variety of scale and focus results in a vast range of approaches being used to evaluate these initiatives. The larger scale the evaluation, the more formal and summative the approach that tends to be taken. Evaluations such as the UK National Student Survey (NSS) involve qualitative and quantitative data-gathering through questionnaires administered to thousands of students at the end of their degree. Often in the higher education sector, evaluation is taken as referring to formal evaluation of courses, programmes and the wider student experience, most commonly undertaken at the end of the process. Increasingly, evaluation also takes place part of the way through courses and programmes, formally or informally, in attempts to ensure that those students responding benefit directly from any changes made in response to their comments. This shift towards undertaking mid-course formative evaluation often involves the use of more informal and creative methods of evaluation with less institutionally instigated and compulsory formats required. This might imply that institutions perhaps place greater value on summative evaluations. Like Cousin, Bamber (2013, p.12) claims that *"evaluation is about attributing value and worth to our activities, to indicate what differences we have made"*, and teachers may find themselves placing greater value on formative evaluations that they have greater control over, and that enable them to make changes for the remainder of a course. Students may also place greater value on formative evaluation mid-way through a course if this means changes can be made that will benefit them directly, often leading to students experiencing increased ownership of evaluation.

Another common approach to evaluating teaching is peer observation of teaching, or peer review. This usually involves a member of staff offering feedback to another member of staff on their teaching, or on their course/programme documentation. The term peer can be widely interpreted in peer observation of teaching (Bovill and Cairns, 2014; Weller, 2009) as either a departmental colleague, a teaching specialist from a Learning and Teaching Centre, or a participant taking part in a Postgraduate Certificate in Learning and Teaching in Higher Education or equivalent programme.

There are many different approaches to evaluation, but let us turn now to explore why students are being increasingly involved in evaluation processes.

Why involve students in evaluation processes?

The expectation to evaluate teaching and learning, and specifically student engagement in teaching and learning, is evident in a number of higher education systems around the world. In addition to the widely known large-scale surveys such as the NSS in the UK and the National Survey of Student Engagement in the US (Kuh, 2009), most degree programmes and modules are evaluated through endpoint evaluations. Student–staff liaison committees are also common forms of evaluating the wider student experience. We also now routinely see 'you said, we did' headlines across campuses, communicating to students how their input to evaluation and feedback activities has resulted in action.

Much of this activity is premised on the idea that evaluation of teaching and learning is something carried out 'on', or 'done to' students; institutions seek feedback on issues (and in ways) that it decides are important. In this framing of evaluation, the institution (and staff) are powerful gatekeepers. Students are considered to be respondents in this approach. Rooted in this conception are assumptions that the evaluators (usually staff/academics) are best placed to formulate the focus of what is to be evaluated, the methods to be used, how to make sense of and prioritise results, and the course of action to be taken (or not) as a result. The outcomes of evaluations can have important consequences, including resource allocation, (dis)continuation of courses and future curriculum design, all of which ultimately affect students. The position of the evaluator, therefore, is an important and privileged one.

Otis and Hammond (2010) argue that Participatory Action Research (PAR) *"supports the inclusion of students' insider knowledge of their expertise as learners. PAR also calls for the construction of new knowledge that arises when all stakeholders, including students, collaborate in inquiry processes leading to positive changes in education"* (Otis and Hammond 2010, pp.32–33). This research methodology is underpinned by arguments similar to those we see to support the engagement of students in evaluation of learning and teaching. Otis and Hammond propose that the principles of PAR, *"participatory, collaborative, democratising, action oriented, and cyclical"* suggest not only a methodological approach to include students in research (and by extension, evaluation), but also provide a moral imperative to do so. We also recognise a political imperative to ensure that diverse student perspectives are included in evaluations. Perhaps some of the strongest calls for student involvement come from recognising the potential benefits to students, staff and institutions. Involving students in evaluation:

- provides new insights to staff and institutions about what is important and relevant to students;
- develops greater understanding of the learning or student engagement activity being evaluated through inclusion of more perspectives in different stages of the evaluation;
- creates opportunities for dialogue; and
- helps develop shared responsibility and ownership.

The student–staff partnership literature supports involving students more fundamentally in their learning (Bryson, 2014; Cook-Sather et al., 2014; Werder and Otis, 2010). The literature demonstrates the value of providing spaces where assumptions about learning and teaching and student engagement are explored and challenged, and of taking account of different perspectives and experiences. We would argue that involving students in evaluation can bring many benefits. For example, students are able to clarify areas of learning and teaching that they consider to be more relevant or important and these insights can lead to better informed evaluations. Evaluations in which students are more meaningfully involved can complement or counter other formalised evaluation mechanisms.

The unique perspectives that different students bring to evaluations can inform both the focus and the methodological approach taken. As a direct result of these unique perspectives and different motivations, evaluations can become richer by benefitting from going in directions that staff and institutions haven't considered (due to their own perspectives previously dominating the evaluation agenda). By combining the perspectives, interests and values of staff, students and institutions, evaluations can lead to developing a much deeper and greater understanding of the topic, activity or outcomes at the centre of inquiry. Involving students in the meaning-making processes that take place in evaluation, as well as involving students in the actions taken as a result, is particularly important if we want to make sure we spend effort changing things that are really important for enhancing student engagement. Students can be involved in any or all of the stages of evaluation we have outlined earlier, helping to frame topics of evaluation through to making sense of data that is collected, but careful thought should be given to which students are being involved at which stages and why, in the same way that careful consideration should be given to which staff are involved at which stages and why. Not all students or staff need be involved in all stages in the same ways (Bovill, 2017; Könings, Bovill and Woolner 2017). Involving students in evaluation, and particularly formative evaluation, provides opportunities to discuss the purpose and focus, methods, outcomes and next steps and can develop a sense of shared responsibility and ownership of evaluation. Involving students gives them a stake in what happens – an opportunity to exercise some agency over their learning – and to share responsibility for what happens as a result.

How can students become more involved in evaluating learning and teaching?

To illustrate the ways in which students are becoming involved in evaluation, we return to some of the existing approaches to evaluation outlined earlier. We provide here some examples that demonstrate how existing forms of evaluation can be built upon and augmented in ways that enhance dialogue and involve greater numbers of students than have typically been involved in representation systems or small student-engagement projects.

At national level, many countries use large-scale surveys such as the NSS (UK), which are completed by very large numbers of students. The student data gathered is used to inform university league tables and other measurements of quality, teaching, learning and student experience within institutions. Whilst these surveys are completed by very large numbers of students, they offer little opportunity for meaningful student involvement in the evaluation process. However, some institutions are recognising the value of engaging students as partners to discuss departmental NSS outcomes and ways to improve future survey outcomes (Marie and Azuma 2018).

Within higher education institutions, many programmes and courses throughout the world use staff–student liaison committees (SSLCs) (or their equivalents) as an integral part of university quality assurance and evaluation of learning and teaching. These formal committee meetings offer a regular opportunity (typically once per semester) for students to raise issues about learning, teaching and 'the student experience' through their class or year representatives. Some universities are inviting a student representative to chair the committee, and others are ensuring any discussion papers are prepared in collaboration with student representatives and discussed with the wider student body. However, these formal systems of student representation and governance ((3) in our student engagement dimensions) often limit the extent to which all student voices can be heard.

Another very common form of evaluation where all students are invited to participate is the end of course or summative programme questionnaire. This is often a standardised form across a higher education institution, which enables all students to express their perspectives on a course or programme. These questionnaires are routinely determined and written by staff. Often there are opportunities to include one or two context-specific questions but, these additional questions are also usually determined by the staff member teaching the course. Clearly the style of questionnaire and relative balance of closed and open-ended questions determines how, and the extent to which, students can express their views. Whether student voices are heard and acted upon as a result of end of course questionnaires is also highly dependent upon individual staff having easy access to the results of the often automated questionnaires, and if they do have access, individual staff motivations about what to do with the data gathered. Indeed, staff attitudes towards students and student feedback has an enormous influence on the different approaches to evaluation that are adopted and how much participation or partnership is encouraged. It is important to note that teaching and course evaluations are used as part of promotion and tenure discussions in the North American context and therefore yield significant power over faculty emotions and careers. Many staff are increasingly recognising the importance of students' perspectives on their course experiences and on the solutions that can be found to teaching and learning challenges. This often leads staff to question whether summative evaluation questionnaires are the most engaging and effective approach to evaluate learning and engagement.

Formative feedback has traditionally offered students the opportunity for greater ownership of the evaluation process by opening up the possibility of influencing the course or project that they themselves are part of. Mid-semester feedback and other types of formative evaluation can sometimes use similar approaches to end of course questionnaires. However, they do seem to be less formal than summative feedback, and because of this, they can enable staff to have more freedom to use different evaluation methods. One common example of a simple evaluation method used part way through a course is the stop, start, continue questionnaire where students are asked to feed back to tutors what they would like them to stop, start and continue doing in their teaching approach (George and Cowan 1999). In an adaptation of this approach, it's possible to suggest that any changes that could be made going forward, might not just be changes made by the teacher. Bovill (2011) argues that by asking the students to also write down what they should start, stop and continue doing to support their own and others' learning, there is a strong message that improvements to learning and teaching are a shared responsibility between staff and students.

In another approach to evaluation, teachers sometimes invite a neutral staff member, perhaps from the university's Learning and Teaching Centre, to meet with students and gather information about what could be done differently to enhance student engagement and learning in a course or programme, including asking students what their role is, or what their role could be, to improve learning within the course. Other colleagues are inviting students to run focus groups with their peers to gather feedback on course and project experiences. When students ask other students about their learning experiences, students can feel less restrained in the feedback they will give. Bovill and Woolmer (2016) have used an approach where the students are asked to suggest evaluation questions that the teacher needs to pose to the class in order to gain constructive feedback from the course or project. Where student numbers allow, another approach is to invite students to work together to evaluate their own course (Bovill, Aitken, Hutchison, Morrison, Roseweir, Scott and Sotannde, 2010) ((6) in our student engagement dimensions). This works well where students are invested in evaluation for some reason, e.g. they are learning about research and evaluation, or they have been engaged deeply in other elements of designing the learning experience. Another idea is to have a discussion with students before running a course, to discuss the focus and approaches students and staff wish to enact.

This provides a valuable opportunity for students to influence their own learning experiences.

Building on these formative approaches, there are growing numbers of universities that are involving students in peer observation of teaching schemes. One of the first schemes was the Students as Learners and Teachers (SaLT) project at Bryn Mawr College, Pennsylvania (USA) run by Alison Cook-Sather (Cook-Sather, 2009). This scheme, and others that have emulated it since, offer another approach to evaluating teaching and involving students. Traditionally, the peer in a peer observation of teaching is a member of teaching staff who observes a colleague teaching. In a twist on the traditional approach to peer observation, students are trained to offer feedback to teachers on their teaching and on how effectively they are engaging students. These schemes offer a powerful way to challenge the stereotypical relationship between teachers and students, and in research from a 'students as colleagues' observation scheme from Edinburgh Napier University (UK), teaching staff often found the student peer feedback they received to be more useful than the staff peer feedback (Huxham, Scoles, Green, Purves, Welsh and Gray 2017).

Students are also increasingly involved in the Scholarship of Teaching and Learning (SoTL) and educational research as a form of evaluation of student engagement and student learning. In many cases they are involved in all stages of research, but in common with many student partnership and engagement initiatives, some examples of student involvement in SoTL, research and evaluation only involve a small number of students ((5) in our student engagement dimensions). Less commonly large numbers of students, or a whole group or class of students are involved in SoTL ((6) in our student engagement dimensions). In most cases there is a genuine desire to ensure that students are authentically involved in processes of research into things that affect them (Otis and Hammond, 2010). Involving students in as many stages as possible of evaluation activity offers opportunities for students and staff to work together to identify topics of inquiry, gather data, and make sense of results through collaborating in the analysis of data. In addition, there may be opportunities for students to remain involved in implementing the outcomes of evaluation activities (Woolmer, Sneddon, Curry, Hill, Fehertavi, Longbone and Wallace 2016). These different approaches to increasing student participation are summarised in Table 6.1.

Implications and conclusions

If we return to Bamber's (2013) idea that through evaluation we are attributing value and indicating the difference we have made to something, then involving students in that process enables a key stakeholder in the learning process to influence what we value, how we change learning and how any difference that is made is experienced. Diverse student perspectives provide us with a greater range of ideas and creativity within evaluation, and increased dialogue between staff and students benefits not just evaluation, but student belonging, the building

Table 6.1 Increasing student participation in evaluation

Activity	Formative or Summative	Focus: Governance or Pedagogy	Students involved: selected or whole cohort/class	Opportunities to increase student engagement
National Surveys	Summative	Governance or Pedagogy	Whole cohort	Student involvement in interpreting/analysing results and planning future action.
Liaison Committees	Formative or Summative	Governance or Pedagogy	Elected	Ensure election processes robust and inclusive, ensure reps are representative and mechanisms exist for representatives to engage systematically with whole cohorts
End of course evaluations	Summative	Governance or Pedagogy	Whole cohort	Involve students in designing questions to be included in evaluation, and data collection, and analysis and future actions.
Mid course evaluations	Formative.	Pedagogy	Whole class	Involve students in designing evaluation, data collection, analysis and future actions. Create opportunities for dialogue and enhanced ownership (often more freedom than with end of course evaluations)
Peer observation	Formative	Pedagogy	Selected	Students conduct peer observation and provide feedback to staff. (Process usually supported and guided by external co-ordinator).
Scholarship of Teaching and Learning	Both	Pedagogy	Selected or whole class	Involve either a small group or a whole class of students in designing questions for evaluation, and/or data collection, and/or analysis, and/or future action. Involve students in 'going public' in dissemination and publication.

of academic community, teaching quality and learning outcomes (Gibbs 2012; Mårtensson, Roxå and Stensaker 2014).

We recognise that involving students can be challenging, not least in terms of navigating the various power relationships involved and the existing institutional structures needed, as documented in the PAR literature and work by Bovill, Cook-Sather, Felten, Millard and Moore-Cherry (2016). However, we argue that the underpinning values of PAR and of the involvement of students in higher education evaluation is an important principle to add to Ahmad et al.'s list of evaluation principles. Many of these challenges are also outweighed by the benefits from working with students to evaluate learning and teaching. The insights and perspectives students bring, the different forms of data collected by students from other students, and the greater understanding created for the benefit of both staff and students are compelling reasons for engaging students in evaluation processes.

Our own experience and the examples we have included suggest the following are important considerations for student involvement in evaluation.

- Make space for informal and transparent conversations with students about learning and teaching, and about student engagement. Research suggests these conversations are the bedrock of positive relationships and outcomes for students.
- Build positive staff attitudes towards students – if we want to engage students, staff need to be engaged and interested in students.
- Acknowledge and be open to the valuable perspectives students bring to discussions about student engagement and learning and be prepared to respond and act upon some suggestions, and explain why it might not be possible to act upon others.
- Be mindful of issues of equity and inclusion, paying attention to the voices of students not often represented/under-represented in learning and evaluation.
- Have high expectations of what students will and want to contribute, as they will usually meet and exceed your expectations.
- Be aware that when students are engaged in evaluation meaningfully, their engagement often extends into a deeper and wider engagement with other areas of learning and with their overall university experience.

By increasing the opportunities for students to evaluate learning and teaching, and student engagement initiatives, we all benefit from students' perspectives. Our own experiences of working with students to evaluate learning and teaching has led us to collaborate in investigating areas of work that we had not previously considered exploring, and has revealed valuable things we did not know. The benefits of including students' perspectives in evaluation strongly supports the argument for continuing to provide more opportunities for dialogue and informal conversations between staff and students about learning, teaching and student engagement.

References

Ahmad, A., Fenton, N., Graystone, L., Acai, A., Matthews, K. and Chalmers, D., 2018. *Investigating Impact in Higher Education*. Higher Education Research and Development Society of Australia.

Bamber, V. (ed.), 2013. Evidencing the value of educational development, *SEDA Special* 34.

Bovill, C., 2011. Sharing responsibility for learning through formative evaluation: moving to evaluation as learning. *Practice and Evidence of the Scholarship of Teaching and Learning in Higher Education*, 6 (2) 96–109.

Bovill, C., 2017. A framework to explore roles within student–staff partnerships in higher education: which students are partners, when and in what ways? *International Journal for Students as Partners* 1 (1) 1–5. Retrieved from: https://doi.org/10.15173/ijsap.v1i1.3062

Bovill, C. and Cairns, A., 2014. *Peer observation of teaching as a form of strategic academic development*. Paper presentation, International Consortium on Educational Development Conference, Stockholm, Sweden, 16–18 June. Retrieved from: http://iced2014.se/proceedings/1576_Bovill.pdf

Bovill, C. and Woolmer, C., 2016. *Bottom-up and emergent institutional change: evaluating a student engagement course and a new network for academic staff*. Paper presentation, RAISE Conference, Loughborough, 8–9 September.

Bovill, C., Aitken, G., Hutchison, J., Morrison, F., Roseweir, K., Scott, A. and Sotannde, S., 2010. Experiences of learning through collaborative evaluation from a Postgraduate Certificate in Professional Education. *International Journal for Academic Development* 15 (2) 143–154. Retrieved from: https://doi.org/10.1080/13601441003738343

Bovill, C., Cook-Sather, A., Felten, P., Millard, L. and Moore-Cherry, N., 2016. Addressing potential challenges in co-creating learning and teaching: overcoming resistance, navigating institutional norms and ensuring inclusivity in student–staff partnerships. *Higher Education* 71(2), 195–208. Retrieved from: https://doi.org/10.1007/s10734-015-9896-4

Brooman, S., Darwent, S. and Pimor. A., 2015. The student voice in higher education curriculum design: is there value in listening? *Innovations in Education and Teaching International* 52 (6) 663–674. Retrieved from: https://doi.org/10.1080/14703297.2014.910128

Bryson C. (Ed) 2014. *Understanding and developing student engagement: perspectives from universities and students*. Abingdon: Routledge, 2014.

Cook-Sather, A., 2009. From traditional accountability to shared responsibility: The benefits and challenges of student consultants gathering midcourse feedback in college classrooms, *Assessment and Evaluation in Higher Education*, 34 (2) 231–241. Retrieved from: https://doi.org/10.1080/02602930801956042

Cook-Sather, A., Bovill, C. and Felten, P., 2014. *Engaging students as partners in learning and teaching: a guide for faculty*. San Francisco, CA: Jossey Bass.

Cousin, G., 2009. *Researching learning in higher education: an introduction to contemporary methods and approaches*. London: Routledge.

George, J. and Cowan, J., 1999. *A handbook of techniques for formative evaluation. Mapping the student's learning experience*. London: Kogan Page.

Gibbs, G., 2012. *Implications of 'Dimensions of quality' in a market environment*. York: Higher Education Academy.

Huxham, M., Scoles, J., Green, U., Purves, S., Welsh, Z. and Gray, A., 2017. 'Observation has set in': comparing students and peers as reviewers of teaching. *Assessment and Evaluation in Higher Education* 42 (6) 887–899. Retrieved from: https://doi.org/10.1080/02602938.2016.1204594

Könings K.D., Bovill, C. and Woolner, P., 2017. Towards an interdisciplinary model of practice for participatory building design in education *European Journal of Education* 52 (3) 306–317. Retrieved from: https://doi.org/10.1111/ejed.12230

Kuh, G. D., 2009. What student affairs professionals need to know about student engagement. *Journal of College Student Development*, 50 (6) 683–706. Retrieved from: https://doi.org/10.1353/csd.0.0099

MacFarlane, B. and Tomlinson, M., 2017. Editorial: Critical and Alternative Perspectives on Student Engagement. Higher Education Policy, 30, 1–4. Retrieved from: https://doi.org/10.1057/s41307-016-0026-4

Marie, J. and Azuma, F., 2018. Partnership support for departments with low satisfaction. *Student Engagement in Higher Education Journal* 2 (1).

Mårtensson, K., Roxå, T. and Stensaker, B., 2014. From quality assurance to quality practices: an investigation of strong microcultures in teaching and learning, *Studies in Higher Education*, 39 (4) 534–545. Retrieved from: https://doi.org/10.1080/03075079.2012.709493

Mercer-Mapstone, L, Dvorakova, S.L, Matthews, K.E., Abbot, S., Cheng, B., Felten, P., Knorr, K, Marquis, E., Shammas, R. and Swaim, K., 2017. A systematic literature review of students as partners in higher education. *International Journal for Students as Partners* 1 (1) 1–23. Retrieved from: https://doi.org/10.15173/ijsap.v1i1.3119

Otis, M. M, and Hammond, J., 2010. Participatory Action Research as a rationale for student voices in the Scholarship of Teaching and Learning in Werder, C., and Otis, M.M (ed.), 2010. Engaging student voices in the study of teaching and learning. Sterling, VA: Stylus.

Pawson, R., and Tilley, N., 1997. An introduction to scientific realist evaluation. In E. Chelimsky and W. R. Shadish (eds.), Evaluation for the 21st century: A handbook (p.405–418). Sage Publications. Retrieved from: https://doi.org/10.4135/9781483348896.n29

Saunders, M., 2000. Beginning an evaluation with RUFDATA: Theorising a practical approach to evaluation planning. *Evaluation*, 6 (1) 7–21. Retrieved from: https://doi.org/10.1177/13563890022209082

Weller, S., 2009. What does "peer" mean in observation for the professional development of higher education lecturers? *International Journal of Teaching and Learning in Higher Education* 21 (1) 25–35.

Werder, C. and Otis, M. M. (eds.), 2010. Engaging student voices in the study of teaching and learning. Sterling, VA: Stylus.

Wolf-Wendel, L., Ward, K. and Kinzie, J., 2009. A tangled web of terms: The overlap and unique contribution of involvement, engagement, and integration to understanding college student success. *Journal of College Student Development*. 50:4, 407–408. Retrieved from: https://doi.org/10.1353/csd.0.0077

Woolmer, C., Sneddon, P., Curry, G., Hill, B., Fehertavi, S., Longbone, C., and Wallace, K., 2016. Student–staff partnership to create an interdisciplinary science skills course in a research intensive university. *International Journal for Academic Development*. 21 (1) 16–27. Retrieved from: https://doi.org/10.1080/1360144x.2015.1113969

Part II

International perspectives of theory into practice

Student engagement through classroom-focused pedagogical partnership

A model and outcomes from the United States

Alison Cook-Sather

Introduction

Student engagement is necessarily shaped by the context in which any given learner might engage and by how that context intersects with the learner's own intersecting identities, previous educational (and life) experiences, and goals. In the United States, higher education comprises institutions that vary by type (small, private, selective, liberal arts colleges; large, public, research universities; work-oriented, community colleges; and more), operate with relatively limited supervision and control by governmental bodies, are mostly privately funded, and are highly competitive (Felten, 2018). In this context, student engagement has been conceptualized primarily in relation to the potential of high-impact practices (Kuh, 2008) and of active-learning strategies (Freeman, Eddy, McDonough, Smith, Okoroafor, Jordt, and Wenderoth, 2014) as those are enacted in individual classrooms, which varies widely within and across institutions. A relatively new phenomenon variously called "*pedagogical partnership*" and "*students as partners*" offers an especially powerful form of engagement built on context-specific collaborations between students and staff (Cook-Sather, Bovill, and Felten, 2014; Healey and Healey, 2018).

Colleagues and I have defined pedagogical partnership as "*a collaborative, reciprocal process through which all participants have the opportunity to contribute equally, although not necessarily in the same ways, to curricular or pedagogical conceptualisation, decision making, implementation, investigation, or analysis*" (Cook-Sather, Bovill, and Felten, 2014, pp.6–7). Scholars around the world have made a range of arguments about the relationship between student engagement and pedagogical partnership. Some have argued that partnership is a path toward student engagement (Bovill and Felten, 2016; Bryson, 2014; Millard, Bartholomew, Brand and Nygaard, 2013; Taylor, Wilding, Mockridge and Lambert, 2012). Others situate student engagement, partnership, and co-creation in dynamic interaction with one another (Bovill, Cook-Sather, Felten, Millard, and Moore-Cherry, 2016). Still others propose redefining student engagement as partnership (Matthews, 2016). I have argued for thinking about the engagement of academic staff as well as students within partnership (Cook-Sather, 2013), and colleagues and I have found within the US context and elsewhere that partnership can make both classrooms and institutions more inclusive and responsive, thereby not only better engaging but also valuing students traditionally under-represented in and under-served by higher education (Cook-Sather, 2015; Cook-Sather and Agu, 2013; de Bie, Marquis, Cook-Sather, and Luqueño, forthcoming.

In this chapter I present one model of pedagogical partnership – classroom-based, pedagogical consultancy – developed through the Student as Learners and Teachers (SaLT) program. Created in 2006 at Bryn Mawr and Haverford Colleges, two selective, liberal arts colleges located in the Mid-Atlantic region of the United States, SaLT pairs academic staff with undergraduate students not enrolled in those staff members' courses in one-on-one, semester-long, pedagogical partnerships focused on explorations, affirmations, and, where appropriate, revisions of approaches to teaching and learning (Cook-Sather, 2016). Drawing on ethics-board approved research on this program and on essays published by student and staff partners who have participated in SaLT and programs like it, I share:

(1) outcomes in relation to the engagement partnership promotes (a) in student partners and (b) in the students enrolled in courses upon which student and staff partners focus;
(2) preliminary findings on the potential for pedagogical partnerships to foster greater equity and inclusion; and
(3) suggestions for where to find advice for developing classroom-focused pedagogical partnerships.

Pedagogical partnerships focused on classroom practice in the US context

Because there are no mandates and few models for pedagogical partnerships between academic staff and students in higher education in the United States, institutions must take their own initiative in developing and legitimating pedagogical partnership. Some approaches have linked partnership work with their institutional missions (e.g., Goldsmith, Hanscom, Throop, and Young, 2017; Oleson, 2015; Volk, 2016). Others have framed it as an extension of their commitment to developing engaging and effective curricula (Delpish, Holmes, Knight-McKenna, 2010; Mihans, Long, and Felten, 2008). Still others have argued for the potential of partnership to inform the Scholarship of Teaching and Learning (Felten, 2013; Werder and Otis, 2010).

In the United States, classroom-focused pedagogical partnership programs have developed at small, selective, liberal arts colleges, such as Berea, Lewis and Clark, Oberlin, Reed, Smith, and Ursinus Colleges (USA); at private universities, such as Trinity University (USA) and University of Denver (USA); and at large, public, state universities, such as University of Virginia (USA) and Florida Gulf Coast University (USA). All of these programs have been inspired by the SaLT program.

Through one-on-one, semester-long partnerships, student partners visit their staff partners' classes, typically once a week; meet weekly with their staff partners; and meet weekly with other student partners and program directors. The goal in each of these forums is to affirm what is working well in staff partners' classrooms and consider how to deepen, extend, or expand inclusive and engaging pedagogical approaches. Students apply for this position; receive a set of guidelines for developing partnerships with academic staff members; are oriented through workshops and/or the weekly meetings with other student partners and program directors; and are compensated for their work with hourly pay, stipends, or academic credit (Cook-Sather, Bahti, and Ntem, forthcoming).

Student engagement through classroom-focused pedagogical partnership

A variety of publications documents how classroom-focused pedagogical partnership can deepen engagement of student partners themselves and also support the deepening of engagement among students enrolled in the courses upon which staff and student partners focus (Cook-Sather, Bovill, and Felten, 2014; Luker and Morris, 2016; Mercer-Mapstone, Dvorakova, Matthews, Abbot, Cheng, Felten, Knorr, Marquis, Shammas, and Swaim 2017; Schlosser and Sweeney, 2015).

Pedagogical partnerships create opportunities for students and staff to "*engage in more active dialogue*" about teaching and learning (Goldsmith et al., 2017). When staff and students are "*engaging actively in collaboration around teaching goals*" (Oleson, 2016), students gain skills, insights, confidence, and capacity that affect their engagement within and beyond the classroom. Student partners develop skills that not only help them "*reflect on [their] other classes*" in general but, more specifically, "*understand the rationale behind an activity or behind an assignment*" and thereby better understand "*why I am being asked to engage with this particular text in this particular way.*" As student partners explain, to see "*the pedagogical reasoning*" behind an assignment "*totally deepened my learning*"; partnership helps student partners "*think much more deeply about what I need as a learner.*" Student partners also talk about engaging more fully beyond the classroom because they "*have a lot more comfort talking to professors*": they "*feel like [they] understand both how to approach a teacher*" and that they "*have something to say that's worth hearing.*" The confidence and capacity they develop through pedagogical partnership make student partners feel that they have "*more tools... to engage beyond the way I had been trained to engage – more creativity around how to get... engaged even if I didn't feel a pull*" (all quotations from students in Cook-Sather, 2018b, pp.927–928).

Pedagogical partnership can also deepen the engagement of students enrolled in the courses upon which student and their staff partners focus. Some pedagogical partnerships take as an explicit focus revising practices to better engage students (e.g., Bunnell and Bernstein, 2014). Others explore fostering student engagement as one of many essential dimensions of teaching (e.g., Conner, 2012; Colón García, 2017; Singh, 2018). Regardless of the explicit focus of the pedagogical partnership, student partners often comment on engagement in their observation notes (see Cook-Sather, Schlosser, Sweeney, Peterson, Cassidy, and Colón García, 2017), and student partners identify positive changes focused on promoting greater engagement, such as: "*When you reached out to the quieter students in the class, we saw a significant change in how they participated*" (Abbott and Been, 2017). Student partners are specific about what promotes engagement: "*there was overwhelming positive commentary from the students about the variety of activities… [and] they found the class to be incredibly engaging because of those*" (Brunson, 2018).

Through regular dialogue with their student partners, staff partners clarify for themselves the kind of engagement they hope for from students:

> *[My student partner] noted how I use the word 'lingering,' for example, when I want the class to sit with something longer. It was tremendously useful to realize that, in fact, I do want students to linger: to change the tempo of their engagement with literature, as well as with the world that literature brushes up against.*
>
> (Reckson, 2014)

They also develop greater clarity regarding how to achieve the kind of engagement they hope for. A staff partner described how her student partner's observation notes highlighted "*a shift in the atmosphere of engagement and relationship in the room*," which helped the staff partner "*alter my classroom preparations to allow for more exploratory discussion, grow comfortable with waiting in silence for things to emerge, and look closely for those flashes of engagement before they disappeared*" (Bressi Nath, 2012).

Pedagogical partnership can promote equity and inclusion

Several ethics-approved studies focused on the experiences of under-served and under-represented students who have participated in the SaLT program have found that pedagogical partnerships can provide "*counter-spaces*" – arenas in which the experiences of students of colour, as well as of other students who have been under-represented in and under-served by institutions of higher education, "*are validated and viewed as important knowledge*" (Solórzano, Ceja and Yosso, 2000, p.70). Through pedagogical partnership, students who bring these identities are recognised as "*holders and creators of knowledge*" (Delgado-Bernal,

2002, p.106; Cook-Sather, 2015; Cook-Sather and Agu, 2013; Cook-Sather and Felten, 2017). Pedagogical partnerships and the pedagogical approaches that can be co-created through them can begin to address the long legacies of discrimination and structural inequality that have impacted students' sense of inclusion in or exclusion from the institutions they attend (Cook-Sather, Des-Ogugua, and Bahti, 2018). In addition, through pedagogical partnership, students for whom higher education is not only unwelcoming but also unfamiliar can build capacity to navigate institutions created by and for a far less diverse population (de Bie et al., forthcoming.

When attention is paid to ensuring that a diversity of students have the opportunity to take up the role of student partner, pedagogical partnerships can support academic staff in soliciting "*unheard voices*" (Harper and Quaye, 2009), developing "*culturally sustaining pedagogy*" (Paris and Alim, 2014), and creating new spaces in which diversity and difference are seen as the very conditions for engagement rather than add-ons or as separate issues (Felten, Bagg, J., Bumbry, M., Hill, J., Hornsby, K., Pratt and Weller 2013). When intentionally constructed, pedagogical partnership can afford students from under-represented and equity-seeking groups "*'a seat at the proverbial table'*" (student quoted in Cook-Sather and Agu, 2013, p.277) and affirm that those students' "*'commitment to make spaces safer for underrepresented groups'*" can "*'drive important transformation in classrooms and in the student–teacher relationship'*" (students quoted in Cook-Sather and Agu, 2013, pp.277–278).

Individual staff and student partners can do essential work toward creating more equitable and inclusive classrooms. One staff partner reflected on how pedagogical partnerships can "*create the space necessary to address with students how issues of equity and inclusion affect their classrooms and fields.*" She noted that "*these are delicate conversations, which should be handled with care and respect, but my experiences over the past year have shown me that students are eager to listen and engage.*" This staff member's work with her student partner, Meron, supported her in creating space for such conversations. In her words: "*My partnership with Meron was essential for developing the brave space necessary to have these conversations, validating how my personal experiences influence my teaching, and supporting the changes I attempt to make.*" (All quotes from Perez, 2016.)

Practical steps toward creating pedagogical partnerships

As pedagogical partnerships become increasingly recognized as a promising approach to promoting engagement, greater equity, and educational development in higher education, those hoping to develop such partnerships seek guidance on what to consider and where to begin. Cook-Sather, Bovill, and Felten (2014) offer theory and empirical evidence to support efforts in student–staff partnerships, describe a range of possible levels of partnership that might be appropriate in different circumstances, and include responses to a range of questions as well as advice from academic staff, students, and administrators who have hands-on experience with partnership programs. Healey and Healey (2018) suggest considering four inter-related areas that underpin the context-dependent nature of pedagogical partnership work:

(1) the meaning of partnership;
(2) the emotions, motivations, attitudes, behavior, and values of the participants;
(3) the aim, scale, and timeframe of the project or initiative; and
(4) the conceptual framework adopted.

Cook-Sather, Bahti, and Ntem (2017) offer detailed discussions of how to develop pedagogical partnership programs. They suggest that those planning to develop or extend pedagogical partnership programs clarify the reasons for such programs and what might get in the way. They recommend surfacing the main problematic assumptions people make about this work; considering how to situate and structure the program, including how the program might fit into the larger institution and what relationship the program might have to other programs; and developing a plan for how to get started and for sustainability. They advise deciding what the shared and respective responsibilities of facilitating pedagogical partnerships will be; mapping out the particular responsibilities of participants; and generating a set of approaches that student and staff partners can use. Finally, they recommend developing preliminary plans for how to manage the most common logistical and emotional challenges of partnership and developing some approaches to evaluating partnership work.

Conclusion

Because forms of pedagogical partnership work emerging in higher education contexts in the United States are not guided by any national policies, and because there is such a range of types of institutions of higher education, each institution needs to develop a different approach to supporting pedagogical partnership. The basic design of SaLT has proven to work well across several kinds of institutions in the United States, although each institution has also adapted it in particular ways to be responsive to their institutional, staff, and student needs. All of them have found that pedagogical partnerships, *"situated at the intersection of student engagement and academic development, are uniquely positioned to foster belonging for students and academic staff, particularly for those who have traditionally been marginalised in higher education"* (Cook-Sather and Felten, 2017). Sense of belonging (Cohen and Garcia, 2008; Strayhorn, 2008; Asher and Weeks, 2014) is linked to student engagement and can help institutions of higher education expand understandings of success as relational – the shared responsibility of all involved for all involved – as well as individual (Cook-Sather, 2018).

While there are challenges involved in such work (Bovill, Cook-Sather, A., Felten, P., Millard and Moore-Cherry 2016, Cook-Sather, Bahti, and Ntem, forthcoming), research suggests that the benefits far outweigh the challenges not only in the United States but also in other contexts about which scholars have published, including Australia, Canada, Malaysia, Sweden, and the United Kingdom (Barrineau, Schnaas, U., Engström, and Härlin, 2016; Cook-Sather, Bovill, and Felten, 2014; Healey, Flint, and Harrington, 2014; Kaur, Awang-Hashim, and Kaur, 2018; Marquis, Puri, Wan, Ahmad, Goff, Knorr and Woo, 2016; Mercer-Mapstone et al., 2017). Pedagogical partnerships focused on classroom practices not only deepen engagement but also foster in student partners a productive sense of empowerment and empathy (Cook-Sather and Mejia, 2018). Furthermore, they have the potential to enhance student–staff relationships, promote greater equity and inclusion (de Bie et al., forthcoming), and transform colleges and universities into more egalitarian learning communities (Matthews, Cook-Sather, and Healey 2017). For these reasons, they are one of the most exciting developments in higher education not only in the United States but also around the world.

References

Abbott, C., and Been, L. E., 2017. Strategies for transforming a classroom into a brave and trusting learning community: a dialogic approach. *Teaching and Learning Together in Higher Education*, 22. Retrieved from: https://repository.brynmawr.edu/tlthe/vol1/iss22/3/

Asher, S.R. and Weeks, M.S., 2014. Loneliness and belongingness in the college years. In Coplan, R. J. and Bowker, J. C. (eds.) *The handbook of solitude: Psychological perspectives on social isolation, social withdrawal, and being alone*, pp.283–301. Hoboken, NJ: Wiley Blackwell

Barrineau, S., Schnaas, U., Engström, A., and Härlin, F., 2016. Breaking ground and building bridges: a critical reflection on student–faculty partnerships in academic development. *International Journal for Academic Development*, 21 (1). Retrieved from: https://doi.org/10.1080/1360144x.2015.1120735

Bovill, C., Cook-Sather, A., Felten, P., Millard, L., and Moore-Cherry, N., 2016. Addressing potential challenges in co-creating learning and teaching: overcoming resistance, navigating institutional norms and ensuring inclusivity in student–staff partnerships. *Higher Education*, 71 (2), 195–208. Retrieved from: https://doi.org/10.1007/s10734-015-9896-4

Bovill, C., and Felten, P., 2016. Cultivating student–staff partnerships through research and practice. *International Journal for Academic Development*, 20 (1), 1–3. Retrieved from: https://doi.org/10.1080/1360144X.2016.1124965

Bressi Nath, S., 2012. Finding voices in reflection: How my work through the TLI changed my classroom dynamics. *Teaching and Learning Together in Higher Education*, 6. Retrieved from: https://repository.brynmawr.edu/tlthe/vol1/iss6/8/

Brunson, M., 2018. The formation and power of trust: how it was created and enacted through collaboration. *Teaching and Learning Together in Higher Education*, 23. Retrieved from: https://repository.brynmawr.edu/tlthe/vol1/iss23/2/

Bryson, C. (Ed.), 2014. *Understanding and developing student engagement*. London: Routledge. Retrieved from: https://doi.org/10.4324/9781315813691

Bunnell, S., and Bernstein, D., 2014. Improving engagement and learning through sharing course design with students: a multi-level case. *Teaching and Learning Together in Higher Education*, 13. Retrieved from: https://repository.brynmawr.edu/tlthe/vol1/iss13/2/

Cohen, G.L. and Garcia, J., 2008. Identity, belonging, and achievement: A model, interventions, implications. Current Directions in Psychological Science, 17(6), pp.365–369.

Colón García, A., 2017. Building a sense of belonging through pedagogical partnership. *Teaching and Learning Together in Higher Education*, 22. Retrieved from: https://repository.brynmawr.edu/tlthe/vol1/iss22/2/

Conner, J., 2012. Steps in walking the talk: how working with a student consultant helped me integrate student voice more fully into my pedagogical planning and practice. *Teaching and Learning Together in Higher Education*, 6. Retrieved from: https://repository.brynmawr.edu/tlthe/vol1/iss6/6/

Cook-Sather, A., 2013. Catalyzing multiple forms of engagement through student–faculty partnerships exploring teaching and learning. In E. Dunne and D. Owen (eds.), *The Student Engagement Handbook: Practice in Higher Education*. Bingley: Emerald Publishing Group.

Cook-Sather, A., 2015. Dialogue across differences of position, perspective, and identity: reflective practice in/on a student–faculty pedagogical partnership program. *Teachers College Record*, 117 (2).

Cook-Sather, A., 2016. Undergraduate students as partners in new faculty orientation and academic development. *International Journal of Academic Development*, 21 (2), 151–162. Retrieved from: https://doi.org/10.1080/1360144x.2016.1156543

Cook-Sather, A., 2018. Listening to equity-seeking perspectives: how students' experiences of pedagogical partnership can inform wider discussions of student success. *Higher Education Research and Development*, 37 (5), 923–936. Retrieved from: https://doi.org/10.1080/07294360.2018.1457629

Cook-Sather, A., and Agu, P., 2013. Students of color and faculty members working together toward culturally sustaining pedagogy. In J.E. Groccia and L. Cruz (eds.), *To improve the academy: Resources for faculty, instructional, and organizational development* (pp.271–285, Vol. 29). San Francisco, CA: Jossey-Bass/Anker.

Cook-Sather, A., Bahti, M., and Ntem, A., 2019. *Pedagogical Partnerships: A How-To Guide for Faculty, Students and Academic Developers in Higher Education*. Elon, NC: Elon University Center for Engaged Learning.

Cook-Sather, A., Bovill, C., and Felten, P., 2014. *Engaging Students as Partners in Learning and Teaching: A Guide for Faculty*. San Francisco, CA: Jossey-Bass.

Cook-Sather, A., Des-Ogugua, C., and Bahti, M., 2018. Articulating identities and analyzing belonging: a multistep intervention that affirms and informs a diversity of students. *Teaching in Higher Education*, 23 (3), 374–389. Retrieved from: https://doi.org/10.1080/13562517.2017.1391201

Cook-Sather, A., and Felten, P., 2017. Ethics of academic leadership: guiding learning and teaching. In Frank Wu and Margaret Wood (eds.), *Cosmopolitan Perspectives on Becoming an Academic Leader in Higher Education* (pp.175–191). London: Bloomsbury Academic.

Cook-Sather, A., and Mejia, Y., 2018. Students experience empowerment and empathy through pedagogical partnership. Retrieved from: www.bera.ac.uk/blog/students-experience-empowerment-and-empathy-through-pedagogical-partnership (accessed 23 July 2019).

Cook-Sather, A., Schlosser, J. A., Sweeney, A., Peterson, L. M., Cassidy, K. W., and Colón García, A., 2017. The pedagogical benefits of enacting positive psychology practices through a student–faculty partnership approach to academic development. *International Journal for Academic Development*, 23 (2), 123–134. Retrieved from: https://doi.org/10.1080/1360144x.2017.1401539

de Bie, A., Marquis, E., Cook-Sather, A., and Luqueño, L. (forthcoming) Valuing knowledge(s) and cultivating confidence: contributions of student–faculty pedagogical partnerships to epistemic justice. International Perspectives in Higher Education: Strategies for Fostering Inclusive Classrooms. *Innovations in Higher Education Teaching and Learning.*

Delgado-Bernal, D., 2002. Critical race theory, Latino critical theory, and critical raced-gendered epistemologies: recognizing students of color as holders and creators of knowledge. *Qualitative Inquiry*, 8 (1), 105–126. Retrieved from: https://doi.org/10.1177/107780040200800107

Delpish, A., Holmes, A., Knight-McKenna, M., et al., 2010. Equalizing voices: student–faculty partnership in course design. In C. Werder and M. M. Otis (eds.), *Engaging student voices in the study of teaching and learning* (pp.96–114). Sterling, VA: Stylus.

Felten, P., 2018. Student engagement in the United States: From customers to partners? In M. Tanaka (ed.), *Student Engagement and Quality Assurance in Higher Education: International Collaborations for the Enhancement of Learning.* Routledge. Retrieved from: https://doi.org/10.4324/9780429025648

Felten, P., 2013. Principles of good practice in SoTL. *Teaching and Learning Inquiry*, 1 (1), 121–125. Retrieved from: https://doi.org/10.20343/teachlearninqu.1.1.121

Felten, P., Bagg, J., Bumbry, M., Hill, J., Hornsby, K., Pratt, M. and Weller, S. 2013. A call for expanding inclusive student engagement in SoTL. *Teaching and Learning Inquiry*, 1 (2), 63–74. Retrieved from: https://doi.org/10.20343/teachlearninqu.1.2.63

Freeman, S., Eddy, S., McDonough, M., Smith, M., Okoroafor, N., Jordt, H., and Wenderoth, M., 2014. Active learning increases student performance in science, engineering, and mathematics. Proceedings of the National Academy of Science of the United States of America, 111 (23), 8410–8415.

Goldsmith, M., Hanscom, M., Throop, S. A., and Young, C., 2017. Growing student–faculty partnerships at Ursinus College: a brief history in dialogue. *International Journal for Students as Partners*, 1 (2). Retrieved from: https://doi.org/10.15173/ijsap.v1i2.3075

Harper, S. R., and Davis, C. H. F. III., 2016. Eight actions to reduce racism in college classrooms. American Association of University Professors. Retrieved from: www.aaup.org/comment/3881#.WhTRGbT81E5 (accessed 23 July 2019).

Harper, S.R. and Quaye, S.J., 2009. Beyond sameness, with engagement and outcomes for all. In Harper, S.R. and Quaye, S.J. (eds.), *Student engagement in higher education*, pp.1–15. New York and London: Routledge.

Healey, M., Flint, A., and Harrington, K., 2014. *Students as partners in learning and teaching in higher education*. York: Higher Education Academy.

Healey, M., and Healey, R., 2018. 'It depends': exploring the context-dependent nature of students as partners. *International Journal for Students as Partners*, 2, 1. Retrieved from: https://doi.org/10.15173/ijsap.v2i1.3472

Kaur, A., Awang-Hashim, R., and Kaur, M., 2018. Students' experiences of co-creating classroom instruction with faculty: a case study in eastern context. *Teaching in Higher Education*, 24(4), 461–477. Retrieved from: https://doi.org/10.1080/13562517.2018.1487930

Kuh, G. D., 2008. *High-impact educational practices: what they are, who has access to them, and why they matter.* Washington, DC: Association of American Colleges and Universities.

Luker, M., and Morris, B., 2016. Five things I learned from working with the Student-Consultant for Teaching and Learning Program. *Teaching and Learning Together in Higher Education, 17.* Retrieved from: https://repository.brynmawr.edu/tlthe/vol1/iss17/2/

Marquis, E., Puri, V., Wan, S., Ahmad, A., Goff, L., Knorr, K. and Woo, J., 2016. Navigating the threshold of student–staff partnerships: a case study from an Ontario teaching and learning institute. *International Journal for Academic Development*, 21 (1), 4–15. Retrieved from: https://doi.org/10.1080/1360144x.2015.1113538

Matthews, K. E., 2016. Students as partners as the future of student engagement. *Student Engagement in Higher Education Journal,* 1 (1), 1–5. Retrieved from: https://journals.gre.ac.uk/index.php/raise/article/view/380

Matthews, K. E., Cook-Sather, A., and Healey, M., 2017. Connecting learning, teaching and research through student–staff partnerships: toward universities as egalitarian learning communities. In V. Tong, A. M. Standen, and M. Sotiriou (eds.), *Research Equals Teaching: Inspiring Research-Based Education through Student–staff Partnerships.* London: UCL Press.

Mercer-Mapstone, L., Dvorakova, L.S., Matthews, K.E., Abbot, S., Cheng, B., Felten, P., Knorr, K., Marquis, E., Shammas, R., and Swaim, K., 2017. A systematic literature review of students as partners in higher education. *International Journal of Students as Partners,* 1 (1), 1–23. Retrieved from: https://doi.org/10.15173/ijsap.v1i1.3119

Mihans, R., Long, D. and Felten, P., 2008. Power and expertise: student–faculty collaboration in course design and the scholarship of teaching and learning. *International Journal for the Scholarship of Teaching and Learning,* 2 (2). Retrieved from: https://digitalcommons.georgiasouthern.edu/cgi/viewcontent.cgi?referer=andhttpsredir=1andarticle=1110andcontext=ij-sotl

Millard, L., Bartholomew, P., Brand, S., and Nygaard, C., 2013. Why student engagement matters. In C. Nygaard, S. Brand, P. Bartholomew and L. Millard (eds.), *Student engagement: Identity, motivation and community* (pp.1–15). Farringdon: Libri.

Oleson, K. C., 2016. Introduction – Collaborating to develop and improve classroom teaching: Student-consultant for teaching and learning program at Reed College. *Teaching and Learning Together in Higher Education,* 17. Retrieved from: http://repository.brynmawr.edu/tlthe/vol1/iss17/1

Paris, D. and Alim, S., 2014. What are we seeking to sustain through culturally sustaining pedagogy? A loving critique forward. *Harvard Educational Review,* 84 (1), 85–100. Retrieved from: https://doi.org/10.17763/haer.84.1.982l873k2ht16m77

Perez, K., 2016. Striving toward a space for equity and inclusion in physics classrooms. *Teaching and Learning Together in Higher Education,* 18. Retrieved from: https://repository.brynmawr.edu/tlthe/vol1/iss18/3/

Reckson, L. V., 2014. The weather in Hemingway. *Teaching and Learning Together in Higher Education,* 11. Retrieved from: https://repository.brynmawr.edu/tlthe/vol1/iss11/6/

Schlosser, J., and Sweeney, A., 2015. One year of collaboration: Reflections on student–faculty partnership. *Teaching and Learning Together in Higher Education*, 15. Retrieved from: https://repository.brynmawr.edu/tlthe/vol1/iss15/2/

Singh, M., 2018. Moving from "us vs. them" to "us" through working in pedagogical partnership. *Teaching and Learning Together in Higher Education*, 23. Retrieved from: https://repository.brynmawr.edu/tlthe/vol1/iss23/5/

Solórzano, D., Ceja, M. and Yosso, T., 2000. Critical race theory, racial microaggressions, and campus racial climate: The experiences of African American college students. *Journal of Negro Education*, 69 (1/2), 60–73. Retrieved from: www.jstor.org/stable/2696265?seq=1#metadata_info_tab_contents

Strayhorn, T. L., 2008. The role of supportive relationships in facilitating African American males' success in college. Naspa Journal, 45(1), pp.26–48.

Taylor, P., Wilding, D., Mockridge, A. and Lambert, C., 2012. Reinventing engagement. In I. Solomonides, A. Reid and P. Petocz (eds.), *Engaging with learning in higher education* (pp. 259–278). Farringdon: Libri.

Volk, S., 2016. Student–faculty partnerships: collaborating to improve teaching and learning. Retrieved from: http://languages.oberlin.edu/blogs/ctie/2016/05/01/student–faculty-partnershipscollaborating-to-improve-teaching-and-learning/

Werder, C., and Otis, M. M. (Eds.) 2010. *Engaging student voices in the study of teaching and learning*. Sterling, VA: Stylus.

Chapter 8

From the 'micro' to the 'mega'

Toward a multi-level approach to supporting and assessing student–staff partnership

Elizabeth Marquis, Christine Black, Rachel Guitman, Mick Healey and Cherie Woolmer

Introduction

Student–staff partnership describes a process in which students collaborate actively with staff[1] in higher education to advance pedagogical activities such as curriculum design, pedagogic consultancy, subject-based research, or the scholarship of teaching and learning (Healey, Flint and Harrington, 2014). The goal of such work is to disrupt traditional teacher–learner hierarchies, and to promote active engagement from the student, as opposed to passive reception. Partnership can thus be seen as one strand of a growing, international body of work focused on student engagement in higher education. Student–staff partnership relationships are founded on values of mutual respect, reciprocity, and shared responsibility (Cook-Sather, Bovill and Felten, 2014). These values form the basis for meaningful, power-shifting student–staff relationships.

A range of scholarly literature focuses on the benefits and potential of student–staff partnerships based on the aforementioned principles (Bovill, Cook-Sather and Felten, 2011; Healey, Flint and Harrington 2014, Cook-Sather and Luz 2015, Marquis, Puri, Wan, Ahmad, Goff, Knorr, Vassileva and Woo, 2016; Matthews 2016). As Bovill, Cook-Sather and Felten (2011) note, collaboration with students in higher education places students in active and participatory roles, enhancing learning outcomes. Indeed, the partnership approach has great potential for empowering students and promoting student agency, in contrast to traditionally hierarchical approaches (Bovill et al., 2011). As well, partnerships have substantial benefits for the staff involved. These include increased connection to students, enhanced understanding of student points of view, and motivation to engage more fully in teaching roles (Bovill et al., 2011). For both students and staff, partnership relationships enable effective communication, with both parties feeling heard and understanding the other's perspective.

While partnership has been shown to have a range of positive outcomes – both in terms of the processes it entails and the outputs it supports – much of the existing research tends to focus on small-scale initiatives and to document the benefits of partnership for the individuals immediately involved (Mercer-Mapstone, Dvorakova, Matthews, Abbot, Cheng, Felten, Knorr, Marquis, Shammas and Swaim, 2017). While this attention to individual outcomes is necessary and valuable, it is perhaps insufficient to support fully the claims that partnership has the potential to influence culture within an institution (Matthews, Cook-Sather and Healey, 2018). Much existing work focusing on learning, teaching, and the scholarship of teaching and learning (SoTL), for example, demonstrates that individual change or development often fails to permeate or persist in departmental teaching cultures (Roxå and Mårtensson, 2012; Fanghanel, 2013), and/ or argues that efforts to support teaching and learning need to be woven into broader institutional cultures (Bamber, Trowler, Saunders and Knight, 2009; Williams, Verwoord, Beery, Dalton, McKinnon, Strickland, Pace and Poole, 2013; Amundsen, Emmioglu, Hotton, Hum and Xin, 2016). Given the ways in which institutional resistance and entrenched hierarchies have been shown to pose particular barriers to partnership work (Bovill, Cook-Sather, Felten, Millard and Moore-Cherry 2016; Marquis, Black and Healey, 2017), attention to such institutional weaving may be especially important if partnership is to realize its capacity to transform universities into more egalitarian spaces (Cook-Sather and Luz, 2015; Cook-Sather and Felten, 2017) that push back against the neoliberal forces currently shaping higher education institutions (McCulloch, 2009; Neary, 2014).

At McMaster University (Hamilton, Canada), we have developed a range of initiatives to foster partnership work, which, together, aim to support partnership at different institutional and inter-institutional levels. Nevertheless, we have yet to engage in systematic mapping of these initiatives in relation to one another or reflection on the extent to which they contribute, as a set, to supporting the growth of partnership culture in our context and beyond. In what follows, then, we offer a preliminary attempt at such assessment, describing three central partnership initiatives supported by McMaster's teaching and learning institute, and drawing on research about those initiatives, as well as our own reflections, to assess their cumulative effects. In so doing, we draw on what Friberg (2016) calls the '4M Framework,' positioning this model as a potentially valuable and previously under-utilized resource for individuals interested in developing or analysing partnership work. By applying this framework to examine key partnership initiatives in one context, we aim to model the potential value of this approach both for highlighting the levels at which institutional initiatives focus and generating insight into the interconnectedness of these levels.

The 4M Framework

The 4M Framework offers one way of responding to the need to consider how institutional change and educational development processes play out at a variety of institutional and inter-institutional levels. In particular, it focuses on how efforts aimed at development and change function in relation to what have been called the micro-, meso-, and macro-levels of institutions, as well as the mega-level, which extends beyond immediate institutional contexts to include broader national and international frames. As Verwoord and Poole (2016) note, scholars have conceptualized these strata in varying ways. Roxå and Mårtensson (2012), for example, suggest the micro-level consists of individuals, while the meso-level describes collections of people organized into significant networks or workgroups. Conversely, Williams et al. (2013) and Verwoord and Poole (2016) define the micro-level as individuals and groups in 'on the ground' teaching and learning roles, while reserving the labels 'meso' for middle management (e.g., Department Chairs and Deans) and 'macro' for senior institutional leaders, respectively. In this chapter, we take a slightly broader view, echoing Simmons (2009; 2016) and Wuetherick and Yu (2016) by using 'micro' to refer to individual staff, students, and courses, 'meso' to denote programs and departments, 'macro' to describe institutions, and 'mega' to indicate extra-institutional contexts (see Figure 8.1).

As Simmons (2016) and Friberg (2016) demonstrate, attention to these levels can reveal significant insights about how and where development and advocacy initiatives are affecting university teaching and learning cultures and where opportunities for growth and development lie. While some scholars have raised questions about how thoroughly integrated partnership activities are within institutional cultures (Flint, 2016), we are unaware of partnership scholarship that

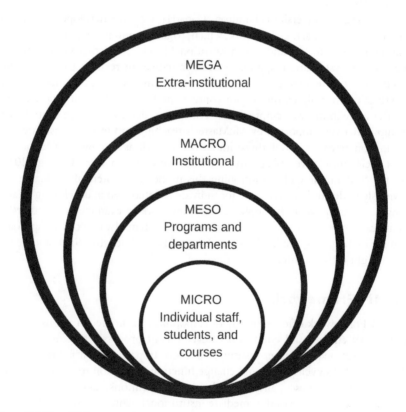

Figure 8.1 The 4M Framework

applies the 4M model to assess and refine partnership activities in this way. The following discussion thus offers preliminary consideration of how three large-scale partnership initiatives at McMaster operate and interact to support partnership from the 'micro' to the 'mega', identifying both strengths and gaps in the model we have developed.

McMaster University initiatives

Our approach to supporting pedagogical partnerships at McMaster has been organic in many senses, but strategic in others, and has, consequently, led to incremental growth within the institution over a period of five years. While partnership occurs in many ways and in various contexts at the university, we focus in this chapter on three flagship initiatives supported by the university's central teaching and learning institute: the Student Partners Program (SPP), the International Students as Partners Institute (ISaPI), and the *International Journal for Students as Partners* (*IJSaP*).

McMaster's Student Partners Program (SPP)

The Student Partners Program (SPP) began in 2013–14 as a collaboration between the Arts and Science Program at McMaster and the Teaching and Learning Institute. The SPP was designed to establish meaningful partnerships between students and staff on teaching and learning projects. Each year, there are three opportunities for students and staff to submit project proposals, which outline the details of their projects as well as their connections to partnership principles. Through this process, we attempt to ensure that partnership projects included in the program allow for meaningful engagement and connections, and do not fall into patterns common to unpaid internships or more traditional research assistant relationships. A team of staff and students reviews submitted proposals, and successful projects receive funding to support student involvement in the work. Typically, students work for approximately five hours per week on their projects, in paid positions.

Since the program's inception, participating staff and students have worked on projects that may involve, but are not limited to, designing and developing courses and curricula, creating resources, and collaborating on pedagogical research. Many have co-authored research articles and co-presented at conferences (e.g., Ahmad, Ali, VanMaaren, Barrington, Merritt and Ansilio, 2017; Johnstone, Marquis and Puri, 2018; Marquis, Redda and Twells, 2018), demonstrating partnership in the academic community. Participants have been drawn from all faculties on our campus, and have included students ranging from first year undergraduates through to senior PhD candidates. The program has grown substantially since its establishment, and in 2017–18 more than 200 staff and students were involved. Given this scope, and the substantial and tangible benefits connected to partnership, this program has been gaining attention in the higher education sector (Healey, Flint and Harrington, 2016; Cook-Sather, Bahti and Ntem, forthcoming). See Marquis et al., 2016, Marquis, Haqqee, Kirby, Liu, Puri, Cockcroft, Goff and Knorr, 2017 for further detail.

International Students as Partners Institute (ISaPI)

The International Institute on Students as Partners was developed in 2015 by two staff members and one student working in partnership via the SPP. The aim of this institute was to gather people from different countries together, and create a space where partnerships and projects could flourish. As a result of this partnership project, the first International Institute was held in May 2016, with nearly 100 participants from seven countries. These participants could participate in either one or two workshops or a three-day Change Institute. Each of the workshops focused on engaging students as partners in a different context or domain, including learning, teaching and assessment, subject-based research and inquiry, SoTL, and curriculum design and pedagogic consultancy (see Healey, Flint and Harrington, 2014). Local and international students and staff worked together to organize and facilitate these workshops. The Change Institute invited teams consisting of four to six students and staff to work on developing a specific partnership initiative they could implement on their home campus. Student and staff facilitators worked to support teams and their project development. Participants in the Change Institute came from a range of different countries and institutions, making ISaPI a global event.

Given the successes of this initial offering, ISaPI has since become an annual event, and continues to draw participants from around the world. In its first two years, 170 students and staff have participated (some both times), coming from ten countries worldwide. See Acai, Kirby and Shammas 2017; Marquis, Black and Healey, 2017; Marquis, Guitman, Black, Healey, Matthews and Dvorakova, 2018 for more detail).

International Journal for Students as Partners (IJSaP)

The idea to establish *IJSaP* arose from conversations at the first ISaPI meeting in May 2016. It was clear there was demand for an international scholarly journal where we could continue the debates and exchanges of ideas, practices and policies stimulated by ISaPI. Our vision was to create an 'inclusive scholarly knowledge-building community' (Brew 2006, xiii), which would bring staff and students together in partnership, not only as authors, but also as reviewers and editors; and hence challenge the traditional absence of students from academic publishing (Healey, Healey and Cliffe, 2018).

The Teaching and Learning Institute at McMaster offered to host the journal, seeing this as a logical next step in a strategy to make partnerships central to the operation of the Institute and to demonstrate leadership in teaching and learning. McMaster University Library Press agreed to publish *IJSaP* as an open access journal with no author charges. The international dimension was built into the structure by having editorial teams in four different countries – Australia, Canada, UK and US – and an International Advisory Group of academics, learning support staff and students, initially from eight countries (Cliffe, Cook-Sather, Healey, Healey, Marquis, Matthews, Mercer-Mapstone, Ntem, Puri and Woolmer, 2017).

The journal is guided by the principles and values underlying student partnership (Higher Education Academy, 2015; Matthews, 2017), emphasizing inclusivity, with students and staff working together in partnership as co-editors, and sharing power in that all major decisions are discussed together in a transparent manner. Articles are reviewed by both students and staff, who, if inexperienced, are supported with co-developed resources. The experience has been rewarding, but also at times challenging. For example, we have had to confront and navigate existing norms and assumptions about publishing and expertise, take time to learn about the different perspectives and experiences we each bring, and work to genuinely integrate a wide variety of perspectives while still moving forward with clarity (Cliffe et al., 2017). It takes time to develop the mutual respect and trust needed for successful partnership.

McMaster initiatives from the micro to the mega

To demonstrate and explore the potential of the 4M model for those interested in partnership work, we now discuss how the initiatives described above address each of the 4M levels in turn. We recognize that initiatives rarely influence just one stratum of an organization. The reality is much messier than that, and we attempt to account for this where relevant in the discussion. However, we think there is merit in systematically assessing the initiatives across the respective levels of the 4M framework as this enables stakeholders, who each have their own interests, to see evidence of the cumulative impact of this work. It also allows us to identify ways to enhance our efforts to contribute to a sustained commitment to the practice and scholarship of partnership at McMaster and beyond. We thus present a detailed analysis of the successes and limitations of the McMaster initiatives at each of the four levels, with the hope that this offers an example of how the framework might be used by others to grow and refine partnership in their contexts.

Micro-level

Projects funded through the Institute's SPP are identified predominantly by staff and often focus on activities that impact upon the micro-level of the institution. These activities include course (re)design and review and SoTL focusing on teaching effectiveness or other issues of relevance to student learning in particular classes (Hutchings, 2000). One benefit of micro-level engagement is that there are high levels of ownership and relevance for the parties involved; the needs and priorities are locally defined, with the only parameters being that students and staff work together in partnership on teaching and learning issues.

While ISaPI and *IJSaP* clearly extend beyond the McMaster community, they too make space for, and aim to support and celebrate, work happening at the micro-level of institutions internationally. Some attendees at ISaPI are interested primarily in learning about partnership and applying it in their own teaching, learning, or SoTL research, for instance, while *IJSaP* explores micro-level partnership practice in many of the case studies, reflective essays, and research articles it publishes. In so doing, these venues help to bring micro-level initiatives to the mega-level, where they might, in turn, influence others' micro-level practices. At the same time, the running of these initiatives engages staff and students from multiple institutions worldwide, providing developmental support to people working as reviewers, editors, and facilitators, and influencing their individual capacity to work in and develop partnership as a result.

Echoing much of the partnership literature, our research also documents considerable micro-level benefits connected to the SPP and ISaPI, including the development of meaningful relationships between staff and students, the enhancement of particular courses or projects through the integration of multiple perspectives, and the development of new skills and knowledge for participants (Marquis et al., 2016; 2017; Marquis, Black and Healey 2017; SPP 2018). Students have described developing greater confidence in their own knowledge and potential to contribute to scholarly endeavors (Marquis, Jayaratnam, Mishra, and Rybkina, 2018; de Bie, Marquis, Cook-Sather and Luqueño forthcoming, Cook-Sather, Prasad, Marquis and Ntem, 2019), as well as enhancing their approaches to teaching and learning after participating in the SPP (Marquis et al., 2016; de Bie et al., forthcoming). Likewise, staff participants have discussed becoming more aware of student perspectives, reassessing their sense of student capacities, and developing a willingness to engage students more actively in teaching and learning endeavors (Marquis, Power and Yin 2018).

Again, these outcomes demonstrate the micro-level potential of initiatives like the SPP and ISaPI. Indeed, insofar as some of the individuals participating in the research described above were working on partnership projects keyed to the meso-, macro-, or mega-levels, these findings emphasize the possibility that micro-level benefits can accrue from partnership working regardless of the level at which it is pitched. This is a promising finding for programs like the SPP, suggesting its broad potential to support meaningful individual outcomes for participants while fostering a range of kinds of partnership work. At the same time, the considerable expansion of the program since its inception points to the possibility of such micro-level benefits being realized on an increasingly broad institutional (macro) scale.

Nevertheless, areas for growth and refinement at the micro-level remain. On the one hand, recent research conducted at McMaster demonstrates that many students remain unaware of the SPP or uncertain about what it involves (Marquis, Jayaratnam et al., 2018). At the same time, the budget limitations of the program mean that some students and staff who apply to take part cannot be funded. This certainly limits the potential of the program (in its current form) to weave partnership into the institution and may raise concerns about equity and access despite the large number of people taking part (Marquis, Jayaratnam et al., 2018). Moreover, the rapid growth of the program has come with the trade-off that the institute staff who oversee it are less immediately connected to the individual projects taking place than they once were, and thus less able to provide extensive support for participants or determine conclusively the extent to which a partnership ethos is realized effectively in each project. Lastly, our ongoing research has also documented common challenges connected to partnership working for individuals supported by the SPP and/or ISaPI. Many of these, such as time barriers and institutional resistance (Marquis et al., 2016; Marquis, Black and Healey, 2017), may militate against effectively realizing partnership approaches, pointing clearly to the need to consider how these individual outcomes might be affected by pressures from, or efforts at, other institutional levels – particularly the meso.

Meso-level

While the SPP, ISaPI, and *IJSaP* likewise aim to support meso-level partnership initiatives (i.e., those focused on programs and departments), the evidence of engagement and impact at this level is less extensive. On one hand, two specific streams of the SPP have been strategically designed to include departmental or program-wide engagement. One of these focuses on partnership in program review and quality enhancement processes; the other (which is affiliated with a Leadership in Teaching and Learning (LTL) Fellowship offered by the institute) engages students in working with academic staff on either course- or department-focused projects. The LTL Fellowship program is informed by socio-cultural approaches to institutional change (Roxå and Mårtensson, 2009; Mårtensson, Roxå and Olsson 2011), and thus aims to create spaces for Fellows to develop networks across campus and share the outcomes of their projects with others in their departmental or Faculty contexts (Fenton, Goff and Zeadin, 2016).

Other examples that illustrate the capacity of the initiatives described above to engage and impact at the meso-level are more ad hoc. Teams of staff and students have proposed topics for inclusion in the SPP that focus on advancing department-wide priorities, for example, just as some teams submitting projects for inclusion in the 'change institute' component of ISaPI have focused on program- or department-level initiatives. Our research about the SPP and ISaPI has also documented instances in which participants became advocates of partnership initiatives in their departments, encouraging colleagues to participate or administrators to persuade other staff to engage (Marquis, Power and Yin, 2018; Marquis et al., 2018). These examples, which resonate with scholarship about individual staff 'leading up' in SoTL (Miller-Young, Anderson, Kiceniuk, Mooney, Riddell, Schmidt Hanbidge, Ward, Wideman and Chick, 2017) are comparatively sparse, however, and more research needs to be conducted about when and why some departments become engaged in initiatives like the SPP and ISaPI, and when and why they do not. Given that departmental cultures also have the capacity to 'undo' or ignore individual-level change (Roxå and Mårtensson, 2012; Williams et al., 2013), this seems an especially important gap for us to continue to address. Looking ahead, we might consider further how to support individual champions to spread partnership work, explore additional opportunities for encouraging department-specific initiatives, and contribute to broader efforts to support change or celebrate successes in departmental cultures. In this respect, our arguments here are not unlike those of SoTL scholars who have demonstrated both the particular challenges and the potential significance of the meso-level (Verwoord and Poole, 2016; Simmons, 2016). As Williams et al. (2013, p.52) point out, "*if departments are the places where barriers to change exist, they are also important loci for change.*"

Macro-level

From one perspective, the SPP itself is evidence of significant macro-level support for partnership at McMaster. The program, operating via the central teaching and learning institute, provides substantial funding for partnership projects across campus, thereby seeding such work and demonstrating institutional recognition of its importance. This recognition has also been illustrated through the university's commitment to publish the journal, and provide ongoing funding for ISaPI, as well as through increasing recognition of the SPP and of partnership in institutional documents. As scholarship has suggested (Miller-Young et al., 2017), such high level support can play an important role in weaving teaching and learning initiatives into institutional fabrics; it is a key enabler for activity to take place at all other levels of the 4M model.

At the same time, we have also attempted to include projects keyed to the macro-level within the SPP, ISaPI, and *IJSaP* wherever possible. Some projects supported by the SPP overlap with major institutional priorities, such as community engaged learning (McMaster, 2012), for example, and/or with work being done centrally, in the Teaching and Learning Institute, to support teaching and learning cultures across campus. Projects included in the 'change institute' component of ISaPI or published in *IJSaP* (Lowe, Shaw, Sims, King and Paddison 2017; Shaw, Rueckert, Smith, Tredinnick and Lee 2017) have likewise involved institution-wide efforts in several cases, and one section of ISaPI is devoted to supporting participants in embedding their projects institutionally. Research connected to ISaPI has documented how participants have benefitted from the time and tools provided at the event to successfully move these institution-level initiatives forward upon returning to their home campuses, while also suggesting that other ISaPI participants have valued the opportunity to share strategies for navigating institutional barriers with other participants (Marquis, Guitman et al., 2018). These are promising preliminary indicators of macro-level effects.

Like many of the meso-level projects discussed above, however, the majority of the macro-level projects involved in the SPP or ISaPI arise largely because individuals and teams happen to submit them, rather because of proactive planning on our part. This is something we could continue to explore going forward, considering if and how we might do more to encourage and support partnership projects connected to institutional initiatives and priorities. We might also continue to consider means of systematizing and recognizing partnership at the institutional level, such as advocating for the inclusion of partnership in strategy documents and academic staff assessment policies, or finding ways to make participation in programs like the SPP more widely known and expected.

Mega-level

IJSaP and ISaPI are most obviously aligned with this level as they facilitate extra-institutional engagement. In research exploring ISaPI (Marquis, Black and Healey, 2017; Marquis, Guitman, Black, Healey, Matthews and Dvorakova, 2018), for instance, participants highlighted the role it played in allowing them to become part of a broader, international movement in higher education. This community was seen as significant in itself, and also central to helping participants navigate the complexities of partnership at the micro-, meso-, and macro-levels on their home campuses. Likewise, in providing a platform for the dissemination of partnership scholarship from around the world, *IJSaP* also contributes to the development of the international community, showcases partnership conducted at each of the 4M levels, and circulates ideas and evidence that might be translated back into practice in various institutional contexts. Again, then, the interplay amongst the various initiatives across the 4M levels becomes apparent.

More locally, we also aim to contribute to the mega-level at McMaster via ongoing research on partnership and the SPP, and by supporting and encouraging McMaster students and staff to engage in co-presentation and publication of scholarship connected to their projects. Each year, we fund a number of students to co-present at local and international conferences, and we also support staff and student authors in writing about their partnership activities for publication (e.g., many individuals develop and submit manuscript submissions as part of their SPP funding). Several SPP participants have also served as reviewers for *IJSaP*. Of course, our capacity to support conference attendance and travel are constrained by budget limitations, so issues of scope and equity of access remain challenges to consider, as does the necessity for continued institutional support and funding.

We see significant positive outcomes attached to the role McMaster plays at the mega-level. We are clearly operating in ways that help to bring others together, either to learn more about partnership approaches or to develop and refine their own practice, and thus contributing to a growing international community of scholars and practitioners. Nevertheless, we see the potential to build on this work by continuing to develop ways of translating our own and others' research findings into practice on our campus, more effectively marshaling mega-level evidence to support meaningful partnership at the micro-, macro-, and meso-levels.

Conclusion

In this chapter, we have applied the 4M Framework to assess three innovative SaP initiatives at McMaster University. We have focused particularly on the SPP and ISaPI, as we have undertaken research on their impact, whereas research and reflection on *IJSaP* is only just beginning (Healey, Cliffe, Healey, Mercer-Mapstone and Woolmer, 2018). The way in which each of the initiatives has played out is dependent on the context in which they have been developed (Healey and Healey, 2018). However, one of the insights provided by adopting the 4M Framework is the interaction between the different levels. Whereas the SPP operates primarily at the micro-level, the other two initiatives are more focused at the macro- and mega-levels. Each has elements of all of the four levels, however, and we argue that recognition of this interaction is essential if the initiatives are to be effective.

Moreover, drawing from our experience of mapping and assessing these initiatives against the four levels of the 4M Framework, we argue that this model offers a meaningful tool for considering the development and refinement of initiatives to embed student–staff partnership in higher education contexts, and perhaps for evaluating the ways in which initiatives might cumulatively influence culture. Considering our own programs in relation to this framework has both highlighted key successes (some of which were not immediately obvious before writing this chapter) and documented potential areas for targeted enhancement (such as a more extensive focus at the meso-level). We thus encourage other partnership practitioners to consider drawing on this framework to support a similar analysis of partnership initiatives in their own contexts.

Note

1 Throughout this chapter we use 'staff' broadly, to refer to academic staff (referred to as faculty in North American contexts) and/or professional staff

References

Acai, A., Kirby, S. and Shammas, R., 2017. Reflections on an international "change institute" for students as partners: A student perspective. *International Journal for Students as Partners*, 1(1).

Ahmad, A., Ali, A., VanMaaren, J., Barrington, J., Merritt, O. and Ansilio, K., 2017. Partnership in practice: Implementing Healey's conceptual model. *International Journal for Students as Partners*, 1(2). Retrieved from: https://doi.org/10.15173/ijsap.v1i2.3197

Amundsen, C., Emmioglu, E., Hotton, V., Hum, G. and Xin, C., 2016. The intentional design of a SoTL initiative. *New Directions for Teaching and Learning*, 146, 31–38. Retrieved from: https://doi.org/10.1002/tl.20184

Bamber, V., Trowler, P., Saunders, M. and Knight, P., 2009. *Enhancing learning and assessment and curriculum in higher education*. Maidenhead: Society for Research into Higher Education and Open University Press. Retrieved from: https://doi.org/10.1111/j.1467-9647.2011.00728.x

Bovill, C., Cook-Sather, A. and Felten, P., 2011. Students as co-creators of teaching approaches, course design, and curricula: Implications for academic developers. *International Journal for Academic Development*, 16(2), 133–145. Retrieved from: https://doi.org/10.1080/1360144x.2011.568690

Bovill, C., Cook-Sather, A., Felten, P., Millard, L. and Moore-Cherry, N., 2016. Addressing potential challenges in co-creating learning and teaching: Overcoming resistance, navigating institutional norms and ensuring inclusivity in student–staff partnerships. *Higher Education*, 71(2), 195–208. Retrieved from: https://doi.org/10.1007/s10734-015-9896-4

Brew, A. (2006) *Research and teaching: beyond the divide*. London: Palgrave Macmillan.

Cliffe, A., Cook-Sather, A., Healey, M., Healey, R., Marquis, B., Matthews, K.E., Mercer Mapstone, L., Ntem, A., Puri, V. and Woolmer, C., 2017. Launching a journal about and through students as partners. *International Journal for Students as Partners*, 1(1). Retrieved from: https://doi.org/10.15173/ijsap.v1i1.3194

Cook-Sather, A., Bahti, M. and Ntem, A. (forthcoming). *A how-to guide to teaching and learning together in higher education: Developing and supporting student–faculty partnerships focused on classroom teaching and curriculum design and redesign.*

Cook-Sather, A., Bovill, C. and Felten, P., 2014. *Engaging students as partners in learning and teaching: A guide for faculty*. San Francisco, CA: Jossey Bass.

Cook-Sather, A. and Felten, P., 2017. Ethics of academic leadership: Guiding learning and teaching. In F. Su and M. Woods (eds.), *Cosmopolitan perspectives on becoming an academic leader in higher education*. London: Bloomsbury, 175–191. Retrieved from: https://doi.org/10.5040/9781474223058.ch-010

Cook-Sather, A. and Luz, A., 2015. Greater engagement in and responsibility for learning: What happens when students cross the threshold of student–faculty partnership. *Higher Education Research and Development*, 34(6), 1097–1109. Retrieved from: https://doi.org/10.1080/07294360.2014.911263

Cook-Sather, A., Prasad, S. K., Marquis, E. and Ntem, A., 2019. Mobilizing a culture shift on campus: Underrepresented students as educational developers. *New Directions for Teaching and Learning*, 159, 21–30.

de Bie, A., Marquis, E., Cook-Sather, A. and Luqueño, L., forthcoming. Valuing knowledge(s) and cultivating confidence: Contributing to epistemic justice via student–faculty pedagogical partnerships. In J. Hoffman and P. Blessinger (eds.), *International perspectives in higher education: Strategies for fostering inclusive classrooms*. Bingley: Emerald Group Publishing. Retrieved from: https://doi.org/10.1108/s2055-364120190000016004

Fanghanel, J., 2013. Going public with pedagogical inquiries: SoTL as a methodology for faculty professional development. *Teaching and Learning Inquiry*, 1(1), 59–70. Retrieved from: https://doi.org/10.2979/teachlearninqu.1.1.59

Fenton, N., Goff, L., and Zeadin, M., 2016. Developing a leadership in teaching and learning fellowship program at an Ontario university. Presentation at the Society for Teaching and Learning in Higher Education Conference, London.

Flint, A., 2016. Moving from the fringe to the mainstream: opportunities for embedding student engagement through partnership. *Student Engagement in Higher Education Journal*, 1(1).

Friberg, J., 2016. Might the 4M framework support SoTL advocacy? Retrieved from: https://illinoisstateuniversitysotl.wordpress.com/2016/07/11/might-the-4m-framework-support-sotl-advocacy/ (accessed 23 July 2019).

Healey, M., Flint, A. and Harrington, K., 2014. *Engagement through partnership: Students as partners in learning and teaching in higher education.* York: HE Academy. Retrieved from: www.heacademy.ac.uk/engagement-through-partnership-students-partners-learning-and-teaching-higher-education

Healey, M., Flint, A. and Harrington, K., 2016. Students as partners: Reflections on a conceptual model. *Teaching and Learning Inquiry*, 4(2). Retrieved from: https://doi.org/10.20343/10.20343/teachlearninqu.4.2.3

Healey, M. and Healey, R.L., 2018. 'It depends': Exploring the context-dependent nature of students as partners practices and policies. *International Journal for Students as Partners*, 2(1). Retrieved from: https://doi.org/10.15173/ijsap.v2i1.3472

Healey, R.L., Cliffe, A., Healey, M., Mercer-Mapstone, L. and Woolmer, C., 2018. Engaging students as partners in academic publishing. Presentation at ISSoTL18 Conference, Bergen, Norway.

Healey, R.L., Healey, M. and Cliffe, A., 2018. Engaging in radical work: Students as partners in academic publishing. *Efficiency Exchange*. Retrieved from: www.efficiencyexchange.ac.uk/12775/engaging-radical-work-students-partners-academic-publishing/ (accessed 23 July 2019).

Higher Education Academy, 2015. *Framework for student engagement through partnership.* York: HE Academy. Retrieved from: www.heacademy.ac.uk/sites/default/files/downloads/student-enagagement-through-partnership-new.pdf

Hutchings, P. (ed.), 2000. *Opening lines: Approaches to the scholarship of teaching and learning.* Menlo Park, CA: Carnegie Foundation for the Advancement of Teaching.

Johnstone, K., Marquis, E., and Puri, V., 2018. Public pedagogy and representations of higher education in popular film: New ground for the scholarship of teaching and learning. *Teaching and Learning Inquiry*, 6(1). Retrieved from: https://doi.org/10.20343/teachlearninqu.6.1.4

Lowe, T., Shaw, C., Sims, S., King, S. and Paddison, A., 2017. The development of contemporary student engagement practices at the University of Winchester and Winchester Student Union, UK. *International Journal for Students as Partners*, 1(1). Retrieved from: https://doi.org/10.15173/ijsap.v1i1.3082

Marquis, E., Black, C. and Healey, M., 2017. Responding to the challenges of student–staff partnership: Reflections of participants at an international summer institute. *Teaching in Higher Education*, 22(6), 720–735. Retrieved from: https://doi.org/10.1080/13562517.2017.1289510

Marquis, E., Guitman, R., Black, C., Healey, M., Matthews, K.E. and Dvorakova, S., 2018. Growing partnership communities. What experiences of an international institute suggest about developing student–staff partnership in higher education.

Innovations in Education and Teaching International. Retrieved from: https://doi.org/10.1080/14703297.2018.1424012

Marquis, E., Haqqee, Z., Kirby, S., Liu, A., Puri, V., Cockcroft, R., Goff, L. and Knorr, K., 2017. Connecting students and staff for teaching and learning inquiry: The McMaster student partners program. In B. Carnell and D. Fung (eds.), *Disciplinary approaches to connecting the higher education curriculum.* London: UCL Press, 203–216. Retrieved from: https://doi.org/10.2307/j.ctt1xhr542.20

Marquis, E., Jayaratnam, A., Mishra, A. and Rybkina, K., 2018. "I feel like some students are better connected": Students' perspectives on applying for extra-curricular partnership opportunities. *International Journal for Students as Partners*, 2(1). Retrieved from: https://doi.org/10.15173/ijsap.v2i1.3300

Marquis, E., Power, E. and Yin, M., 2018. Promoting and/or evading change: The role of student staff partnerships in staff teaching development. *Journal of Further and Higher Education.* Retrieved from: https://doi.org/10.1080/0309877X.2018.1483013

Marquis, E., Puri, V., Wan, S., Ahmad, A., Goff, L., Knorr, K., Vassileva, I. and Woo, J., 2016. Navigating the threshold of student–staff partnerships: A case study from an Ontario teaching and learning institute. *International Journal for Academic Development* 21(1), 4–15. Retrieved from: https://doi.org/10.1080/1360144x.2015.1113538

Marquis, E., Redda, A. and Twells, L., 2018. Navigating complexity, culture, collaboration, and emotion: Student perspectives on global justice and global justice education. *Teaching in Higher Education* 23(7), 853–868. Retrieved from: https://doi.org/10.1080/13562517.2018.1437133

Mårtensson, K., Roxå, T. and Olsson, T., 2011. Developing a quality culture through the scholarship of teaching and learning. *Higher Education Research and Development*, 30(1), 51–62. Retrieved from: https://doi.org/10.1080/07294360.2011.536972

Matthews, K. E., 2016. Students as partners as the future of student engagement. *Student Engagement in Higher Education Journal*, 1(1).

Matthews, K. E., 2017. Five propositions for genuine students as partners practice. *International Journal for Students as Partners* 1(2). Retrieved from: https://doi.org/10.15173/ijsap.v1i2.3315

Matthews, K. E., Cook-Sather, A. and Healey, M., 2018. Connecting learning, teaching, and research through student–staff partnerships. Toward universities as egalitarian learning communities. In V. C. H. Tong, A. Standen, and M. Sotiriou (eds.), *Shaping higher education with students. Ways to connect research and teaching.* London: UCL Press, 23–29. Retrieved from: https://doi.org/10.2307/j.ctt21c4tcm.7

McCulloch, A., 2009. The student as co-producer: Learning from public administration about the student-university relationship. *Studies in Higher Education*, 34(2), 171–183. Retrieved from: https://doi.org/10.1080/03075070802562857

McMaster Forward with Integrity Advisory Group, 2012. Forward with integrity: The emerging landscape. Retrieved from: https://president.mcmaster.ca/wp-content/uploads/2016/04/AG_Report_FWI_Emerging_Landscape_11Jul12.pdf (accessed 23 July 2019).

Mercer-Mapstone, L., Dvorakova, S.L., Matthews, K.E., Abbot, S., Cheng, B., Felten, P., Knorr, K. Marquis, E., Shammas, R. and Swaim, K., 2017. A systematic literature review of students as partners in higher education. *International Journal for Students as Partners*, 1(1). Retrieved from: https://doi.org/10.15173/ijsap. v1i1.3119

Miller-Young, J.E., Anderson, C., Kiceniuk, D., Mooney, J., Riddell, J., Schmidt Hanbidge, A., Ward, V., Wideman, M.A. and Chick, N., 2017. Leading up in the scholarship of teaching and learning. *Canadian Journal for the Scholarship of Teaching and Learning*, 8(2). Retrieved from: https://doi.org/10.5206/ cjsotl-rcacea.2017.2.4

Neary, M., 2014. Student as producer: Research-engaged teaching frames university-wide curriculum development. *CUR Quarterly*, 35(2), 28–34.

Roxå, T. and Mårtensson, K., 2009. Significant conversations and significant networks – Exploring the backstage of the teaching arena. *Studies in Higher Education*, 34(5), 547–559. h Retrieved from: ttps://doi.org/10.1080/03075070802597200

Roxå, T., and Mårtensson, K., 2012. How effects from teacher training of academic teachers propagate into the meso level and beyond. In E. Simon and G. Pleschova (eds.), *Teacher development in higher education: Existing programs, program impact, and future trends*. London: Routledge, 213–233. Retrieved from: https://doi. org/10.4324/9780203096826

Shaw, N., Rueckert, C., Smith, J., Tredinnick, J. and Lee, M., 2017. Students as partners in the real world – A whole-institution approach. *International Journal for Students as Partners*, 1(1). Retrieved from: https://doi.org/10.15173/ijsap. v1i1.3079

Simmons, N., 2009. Playing for SoTL impact: A personal reflection. *International Journal for the Scholarship of Teaching and Learning*, 3(2), 15. Retrieved from: https://doi.org/10.20429/ijsotl.2009.030230

Simmons, N., 2016. Synthesizing SoTL institutional initiatives toward national impact. *New Directions for Teaching and Learning*, 146, 95–102. Retrieved from: https://doi.org/10.1002/tl.20192

SPP, 2018. Unpublished program case studies.

Verwoord, R. and Poole, G., 2016. The role of small significant networks and leadership in the institutional embedding of SoTL. *New Directions for Teaching and Learning*, 146, 79–86. Retrieved from: https://doi.org/10.1002/tl.20190

Williams, A. L., Verwoord, R., Beery, T. A., Dalton, H., McKinnon, J., Strickland, K., Pace, J. and Poole, G., 2013. The power of social networks: A model for weaving the scholarship of teaching and learning into institutional culture. *Teaching and Learning Inquiry*, 1(2). Retrieved from: https://doi.org/10.2979/ teachlearninqu.1.2.49

Wuetherick, B. and Yu, S., 2016. The scholarship of teaching and learning in Canadian higher education. *New Directions for Teaching and Learning*, 146, 23–30.

Chapter 9

A students-as-partners approach to developing a work-integrated learning program for science

Susan Rowland

Introduction

This chapter is an account of a students-as-partners approach that my collaborators and I took to developing a novel Work-Integrated Learning (WIL) program for science students. The pilot implementation of the program was completed in consultation with a group of student volunteer partners who helped us develop, road-test, and evaluate the activities. Before beginning this account it is important to flag the difference between the concepts of *engaging students*, and *engaging students as partners* – they are related, but different, ideas. Coates (2005) summarizes the concept of student engagement as something "*based on the constructivist assumption that learning is influenced by how an individual participates in educationally purposeful activities.*" Although he describes engaged learning as a "*joint proposition*", he also notes it "*depends on institutions and staff providing students with the conditions, opportunities and expectations to become involved*" (p.26). This conception of engagement focuses on what students "do", which is foundational to quality pedagogy (Biggs, 1999). What it does *not* address is the question of what students *bring to*, and *create during*, their education. It also does not explicitly offer an avenue for students to help form their education to fit their needs.

The approach described in this chapter invites students to partner with the university, and to bring their own ideas and questions to the curriculum so both staff and students can learn as a group. The project was based on the philosophy laid out by Matthews (2016), who describes a partnership as something in which, "*students and teachers are both curious and able learners, albeit with varying levels of knowledge, capabilities, and with differing experiences*" (p.3). Importantly, the educators in this project felt that the experiences, input, and engagement the students brought to the activity were crucial to its improvement. As conceptualized by Healey, Flint, and Harrington (2016), the focus of this students-as-partners engagement was on co-creation, and collaborative enquiry. This chapter examines the WIL pilot program, the students' partnership activities, the contributions they brought to the project, and the way their input has helped position the program for large-scale rollout at the university. The chapter will also discuss how student partnership in the project was facilitated so that readers have a sense of how they might involve students in an initiative of this nature.

Background

A short background about the context for this initiative will be helpful for readers. Australian universities operate in a high-scrutiny environment. In 2008, the Australian Government legislated an uncapping of government-supported university places, which dramatically increased student enrolments. This *demand driven system* is an opportunity for both students and universities. It has also increased the costs of federal support for education, with real impact on the national budget (Dow, 2013). As a result, the government now demands more accountability from universities, particularly in the graduate employability space (Commonwealth of Australia 2009; DIISRTE, 2011). Consequently, universities have developed an intense interest in providing WIL, because industry experience during undergraduate education correlates with improved employment outcomes for graduates (Cappelli, 2014; Nunley et al., 2016). By providing WIL, universities are better able to support the needs of students and satisfy reporting requirements. This was a significant part of the rationale for the project reported in this chapter. Bringing a students-as-partners approach to the project also fits with the employability agenda; partnership work helps develop students' sense of self-efficacy, their communication skills, and their ability to help identify and solve problems. All of these skills and attributes are desired by science, technology, engineering, and math (STEM) employers (Deloitte Access Economics, 2014).

The project was conducted within the Faculty of Science at the University of Queensland (AUS). The Faculty of Science is the administrative unit for the six science-related schools at the university. The schools teach around 14,000 individual students each year; around 8,000 of these students are enrolled in degree programs administered by the faculty or its schools. The project aimed to reach these students, particularly the individuals enrolled in the generalist science degrees. The project aimed to develop a WIL program that could accommodate hundreds or thousands of students at one time, rather than the 30 to 50 accommodated in the formal WIL courses offered at the time in the Faculty of Science. The program was called SCI WIL WORK; the first part of the name is an abbreviation for Science Work-Integrated Learning, while the WORK part refers to the idea that students are using their current paid word as the stimulus for learning. The goal of the project was to develop and test activities to see if students found them valuable for WIL, and to examine what students learned from each activity. The entire pilot was financed through a small grant from the Australian Council of Deans of Science (A$10,000) and a matched contribution from the Faculty of Science (A$10,000). The University also provided in-kind costs in the form of the core team salaries. The grant funds were spent on employing grant team members and on small financial and food rewards for the student partners.

Why develop a new WIL program in science?

WIL is a well-established pedagogy (Patrick, Peach, Pocknee, Webb, Fletcher and Pretto, 2008) and, on the surface, it would seem that a *new* form of WIL is unnecessary for science students. There were two key issues, however, that drove the initiation of this partnered project. First, students in the Faculty of Science at our university were concerned about their graduate employment prospects. Second, the Australian Office of the Chief Scientist published a report (Edwards, Perkins, Pearce and Hong, 2015) that showed poor participation in WIL for science students generally, and an "*almost negligible*" (p.60) participation in industry placements for students in the natural and physical sciences.

There are several reasons why science students have poor WIL participation; perhaps the most important of these is the difficulty of providing appropriate industry placements for the large numbers of students who enroll in the generalist Bachelor of Science degree. Our solution to this problem was to design SCI WIL WORK as a non-traditional science WIL program that both incorporated and expanded the conception of WIL explained by Edwards et al. (2015). Edwards and co-workers found that, in Australian universities, WIL most commonly includes "*Integrating theory with the practice of work; Engagement with industry and community partners; Planned, authentic activities; and Purposeful links to curriculum and specifically designed assessment*" (p.46). SCI WIL WORK honored these approaches, but asked students to use their *existing, non-science* work as the focus for workplace-related learning. This is a radical departure from the traditional use of a *discipline-associated* industry placement as the focus for WIL.

When SCI WIL WORK was proposed as a WIL opportunity, some colleagues in the Faculty of Science openly questioned whether non-science work could legitimately "*count*" as science-related activity. We questioned it ourselves at some points, and vacillated over whether to only allow science-related work as the stimulus activity. In the end, however, it was decided that limiting the type of work that students could draw on would also limit the numbers (and types) of students who could participate in the pilot. Hence, students were invited to participate in SCI WIL WORK if they were undertaking *any* work or volunteering activity; this inclusive approach legitimized students' 'transgressions' into non-science workplaces, and allowed them to examine their truly transferable skill sets.

The project team

The SCI WIL WORK team came from a variety of backgrounds, and the mix of people was important for the success of the project. The non-student team consisted of:

(i)   the author, a teaching-focused academic in science with a research interest in professional development, learning through authentic practice, and employability;

(ii) a senior academic administrator and teacher in the Faculty of Science;

(iii) an administrative staff member with strong ties to the student community and extensive experience with organizing student enrichment activities;

(iv) an academic (and academic developer) with a strong interest and theoretical background in employability for students in generalist programs;

(v)   a science communicator who helped produce clear, concise support materials for the students; and

(vi) a recent Bachelor of Science graduate, who provided an important perspective by asking "*What would I have liked to know before I graduated?*" and developing materials that addressed this question.

The student partner team was larger than the staff team. It consisted of:

(i)   an Honors (fourth-year) student who completed a full year of research on the project and wrote a research thesis;

(ii) an undergraduate (third-year) researcher who attended all the classes and helped with several aspects of evaluating the project; and

(iii) undergraduate students who completed the program activities, suggested additional activities, engaged in on-project feedback, and participated in post-project reflective interviews. The project began with 29 participants who expressed interest in SCI WIL WORK, 18 of whom attended Workshop 1. By the end of Workshop 5, 11 students remained engaged.

How were students engaged as partners?

In this section I will briefly explain the SCI WIL WORK project as a way to contextualize the students' engagement. After this, I will present a series of vignettes, each of which exemplifies an important facet of the students-as-partners engagement. The timeline and sequence of activities in the overall project are shown in Figure 9.1; details of the curriculum and workshop activities are shown in Table 9.1.

Vignettes of student engagement through partnership

This section describes three areas of student partnership and engagement that occurred during this project. The goal of each vignette is to examine *how* students engaged, *why* they engaged (or stopped engaging), and *what* they gained or taught us as a result of their engagement. This section aims to provide information that is useful to educators who want to engage student partners in a similar program.

Part 1 Pre-implementation (Preparation) May–Jul Y1	• Develop learning objectives and curriculum for pilot SCI WIL WORK • Obtain ethics approval • Recruit student participants • Build Learning Management System site • Develop theoretical framework to examine desired learnings
Part 2 Implementation (Pilot delivery) Aug–Nov Y1	• Deliver Workshops 1–5 (10 class hours) • Revise and elaborate on planned curriculum in response to student input and engagement • Collect artefacts from the students' activity (e.g., student-generated interviews with science graduates, CVs, reflections, question responses) • Conduct post-mentoring interviews with students to understand their experience and challenges • Conduct post-course interviews with students for deeper examination of learnings and lived curriculum
Part 3 Post-implementation (Analysis and evaluation) Dec Y1–May Y2	• Implement coding strategy to analyse qualitative data from student-generated learning artefacts and interview transcripts (mapping against framework) • Map student achievements to enacted curriculum • Write research report and presentation • Contribute results to guidelines for best practice of SCI WIL WORK implementation

Figure 9.1 Timeline and sequence of activities for the project

Note: The staff completed Part 1 without substantial student input and Part 2 in consistent partnership with the students. The Honors student researcher and undergraduate researcher completed the tasks in Parts 2 and 3 in partnership with the staff team. The undergraduate student pilot participants contributed to Part 2.

Vignette 1: Engagement through recruitment and retention approaches

The academic team for this project had extensive experience with recruiting students for projects. This experience had shown that students tend to be more serious about an activity if they are admitted after making an initial declaration of their reasons for participating. Consequently, when the entire student population of the Faculty of Science (around 8,000 students) was emailed with details of the project, we asked students to submit an Expression of Interest (EOI) through an online survey facility. Students were asked for an EOI (250 words max) that addressed this question: "*Why are you interested in participating in the Employability Skills in Science project?*" As a barrier to entry, this short EOI is small enough to allow broad participation, but apparently large enough to focus students' ideas about their participation-related ambitions.

The 29 student EOIs revealed a broad range of motivations for participation. As expected, most students wanted to generally improve their employability or their skills around gaining or keeping employment. Around half wanted to understand how to articulate their current skill set in a way that employers would value. Importantly, however, eight students wanted to help with course development; they cited several reasons for this, including helping and meeting other students, engaging with academics in building an educational offering, and driving cultural change around valuing work as learning. Some showed a deep awareness of the modern employment landscape, and the need to adapt curricula to the market. One applicant said he wanted to understand his transferable skill set through collaborative reflection because:

Table 9.1 Details of the curriculum for SCI WIL WORK Workshops 1–5

Session	Activities
Workshop 1: Seminar Week 4; 18 students **Getting to know you**	**Pre:** Submit current CV. **During:** Students introduced themselves to each other in an informal 'networking' situation (with pizza and drinks). The class discussed: (i) networking and conversational technique; (ii) rules of the classroom (co-created); (iii) qualities desired by employers (student opinions and evidence-based data); (iv) their own strengths and weaknesses and their current CV; (v) peer mentoring activity (with speed dating to make mentor/mentee connections). **Post:** Readings around science graduate employability, with associated questions.
Workshop 2: Seminar Week 5; 15 students **What can you do with your science degree?**	**Pre:** Submit answers to question set (discussed in class). **During:** The class discussed: (i) skills students gain from a BSc and how the scientific mindset and aptitudes apply in non-science roles; (ii) an action plan to address one personal weakness; Repeat speed dating to finalise peer mentoring pairings. **Post:** Readings around science identity and personal development plans, with associated questions. Peer mentoring sessions and reflections.
Workshop 3: Seminar Week 7; 13 students **Where do you fit in and what are you going to do about it?**	**Pre:** Submit peer mentoring reflections and responses to readings (discussed in class). **During:** The class discussed: (i) progress of actions to address their weaknesses; (ii) what they enjoy or dislike about their current employment; (iii) their networks (friends vs professional connections); (iv) upcoming homework assignments. **Post:** Students worked on assigned activities (interview a science graduate; find a science job advertisement and produce a mock application). Students also participated in an interview about peer mentoring with the undergraduate researcher.
Workshop 4: Seminar Week 9; 13 students **Let's hear from some science graduates**	**Pre:** Submit job application for feedback **During:** The class discussed: (i) addressing selection criteria in the job application; (ii) their progress in finding an interviewee; (iii) their 'Me in Three' talk preparation; (iv) potential questions for the panel of science graduates; (v) interviewing and listening skills. Six recent science graduates visited the workshop; they answered students' questions about their journey to work. **Post:** Students prepared their 'Me in Three' talk, and continued work on their interview.
Workshop 5: Seminar Week 12; 12 students **Me in Three**	**Pre:** Submit the science graduate interview and the 'Me in Three' script. **During:** Students presented their 'Me in Three' talk and (i) received academic and peer feedback; and (ii) the group reflected on their strengths and weakness and discussed how to communicate these to employers. The facilitators conducted a mock job interview with one student; the group reflected on and discussed their performance. **Post:** Students submitted revised CV and completed an exit interview.

Australian science is transitioning to a state of emphasis on 'science-utility' rather than 'science-purity'. Political, industrial and university dialogue is saturated with claims advocating… STEM training in order to sustain jobs and foster translational innovation. Consequently, employers are not merely seeking graduates with high discipline knowledge, but those with diversified skill-sets and broad experiential learning.

The EOIs showed that pitching an experience as an opportunity to create systemic change through collaboration is effective with students, as several recruits wanted to give back and be part of a learning community.

The retention note in this vignette is short, but pithy. There was some attrition during the program (see the numbers in Table 9.1). The primary reason students left the SCI WIL WORK program was over-commitment. Students rightly chose to prioritize their studies and their paid work over a voluntary activity, even though they were gaining five dinners, a small financial incentive (~A$120), and significant employability learning through their participation. Some students just stopped attending the workshops (or did not attend Workshop 1 after their initial EOI was acknowledged), but several students wrote to us with apologies – for example:

With deep regret I believe I have to withdraw from the WIL study. I intend to graduate at the end of this semester and I need to dedicate myself fully to study. If it is at all possible, I would still like to be retained on the mailing list and community site as I have found the material provided to be eye-opening and the exercises and questions invaluable for reflection even at this early stage of the project. I just can't guarantee that I can put aside time to complete the tasks when the study requires them. I think the study is a fantastic initiative that will obviously succeed in assisting graduate confidence and employability and can only say I wish it had been available to me in previous years.

Maintaining high levels of student engagement is considerably dependent on the reward that students perceive around an activity. Many students are juggling study, work, family, and other obligations. Course credit and paid employment are both strong motivators of sustained engagement, and the SCI WIL WORK activities will be offered for course credit in the future.

Vignette 2: Engagement through open, respectful, classroom discussion

Unlike many science classrooms in Australia, the SCI WIL WORK teaching environment was predicated on the idea that students' ideas and opinions are core components of the curriculum. At every possible turn, students were asked to contribute their ideas after they had read literature or completed activities that helped them understand themselves. This taught us a lot about the way students think, and about the spaces we could help them explore as we developed the curriculum.

As an example: students were presented with a list of science graduate employment outcomes (Harris, 2012; see also Table 9.1), then asked which jobs surprised them. One student voiced their surprise at a listed job because "*scientists are not creative*". As scientists, the staff team members were surprised by this! We consider science to be very creative, and Florida (2002, 2003) places scientists in the "*super-creative core*" of the creative class. When we (as moderators) questioned the student's observation, the whole student group embarked on a 20-minute discussion about their own creativity, the nature of creativity, and the ways scientists create as part of their work. Although this derailed the planned activities for the workshop, it was enormously valuable. It gave students insight into who they were, and taught them to embrace their creative natures (rather than trying to suppress them because they were not fulfilling stereotypical 'sciencey' behaviors).

Australian science students are not generally used to contributing their own ideas in an open forum. To engage the student partners in SCI WIL WORK we needed to re-shape their natural (or learned) tendency to hide their own ideas behind the scientific facts they were sure of. This took some work. During open classroom discussions the moderators carefully maintained a safe space, with a code of conduct that the students co-developed. The students bought into this co-development approach – they worked as a group to build all the rules for their class time. They were particularly keen to take five minutes to meet the new people at their table at the beginning of each workshop. This simple step can be easily overlooked in a busy class session, but it is extremely important.

In addition to the class code of conduct, students were also asked to reflect on whether they were dominating conversations, or not contributing to the group, and to address these traits through active management of their behavior. This prompted some interesting moments in the class. After a particularly impassioned discussion in the room, a quiet member of the class explained how she was struggling in the conversational classroom:

> *I'm sitting here, watching how people talk and just say their ideas out loud. I'm in awe of that. I don't know how to do it, but I wish I did. I just can't keep up with the speed that everyone expresses their ideas. By the time I have got an idea formed in my head the conversation has moved on. I'm trying to learn from the people here who can do it.*

Other students backed up her statement, expressing similar fears and thoughts of inadequacy. In response, the moderators explained that it was good to be a thoughtful listener and also paid more attention to directing traffic in the classroom conversations so that all students had an opportunity to contribute. More vocal students were asked to take a back seat, to give them practice at contribution through listening and considering the ideas of others. More reticent members of the group were asked to share an idea or opinion without significant preparation, to give them practice at speaking without perfecting their ideas first. Every student was required to speak, listen, and reflect repeatedly. Because the classroom was a safe and respectful environment, the students encouraged their classmates in this work. Importantly, during the Peer Mentoring activity (between Workshops 2 and 3) some students shared knowledge about communication skills with their peers. Although respectful classroom discussion seems like a simple approach to student engagement, it is very rewarding for students to be heard. It encourages and helps them to develop ideas about who they are, what they believe, and what they can give to the world. As students build this conception of self-as-contributor they become more engaged partners.

Vignette 3: Engagement through for-credit research projects

Students working with the implementer group completed two full Scholarship of Teaching and Learning (SoTL) research projects around SCI WIL WORK; both studies were approved by the university Human Research Ethics Committee. One study focused on the peer mentoring activity, while the other addressed the participants' learning of career management skills from the program. Both of these projects were conducted primarily by the student researchers. One student was an undergraduate researcher, and the other was a fourth-year Honors degree candidate. Both students obtained course credit in a Bachelor of Science or related program for their work.

The student researchers collected data from multiple artefacts that the SCI WIL WORK students produced during their program activities (see Table 9.1 for items). The student researchers also interviewed all of the student participants individually about their involvement; and transcribed, then analysed these interviews. The academic team members were impressed with the growth and professionalism exhibited by the student researchers during their projects. The data collected were of publishable quality, and the students received high grades from independent assessors.

This kind of research is ideally conducted by student partners. The student interviewees were able to speak freely and confidentially to a peer interviewer, and their reflections were not clouded by the power dynamics that occur in a student-academic interview. All of the interview data were de-identified before the academic implementers saw it, which enhances students' ability to express contentious or potentially unpopular opinions about academic work. As a result, the interview responses from the students were particularly generous and data-filled. The results are fascinating and educational for the academic partners in the project, and they will drive production of teaching materials that better serve the students. The student researchers developed many transferable skills during their work, and the studies are now yielding papers, which further benefit the student researchers.

Conclusion

This chapter describes the implementation of a pilot WIL program in science that allowed students to draw on their extant non-science work as a stimulus for reflection. It provided multiple opportunities for student engagement and partnership which benefited both the students and the staff involved in the project. Importantly, the project addressed the employability agenda of the host university – an agenda shaped by the extant national conversation around graduate outcomes (Commonwealth of Australia 2009; DIISRTE, 2011).

Without student engagement, this project would not have been possible. The participants shaped the activities in the program (as participants) and investigated the learning outcomes of their peers (as researchers). The student feedback on the program and the results from the research have both been used as evidence for the development of new approaches to curriculum and co-curricular offerings in the Faculty of Science. The involvement of the students opened the eyes of the academic participants. We found that our ideas about what students needed were not always correct and we were consistently surprised by the activities that interested the students. Most importantly, many of the implementation team had forgotten their own sense of confusion (and trepidation) around the process of landing a first job in science. The student participants reminded us; their "*differing experiences*" Matthews (2016) (p.3) were enormously important in pinpointing holes in the envisaged curriculum for SCI WIL WORK.

As a result of the project, the Faculty of Science appointed a new academic leader in the employability space (the author) who is now developing a suite of for-credit and co-curricular offerings that harness the enthusiasm and skills demonstrated by the student participants. The Faculty now offers an annual 'Students as Partners' program that provides students with scholarship payments that enable collaboration with staff. So far, the projects have supported curriculum reform, trials of employability activities, development of student leadership opportunities, and strategic planning activities. The Faculty has also developed a leadership and mentoring program for students; over 100 students participated in the first iteration, and a follow-up Science Leaders Academy will launch this year.

The SCI WIL WORK project reported in this chapter has been an example of student engagement, in that we provided "*students with the conditions, opportunities and expectations to become involved*" (Coates, 2005, p.26). It is, however, much more than this. The students impressed the implementing team with their enthusiasm, their ability to articulate ideas, and their willingness to contribute to a joint venture in curriculum creation. They also opened the implementers' eyes to the needs of all students. As a result, the partnership has provided opportunities for both staff and students to improve the educational experience across the Faculty of Science in practical, meaningful, and sustainable ways.

References

Biggs, J., 1999. What the student does: teaching for enhanced learning. *Higher Education Research and Development*, 18(1), 57–75. Retrieved from: https://doi.org/10.1080/0729436990180105

Cappelli, P., 2014. *Skill Gaps, Skill Shortages and Skill Mismatches: Evidence for the US. NBER Working Paper No. 20382.* Cambridge, MA: National Bureau of Economic Research. Retrieved from: www.nber.org/papers/w20382

Coates, H., 2005. The value of student engagement for higher education quality assurance. *Quality in Higher Education*, 11(1), 25–36. Retrieved from: https://doi.org/10.1080/13538320500074915

Commonwealth of Australia, 2009. *Transforming Australia's higher education system*. Canberra: Department of Education, Employment and Workplace Relations. Retrieved from: http://hdl.voced.edu.au/10707/131634

Deloitte Access Economics, 2014. *Australia's STEM Workforce: a survey of employers*. Canberra: Office of the Chief Scientist. Retrieved from: www.chiefscientist.gov.au/wp-content/uploads/DAE_OCS-Australias-STEM-Workforce_FINAL-REPORT.pdf

DIISRTE, 2011. *Development of performance measurement instruments in higher education. Discussion paper*. Canberra: Department of Industry, Innovation, Science, Research and Tertiary Education. Retrieved from: www.deewr.gov.au?HigherEducation/Publications/Pages/Home.aspx

Dow, C., 2013. *Higher education: sustainability of a demand-driven system*. Parliamentary Library Briefing Book. Canberra: Parliament of Australia Library. Retrieved from: www.aph.gov.au/About_Parliament/Parliamentary_Departments/Parliamentary_Library/pubs/BriefingBook44p/HigherEducation

Edwards, D., Perkins, K., Pearce, J., and Hong, J., 2015. *Work Integrated Learning in STEM in Australian Universities: Final Report submitted to the Office of the Chief Scientist*. Australia: ACER. Retrieved from: www.acer.org

Florida, R., 2002. *The rise of the creative class: and how it's transforming work, leisure, community and everyday life*. New York: Perseus Book Group.

Florida, R., 2003. Cities and the creative class. *City and Community*, 2(1), 1–19.

Harris, K. L., 2012. *A background in science. What science means for Australian society. A study commissioned by the Australian Council of Deans of Science*. Melbourne: Centre for the Study of Higher Education.

Healey, M., Flint, A., and Harrington, K., 2016. Students as partners: Reflections on a conceptual model. *Teaching and Learning Inquiry*, 4(2). Retrieved from: https://doi.org/10.20343/10.20343/teachlearninqu.4.2.3

Nunley, J. M., Pugh, A., Romero, N., Seals Jr, A., 2016. College major, internship experience, and employment opportunities: Estimates from a résumé audit. *Labour Economics*, 38 (January 2016), 37–46. Retrieved from: https://doi.org/10.1016/j.labeco.2015.11.002

Matthews, K. E., 2016. Students as partners as the future of student engagement. *Student Engagement in Higher Education Journal*, 1(1).

Patrick, C. J., Peach, D., Pocknee, C., Webb, F., Fletcher, M., Pretto, G., 2008. *The WIL [Work Integrated Learning] report: A national scoping study [Australian Learning and Teaching Council (ALTC) Final report]*. Brisbane: Queensland University of Technology. Retrieved from: www.altc.edu.au and www.acen.edu.au

Chapter 10

Going beyond student voice through meta-level education transformation

Adam Fletcher

More than ever before, educators, educational administrators and political leaders are showing interest in the roles of students throughout educational institutions and the wider education system as a whole. This system, from national offices to individual classrooms, has unlimited potential for engaging students as partners throughout its countless contours, including what I call the '4 Ps' of schools: Policies, procedures, personnel and practices. While much of this activity has been studied in the past 40 years, there have been few attempts to coalesce these divergent approaches into a consolidated strategy for school improvement.

The following theory is called Meaningful Student Involvement and, since 2001, it has been moving from theory into practice worldwide. This chapter will explore this activity in North American contexts. However, because of its positioning as a pro-democratic, anti-exclusionary educational approach, the recommendations and considerations herein can be relevant to global audiences (El Bouhali, 2015).

Meaningful Student Involvement is the process of engaging students as partners in every facet of school change for the purpose of strengthening their commitment to education, community, and democracy (Chopra, 2014; Dewey, 1916; Fletcher, 2003; Freire, 1987). The contention behind this theory is plain: by establishing intentional, active and substantive partnerships with every single student in every single learning environment, everywhere, all of the time, our schools and our societies can be healthier for everyone's hearts and minds today and in the future (Fletcher, 2017).

In order to actualize the full effect of Meaningful Student Involvement, we must go beyond student voice though, and embrace the reality of student engagement, which can only happen through meta-level education transformation (Fielding, 2004; Flutter and Rudduck, 2006; Chopra, 2014). This chapter explores how that happens, what it looks like, how it is challenged, and what the future could look like. The following section explores the differences between student voice, Meaningful Student Involvement and otherwise.

1. Student voice is not enough

Student voice is any expression of any learner about education that can happen any-where, anytime about anything related to learning, and can take countless forms. Students testifying to school governments, fighting in hallways, writing reports on education, and vaping in bathrooms can all be interpreted as student voice. Student voice does not require adult approval or acceptance; instead, it includes both the raw and genuine expression of students about education as well as the shiny, tokenistic presentations. Because of the disjunction between how students present their expression and what, who and how educators listen to students, student voice is not enough to transform education (Bain and Golmohammadi, 2016). Another student voice survey or focus group is not going to radically undermine the hierarchical nature of schooling from the youngest years through graduation, into higher education and beyond.

Our society demands nothing less though. Year over year, generation after generation, we have seen the inadequate basis of schools to accomplish a sus-tainable democratic society. Instead, we have witnessed the continued under-mining of our governments, our laws, our social safety net, and our cultural norms. Despite the strengthening of our society through increased diversity and broadened social enlightenment, our systems strain under the burden of crass capitalism that places individual wealth before the health of communities and our world as a whole (El Bouhali, 2015). We need to radically rebalance the injustice of hatred, racism, classism, sexism, xenophobia and more. One of the very best ways to do this is by transforming the entire education system including uni-versities, and some of the best ways that happens is within the locus of control for individual educators, education institution administrators, education system leaders, and politicians. Of course, students themselves can occupy vital roles too (Fielding, 2004; Tomozii and Topală, 2014; Fletcher 2017).

Before we can transform the education system, including universities, we must understand what it is. The following section explores the dimensions, avenues and outcomes of the education system.

2. Understanding the education system

Over the past century, systems of education have emerged throughout the Western world, many of which possess the same attributes. Rather than explore them in general, this article explores the education system in North America where Meaningful Student Involvement is spreading. Because of the similar assumptions undergirding education systems around the world, these findings can be applied internationally (El Bouhali, 2015; Freire, 1987; Fielding, 2004; Mahar, 2007; Tomozii and Topală, 2014).

As has been shown repeatedly, education begins informally from the youngest ages, and is led by parents or caregivers first. The education system starts with any formal attempts to influence, guide or direct a child's learning, whether through popular culture or specific classroom approaches. In most communities today, that means preschool programs promoting infant and toddler development. When children leave the home and assume their formal titles as 'learners', they enter the education system through a classroom (Fives and Manning, 2005), usually with a single teacher, focused on a plethora of topics. That teacher uses numerous teaching methods and curricula to propagate learning, and then assesses students using a range of tests, some standardized across all schools and others created by individual teachers. In all grade levels from kindergarten through twelfth grade, principals and headmasters manage those teachers, ensuring school efficiency, high completion and graduation rates, and ensuring budgetary alignment with district, state and federal education priorities. They also ensure individual schools comply with policies and laws and supervise the overall well-being of buildings. These individual schools are the underpinning of the education system in the United States.

At the federal level, the president of the United States appoints a cabinet secretary to manage their education agenda. That education secretary has an agency to carry out the president's agenda, which is complemented by the budget and goals set forth by the U.S. Congress. This education agency administers those funds through a series of programs, which in turn insist compliance with the federal agenda by individual classroom teachers, and every level of the education system between individual students and the president. The U.S. Supreme Court maintains checks and balances throughout the education system, while popularly elected district and state school boards ensure the prevalence of local priorities in schools. These priorities almost always align with federal priorities, with few instances of deviance across the entire country. The local education systems across the country divvy federal money and state money and district money through the administration of programs in individual schools at every grade level. These programs ensure curriculum, supplies, personnel, facilities and other aspects of school operation; they also reveal the political, cultural and social, economic and other agendas of the local, state and federal governments.

In the United States, public higher education institutions are funded through similar channels. The federal education agency maintains oversight of public higher education institutions, and ensures that private colleges and universities are operating within a range of acceptable behavior and outcomes, too. Private higher education institutions have more discretion over their day-to-day operations though, and operate outside the oversight of publicly elected officials, such as school board members on the district and state levels. There are bureaucracies apparent within those organizations too, though, ensuring plenty of opportunities for students to affect education transformation there, as well.

Understanding the meta-level education transformation inherent within Meaningful Student Involvement means grasping the outsized effect of national education policies and acknowledging the breadth of possibilities. The following section explores those areas.

3. The meta-level logic of meaningfulness

As many have argued before, the goal of all learning institutions everywhere, all of the time should be student engagement (Dewey, 1916; Counts, 1978; Freire, 1987; Fletcher, 2017). Meaningful Student Involvement can be a clear pathway to that outcome. While schools have continually assessed memorization skills, learning processes and student compliance with educator expectations, they have failed to address the underlying necessity of student engagement (Bain and Golmohammadi, 2016; Marks, 2000; Price and Baker, 2012). Aside from being wholly ineffectual at measuring student ability, these evaluations are largely manipulative, forcing students to learn subjects they are disinterested in without the punishment of being labelled failures. A more relevant, holistic and just measurement would assess student engagement in learning across their entire educative experience.

In order to do that, we have to recognize that student engagement has too many definitions right now. Rather than fixate on psychological investment, classroom time-on-task ability, or intangible enthusiasm markers, we need a simple, pragmatic sense of what student engagement is (Fives and Manning, 2005; Price and Baker, 2012). That is why SoundOut devised the following definition, which has been shared with countless educators through professional development sessions: Student engagement is the act of learners choosing the same things repeatedly in the context of learning. These things can include emotions, social connections, physical activities, etc. They can also be tangible or esoteric; practical or pie-in-the-sky; perceived as positive or negative; and productive or unproductive in the classroom setting (Fives and Manning, 2005). There are literally no bounds to what students can be engaged in.

Meaningful student involvement can foster student engagement within classrooms, throughout entire education institutions, and across whole education systems. Students can be directly affected by participating in a variety of types of involvement, including education planning, pedagogical research, classroom teaching, learning evaluation, systemic decision-making, and education advocacy (Flutter and Rudduck, 2006). These activity types can act as entry points for engagement, providing iterative learning opportunities for students to understand the broader aspects of learning, teaching and leadership beyond their immediate classroom experiences. In this way, a theory of change emerges through the activities. As other researchers have found, Meaningful Student Involvement can inform each of these approaches individually as well as together, enhancing and unifying the approach significantly (Chopra, 2014; Fielding, 2004; Flutter and Rudduck, 2006).

As illustrated in Figure 10.1, the first part of this theory of change is the activity of learning about Meaningful Student Involvement itself. This learning should involve students and educators together, and should explore the Frameworks for Meaningful Student Involvement. Similar to the contention presented by Bain and Golmohammadi, as part of that learning process, students should take

1. STUDENTS AND EDUCATORS LEARN ABOUT
MEANINGFUL STUDENT INVOLVEMENT
• Students take action to improve education through
Planning, Research, Teaching, Evaluation, Decision-Making, Advocacy
• Educators become partners, supporting meaningful student involvement
as advocates, allies and stakeholders

2. SCHOOLS ARE TRANSFORMED

INITIAL PEOPLE AFFECTED	INITIAL PLACES CHANGED
• Participating students	• Directly involved classrooms
• Educators	• Directly involved school
• Support staff	• Directly involved agencies
• Administrators and others	

3. EDUCATION SYSTEM IS TRANSFORMED

SECONDARY PEOPLE AFFECTED	SECONDARY PLACES CHANGED
• Additional students	• Directly involved classrooms
• Educators	• Directly involved school
• Support staff	• Directly involved agencies
• Administrators and others	

4. EDUCATION TRANSFORMATION IS SUSTAINED
TERTIARY PEOPLE AFFECTED
• Students as they become adults, voters,
professionals and taxpayers
• Educators and others as they
progress in their careers
• Parents and other adults surrounding
students as they vote, pay taxes and talk in public

Figure 10.1 Meaningful Student Involvement Logic Model

action to improve education and educators should become partners who support Meaningful Student Involvement as advocates, allies and stakeholders (Bain and Golmohammadi, 2016). The second part of this logic model is resultant from the first: Schools are transformed. This illustrates the first order of change within a learning environment where Meaningful Student Involvement has occurred, and assumes that participating students, educators, support staff and others are positively changed through the type of activity(s) initiated by students (Maatta and Uusiautti, 2018). The initial places changed by Meaningful Student Involvement were directly involved, and may include classrooms, buildings, and/or education agencies. Showing a ripple effect, the second order of change involves students beyond the initial group who participated who may be positively affected by the changes instituted, along with additional educators, support staff and others who were not directly involved, but reaped the rewards of the educational improvement activities inherent within Meaningful Student Involvement. The tertiary level affected is more obtuse, but nevertheless important to the model. It consists of students, participating and otherwise, as they graduate from school and become adults, voters, professionals and taxpayers, as well as participating educators and others as they progress in their educational careers. Additionally, parents and other adults surrounding students may be affected as they vote, pay taxes and talk in public about education.

The potential of this engagement is nearly limitless, as the effects of Meaningful Student Involvement can potentially ripple endlessly through generations of students across countless educational settings. With that potentiality though, the question easily emerges of what Meaningful Student Involvement actually looks like.

4. Characteristics of meaningful student involvement

In early research, SoundOut recorded a series of patterns whenever students and educators talked about involvement in the education system being meaningful (Fletcher, 2008). There were six basic characteristics within this pattern. For almost two decades now, SoundOut has used them to show exactly what is present in schools where Meaningful Student Involvement is an organizing premise for school transformation.

The first characteristic of Meaningful Student Involvement is system-wide approaches to Meaningful Student Involvement. This means that all students in all learning settings are meaningfully involved throughout their education in *any* form. This characteristic is evident when every education improvement activity includes opportunities for all students in every level to be involved through system-wide planning, research, teaching, evaluation, decision-making, and advocacy. It is also evident when meaningful involvement starts in kindergarten and extends to and through higher education (Hamilton, 2018; Krause, 2005). There are a variety of opportunities throughout each student's individual learning experience that also connect students across the learning experiences of their peers that happen within their education institution, throughout their local region, across states and around the world (Mahar, Warne, Collins, Manefield and Moore, 2007). There are a variety of opportunities for meaningful involvement in classroom management, interactions with peers and adults throughout the school, and ongoing throughout their educational careers, as well as opportunities for student/adult partnerships in learning communities that feature student-specific roles in building leadership, and intentional programs designed to increase student efficacy as partners in educational improvement.

The second characteristic of Meaningful Student Involvement is high levels of student authority through Meaningful Student Involvement. This is apparent when students' ideas, knowledge, opinions and experiences in schools and regarding education are actively sought and substantiated by educators, administrators, and others throughout the educational system. Educators, support staff, administrators and politicians actively acknowledge, validate and authorize students' ability to improve schools, while students are deliberately taught about learning, about the education system, about student voice and Meaningful Student Involvement, and about improving learning, teaching and leadership throughout education. Schools' commitment to Meaningful Student Involvement is obvious through sustainable activities, comprehensive planning and effective assessments, and those assessments measure shared and individual perceptions and outcomes of Meaningful Student Involvement (Fletcher, 2017).

The presence of interrelated strategies that integrate Meaningful Student Involvement is the third characteristic. This characteristic is present when students are incorporated into ongoing, sustainable school reform activities. There are deliberate opportunities for learning, teaching and leadership for all students throughout the educational system. In individual learning spaces, this can mean integrating student voice into classroom management practices; giving students opportunities to design, facilitate, and evaluate the curriculum; or facilitating student learning about school systems. Having equitable opportunities to participate with educators in formal educational improvement activities is another example of this characteristic, as well as students having complete, equitable voting rights in administrative leadership activities. Whatever the opportunities are, ultimately it means they are all tied together with the intention of improving education for all learners all the time. Every learning institution, whether within primary, secondary or higher education, should be in a continuous mode of improvement, and every single improvement effort should seek nothing less than to engage students as partners. Doors are opened for classroom teachers, institution leaders and other educators to fully and completely partner with students, and each of these strategies is integrated through a formal education improvement plan relating to other efforts within an education institution (Fives and Manning, 2005). Each of these strategies is obvious within regular policies and procedures in schools, districts, and/or state agencies.

The fourth characteristic of Meaningful Student Involvement is sustainable structures of support for implementing learning, teaching, and leadership. Policies and procedures are created and amended to promote Meaningful Student Involvement throughout education institutions, including specific funding opportunities that support student voice and student engagement. This characteristic includes ongoing professional development for educators focused on Meaningful Student Involvement, and a new vision for students that is integrated and infused into classroom practice, building procedures, district/state/federal policy. Ultimately it engenders new cultures that constantly focus on students by constantly having students on board. Sustainability within schools is actively observed, examined, critiqued and challenged by students and adults as the intermixing of culture and structure through structures of support, including student action centers that train students and provide information to student/adult partners. Such structures also include a curriculum specifically designed to teach students about school improvement and student action, as well as fully funded, ongoing programs that support Meaningful Student Involvement.

Personal commitment is the fifth characteristic of Meaningful Student Involvement. This is apparent when students and adults acknowledge their mutual investment, dedication, and benefit, and acknowledgment is visible in learning, relationships, practices, policies, school culture, and many other ways. It is also apparent since Meaningful Student Involvement is not just about students themselves. It insists that from the time of their pre-service education, teachers, administrators, paraprofessionals, counselors, and others see students as substantive, powerful, and significant partners in all the different machinations of schools; when they have this commitment every person will actively seek nothing other than to fully integrate students at every turn. This commitment also results in students who were previously seen as outsiders no longer being viewed as different and separate, both through intention and action. Particular emphasis is placed on engaging low-income students, students-of-colour and low-achieving students in buildings where predominantly white, upper-income and/or high-achieving students have been perceived as having greater value or more importance than other learners. Sharing and re-affirming personal commitment is a cultural norm within the environment where Meaningful Student Involvement happens (Maatta and Uusiautti, 2018).

The sixth characteristic of Meaningful Student Involvement is strong learning connections (Flutter and Rudduck, 2006). Classroom learning and student involvement are connected by classroom learning and credit, ensuring relevancy for educators and significance to students when deliberate connection ties together the roles for students with the purpose of education. It also substantiates student/adult partnerships and signifies the intention of adults to continue transforming learning as learners themselves evolve. This characteristic shows that Meaningful Student Involvement should not be an 'add-on' strategy for educators – it should be integrated throughout their daily activities, with classroom teachers acknowledging school-focused projects and education involvement by students with credit. This new vision for students provides all people in schools, young and adult, with opportunities to collaborate in exciting new ways while securing powerful new outcomes for everyone involved, most importantly students themselves.

These six characteristics have several potential responsibilities: they can ensure that student engagement is the goal of Meaningful Student Involvement; straddling theory and practice, they can enhance student involvement to ensure meaningfulness; and they can make sure student engagement is neither myopic and narcissistic nor overreaching and non-beneficial to specific students themselves. Finally, they can lay a firm foundation for action and provide reasonable guidelines for assessment.

5. Challenges to meaningfulness

There are several roadblocks to Meaningful Student Involvement. The complications of education policy alone actively assure educators' and education leaders' inaccessibility, unavailability and indifference to student voice, let alone to engaging students as partners throughout education vis-à-vis Meaningful Student Involvement (Mitra, 2009; Fletcher, 2017). It is essential to understand these challenges, as they can inhibit and prohibit meaningfulness for every single student within a learning institution.

However, understanding the complex ways meaningfulness does not happen may require simplifying the reasons for the challenges. Alfie Kohn might do this best when he suggests the barriers are multi-layered: the culture of education stops schools from being meaningful; educators and administrators stop education from being meaningful; and students themselves may prevent Meaningful Student Involvement (Kohn, 1993). Following is an exploration of these challenges of meaningfulness in student involvement.

A. Culture

Education culture can mean many things, including opinions, ideas, attitudes, feelings and actions that emerge among students, between students and adults, and among adults. (Kipp, Quinn, Lancaster, Malone, Lashway, Lochmiller and Sharratt 2014). The relationships between people matter, and inform the socio-emotional landscape through which learning, teaching and leadership happens. It is vital to understand the ways education culture becomes evident, including one-on-one interactions, classroom teaching practices, systemic decision-making and so on (Chopra, 2014; Fives and Manning, 2005). Culture can act as a barrier in countless ways, including overt measures such as the 4P's mentioned earlier; and subversive measures including student coercion, educators' perspectives towards students, etc.

Tokenism is a significant factor affecting student involvement that is affected by the culture of schools today (Fletcher, 2015), including higher education specifically (Hamilton, 2018; Henslee, Leao, Miller, Wendling and Whittington, n.d.; Krause, 2005). With the appearance and images of students used to promote colleges, recruit students and otherwise benefit the overall image of higher education, there is a growing awareness that having students in attendance without any power, potential or possibilities for meaningful involvement can actually be detrimental to students themselves (Hamilton, 2018; Henslee, n.d.), as well as for the education system overall (Fletcher, 2017). Moving beyond surveys and focus groups, transforming outmoded student governance practices, and diving into the depth and breadth of Meaningful Student Involvement may be the only way for learning institutions to authentically and sustainably engage students as partners with educators and others.

B. Educators and administrators

Educators and administrators in schools can stop Meaningful Student Involvement in numerous ways. In SoundOut's work, the overall attitudes and perceptions of adults towards students disallows meaningfulness in opportunities for involvement. For instance, when student governments are merely allowed to share ideas, give counsel and otherwise not make substantive decisions, educators and administrators block Meaningful Student Involvement. Similarly, the practice of manipulating students to become involved through grades, classroom credit or other mechanisms is a barrier, along with limiting students to making inconsequential decisions about education. This can look like allowing students to plan dances and choose school mascots, and not making space for students on curriculum planning committees or in budgeting decisions. Meaningful Student Involvement requires the active, intentional and substantial engagement of students throughout every level of education practice, management, evaluation and administration, and beyond (Fletcher, 2008).

Educators and administrators are particularly likely to resist Meaningful Student Involvement, if only in a sense of self-preservation. SoundOut has identified three primary ways this happens: the first is by profiting off student voice; the second is by maintaining authority; the third is by acting as a vacuum (Bain and Golmohammadi, 2016).

By using the phrase Meaningful Student Involvement, many educators and education administrators are asserting they are interested in listening to the unfettered opinions, ideas, experiences, and wisdom of students. However, their approaches are similar to that of many companies that market to young people, in that they are listening for profit. They continue to maintain or develop funding opportunities for these activities by using student voice. A rather cynical perspective, this barrier may be the most insidious of all.

The second way educators and administrators are barriers happens when adults maintain authority through Meaningful Student Involvement. By using anti-transparent responses to students, this merely perpetuates the modus operandi of schools, which is to do *to* and *for* students, rather than to work *with* students as partners. The approach advocated for by the vast majority of existent student voice programs is adult-dictated, adult-agenda oriented, and ultimately will only benefit adults; which actually reinforces adult authority. This is obviously antithetical to Meaningful Student Involvement, acting as an enormous barrier.

When educators and administrators act as vacuums to student voice, they are challenging Meaningful Student Involvement. Ultimately, the approach of using student voice to reinforce adults' preconceptions is the same for students as yelling into an empty well. Students speak into a vacuum where they do not know the outcomes of their contributions to educators, leaders, and advocates, and there is little or no accountability, and there is little or no substantive student presence (Fletcher, 2017).

6. Conclusion

The goal of Meaningful Student Involvement anywhere in education should be to build the capacity of students to cause change within the education systems and communities to which they belong. At the same time, the education system should be continuously, radically, intentionally and holistically transformed, and students should be the main partners in accomplishing this. As this chapter has shown, that is wholly possible, with thorough, authentic and committed research, scholarship and action.

Unfortunately, many student voice programs today actually negate students' abilities to cause that change by capturing student voice and binding it to the hands of educators and administrators. This disengages learners, taking away the little authority that students should have. Rather than alienating students from the process of educational transformation, we should seek to do nothing less than enliven any level of interest students may have in the first place. Meaningful Student Involvement provides a clear avenue through which to do this.

References

Bain, J. and Golmohammadi, L., 2016. Integrating Student Voice in Higher Education Assessment Practice: Negotiating the dialogic vacuum, BERA Annual Conference 2016. Leeds, United Kingdom, September 13–15. Retrieved from: https://research.gold.ac.uk/20272/1/BERA%20Presentation.pdf (accessed 10 April 2019).

El Bouhali, C., 2015. The OECD neoliberal governance, In Abdi, A., Shultz, L. and Pillay, T. (Eds.) *Decolonizing global citizenship education*. Rotterdam: Sense Publishers. pp.119–129. Retrieved from: https://doi.org/10.1007/978-94-6300-277-6_10

Chopra, C. H., 2014. New pathways for partnerships: An exploration of how partnering with students affects teachers and schooling (Doctoral dissertation). Retrieved from: https://digital.lib.washington.edu/researchworks/bitstream/handle/1773/25487/Chopra_washington_0250E_12871.pdf?sequence=1%20 (accessed 10 April 2019).

Counts, G. S., 1978. *Dare the school build a new social order?* Carbondale: Southern Illinois University Press. Retrieved from: https://doi.org/10.1057/9781137015914.0007

Dewey, J., 1916. *Democracy and education*. New York: Macmillan.

Fielding, M., 2004. Transformative approaches to student voice: Theoretical underpinnings, recalcitrant realities, *British Educational Research Journal*, 30, 2, 295–311. Retrieved from: https://doi.org/10.1080/0141192042000195236

Fives, H. and K. Manning, D., 2005. Teachers' Strategies for Student Engagement: Comparing Research to Demonstrated Knowledge. Paper presented at the 2005 Annual Meeting of the American Psychological Association, Washington, DC. Retrieved from: https://msuweb.montclair.edu/~fivesh/Research_files/FivesandManning_2005_APA.pdf

Fletcher, A., 2003. *Meaningful student involvement guide to students as partners*. Olympia: SoundOut.

Fletcher, A., 2008. The architecture of ownership, *Educational Leadership*, 66, 3. Retrieved from: www.ascd.org/publications/educational-leadership/nov08/vol66/num03/TheArchitecture-of-Ownership.aspx (accessed 10 April 2019).

Fletcher, A., 2017. *Student Voice Revolution: The meaningful student involvement handbook*. Olympia: CommonAction.

Flutter, J. and Rudduck, J., 2006. Student voice and the architecture of change: Mapping the territory. Retrieved from: www.educ.cam.ac.uk/research/projects/researchdevelopment/07_06rudduck1.doc (accessed 10 April 2019).

Freire, P., 1987. *Pedagogy of freedom: Hope, democracy and civic courage.* Lanham, MD: Rowman.

Hamilton, A., 2018. The need for student engagement. *New Directions for Teaching and Learning*, 154, 21–31. Retrieved from: https://doi.org/10.1002/tl.20288

Henslee, C., Leao, M., Miller, K., Wendling, K.A. and Whittington, S., n.d. *Do You See What I See? Undergraduate Students' Perceptions of IUPUI Campus Viewbooks and Experiences.* Retrieved from: https://education.indiana.edu/students/graduates/program-specific/higher-education-and-student-affairs/_docs/2016%20SPA%20at%20IU%20Journal.pdf (accessed 10 April 2019).

Kipp, G., Quinn, P., Lancaster, S., Malone, G., Lashway, L., Lochmiller, C., and Sharratt, G., 2014. *The AWSP Leadership Framework User's Guide.* Olympia: Association of Washington School Principals. Retrieved from: www.awsp.org/docs/default-source/member-support-documents/Leadership-Framework/users-guide/awsp_leadership_framework_users_guide_final_webres.pdf (accessed 10 April 2019).

Kohn, A., 1993. Choices for children: why and how to let students decide. *Phi Delta Kappan*, 8, 20. Retrieved from: www.alfiekohn.org/article/choices-children/ (accessed 15 October 2019).

Krause, Kerri-Lee., 2005. Understanding and promoting student engagement in university learning communities. Centre for the Study of Higher Education. Retrieved from: www.cshe.unimelb.edu.au/pdfs/Stud_eng.pdf (accessed 10 April 2019).

Maatta, K. and Uusiautti, S., 2018. *The Psychology of Study Success in Universities.* Routledge.

Mahar, S., Warne, C., Collins, J., Manefield, R. and Moore, J., 2007. *Student Voice: A historical perspective and new directions.* Melbourne: Department of Education Office for Education Policy and Research Division. Retrieved from: www.researchgate.net/publication/265173461_Student_Voice_A_Historical_Perspective_and_New_Directions (accessed 15 October 2019).

Marks, H., 2000. Student Engagement in Instructional Activity: Patterns in the Elementary, Middle, and High School Years, *American Educational Research Journal*, 37, 1. Retrieved from: https://doi.org/10.2307/1163475

Mitra, D. L., 2009. Student voice and student roles in education policy reform, In D. Plank, G. Sykes, and B. Schneider (Eds.), *AERA handbook on education policy research* (pp.819–830). London: Routledge. Retrieved from: https://doi.org/10.4324/9780203880968.ch63

Price, K., and Baker, S. N., 2012. Measuring students' engagement on college campuses: Is the NSSE an appropriate measure of adult students' engagement? *Journal of Continuing Higher Education*, 60, 1, 20–32. Retrieved from: https://doi.org/10.1080/07377363.2012.649127

Tomozii, S.E. and Topală, I., 2014. Why do we need to change the educational paradigms? *Procedia-Social and Behavioral Sciences*, 142, 586–591. Retrieved from: https://doi.org/10.1016/j.sbspro.2014.07.670

Chapter 11

Critically reflecting on identities, particularities and relationships in student engagement

Peter Felten

The concept of student engagement has become a catch-all used in many countries around the world to describe diverse practices that enhance learning and improve outcomes in higher education. In the U.S., for example, variations on the word *"engagement"* are ubiquitous in university and college marketing materials, and the educational practices related to this concept are mushrooming through institutional strategic plans and curricula (Felten, Gardner, Schroeder, Lambert, and Barefoot, 2016). Engaged learning is everywhere.

Engagement as a framework has roots in research and theorizing by Alexander Astin on *"student involvement."* Astin concluded that *"The extent to which students can achieve particular developmental goals is a direct function of the time and effort they devote to activities designed to produce these gains"* (1984, p.301). Scholars, including George Kuh, built on this insight to define *"student engagement"* as a result of two factors: the time and effort students dedicate to educationally purposeful activities, and an institution's programs and pedagogies designed to influence student behavior (Kuh, Kinzie, Schuh, Whitt, and Associates, 2010; Wolf-Wendel, Ward, and Kinzie 2009). Put most simply, student engagement results from the combination of student effort and institutional programs.

The concept of student engagement has such traction in higher education in large part because it acts as a heuristic – a useful tool that supports problem-solving and reflection, particularly for institutional actors. The student engagement equation (student effort plus institutional programs equals learning outcomes) is an appealing and practical rule-of-thumb for individuals and groups tasked with academic planning and administration. Engagement is everywhere because it is practical and useful.

Even as academic leaders and marketers have embraced this concept as something of *"an uncritically accepted academic orthodoxy"* (Zepke 2014, p.699), scholars have devoted considerable time and effort to *"disentangle the strands of student engagement"* (Kahu 2013, p.766), evaluating behavioral, psychological, socio-cultural, and holistic perspectives on engagement. This scholarly analysis is appropriate, but perhaps we are hoping for too much if we expect student engagement to withstand rigorous theoretical critique. Rather, as Lee Shulman

(2002) wrote about many commonly used educational heuristics (before student engagement became one):

> *They help us think more clearly about what we're doing, and they afford us a language through which we can exchange ideas and dilemmas... They are powerful as long as we don't take them too seriously, as long as we don't transform mnemonic into dogma or heuristic into orthodoxy.*

(p.42)

Conceiving of student engagement as a practical but imperfect tool that should not be taken "*too seriously*" encourages skepticism and distance in both practice and scholarship. In an attempt to adapt such a stance, in this essay I will argue that student engagement as a heuristic is particularly problematic on issues of both student identity (who?) and activity (doing what?). These two aspects of engagement can be vexing for both practitioners and scholars because taken together they seem to imply that, in the words of Coates (2005), "*individual learners are ultimately the agents of discussions of engagement*" (p.26). Framing students in this way, however, falsely implies that students are completely autonomous actors within higher education, as Matthews explains (2016). That misses the significance of human relationships in the learning and lives of students. To better understand and act upon the complexity of engagement, scholars and practitioners should focus their attention on the qualities of relationships – both student–faculty/staff and also student peer–peer relationships – that profoundly shape student experiences in and outcomes from higher education.

Two problems with student engagement

Two persistent and significant tensions exist at the heart of both research and practice related to student engagement.

1. Who is being engaged?

Student engagement as a construct assumes generic students, obscuring or perhaps ignoring how student identities influence learning and experiences. Student engagement research often washes away variability among students, concluding that certain practices will be high impact for all. That might appear to be true in large data sets, but the lived experiences of many in higher education suggest that student identities play a significant role in shaping learning. Writing a decade ago, Bryson and Hand critiqued the engagement literature for the implicit assumption that students were "*a member of a stereotyped, homogenous mass*" (2007, p.13). Echoing this, Zepke (2014), drawing on an article by Thomas about student retention (2002), reminded researchers "*to keep in mind more the impact of [student] ethnicity, age, gender, socio-economic status, lifestyle and beliefs on engagement*" (p.704).

Taking this general critique one significant step further, Patton, Harper, and Harris (2015) used Critical Race Theory to underscore what they describe as the *"racelessness"* of most student engagement research in the United States. They demonstrate how racial identities in the U.S. can substantially yet variably influence student engagement. In a predominantly White residence hall, for instance, experiences within a living-learning community might positively enhance engagement and belonging for some students but leave others feeling isolated and alienated. Being labeled with a racial slur also *"is undoubtedly a high-impact experience,"* as are the *"peer pedagogies"* employed as students of colour teach *"other students of color about the realities of race on campus and the skills necessary to survive racist institutional settings"* (Patton, Harper, and Harris, 2015, pp.209–210).

Critical Race Theory not only focuses attention on a central factor in student identity that is often missing from student engagement discourse, it also emphasizes the necessity of recognizing the capacities all students bring with them to higher education. Rather than concentrating on deficits of students from certain identity categories (O'Shea, Lysaght, Roberts, and Harwood, 2016), Critical Race Theory demonstrates the importance of employing a lens of *"cultural wealth"* that foregrounds the *"array of knowledge, skills, abilities, and contacts"* all students possess (Yasso 2005, p.77). For instance, Harper (2009) illustrates what U.S. institutions might learn about student engagement if they studied high achieving Black male students, rather than tacitly viewing all Black men through the lens of academic deficits. Student identities are too substantial a factor in engagement to be left out of the equation or to be understood from a single perspective.

2. What are they doing when they are (not) engaged?

Engagement research and practices are general, but student experiences with engagement are particular. Large-scale quantitative analysis is the foundation of student engagement research. Using huge data sets, Kuh (2008) defined a set of *"High-Impact Educational Practices"* (HIPs) that are most likely to produce positive outcomes for undergraduates in the United States. The HIPs range from first-year seminars and writing-intensive courses to internships and field experiences. Digging into the research on these practices, however, reveals that not everything in the category of a HIP yields significant learning for all students. In a longitudinal study of students at multiple U.S. institutions, Cuba and colleagues concluded that student engagement is *"particularistic"* and *"linked to specific classes, assignments, professors, pedagogies, subjects, and methodologies"* (2016, p.144). No single general practice was high impact for all of the students in this study.

Similarly, Trowler and Trowler concluded in their literature review that engagement research is so *"general and non-specific"* that *"what works in one place may not work, and may even be counter-productive, in another"* (2010, p.6, 7). That conclusion has been repeatedly demonstrated in U.S. research. For instance, Finley and McNair (2013) show that simply labeling something a "*learning community*" (or any other High-Impact Practice) does not ensure the desired outcomes. Instead, the quality of the experience matters immensely. Scholars have developed several frameworks for defining a high-quality HIP (e.g., Kuh and O'Donnell 2013; Kuh, O'Donnell, and Schroeder 2017), but the variation and generality of these lists suggests that the quality of the experience structured by the institution alone is not enough to ensure deep learning for all students. Put another way, quality is necessary but not sufficient for a high-impact practice. Student experiences and outcomes are too variable to confidently assert that certain practices are high impact for all.

Relationships at the heart of student engagement

Student identity and activity matter too much for students to be treated generically in the engagement equation. The amount and quality of time and effort a student devotes can transform a mundane activity into a high-impact one, or turn a research-based high-impact practice into a dud. At the same time, aspects of a student's identity and background also can profoundly influence whether a specific experience is or is not deeply meaningful.

Recognizing this complexity at the core of conceptualization of student engagement, what are scholars and practitioners to do? I suggest that we need to concentrate our attention on human relationships in student engagement.

Matthews (2016) has made the persuasive case for "*more collaborative forms of engagement between students and academics*" and calls for viewing engagement through the lens of students as partners (p.2). The emerging literature on students as partners can and should inform engagement scholars and practice by offering new or reframed theory and constructs (Matthews, Cook-Sather, Acai, Dvorakova, Felten, Marquis and Mercer-Mapstone, 2019), practices (Cook-Sather, Bovill, and Felten 2014), and evidence of outcomes (Mercer-Mapstone, Dvorakova, Matthews, Abbot, Cheng, Felten, Knorr, Marquis, Shammas, and Swaim, 2017).

Yet 'students as partners' is too narrow a frame to fully capture the complexity of relationships in student engagement because it centers on student–faculty/staff interactions. Those are highly significant (Kim and Sax 2017), but decades of research demonstrate student peer–peer relationships are the foundation of student learning, belonging, and achievement in higher education (e.g., Astin 1977; Tinto, 1987; Mayhew, Rochenback, Bowman, Seifert and Wolniak, 2016). Peer relationships must be central to the study and practice of student engagement.

Critically attending to relationships, particularly peer-to-peer ones, will require many student engagement practitioners and scholars to shift their attention from the micro (individual student) and the macro (institutional practice) to focus more directly on the meso – the interactions among students, faculty, staff, and others. In practice, this could mean building on the pioneering work of scholars including the mathematician Uri Treisman (1992) who explored the variation of outcomes of different student groups in his courses and discovered that successful students, regardless of their identities, engaged in study practices *"emphasizing group learning and a community life focused on a shared interest in mathematics"* (p.368). Indeed, nearly all of the active learning pedagogies that have been proven to be effective with a wide array of students, particularly in STEM, are rooted in purposeful peer–peer interactions (Freeman, Eddy, McDonough, Smith, Okoroafor, Jordt, and Wedneroth, 2014).

Relationships are at the very heart of student engagement. As scholars and practitioners, we should focus our attention on the ways that these interactions enable or constrain learning. Doing this will significantly address the challenges of identity and particularity that vex current scholarship and practice on student engagement.

References

Astin, A., 1977. *Four critical years: effects of college on beliefs, attitudes, and knowledge*, San Francisco, CA: Jossey-Bass.

Astin, A., 1984. Student involvement: a developmental theory for higher education, *Journal of College Student Personnel*, vol. 25, pp.297–308.

Bryson, C. and Hand, L., 2007. The role of engagement in inspiring teaching and learning, *Innovations in Education and Teaching International*, vol. 44, no. 4, pp.349–362. Retrieved from: https://doi.org/10.1080/14703290701602748

Coates, H., 2005. The value of student engagement in higher education quality assurance, *Quality in Higher Education*, vol. 11, no. 1, pp.25–36. Retrieved from: https://doi.org/10.1080/13538320500074915

Cook-Sather, A., Bovill, C. and Felten, P., 2014. *Engaging students as partners in learning and teaching: a guide for faculty*, San Francisco, CA: Jossey-Bass.

Cuba, L., Jennings, N., Lovett, S. and Swingle, J., 2016. *Practice for life: making decisions in college*, Cambridge, MA: Harvard University Press.

Felten, P., Gardner, J., Schroeder, C., Lambert, L. and Barefoot, B., 2016. *The undergraduate experience: focusing institution on what matters most*, San Francisco, CA: Jossey-Bass.

Finley, A. and McNair, T., 2013. *Assessing underserved students' engagement in high-impact practices*, Washington: Association for American Colleges and Universities.

Freeman, S., Eddy, S., McDonough, M., Smith, M., Okoroafor, N., Jordt, H. and Wedneroth, M., 2014. Active learning increases student performance in science, engineering, and mathematics, *PNAS*, vol. 111, no. 23, pp.8410–8415. DOI:10.1073/pnas.1319030111

Harper, S., 2009. Institutional seriousness concerning black male student engagement: necessary conditions and collaborative partnerships, in S Harper and S Quaye (eds.), *Student engagement in higher education: Theoretical perspectives and practical approaches for diverse populations*, pp.137–156. New York: Routledge.

Kahu, E., 2013. Framing student engagement in higher education, *Studies in Higher Education*, vol. 38, no. 5, pp.758–773.

Kim, Y. and Sax, L., 2017. The impact of college students' interactions with faculty: a review of general and conditional effects, in MB Paulsen (ed.), *Higher education: handbook of theory and research*, vol. 32. Switzerland: Springer International.

Kuh, G., 2008. *High-impact educational practices: what they are, who has access to them, and why they matter*. Washington, WA: Association of American Colleges and Universities.

Kuh, G., Kinzie, J., Schuh, J., Whitt, E. and Associates, 2010. *Student success in college: creating conditions that matter*. San Francisco, CA: Jossey-Bass.

Kuh, G. and O'Donnell, K. (eds.) 2013. *Ensuring quality and taking high-impact practices to scale*. Washington, WA: Association of American Colleges and Universities.

Kuh, G., O'Donnell, K. and Schneider, C., 2017. HIPs at ten, *Change*, vol. 49, no. 5, pp.8–16. Retrieved from: https://doi.org/10.1080/00091383.2017.1366805

Matthews, K., 2016. Students as partners as the future of student engagement, *Student Engagement in Higher Education Journal*, vol. 1, no. 1, pp.1–5. Retrieved from: https://espace.library.uq.edu.au/view/UQ:404147/UQ404147_OA.pdf

Matthews, K., Cook-Sather, A., Acai, A., Dvorakova, S., Felten, P., Marquis, E. and Mercer-Mapstone, L., 2019. Toward theories of partnership praxis: an analysis of interpretative framing in literature on students as partners in teaching and learning, *Higher Education Research and Development*, vol. 38, no. 2, pp.280–293. Retrieved from: https://doi.org/10.1080/07294360.2018.1530199

Mayhew, M., Rochenback, A., Bowman, N., Seifert, T. and Wolniak, G., 2016. *How college affects students, volume 3: 21st century evidence that higher education works*, San Francisco, CA: Jossey-Bass.

Mercer-Mapstone, L., Dvorakova, L., Matthews, K., Abbot, S., Cheng, B., Felten, P., Knorr, K., Marquis, E., Shammas, R. and Swaim, K., 2017. A systematic literature review of students as partners in higher education, *International Journal for Students as Partners*, vol. 1, no. 1, pp.1–23. Retrieved from: https://doi.org/10.15173/ijsap.v1i1.3119

O'Shea, S., Lysaght, P., Roberts, J., and Harwood, V., 2016. Shifting the blame in higher education – social inclusion and deficit discourses, *Higher Education Research and Development*, vol. 35, no. 2, pp.322–336. Retrieved from: http://dx.doi.org/10.1080/07294360.2015.1087388

Patton, L., Harper, S., and Harris, J., 2015. Using critical race theory to (re)interpret widely studied topics related to students in us higher education, in A Martinez-Aleman, B Pusser and E Bensimon (eds.), *Critical approaches to the study of higher education: a practical introduction*, pp.193–219. Baltimore, MD: Johns Hopkins University Press.

Shulman, L., 2002. Making differences: a table of learning, *Change*, vol. 34, no. 6, pp.36–44. Retrieved from: https://doi.org/10.1080/00091380209605567

Thomas, L., 2002. Student retention in higher education: The role of institutional habitus, *Journal of Educational Policy*, vol. 17, no. 4, pp.423–442. Retrieved from: https://doi.org/10.1080/02680930210140257

Tinto, V., 1987. *Leaving college: rethinking the causes and cures of student attrition*, Chicago, IL: University of Chicago Press.

Treisman, U., 1992. Studying students studying calculus: a look at the lives of minority mathematics students in college, *College Mathematics Journal*, vol. 23, no. 5, pp.362–372. Retrieved from: https://doi.org/10.2307/2686410

Trowler, V. and Trowler, P., 2010. *Student engagement evidence summary*, York: Higher Education Academy.

Wolf-Wendel, L., Ward, K. and Kinzie, J., 2009. A tangled web of terms: The overlap and unique contribution of involvement, engagement, and integration to understanding college student success, *Journal of College Student Development*, vol. 50, no. 4, pp.407–428. Retrieved from: https://pdfs.semanticscholar.org/4fb5/e983e9abcbb1e930bb87facc9c43c06872ca.pdf

Yasso, T., 2005. Whose culture has capital?, *Race, Ethnicity, and Education*, vol. 8, no. 1, pp.69–91. Retrieved from: https://doi.org/10.1080/1361332052000341006

Zepke, N., 2014. Student engagement research in higher education: questioning an academic orthodoxy. *Teaching in Higher Education*, vol. 19, no. 6, pp.697–708. Retrieved from: https://doi.org/10.1080/13562517.2014.901956

Part III

Models of student engagement in practice

Chapter 12

Trust me, working alone is challenging

What are the benefits of working in partnership in higher education?

Kiu Sum

'Merging' students and staff for collaborative work has been a revolution in recent years – more specifically, since the work conducted by Colin Bryson with the RAISE network (Bryson, 2014), Healey et al.'s principles of partnership (Healey, Flint and Harrington, 2014), and many higher education institutions' (HEIs) having followed the partnership practice lead from institutions like Bryn Mawr College (USA), Birmingham City University (UK) and the University of Winchester (UK) (Cook-Sather, 2018; Freeman, Millard, Brand and Chapman, 2014; Lowe, Shaw, Sims, King and Paddison, 2017). Since then, the concept of 'student–staff partnership' has developed, modernised and revolutionised the delivery of learning and teaching. One can only imagine the thoughts running through the minds of staff when it first began! Such questions as *"Will students know what they are doing?"* or *"Will students mess up everything that I have planned and worked for all these years?"* were voiced openly in consultations concerning student engagement in quality assurance in 2007 and, no doubt, something similar accompanied learning and teaching developments (Owen, 2013, p.164). It must have been a daunting thought for staff (the more so for teaching academics) to hand over the reins to students for the leading of sessions or projects. A strong foundation of student–staff partnership, trust and faith has since been more commonly accepted, with the role of students now more prominent than it traditionally was. No longer are they just 'learners'; rather, they are the next generation of educators, in so many ways, for the future. They are the ones who will change and shape learning and teaching in higher education (HE). They may be termed 'Students as Co-creators' (Sum, 2018), 'Students as Partners' (Matthews, 2016), 'Student Changemakers' (Marie, Arif, and Joshi, 2016) and other similar titles, as their roles are developed by various learning and teaching groups across HEIs. The key message is that students can be so much more than passive learners, taking an engaged, shared and creative role in transforming education in the HE sector. Students may also simultaneously be employees, commuters, carers, parents and many other things. Society is fast evolving and so are our perceptions of students' roles in our communities. The question is, how do *you* view students' roles?

There has traditionally been a clear understanding that HE staff do – and want to do – things in their own ways when it comes to developing learning and teaching, relying on the knowledge of prior experience to judge what may or may not work. However, now that the numbers of students for whom they are responsible have been growing, year on year, in tandem with frequent rapid changes in the curriculum, they are struggling to maintain a satisfactory work-life balance and need to prioritise their health and wellbeing in order to minimise occupational stress. Staff are more than just staff: they are the gatekeepers to students' education; they shape students' memories in education and work hard where possible to achieve social impact via research and knowledge-exchange. With the increasing demands made upon them by contemporary education – such as more pastoral care, reporting and striving for 'excellence' – it is easy to understand that they might find it challenging to keep themselves up to date with the latest research into pedagogy. There is, therefore, an imperative to support the teaching and non-teaching staff in all institutions, for they are instrumental in generating from amongst our students the next set of leaders.

Students entering the HE phase of their careers also have expectations (though some, unfortunately, don't) of what they want to experience and achieve during the short three or four years of their undergraduate journey. Their moment of fulfilment on the graduation stage, however, comes at great personal, psychological and financial cost. Though they have shaken the hand of an eminent dignitary and celebrated with family and friends, their academic success may well be overshadowed by the harsh reality of trying to progress to their dream career in a crowded and competitive job market, where they often lack the necessary social capital – the power, knowledge, support and resources – to make their way. However, their engagement with student–staff partnership activities can (and does) equip them with skills remarkably relevant and helpful to their future careers when their subject degree alone cannot. There is well-documented evidence of the mutual benefits for students and staff of such partnerships and student engagement globally is certainly rapidly developing (Mercer-Mapstone, 2019; Cook-Sather, Bovill, and Felten, 2014).

Previously, there was a considerable imbalance in the roles of students and staff at university, with decision-making firmly in the hands of the latter, who 'knew best'. Now, however, since the revolution in student engagement partnerships (NUS, 2012), students are more heavily involved in championing student voice and influencing learning and teaching in the HE sector.

Student–staff partnerships in HE, whether they co-design a programme or co-research an aspect of students' experiences, are recognised to be tremendously beneficial for the institutions and their entire communities. Consequently, HE is seeing a shift in pedagogic research, involving students as partners and changes in the language related to learning and teaching development (Gravett, Kinchin and Winstone, 2019). The question I would therefore like to address in this chapter is: "*Why are student–staff partnerships better than academics doing it on their own?*" Using existing examples and personal reflections, this chapter will explore the benefits of working in partnership in HE.

"Every block of stone has a statue inside it, and it is the task of the sculptor to discover it" – or so Michelangelo is alleged to have said. During my long and bumpy educational journey, I reflected on what Michelangelo said. I, for sure, am no Michelangelo, but I could see its validity and its relevance to student engagement. If we to ask university staff to chisel their ideal student out of stone, representing the attitudes and attributes they perceive as perfect, and likewise ask students to make a sculpture of their ideal, flawless member of staff, a comparison of the two works might well have some similarities, but we might also be shocked by the contrasts. However, in the context of student–staff engagement, with its much-enhanced communication and mutual knowledge, understanding, respect and support, perhaps the perception gap would be much narrower and the statues much more alike. Shared knowledge and goals – with student understanding staff perspectives, institutional pressures and practical constraints and staff awareness/ recognition of students' personal experience, individual challenges/ needs and potential for making significant contributions to joint activities – are much more likely to bring intentions to fruition, maximising the impact of anticipated educational change.

I am sure that this will resonate somewhat with everyone and sometimes, I find, working alone can be quite challenging. Yes, I completely understand that to work on your own is, to a certain extent, good for independent learning, problem-solving, resilience, self-motivation and so on. However, working alone day in, day out (sometimes for days on end) and not speaking to or bumping into other people at all, only nodding your head to the security guards when entering or leaving the building – that's definitely isolating for some students. Furthermore, this isolation is hardly helpful to building those lifelong skills that are vital to survival and success in today's society: being socially aware, functioning as part of a team and communicating well with others in a cooperative community. And that is where 'student–staff partnership' fits in – it is not merely a phase or a fashionable trend of the moment, but something with a much more long-lasting positive impact on university experiences, as we may find in the literature (Lowe et al., 2017; Marquis et al., 2016; Marie et al., 2016).

Take RAISE and Jisc for example. These are organisations that place 'student engagement' at the heart of what they do: championing student voice, 'student as partners' and 'students as collaborators'. Drawing on the seminal work of Healey, Flint, and Harrington (2014) in creating principles for the student–staff partnership to follow, committed practitioners have established shared partnership as a process for engagement. It is, however, so much more than just engaging with all the different types of stakeholders. There are many benefits to working in partnership, whether with other students or with members of staff. Partnership is fundamentally a relationship of learning and growing collaboratively in HE, enhancing everyone's university experiences. Through Jisc, various projects have been introduced by the 'Change Agents' Network' (CAN), uniting various projects from different HE institutions and using students effectively to help develop the term 'students as partners' (Jisc, 2019). As such, CAN has grown from strength to strength and this has been evident in the increasing number of actions springing from conversations following the annual CAN conference. I, myself, have had the opportunity to attend and present at the CAN conference, from which I have been able to grow and develop my skills in my pedagogical research. It was through these involvement opportunities with Jisc and RAISE that I was able to see through a different lens and identify what has become a passion: realising the much-needed support that helps to develop student engagement in HE.

Developing successful student–staff partnerships is not merely about bringing students and staff together to work on projects; the process embodies the fundamental inter-relationship of everyone involved in the HE journey – students, teaching and non-teaching staff, professional service staff and many others. It is for everyone to co-create together, learning by this means to engage, share and learn best practice that can be transferred to and applied in different subjects and settings. My own student–staff partnership adventures were exciting, yet I was nervous, not knowing how to approach those with whom I wasn't in daily interaction. Communicating with the wider student population and expecting replies was a challenge in itself, but communicating with members of staff whom I had never met and being aware of their high status within the university was another matter! Believe me, it was a challenge at first, but over time, you realise that they too are humans. The knowledge you gain of the university community outside your own department and seeing through various lenses how the university functions at various levels just highlights how diverse and multi-cultural the activities are. You see the different departments that make a university; you see the personalities and individual characteristics from within the university community that make it like a family; you see the people behind the phone calls and email communications that make a university experience real. The message is simple: no individuals, whether students or staff, are the same. They are not clones of each other, but unique people who each bring something different and exciting to today's HE learning and teaching. And it is the small step of signing up to student–staff partnerships that create a new beginning of change for all.

Whether you are a student or a member of staff, there is encouragement to take up continuing professional development (CPD) wherever possible. It may be hard as a fresher to imagine how doing 'extra CPD' as a student can be beneficial, for you are trying desperately to understand the educational system you face, especially during the information overload that is induction week. But, believe you me, a few years at university pass with the blink of an eye. You turn up, swiping in on day one and the next moment, it seems, you realise that you are swiping in to take your end-of-year exams, having been immersed in long days and late nights of revision or writing up those assessments. As a student, one might ask the question: "*Why should I do CPD now and not wait until I have graduated?*" I once asked that very same question, yet it is at university where your eyes are opened to the many opportunities there are. It is a time for exploring your abilities and skills; a time when you learn and can afford to make silly mistakes and to learn from those, knowing your academics are always there supporting you when you feel down; a time when you discover your career aspirations; and a time to be motivated and inspired to plan what you want to do after university. For members of staff, doing CPD has likewise great benefits to their development and university experiences. As mentioned, they are the developers of the next generation of thinkers and professionals, inspiring and motivating students to do their best, having themselves been through the same challenges previously. CPD is a great mechanism for staff to shape their learning and teaching in HE; to meet the demanding expectations of 21st-century society. They bring to life traditional theories and their applications via novel and interactive sessions; they seek to understand individual student needs; they mould students and equip them with the latest high standards of skills and attributes, encouraging and supporting them to stand out from the crowd. They are more than just educators or teachers: they inspire students to achieve their potential through those staff–student interactions that help both parties to understand each other and how their roles can influence and benefit each other. Similarly, working in student–staff partnerships is exactly that: it is an innovative and alternative means of CPD, enhancing university experience and student–staff engagement.

Pedagogy is shifting – it is becoming the norm to include students in learning and teaching development discussions, projects and enhancements. I have reflected on and drawn attention in this chapter to some of the features of this change: teamwork, understanding individuals as people and CPD. I have highlighted some of the benefits of student–staff partnerships, which continue to have a significant positive influence on university experiences. Partnership is a broad topic, with aspects deserving of further discussion; it certainly is a potent means of tackling the current challenges faced by HE. It's worth bearing in mind that we, as unique individuals, have something to contribute, no matter how small – and even if we're not totally sure what it is. I'm put in mind of the words of Galician poet and writer Rosalia De Castro: "I see my path, but I don't know where it leads. Not knowing where I'm going is what inspires me to travel it."

This chapter has briefly discussed the benefits of student–staff partnership to the initial question "*Why are staff–student partnerships better than academics doing it on their own?*" Working alone is challenging, yet HE has progressed from having no partnerships at all to the position of having integrated and embedded partnership practice; collaborations between staff and students have transformed the way we previously perceived HE learning and teaching pedagogy. The chapter has also identified the benefits of student–staff partnerships, including students' gaining a different perspective of the university experience and simultaneously developing their personal and professional skills. Conversely, staff may not have embraced partnership so quickly, as they have not found it easy to relinquish their previous autonomy within development actions. Those who have more quickly understood partnership's advantages have realised that collaborating with students does give them a unique insight into the student experience and, therefore, enriches their own university experience and their project undertakings. As fresh cohorts of enthusiastic students try to identify their own unique life experiences and educational journeys, HEIs cannot cling to traditional educational strategies. Learning and teaching approaches evolve over time, steadily advancing and meeting the needs and requirements of individuals. Ultimately, it is the students who will benefit from positive change and so incorporating them from the beginning into the developmental processes would be ideal, introducing them to a partnership community with a new ethos and ways of working. Such a student-centric approach, placing learners at the heart of their own educational development, will enable them to see and understand the purpose of their programmes, to which they contribute. We are now seeing more staff and students becoming more engaged in partnership and helping to champion shared activities, providing students with growth in confidence, a sense of belonging and a voice that matters to the educational community.

Having been a student partner myself, I have been aware that many who step into HE institutions are initially surprised by such partnerships, but soon recognise that they represent a unified culture with a very positive and constructive ethos. Indeed, the way we perceive ourselves changes for the better. We, like Michelangelo, need to discover our potential individual identity within the HE monolith and carve it out, so that we may create new legacies for future student generations.

References

Bryson, C., 2014. Clarifying the concept of student engagement. In: Bryson, C. (ed.) *Understanding and developing student engagement* (pp.21–42). Routledge: London.

Cook-Sather, A., 2018. Listening to equity-seeking perspectives: how students' experiences of pedagogical partnership can inform wider discussions of student success. *Higher Education Research and Development*, 37(5), pp.923–936. Retrieved from: https://doi.org/10.1080/07294360.2018.1457629

Cook-Sather, A., Bovill, C., and Felten, P., 2014. *Engaging students as partners in learning and teaching: A guide for faculty*. San Francisco, CA: Jossey-Bass.

Freeman, R., Millard, L., Brand, S. and Chapman, P., 2014. Student academic partners: student employment for collaborative learning and teaching development. *Innovations in Education and Teaching International*, 51(3), pp.233–243. Retrieved from: https://doi.org/10.1080/14703297.2013.778064

Gravett, K., Kinchin, I.M. and Winstone, N.E., 2019. 'More than customers': conceptions of students as partners held by students, staff, and institutional leaders. *Studies in Higher Education*, pp.1–14. Retrieved from: https://doi.org/10.1080/03075079.2019.1623769

Healey, M., Flint, A. and Harrington, K., 2014. *Engagement through partnership: students as partners in learning and teaching in higher education*. York: HEA.

Jisc, 2019. The Change Agents' Network: A network of staff and students working in partnership to support curriculum enhancement and innovation. Retrieved from: https://can.jiscinvolve.org/wp/ (accessed 28 July 2019).

Lowe, T., Shaw, C., Sims, S., King, S. and Paddison, A., 2017. The development of contemporary student engagement practices at the University of Winchester and Winchester Student Union, UK. *International Journal for Students as Partners*, 1(1). Retrieved from: https://doi.org/10.15173/ijsap.v1i1.3082

Marie, J., Arif, M. and Joshi, T., 2016. UCL ChangeMakers projects: Supporting staff/student partnership on educational enhancement projects. *Student Engagement in Higher Education Journal*, 1(1).

Marquis, E., Puri, V., Wan, S., Ahmad, A., Goff, L., Knorr, K., Vassileva, I. and Woo, J., 2016. Navigating the threshold of student–staff partnerships: A case study from an Ontario teaching and learning institute. *International Journal for Academic Development*, 21(1), pp.4–15. Retrieved from: https://doi.org/10.1080/1360144x.2015.1113538

Matthews, K., 2016. Students as partners as the future of student engagement. *Student Engagement in Higher Education Journal*, 1(1).

Mercer-Mapstone, L., 2019. The student–staff partnership movement: striving for inclusion as we push sectorial change. *International Journal for Academic Development*, pp.1–13. Retrieved from: https://doi.org/10.1080/1360144x.2019.1631171

National Union of Students (NUS) (2012) *A manifesto for partnership*, p.8. Retrieved from: www.nusconnect.org.uk/resources/a-manifesto-for-partnership/ (accessed 28 July 2019).

Owen, D., 2013. Students Engaged in Academic Subject Review. In Dunne, E. and Owen, D. (eds.), 2013. *Student Engagement Handbook: Practice in Higher Education*. Bingley: Emerald Group Publishing.

Sum, K., 2018. Growing as a seed. *Student Engagement in Higher Education Journal*, 2 (1) pp.7–11.

Chapter 13

The amplification of student voices via institutional research and evaluation

Liz Austen

Introduction

This chapter focuses on the evidence base which is collected in the name of student voice (often referenced in the singular rather than the plural), with the intention of supporting the transformation of the student learning experience. This exploration looks at how student voices are heard (or not heard) within institutions in the United Kingdom (UK) focusing on the methodologies adopted for research and evaluation with, for, or about students in higher education. This chapter presents a *Typology of Institutional Research and Evaluation* which claim to amplify student voices, outlining a conceptual overview of practices within the UK sector. This synopsis provides a tool for academic leaders and educational developers to map and interrogate the scope of this activity within their own institutions to ensure that activity is designed and implemented from a critical standpoint.

Conceptualising student voice

Student engagement and student voice, as prevalent terms in higher education discourse, are symbiotic concepts. Student engagement (as participation) in institutional voice-giving opportunities can enable student voices to be amplified, listened to and acted upon. Voice-giving, if valued, can create a sense of institutional ownership which may then have benefits for engagement in learning. The activity of students who formally act as representatives of 'the student voice' or those who sporadically provide feedback on their experiences has also been labelled as a process of student engagement (Bryson 2016). At the heart of both these terms is the student as an active participant, but that "*student voice takes engagement beyond the realms of students' own individual learning and into larger conversations about and revisions of educational practice*" (Cook-Sather cited in Dunne and Owen 2013, p.552).

The emergence of 'student voice' as a term within education appeared from the late 1990s–mid 2000s from within the sphere of school- and college-based enhancement.[1] At the outset, student voice was intrinsically ethical and moral and aimed to allow students to democratically participate in institutional processes following a rights-based approach (Cook-Sather 2014; Groundwater-Smith and

Mockler 2016). Higher education has been somewhat adrift of this momentum with a recent focus on the mechanical rather than the ethical (McLeod 2011). Reflecting on the development of policy and practice over the last 20 years, Hall (2017, pp.82–183) concludes:

> *In a sense, the 'student voice' has become a noun—reified into a 'thing' that can be measured and benchmarked, and evidenced through a range of prescribed 'mechanisms'* (Kotsifli and Green, 2010)*... If we remain with our current system, there is potential for student voice to remain actively passive in that this reified 'voice' speaks, but only within pre-defined and legitimised contexts and formats which essentially 'co-opt' these contributions towards managerial/ quality assurance requirements.*
>
> (Roberts and Nash, 2009)

Sabri (2011) makes a similar point, widening the context to ephemeral terms such as 'student choice', 'student voice', 'student experience' and 'student engagement' which all use 'student; as an homogenising *"adjectival noun"* (Sabri, 2011, p.660) which fails to represent the way in which students' experiences are intertwined with their working partnerships with their tutors, other students and other members of the university community. Descriptions of student voice have now become synonymous with notions/systems of representation either sector wide or within institutions (Searle, 2010). The growth of research and evaluation, through external research networks and project funding, and a 'what works' approach to exploring issues in student engagement (Thomas, 2017) have latterly shifted student voice from a process to a measure, ensuring that *strategic* effects and *participatory* impacts are gathered, but less attention is paid to voice as a *right* and as an opportunity to listen *equitably*.[2] This chapter seeks to outline the role that institutional research and evaluation plays in the current conceptualisation and application of student voices.

Institutional research and evaluation (IRE)

Institutional research is defined as *"a broad set of activities that collect, transform, analyse, and use data to generate evidence to support institutional planning, policy formation, quality enhancement, and decision making"* (Woodfield, 2015, p.89). Institutional research (accompanied by evaluation) in the UK higher education sector is supported by a network of institutional practitioners,[3] but is much less well defined within institutions. Institutional researchers in this context are often self-defined, are unlikely to have this phrase in their job title and have a variety of professional and academic backgrounds. In recent years, those working as institutional researchers in the UK (in name or in activity) have seen an increasing demand for projects which amplify student voices for strategic decision making. Whilst institutional enhancement and improvement in student experiences is an obvious aim, another is an increased league table position (through increases in

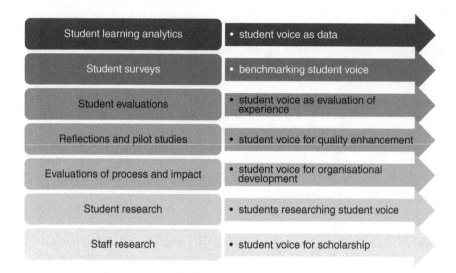

Figure 13.1 Institutional research and evaluation typology: overview

student satisfaction, continuation and attainment) and subsequent market share. Institutional researchers are often tight-roping precariously across both, balancing moral and ethical research principles in an increasingly neoliberal climate.

Austen (2018) recently identified a Typology of Institutional[4] Research and Evaluation (Figure 13.1) which was applied to students as samples/participants or as researchers/analysts/co-producers. This Typology provides an overview of the UK higher education environment in which student voice research and evaluation, used strategically to enhance student experiences, now takes place. It considers "*different types of data, different methods of data collection, and different ethical responsibilities placed on institutional researchers*" (Austen, 2018). This moves beyond Trowler's (2018) categorisation of the elicitation of student voice into "professional (formative)" and "performative (summative)" collations, although her distinction between voice which is sought (the focus of this chapter) and voice which is offered does provide useful clarity. This chapter will discuss each area of the Typology in turn outlining the methodologies employed, the data collected and the ethical governance within each category, before exploring how this data can be used to transform student experiences.

Outlining a typology of student voice research and evaluation

1. Student voice as data

The first category which is relevant to this discussion contains quantitative student data records and learning/learner analytics, sometimes referred to as institutional data. Here, student voices are assumed through the analysis of proxy measures – lifecycle data records of attainment, progression and success, alongside micro level learning habits, activities and outputs such as Virtual Learning Environment (VLE) use, attendance monitoring and library activity. Whilst institutions may claim to know and understand their students from their data profile, this category explicitly *lacks student voices* and reinforces the mechanical/managerial definitions outlined by Searle (2010), McLeod (2011), Sabri (2011) and Hall (2017). The passive generation of big data falls foul to notions of active engagement in voice-amplification and voice-listening/voice-hearing. Methodologically, this data is electronically generated via the monitoring of student activity (rather than self-reported), which students agree to at enrolment. Without data triangulation across a range of methodologies (not just across the range of analytics), there is a risk of confirmation bias on the part of the programmer and the analyst; assumptions about the ideal student (Wong and Chiu 2018) may be pervasive.

However, this cross-sectional data can be easily anonymised for aggregated discussions of module or course performance and can be effectively used longitudinally. Once the data is available for analysis through a dashboard, timely decisions can be made which could impact on a student's current learning experience (rather than an incoming cohort). It does not suffer from the same challenges as self-reported data, and as such, holds some sovereignty within the sector, not least for evidencing impact and progress towards quantitative Key Performance Indicators (KPIs). The dominance of record-based data sets in an educational data hierarchy may, therefore, be difficult to confidently challenge with alternative and contrasting forms of evidence. This data privilege is intensified as it is used as a means of sector differentiation via measures of excellence.

2. Benchmarking student voice

The second category focuses on macro level, self-reported cohort surveys of student experiences administered by an institution, institutional partners (Students' Unions/Associations) and by/on behalf of sector agencies to identify 'single point in time' student voices. These surveys require significant student engagement to obtain data which is representative of the institutional student population. The best-known and most influential survey in the UK is the National Student Survey (NSS), which has been running since 2005 and now contributes to Teaching Excellence Framework appraisals (managed by the UK higher education regulatory body, the Office for Students). Student experience (as a collective noun) is measured by a Likert scale of student satisfaction which in turn is used as a measure of institutional teaching quality. Survey proxies allow for benchmarking across the sector (with positive and negative flags) to enable informed student choice, and within the institution (colour coded with red and green flags) as an identification of need and support. Whilst the NSS is the largest active collection of quantitative and qualitative student voices in the UK, the methodological limitations are well known and include the lack of nuanced questioning to enable enhancement (Buckley, 2012) and the lack of construct validity as a dimension of teaching quality (Gibbs, 2010). Qualitative student comments are often quantified through content analysis and are used to support and contextualise quantitative benchmarks in predetermined themes, rather than analysed inductively. Furthermore, very little attention is given to exploring the extent to which students do not engage with institutional surveys, and who might find that their voices are left unheard by this method.

Institutional researchers are often tasked with administering and analysing sector-led surveys (NSS and other UK surveys such as the UK Engagement Survey, Postgraduate Taught/Research Experience Survey) and designing, administering and analysing institutional surveys. Specific areas of an institution may also run bespoke surveys such as a 'Welcome Survey' or 'Career Readiness Survey', sometimes without awareness of the range of alternative methodological options. The student survey has become the default data-gathering approach within higher education and does lead to action. However, institutional survey response rates are suffering, and more aggressive strategies are being employed as a result of overuse. In spite of this, institutional surveys are now also being explored as an approach to measuring self-reported learning gain, championed by exploratory projects funded by the Office for Students (Kandiko Howson, 2018). The scale of survey capture of student voices (not least, in addition to all other approaches) requires strategic oversight to ensure that ethically and methodologically this approach retains utility for evidence-informed decision-making to enhance student experiences.

3. Student voice as evaluation of experience

The third category remains focused on maintaining and enhancing internal standards, specifically cross-sectional, meso-level evaluations of local experiences. This would include mid and end point module evaluation questionnaires, 'stop start continue' feedback (see Hoon, Oliver, Szpakowska, and Newton, 2015 for a discussion of the value of this method), structured evaluations of teaching performance, student input into quality assurance processes (quality audits and periodic reviews) and student commentary within Student–Staff Committees/ Student Representation Systems (known as Student Voice Mechanisms). This category could also include student-nominated teaching award data sets gathered via qualitative survey responses. These approaches are methodologically varied; these evaluations attempt full cohort samples *and* convenience samples and can include midpoint strategies for enabling change which will impact on those students who have completed the evaluation. Student voices are often more authentic as they are collated by known individuals and depend on a level of trust that the messages will be heard and then acted on. The design and delivery of these evaluations can be institutionally led ('one size fits all') or locally adapted and contextual.

Whilst these approaches are labelled as 'evaluation of experience', they are not commonly designed using the methodological principles of process or impact

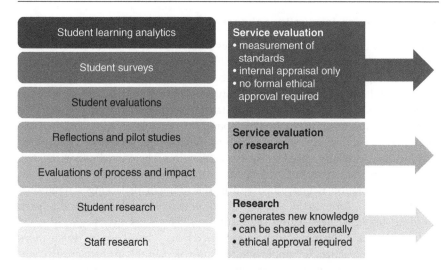

Figure 13.2 Institutional research and evaluation typology: ethical scrutiny

evaluation (see Parsons, 2017). Nor are they discussed as research. These examples are more commonly discussed as 'student feedback'. Any resulting change is then described as 'closing the feedback loop', which has, in itself, become a strategic aim. Without integrated practices and contextual methodological discussions, there is a risk that these evaluations become transactional – or worse, adversarial and ethically compromised.

Figure 13.2 illustrates how the first three types of student voice institutional research and evaluation (IRE) share characteristics which can help govern use and dissemination. This data (unless published externally with permissions) should be primarily used for institutional development and should remain within local discussions, rather than shared externally at conferences or workshops. This is an under-explored ethical dilemma in a sector that actively encourages cross-institutional sharing of local enhancement practices. This work follows the principles of service evaluation – an assurance of local standards for the administering institution to assess how well it is performing against intended aims. Formal ethical approval (via a Research Ethics Committee) may not by required for this type of data collection, but the work must exist within legally defined data protection guidelines and this does not prevent methodological and ethical scrutiny. Hall (2017, p.184) notes that these examples signify good intentions to 'shape services', but the value and worth of such approaches require further consideration. The risk of 'surface compliance', rather than using data for real transformation should be acknowledged, especially if opportunities for students to be empowered by their engagement are overlooked.

Following on from service evaluation, the next categories outline a blurred boundary between service evaluation and research, such that these practices often fall into either category:

4. Student voice for quality enhancement

The fourth category in this Typology uses student voices to aid in the reflection and design of their learning experiences. This work can be carried out by academics who are exploring pedagogical enhancements, assessment co-design within modules, and action research for specific student cohorts. In this category, projects tend to access small samples, collate qualitative case studies, and explore pilots for relatively low risk topics which are time bound and often 'in the moment'. In some cases, alternative 'big' data sources (such as student data, surveys or evaluations) may be used to identify a need for further exploration. There is richness in the data collected here, but it may not be defined as data by those collecting it.

If the exploration is unplanned and in the moment or lacking a traditional research design, formal ethical approval will not have been sought, and as such the data should be kept within the institution. This work may begin, in good faith, as service evaluation, but the parameters may then become much more blurred. Many practices for amplifying student voices in this area are creative and innovative, and often methods are contextually untested. There are a multitude of ethical considerations here concerning engaging students in academic pilots which would seek to balance the risks of harm, benefit and a counterfactual interrogation of what could be done instead.

The authenticity of the data, and the lessons learnt for practice, may convince the practitioner/researcher to explore publication and cross-institutional sharing of good practice. This then presents the challenge of either attempting to seek retrospective ethical approval by Committee or disseminating externally without approval. This negotiation of ethical boundaries can be confusing and demotivating for those involved and this may be one explanation why the full scope of institutional research and evaluation activity within institutions remains unknown and unsurfaced.

5. Student voice for organisational development

This fifth category includes evaluations of process and impact which lead to organisational development. These tend to be evaluations of strategic or financially loaded initiatives, for example access, participation and success initiatives within UK regulatory submissions of Access and Participation Plans. This can include evaluations of interventions which focus on differential student access and outcomes in higher education, for example work to close/eradicate the Black Asian and Minority Ethnic (BAME) degree awarding gap, and the success of outreach work to address social mobility agendas. These interventions have strategic relevance whilst often working within equality and diversity legislation. There is an ethical resonance for both the aims of the evaluation and the applied methodology as those who may seek to benefit from effective interventions (or are at risk from a lack of, or ineffective intervention) are often those who are marginalised in the higher education environment.

Whilst those working across an institution are skilled project managers of creative initiatives, evaluation is often acknowledged as a skills gap. Here we find a category of work which would benefit from formal ethical approval (and is sometimes encouraged). However, these teams may not be methodologically trained, and the formal system of ethical approval can be alienating. When those with expertise in evaluation are commissioned, it is often difficult to move beyond an evaluation of process (how many people attended, what was their experience). Furthermore, elaborate evaluations of impact (financial or theoretical), which are necessary for work with Widening Participation for example, are difficult to do without engagement from the start. Thus, whilst student voices are integral to this methodological approach, there is a risk that they will be under-utilised as evidence of impact.

Evidence-informed enhancement and organisational development is beginning to be recognised as institutionally relevant as the pressure to evidence impact increases. Gradually, institutional evaluators are being asked to support local teams and to build capacity (training and mentoring), or to model effective evaluation practices. In both these scenarios, the assumption is not that the current research and evaluation practice is unethical; rather that the system of ethical governance has not yet evolved to effectively support those working in this area.

6. Students researching student voice

The sixth category involves undergraduate and postgraduate researchers and students employed as institutional researchers/data analysts who employ a student sample or analyse the institution or wider community. This could include research conducted as part of a credit-based assessment (thesis/dissertations). This student work often attracts diverse samples from the institutional student population due to a realistic research design from an insider position. The research of students is often well managed (by supervision or by employment) and the student will benefit through attainment in research projects and the development of research skills. The reflexive considerations of an ethical research position should be considered as part of the ethical approval process, which is often a module-based Category Approval alongside supervisory sign off. This type of research is often overlooked by institutions, who fail to capitalise on the vast amount of policy-relevant student voices generated by student research.

Another variation of the student researcher role is that which is based within academic and central departments via work placements and paid internships. Here, student researchers are often employed to support staff research projects as collaborators, rather than research leaders. Research and analysis conducted by students working for/within a Student Union/Association would also be included here.

7. Student voice for scholarship

The final category of IRE which amplifies student voices is designed by academic staff and contributes as evidence of scholarship for both research and learning/teaching career pathways.[5] Staff research projects sitting within this cat-egory would be governed by the ethical parameters of research – creating new knowledge (see Figure 13.2) – and are particularly pertinent if scholarship is to be defined as "*making transparent, for public scrutiny, how learning has been made possible*" (Trigwell, Martin, Benjamin and Prosser, 2000). In comparison to internal projects for quality enhancement, this research could be funded either externally (by a sector agency) or internally (by institutional, faculty or department project funding). Principal Investigators may sit within faculties and departments as academics or research centre staff and centralised directorates who regularly conduct research and evaluation of strategic relevance. The impact on the institution is often implied, but resulting actions from scholarship activity may be less likely to occur. Whereas the benefits of research-informed teaching are widely documented (Healey and Jenkins, 2009), the current scope of IRE implies that a teaching focus is too narrow, and staff research should be reframed as 'evidence-informed practice within higher education institutions' to acknow-ledge the breadth of application.

From student voice which is sought to student voice which is offered

There are a variety of ways in which students are positioned within student voice research and evaluation and this is primarily an ethical responsibility (Taylor and Robinson, 2009, in Bovill, Cook-Sather, Felten, Millard, and Moore-Cherry, 2016). Within the scholarship of teaching and learning (as outlined by Boyer in 1993) students were once positioned as "*legitimate peripheral participants*" (Trigwell and Shale 2004, p.528), rather than the emergent "*students as partners*" ethos (Healey, Flint, Harrington, 2014). Students have now evolved into potential co-creators of their own learning and of evidence informed practice. Bovill et al. (2016) specif-ically include 'co-researcher' in their typology of student roles adopted in the co-creation of learning and teaching and this could be extended to all work which amplifies student voices. How the student is positioned, not just within learning and teaching, but within all types of IRE in the aforementioned categories in the typology is important. Cook-Sather (2014, p.135) notes with reference to pre HE:

> *When researchers translate themselves into partners with students in the research process, they are no longer the distanced, authoritative, sole authors of the meaning derived from qualitative research approaches such as observations of and interviews with students.*
>
> (Cook-Sather, 2014)

Likewise, students are no longer objects of study but rather subjects, primary actors, or what Delamont (1976) called "*protagonists*".

Whilst identifying research and evaluation within this Typology it is important to consider: is the role of students conceptualised as subject or object? Even qualitative approaches which amplify student voices can risk framing students as heroic subjects, and this idiosyncratic positioning, although powerful to hear, may not necessarily lead to action or empowerment.

Further discussion is also needed to explore whether a model where students are fully integrated into processes of institutional change through empowering engagement as co-researchers, rather than design consultants, is the intention, desire or the most effective model for institutional transformation. This model, based on altruistic rather than consumeristic principles, could begin to challenge the creeping normalisation of student incentives for IRE, which can reinforce power dynamics and influence research findings.

Conclusion

This chapter has presented seven categories of institutional research and evaluation which outline the different approaches currently employed to amplify student voices across the sector. This Typology can be used as a tool to help locate and then map any activity within discrete institutions, to challenge dominant IRE approaches and to critique the positioning of student voices. All categories produce data which can be used for evidence-informed decision-making, but an accurate picture of what exists is needed and is often difficult to uncover. The Typology is constructed in an order which highlights the ethical governance (not the ethical practices) of service evaluation and research activity and each category identifies distinct explanations for how any findings should be used. One of the possible reasons for the invisibility of IRE across an institution may well be a fear of ethical judgement. Supportive networks and communities of practice can provide a forum for a discussion of ethical dilemmas is a constructive and collaborative way. In some institutions, all of the aforementioned research and evaluation practices are supported by a dedicated team who work as consultants, designers, administrators and analysts, from project inception to dissemination, so that a coherent approach can be adopted and capacity can be built institution-wide. An Institutional Research and Evaluation Policy/Strategy and capacity building for academic leaders are useful mechanisms for ensuring that student voices are not used or abused (Jones-Devitt and LeBihan, 2017).

Each type of data collection outlined in this chapter is valid and reliable in its own context. This Typology is therefore presented as non-hierarchical. However, data/evidence hierarchies do exist and data privilege by HE stakeholders needs to be acknowledged. Strategic planners may privilege quantitative data presented in institutional student data sets, supported by benchmarked student surveys, and this is routinely analysed. KPIs are quantitatively dominant, and limitations in time and resource may hinder a wider gaze by these users. Educational developers may privilege student evaluations and local reflections on practice, although the power of the student survey to elicit reactive change cannot be ignored. An unknown is how students engage with their own data landscape and that of the wider institution, and how students as co-researchers can be further valued.

Students are becoming disillusioned with survey burden, but has the counter factual been fully explored? What are the risks of non-participation? And if not surveys, then what? Senior leadership buy in, and the implementation of strategic policies guiding IRE would help to critique data hierarchies, support triangulation, and champion creative and innovative methodologies that provide alternatives to privileged data and further engage and empower the 'heard to hear' (Trowler, 2018). Academic leaders and educational developers are now encouraged to use the Typology presented here to map and scope the activity of their own institution to ensure that diverse student voices are amplified using the most appropriate methods to ensure the most effective evidence-informed decision-making can ensue.

Notes

1   Noting the term 'pupil voice' in UK and Australia
2   Adapting McLeod's 2010 categorisation of the use of voice in educational discourse
3   The UK and Ireland Higher Education Institutional Research (HEIR) network www.heirnetwork.org.uk/
4   In this context 'institutional' refers to resulting work from within Universities and their partner Student Unions/Associations
5   For example, UKPSF: 5 – Engages in professional development, K5 – Methods for evaluating the effectiveness of teaching, V3 – Uses evidence informed approaches and outcomes of research, Higher Education Academy 2015

References

Austen, L. (2018) 'It ain't what we do, it's the way that we do it' – researching student voices, *WonkHE*, 27 February. Retrieved from: http://wonkhe.com/ blogs/it-aint-what   we-do-its-the-way-that-we-do-it-researching-student-voices/ (accessed 24 April 2019).

Bovill, C., Cook-Sather, A., Felten, P., Millard, L., and Moore-Cherry, N. (2016) Addressing potential challenges in co-creating learning and teaching: Overcoming resistance, navigating institutional norms and ensuring inclusivity in student–staff partnerships, *Higher Education*, 71(2), pp.195–208. Retrieved from: https://doi. org/10.1007/s10734-015-9896-4

Boyer, E. L. (1993) *Scholarship reconsidered* (7th ed.), Princeton, NJ: Carnegie Foundation for the Advancement of Teaching.

Bryson, C. (2016) Engagement through partnership: Students as partners in learning and teaching in higher education, *International Journal for Academic Development*, 21(1), pp.84–86. Retrieved from: https://doi.org/10.1080/ 1360144x.2016.1124966

Buckley, A. (2012) *Making it count: Reflecting on the National Student Survey in the process of enhancement*, York: Higher Education Academy. Retrieved from: www. heacademy.ac.uk/system/files/resources/making_it_count.pdf   (accessed   24 April 2019).

Cook-Sather, A. (2014) The trajectory of student voice in educational research. *New Zealand Journal of Educational Studies*, 49(2), pp.131–148. Retrieved from: https://doi.org/10.1007/978-981-13-1858-0_2

Delamont, S. (1976) Interaction in the classroom, contemporary sociology of the school, London: Methuen.

Dunne, E. and Owen, D. (eds.) (2013) *Student Engagement Handbook: Practice in Higher Education*, Bingley: Emerald Group Publishing.

Gibbs, G. (2010) *Dimensions of quality*, York: Higher Education Academy. Retrieved from: www.heacademy.ac.uk/system/files/dimensions_of_quality.pdf (accessed 24 April 2019).

Groundwater-Smith, S. and Mockler, N. (2016) From data source to co-researchers? Tracing the shift from 'student voice' to student–teacher partnerships in Educational action research, *Educational Action Research*, 24(2), pp.159–176. Retrieved from: https://doi.org/10.1080/09650792.2015.1053507

Hall, V. (2017) A tale of two narratives: Student voice-what lies before us? *Oxford Review of Education*, 43(2), pp.180–14. Retrieved from: https://doi.org/10.1080/03054985.2016.1264379

Healey, M., Flint, A. and Harrington, K. (2014) *Engagement through partnership: Students as partners in learning and teaching in higher education*, York: Higher Education Academy. Retrieved from: www.heacademy.ac.uk/system/files/resources/engagement_through_partnership.pdf

Healey, M., and Jenkins, A. (2009) *Developing undergraduate research and inquiry*, York: Higher Education Academy. Retrieved from: www.heacademy.ac.uk/knowledgehub/developing-undergraduate-research-and-inquiry (accessed 24 April 2019).

Higher Education Academy (2015) *UKPSF Dimensions of the Framework*, York: Higher Education Academy. Retrieved from: www.heacademy.ac.uk/system/files/downloads/ukpsf_dimensions_of_the_framwork.df (accessed 24 April 2019).

Hoon, A. Oliver, E. Szpakowska, K. and Newton, P. (2015) Use of the 'Stop, Start, Continue' method is associated with the production of constructive qualitative feedback by students in higher education, *Assessment and Evaluation in Higher Education*, 40(5), pp.755–767. Retrieved from: https://doi.org/10.1080/02602938.2014.956282

Jones-Devitt, S. and LeBihan, J. (2017) *The Use and Abuse of the Student Voice*, York: AdvanceHE. Retrieved from: www.lfhe.ac.uk/en/research-resources/publications hub/index.cfm/SDP2017-05 (accessed 24 April 2019).

Kandiko Howson, C. (2018) *Evaluation of HEFCE's Learning Gain Pilot Projects Year 2*, Report to HEFCE by King's College London. Retrieved from: www.officeforstudents.org.uk/media/1386/evaluation-of-hefce-s-learning-gain-pilotprojects-year-2.pdf (accessed 24 April 2019).

Kotsifli, D. and Green, K. (2010) Making the most of the student voice in further education. Findings from an analysis of surveys and interviews conducted with college student representatives and college staff management teams in England. Cited in Hall, V., 2017. A tale of two narratives: student voice: what lies before us? *Oxford Review of Education*, 43(2), pp.18–193

McLeod, J. (2011) Student voice and the politics of listening in higher education, *Critical studies in Education*, 52(2), pp.179–189. Retrieved from: https://doi.org/10.1080/17508487.2011.572830

Parsons, D. (2017) *Demystifying evaluation: Practical approaches for researchers and users*, Bristol: Policy Press.

Roberts, A. and Nash, J. (2009) Enabling students to participate in school improvement through a Students as Researchers programme, *Improving Schools*, 12(2), pp.174–187.

Sabri, D. (2011) What's wrong with 'the student experience'? *Discourse: Studies in the Cultural Politics of Education*, 32(5), pp.657–667. Retrieved from: https://doi.org/10.1080/01596306.2011.620750

Seale, J. (2010) Doing student voice work in higher education: An exploration of the value of participatory methods, *British Educational Research Journal*, 36(6), pp.995–1015. Retrieved from: https://doi.org/10.1080/01411920903342038

Taylor, C. and Robinson, C. (2009) Student voice: Theorising power and participation, *Pedagogy, Culture and Society*, 17(2), pp.161–175.

Thomas, L. (2017) *Evaluating student engagement*, The Student Engagement Partnership. Retrieved from: http://tsep.org.uk/evaluation-framework/ (accessed 24 April 2019).

Trigwell, K., Martin, E., Benjamin, J. and Prosser, M. (2000) Scholarship of teaching: a model, *Higher Education Research and Development*, 19, pp.155–168.

Trowler, V. (2018) *Responding to student voice: insights into international practice*, QAA Scotland. Retrieved from: www.enhancementthemes.ac.uk/current-enhancement theme/student   engagement-and-demographics/responding-to-student-voice (accessed 24 April 2019).

Wong, B., and Chiu, Y. L. T. (2018) University lecturers' construction of the 'ideal' undergraduate student, *Journal of Further and Higher Education*, pp.1–15. Retrieved from: https://doi.org/10.1080/0309877x.2018.1504010

Woodfield, S. (2015) Institutional research in the UK and Ireland, in Webber, K. and Calderon, A. (eds.), *Institutional research and planning in higher education: Global contexts and themes*, London: Routledge, pp.86–100. Retrieved from: https://doi.org/10.4324/9781315777726

Chapter 14

On the origin of Student Fellows

Reflections on the evolution of partnership from theory to practice

Cassie Lowe and Stuart Sims

> *Whoever is led to believe that species are mutable will do good service by conscientiously expressing his conviction; for only thus can the load of prejudice by which this subject is overwhelmed be removed.*
>
> Charles Darwin, *On the Origin of Species* (1876, p.423)

Student engagement has long been a key strategic priority at the University of Winchester, whose aim is to be 'one of the leaders in the university sector' in this field (University of Winchester Strategic Plan, 2015–2020, p.6). Winchester is a small/medium-sized institution with a broad remit that focuses on humanities, liberal arts, education and health-based courses. It is an institution that prides itself on its values-driven education. This habitat has been the ideal breeding ground for a diverse biosphere of practice across the institution, in various forms, provisions and initiatives, all evolving convergently around working in partnership with students (Healey, Flint and Harrington, 2014; NUS, 2012). Whilst Winchester has been commended (QAA, 2012; 2016) and celebrated for these practices (Guardian Higher Education Awards, 2015; NUS/HEA Partnership awards 2014), adaptation is essential if an institution is to thrive in what can be seen as the hostile ecosystem of contemporary higher education (HE) (Moran and Powell, 2018). In light of this, the staff at Winchester continue to evolve their practice so that it remains relevant and, above all, engaging to students. One such example of Winchester's commitment to student engagement evolution has been the emergence of a 'Centre for Student Engagement', after a team determined that such was vital to ensuring that all students both be aware of all student engagement initiatives and also, therefore, have the opportunity to choose their level of engagement with them (Shaw and Lowe, 2017; Lowe, Shaw, Sims, King and Paddison, 2017). This particular adaptation within the evolution of engagement was driven by student–staff partnership arising from a 'Student Fellows Scheme' (SFS) project, which highlighted the conflicting definitions of 'student engagement' and the need for students to have a single accessible place where they might engage with opportunities. This chapter will discuss the SFS in relation to its evolutionary development in the context of hospitable and hostile environments, both locally and in the wider HE sector. In doing this, we will chart the evolution of the scheme to illustrate the challenges faced and demonstrate that successful adaptations are key to developing a culture of partnership. The authors of this chapter have both coordinated the SFS and acted as staff partners and one has been a Student Fellow. This chapter is informed by reflections from our varied perspectives on the scheme across the years. This chapter will therefore follow the SFS's ever-developing structure, focus, partnership levels and legacy, as the scheme continues to refine itself in the spirit of evolutionary anagenesis.

An environment hospitable to growth

The SFS is Winchester's flagship student engagement initiative, a scheme that is continuously looking for ways to adapt to suit student and staff needs. It is a student–staff partnership initiative, co-directed by the University of Winchester and Winchester Student Union, and provides sixty students with a bursary to work in partnership with a member of staff on a project that will lead to an enhancement of the student experience (Sims, Lowe, Hutber and Barnes, 2014). The SFS was Winchester's response to debates in the United Kingdom (UK) HE sector about partnership and student ownership in order to ensure mutually beneficial change for the institution, its staff and its students (Healey, Flint and Harrington, 2014; Dunne and Zandstra, 2011). 'Partnership' is a concept that has gained significant traction in HE internationally (Mercer-Mapstone, Dvorakova, Matthews, Abbot, Cheng, Felten, Knorr, Marquis, Shammas and Swaim, 2017), but the UK focus took shape through the 'call to arms' presented by the National Union of Students in its *Manifesto for Partnership* (NUS, 2012). This was not a document with a theoretical or even, perhaps, philosophical approach, but a pragmatic and democratic one stimulated by the sense that British HE was changing, as manifest in the funding relationship change in the UK, with the introduction of £9,000 tuition fees in 2012. Alongside this seismic shift in HE, the Quality Assurance Agency's Chapter B5 Student Engagement was published (QAA, 2012) and bodies such as TSEP (The Student Engagement Partnership) and SPARQS (Student Partnerships in Quality Scotland) were active in the sector, focusing energy and institutional motivation on student engagement. This movement called for partnership in resistance to a consumerist model in which students pay fees and are treated as customers (Molesworth, Nixon and Scullion, 2009); it championed partnership as a process (Healey, Flint and Harrington, 2014) and demanded a fundamental revision of the traditional nature of student–staff relationships. With this national, student-driven agenda in mind, the University of Winchester developed a scheme that tried to embody these principles. Key to this was the notion (repeated in bold type in the original document) that "*the sum total of an institution's student engagement mechanisms does not equal partnership*" (NUS, 2012, p.3). It was not enough to meet the rallying cry of this manifesto by badging a partnership label on an existing practice or rebranding something institutions planned to do anyway. This meant a reassessment of the way students and staff collaborated institution-wide. An essential first step towards the promotion of partnership and its establishment as a Winchester ethos was a discrete activity, subsequently built upon and developed within the hospitable national environment that the work of the National Union of Students (NUS) and others had created. The institution's current thriving student engagement activity is the telling result.

The SFS structure has evolved greatly since its inception in 2012. The scheme began as a small-scale, Jisc-funded FASTECH project at the University of Winchester and Bath Spa University (UK) (Hyland, Jessop, El Hakim, Adams, Barlow, Morgan, and Shepherd 2013). Initially, there were only eight projects that ran across semester two and, at this stage in the scheme's existence, the projects were focused solely on technology-enhanced learning (TEL). This particular student engagement emphasis proved successful enough to stimulate stakeholder desire for further SFS projects the following year, on a larger scale and lasting longer. The scheme therefore evolved into an opportunity for sixty students to work on a project from October – after the September recruitment phase – until the Student Fellows Conference in May. The University and the Student Union co-own the day-to-day running of the SFS and its evaluation, as may be discovered in El Hakim, King, Lowe and Sims (2016). That the SFS projects have flourished in the partnership environment at Winchester has led to a change in and expansion of their focus across the years of the scheme. From their TEL beginnings, the projects' foci broadened to any pedagogical initiative and development, such as assessment and feedback (Shaw and Sims, 2017). This particular focus has since mutated into a scheme that has adapted to suit all manner of environments and student and staff needs, engaging over 300 students across five years.

From the primordial soup to sprouting legs

Emerging from its primordial state, the SFS has now climbed up on land to stand tall as a mature partnership initiative. SFS provides a platform for students to work with a member of staff from across the institution – thus actively shaping any part of their student experience – and over 200 projects have been completed since its inception. Projects – whether large or small in scale – that have come from this expansion have had a significant impact on the student experience. Such projects include: spaces and events for students with Autism Spectrum Disorder; a lounge with showers and kitchen facilities for commuting students; an annual festival dedicated to celebrating diversity and various cultures of students across campus. This shift has been driven by demand from the institution and its staff and students, as the effectiveness of the model has become apparent. Though some projects still address pedagogical aspects of the student experience (for example, this year there have been co-designed modules in both the Accounting and Finance and Film Production programmes), as was the case in the previous stages of the evolution of the SFS, the scheme is not limited to this focus. The scope of projects has also grown, with the aim of changing institutional policy and structures – for example, in 2018, a project engaged students in redeveloping the University's Learning and Teaching Strategy. Thanks to the responsive evolution of the scheme, leading to fewer boundaries and greater scope, students and staff alike recognise that they have agency over and ownership of their experience. A key legacy of the scheme has been its adaptability to both student and staff needs on campus and wider trends in the HE sector. (El Hakim et al., 2016, provide further explanation of this practice).

Since 2013, the SFS has had to adapt to considerable change in the cultural climate of students (more on this later in the chapter) and, latterly, to a shift in student needs in relation to structure and timeframe. From 2014 until recently, the projects ran from October to May each academic year, but adjustments are now being made to this timescale, due to students dropping out of the scheme for reasons such as unforeseen circumstances, workload pressure or the need to take up employment to fund their studies. Students are often frustrated at having to withdraw, because they want to see their projects through to completion, but they cannot commit to a full year. Third-year students are particularly affected, for they are completing their final-year projects in the second semester. Their favoured alternative to a protracted project is a short, fast one.

In 2018, the SFS very successfully piloted 'fast-track' projects, allowing students to complete projects with reduced workload and time commitment, and many students and staff applied for semester two projects, to which they felt able to commit. Though smaller in scale, these are just as valuable for getting the student voice heard via work in partnership. Examples of these fast-track projects include: engaging History students in the wider community; ethical approaches to food on campus; innovative approaches to student feedback. For the academic year 2018/19, a full roll-out of the optional 'fast-track' has meant that students can apply with a project that commits them to only a single semester. Such adaptations to the scheme stem from its commitment to student and staff feedback. The University's 'Student Engagement Advisory Group', made up of staff

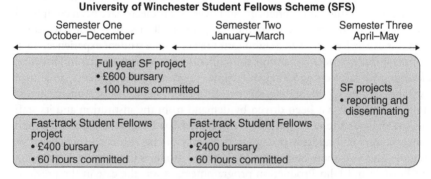

Figure 14.1 Student Fellows Scheme timeline 2018–19

and students, determined the necessary changes and shaped the new structure for the scheme from a range of viable options (Figure 14.1.) It is imperative that the scheme remains a flexible partnership model; it will continue to be responsive to the HE environment and adapt accordingly. Change is necessary for schemes such as this to survive.

Biodiversity and ecology

There are numerous considerations to bear in mind when embarking on the development of partnership activities, particularly if those activities are intended to evolve into something beyond the confines of one discrete activity. The SFS is predicated on the concept that there is a shared sense of what the University is and what it is for (Readings, 1996) and a shared culture to which staff and students contribute, but for which they also share responsibility. This is not a mechanism for just giving students what they want because they have asked for it, but an emphasis upon the need for evidence-based practice (Pring and Thomas, 2004), as a challenge to the developing HE landscape of consumerism. A key part of SFS is encouraging students to engage with other students to demonstrate that there is a need for the change they intend to make and to show why this matters. Not all projects are 'fixing a problem', but are developing innovations that staff and students deem worthwhile. Those that are changing an aspect of the institution do so based on democratic ideals – the change will benefit the many and not the few because the innovators are representing more than just their own voice. This does mean that not all SFS projects make changes. If students have engaged with the wider community and collected empirical evidence that suggests people are happy with the status quo, then it confirms that good practice is already occurring and no change is necessary. This would not be considered an unsuccessful project, but one that adds to a body of evidence to support continuing practices.

Partnership is key to ensuring a democratic approach, both in the organisation of the scheme and the individual student–staff partnerships within. Shared involvement in the management, participation and evaluation of the scheme provides genuine ownership and partnership at all levels. To develop effective and representative change, it is necessary to ensure that anyone in the institution can be involved. That the scheme is co-owned by the Student Union and the University means that decisions made about what projects are viable for the scheme are done in the interests of both of these parties. The important role that the Union plays in championing not only student voice but also democracy is a significant thread running through the scheme. There is also a degree of pragmatism in relation to the way the SFS works. 'Partnership' has been employed as a theoretical framework (Healey et al., 2014), as an ideological imperative (NUS, 2012) and as a 'trend' (Bovill, 2013); however, broadly speaking, the SFS exists to deliver practical benefits and is pragmatic at its core. Pairing staff members with students in order to conduct projects is often seen as a solution to immediate problems or to allow much needed room for innovation. Co-ownership

with the Student Union is fundamental to the scheme's authenticity as an institutional partnership initiative, but it also comes with practical benefits, such as
engaging a wider student audience. The scheme itself needs to be evaluated to
ensure it remains relevant and effective; conducting this with students ensures
that the priorities of students are represented throughout and that the outcomes
benefit students. A partnership ethos permeates the scheme's operation and philosophy to address practically the demands of the environment.

Hostile environments?

As outlined above, one rationale for embedding partnership in a discrete activity
was to take a first step towards broader cultural evolution institutionally. The
potential for a much celebrated scheme to become seen as 'where partnership
happens' can imply that it is the only place partnership should happen. Indeed,
paying students to take part in the SFS immediately sets it apart from other more
organic student–staff partnerships, which is problematic if the paid roles are seen
as having higher status. There is perhaps an inherent danger of partnership only
developing in a closed environment which could bring its evolution to a halt. This
reinforces the importance of normalising working in partnership, so that such
activities do not seem like a localised novelty specific to one department or initiative, but an ethos interwoven into all university activity. This would also seem to
reinforce ideas that partnership is valued only when it is performative. The public
face of student–staff partnership can be very different from the local partnerships
being developed between academics and students, particularly if there is a perception that 'partnership' or 'student engagement' are new 'buzzwords' (Gibbs,
2014; Vuori, 2014) that are foisted upon beleaguered academic staff drowning
in administration and institutional diktats.

Whilst much of the pro-partnership literature depicts it as being democratic
and inclusive (Seale, Gibson, Haynes, and Potter, 2015; Sims, Luebsen and
Guggiari-Peel, 2017; Shaw, Humphry, Atvars and Sims, 2017), the day-to-day
experience of academics may contradict this perception. This is well articulated
by White (2016), who suggests that partnership undermines the authority of
academics and that this is wholly driven by the consumerisation of universities.
The counterargument to this tends to say that partnership is a process of involving
students more in their university experience and that this is not to challenge
existing knowledge or authority. Partnership draws on the fact that students are
experts at being students, even if they lack the pedagogic or disciplinary expertise
of staff (Cook-Sather, Bovill and Felten 2014). Rather, their experience and
expertise are, typically, in being a student. The way this is addressed by SFS when
promoting the scheme is to make it clear to staff and students that partnership
does not necessarily mean equality of time, effort or expertise. Both partners will
contribute to the project, but this will naturally draw upon their capacity to do
so and be informed by their prior experience. Key to this is that project ideas can
be developed by staff, students or existing partnerships, allowing the nature of

the balance to be evident from the outset. This also requires the coordinators of the scheme to play a significant role in negotiating the nature of partnerships and entails supporting staff and students to establish boundaries that respect both the academic freedom and expertise of the staff and the expertise that comes from the experience of the student.

An additional challenge is that, in establishing a discrete activity with funding attached, there is a degree of necessary gatekeeping about what projects are deemed acceptable. Staff and students apply to the scheme with project ideas which are then scrutinised on the basis of their likelihood of success. The various reasons for judging a project to be unsuccessful include: previous projects having been carried out in a similar area (whether successful or not); the scope being too big (particularly in terms of time); the inability to find an appropriate partner (staff or student); the idea not being a good fit with the remit of the scheme. Each of these is subjective and therefore at risk of falling foul of the prejudices and preconceptions of the SFS coordinators. The partnership between the Student Union and University is designed to help ameliorate this dilemma in the SFS. As the scheme is run with a genuine desire to advance student–staff partnership, the agendas of both the University and Union are largely aligned. However, these are two separate organisations and there can be tensions in satisfying both what the institution wants and what those applying to the scheme want.

Conclusion

Throughout this chapter, we have discussed the myriad changes to the SFS in the light of a changing HE sector and shifting institutional needs. As these changes have occurred, we have endeavoured to ensure that these practical adjustments are always made with the intention of advancing the cause of student–staff work in partnership. To turn theory into practice, it is important first to recognise that several factors are brought to bear on both the theory and the practice. In the inherently challenging and complex environment of a university, shifting cultural expectations of how and when it is appropriate to work with students takes time. Whilst there is significant support from across our institution for the principle of working in partnership, this is by no means ubiquitous. As discussed, we must be aware of the risk that such a high-profile scheme may be seen as the only source of partnership. In many ways, a fear of this has driven the expansion of the focus of the scheme from technology to pedagogy and thence to the whole student experience. It has also underpinned endeavours to recruit a wider range of staff and students from all corners of the University. However, these are practical solutions to perhaps a theoretical problem. This could be better addressed by supporting and normalising grassroots part-nership, where there are mechanisms in place to support students and staff who want to work in partnership in their own contexts and not necessarily be attached to an initiative. This does not mean that such initiatives do not have their place in the normalisation of partnership, as they provide evidence that this model works and empower students to be the ones who approach staff with ideas. Balancing the development of partnership in this way also requires balancing competing pressures on the direction of such a scheme. The tension between being theoretically authentic while satisfying the needs of the institution involves a mixture of reflection, compromise and a stubborn adherence to core principles. Establishing a scheme that espouses laudable traits such as normalising partnership, challenging consumerism and generating a shared culture and meaning is highly unlikely to get off the ground. These are certainly principles that should not be compromised, but a practical idealist approach is necessary if change is to be embedded. The prevalence of these challenges raises the importance of self-reflection, evaluation and engagement with a wider community to ensure student–staff partnership remains relevant as both theory and practice. We are aware this discussion has been focused on a particular habitat, namely a small/medium-sized, post-1992 university in the south of England. Just as different species shape their environmental conditions and are shaped by them, exploring the common foundations of partnership cross-institutionally and in greater depth would allow a richer understanding of the evolution of the principles of student–staff partnership.

References

Bovill, C., 2013. Students and staff co-creating curricula: a new trend or an old idea we never got around to implementing? Retrieved from: http://eprints.gla.ac.uk/82348/1/82348.pdf

Cook-Sather, A., Bovill, C. and Felten, P., 2014. *Engaging students as partners in teaching and learning: A guide for faculty.* San Francisco, CA: Jossey-Bass.

Darwin, C., 1992. The Origin of Species, 1876. London: Routledge.

Dunne, E. and Zandstra, R., 2011. *Students as Change Agents in Learning and Teaching.* Bristol: Higher Education Academy/ESCalate.

El Hakim, Y., King, S., Lowe, T. and Sims, S., 2016. Evaluating partnership and impact in the first year of the Student Fellows Scheme, *Journal of Educational Innovation, Partnership and Change*, 2(1). Retrieved from: https://journals.studentengagement.org.uk/index.php/studentchangeagents/article/view/257 (accessed: 7 November 2018).

Gibbs, G., 2014. Student engagement, the latest buzzword. *Times Higher Education.* Retrieved from: www.timeshighereducation.com/news/student engagement-the-latest-buzzword/2012947.article (accessed: 10 March 2018).

Healey, M., Flint, A. and Harrington, K., 2014. *Engagement through partnership: Students as partners in learning and teaching in higher education.* York: Higher Education Academy. Retrieved from: www.heacademy.ac.uk/system/files/resources/engagement_through_partnership.pdf

Hyland, P., Jessop, T., El Hakim, Y., Adams, J., Barlow, A., Morgan, G. and Shepherd, C., 2013. *FASTECH Feedback and Assessment for Students with Technology*, Jisc. Retrieved from: http://jiscdesignstudio.pbworks.com/w/file/70106828/FASTECH%20Final%20evaluation%20report%2010%20Sept.docx (accessed 25 July 2019).

Lowe, T., Shaw, C., Sims, S., King, S., and Paddison, A., 2017. The Development of Contemporary Student Engagement Practices at the University of Winchester and Winchester Student Union, *International Journal for Students as Partners*, 1(1). Retrieved from: https://doi.org/10.15173/ijsap.v1i1.3082

Mercer-Mapstone, L., Dvorakova, S.L., Matthews, K., Abbot, S., Cheng, B., Felten, P., Knorr, K., Marquis, E., Shammas, R. and Swaim, K., 2017. A systematic literature review of students as partners in higher education, *International Journal for Students as Partners*, 1(1). Retrieved from: https://doi.org/10.15173/ijsap.v1i1.3119

Molesworth, M., Nixon, E. and Scullion, R., 2009. Having, being and higher education: The marketisation of the university and the transformation of the student into consumer, *Teaching in Higher Education*, 14(3), 277–287. Retrieved from: https://doi.org/10.1080/13562510902898841

Moran, H. and Powell, J., 2018. *Running a tight ship: can universities plot a course through rough seas?* Report for the Guardian/HSBC/UUK.

National Union of Students (NUS), 2012. A manifesto for partnership. Retrieved from: www.nusconnect.org.uk/resources/a-manifesto-for-partnership (accessed: 7 November 2018).

Pring, R. and Thomas, G., 2004. *Evidence-based practice in education*. London: Open University Press.

QAA, 2012. *UK quality code for higher education–Part B: Assuring and enhancing academic quality–Chapter B5: Student engagement*. Gloucester.

Readings, B., 1996. *The university in ruins*. Cambridge, MA: Harvard University Press.

Seale, J., Gibson, S., Haynes, J. and Potter, A., 2015. Power and resistance: Reflections on the rhetoric and reality of using participatory methods to promote student voice and engagement in higher education, *Journal of further and Higher Education*, 39(4), 534–552. Retrieved from: https://doi.org/10.1080/0309877x.2014.938264

Shaw, C., and Lowe, T., 2017. The Student Participation Map: A tool to map student participations, engagements, opportunities and extra-curricular activities across a Higher Education Institution, *Dialogue: Journal of Learning and Teaching*, 1. 45–50. Retrieved from: https://issuu.com/solentuniversity/docs/dialogue_2016-17 (accessed: 9 November 2018).

Shaw, C. and Sims, S., 2017. Using a Partnership Approach through Student Fellows Projects as an intervention to Assessment and Feedback, *Capture: Learning and Teaching Journal*, 5. Retrieved from: https://issuu.com/theuniversityofwinchester/docs/capture_20vol._205?e=2137537/55140691 (accessed 9 November 2018).

Shaw, C., Humphrey, O., Atvars, T. and Sims, S., 2017. Who They Are and How to Engage Them: A Summary of the REACT Systematic Literature Review of the *Hard to Reach* in Higher Education. *Journal of Educational Innovation, Partnership and Change*, 3(1), 51–64. Retrieved from: https://journals.studentengagement.org.uk/index.php/studentchangeagents/article/view/685 (accessed 5 November 2018).

Sims, S., Lowe T., Barnes, G. and Hutber, L., 2014. The Student Fellows Scheme: A partnership between the University of Winchester and Winchester Student Union, *Educational Developments*, 15(3), 7–10. Retrieved from: www.seda.ac.uk/resources/files/publications_188_Ed%20Devs%2015.3%20FINAL.pdf (accessed 14 November 2018).

Sims, S., Luebsen, W. and Guggiari-Peel, C., 2017. Exploring the role of co-curricular student engagement in relation to student retention, attainment and improving inclusivity. *Journal of Educational Innovation, Partnership and Change*, 3(1), 93–109. Retrieved from: http://dx.doi.org/10.21100/jeipc.v3i1.605

University of Winchester, 2015. The University of Winchester 2015–2020 Strategic Plan. Retrieved from: www.winchester.ac.uk/about-us/our-future/our-strategy/

Vuori, J., 2014. Student engagement: buzzword of fuzzword? *Journal of Higher Education Policy and Management*, 36(5), 509–519. Retrieved from: https://doi.org/10.1080/1360080x.2014.936094

White, M., 2016. Student partnership and a University legitimation crisis. In P. Bamber and J. Moore (eds.), *Teaching Education in Challenging Times: Lessons for Professionalism, Partnership and Practice*, 94–104. Abingdon: Routledge.

Chapter 15

Empowering students as champions in technology enhanced learning (TEL) to improve digital literacies

Fiona Harvey and James Anderson

Digital technologies and the resulting expectations for both students and staff to be digitally literate have put enormous pressure on institutions in terms of how those institutions introduce technology enhanced learning (TEL) within their curriculum (ECORYS, 2016; Becker, Brown, Dahlstrom, Davis, DePaul, Diaz, and Pomerantz, 2018; Fujitsu, 2018). Student expectations to be able to access the web and resources 24/7 means that institutions need to think much more deeply about the implications of working and learning both within and without the institution's walls. One side of this participation in the ubiquitous web is that staff also have been under pressure to explore new technologies and commit to introducing the 'digital' into their curriculum. From a student engagement point of view, this chapter explores the perspectives of a senior academic teaching in a traditionally 'chalk and talk' environment and an education developer who is tasked with supporting academics and students to become engaged in the digital. It highlights issues of engagement for both staff and students in their agreement to participate in the virtual (and physical world). The focus for this exploration is within the traditional, research intensive University of Southampton located on the south coast of England, UK, ranking in the top 1% worldwide. It has approximately 24,500 students with a strong focus on the technology and engineering subjects as well as a diverse range of other disciplines such as art, business and the humanities (University of Southampton, 2016) and the new online University College of Estate Management (UCEM) (UK) the "*leading provider of supported online education for the Built Environment, with 100 years' experience of providing the highest quality learning opportunities*" (UCEM, 2018). This has around 4,000 students from 150 countries around the world.

Over the past few years there has been more and more attention on 'learning online'. The advent of Massive Open Online Courses (MOOCs) whilst not necessarily the 'tsunami' they were predicted to be (Jaschik, 2015), has nonetheless opened up the eyes of many university leaders and faculties to the opportunities that online learning can bring (Gil-Jaurena and Domínguez, 2018). More importantly, if an institution becomes more digital, utilising online spaces and using more TEL, it brings with it opportunities for engaging with students, in ways that would have been very hard to scale in the past. We are in a world now, where technology, the web and the devices that we have are advanced enough and cheap enough to be offered across institutions (Becker et al., 2018, p.30).

Nonetheless, there are challenges associated with the broader use of technology to enhance learning in higher education – not least, impact on the staff and students in terms of skills. Many people, including students, are not as comfortable with using technology in a high stakes environment. By 'high stakes' we refer to the whole degree, from communications with faculty and administrative staff for support and for information, to using it to be tested in the lectures, or even through exams. Part of the problem is not the technology per se, but the skills required to use it. Some have these innate skills: problem solving, flexibility, curiosity, open-mindedness and alike. But some do not, and it is the development of these skills that is as important as technical ability to allow for the practical use of technologies to enhance programmes and engage more effectively.

Across the spectrum of online education delivery, whether it be within a campus-based institution in a blended learning format, or within a totally online programme, the matter of student engagement with learning has always been an issue. In 2009, Kuh stated that student engagement *"represents the time and effort students devote to activities that are empirically linked to desired outcomes of college and what institutions do to induce students to participate in these activities"* (Kuh, 2009, p.683). In a completely online environment, we cite engagement with the virtual learning environment. In a campus-based environment questions can be asked and active learning encouraged through participation of in-class polls to aid discussions, break-out groups or other such activities along with opportunities for engaging with the institution through events and societies. Within an online environment, the online learning platforms are the students' access to the virtual university and they need to be capitalised upon to ensure that the environment is as effective as possible. We can design our programmes to ensure that our students have the best opportunity to engage, by scaffolding learning using techniques such as the five-stage model (Salmon, 2000, p.25) and ensuring that we have created the right amount of balance in the environment to enable students to build up their confidence and skills to make effective use of their online environment. Regardless of our design, we still need to support our staff and students to develop the appropriate skills to engage.

Developing skills to engage with online learning is not easy. Digital skills are not generational and they do not require a particular style. All these myths should be put to bed as soon as possible, as they are unhelpful and tend to lead us down the path to failure. If only life were that simple. In truth, engaging online can be harder than just turning up to a lecture. Being an online student, whether it is a blended approach, where a percentage of the programmes of study are available online as well as a face-to-face or on-campus component, or whether it is completely online, requires a certain amount of personal accountability, time management and determination. There is no one physically making you attend class, no one sat next to you to talk to or for you to ask the odd anonymous question, and ultimately, if you turn off the tools you use to access the content, it's not there anymore. You only have your conscience and your beliefs that you can do this to spur you on.

Framing online tools for engagement is very important and brings in the concept of digital literacies. Our world has changed from the traditional model of 'chalk and talk' view of higher education. Through every other aspect of our interactions with the world, technology has had an impact, from the way we shop to the way we talk to our bank. Nothing is sacred, everything has been touched by the web and education is no different. There is no reason in the world that digital technologies and tools cannot be used within our curriculum offer. Digital technology-based tools can be better, but do not replace the use of traditional educational tools. They can exist together. What we do need to do, however, is change. We believe that change is harder than actually using most of these tools. But through the development of digital literacy skills the use of the web for education and life-long learning is easier and can lead to the broadening of skills and opening of minds to allow our students a better educational experience.

The concept of this resistance to change is nothing new; centuries of developments have led to cries of the dumbing down of education. However, it is important to note that the resistance comes not just from staff in universities, but also to some extent from students. There are many reasons for this, but one of the most interesting is that with the rise of the massification of higher education, our students are becoming more like customers, with expectations being set at the outset of the 'right' to have a degree, regardless of their own input into the process. If we take the example of this expectation, then we have a duty or responsibility to ensure that all our students take advantage of their environment. They should have the opportunity to develop these skills and for our staff to be confident in their application. Burying your head in the sand will not make these requirements go away and the more that we do, the faster the world moves without us. This is not a sustainable option, but there is a solution. Bringing staff and students along through their own digital skills development is vital.

This chapter covers our two differing views of the participation and issues around engaging students with technology to enhance learning. The first view is that of a senior academic within the University of Southampton who, although personally engaged in using social media for learning, is a member of the School of Mathematics and researches pure maths, a discipline not traditionally known for its penchant for engaging with TEL. The second view is that of an academic-related member of staff whose role includes being an advocate for TEL and encouraging its use, who has since moved onto to another very different university which nonetheless has similar issues regarding engagement with technology to enhance programmes. Although the role was to support and encourage the use of TEL with academic staff, it was with the help of students that a new model was created that flipped staff development so that the students were at the heart of their development. The Innovation and Digital Literacies (iChamps) model supported both staff and students (Harvey, 2018). The contrasting view is that of online students and staff who operate entirely online for a small, private university. Their view in fact demonstrates the similarities between these remarkably different universities and shows how attitudes and behaviours across both students and staff are the same, regardless of the status of the university.

These stories are presented as case studies and offer the reader an insight into the challenges and possible solutions to reaching staff and students with the use of TEL.

The institutional view – Professor James Anderson, Associate Dean, University of Southampton (UK)

I approach this view from two different standpoints: one the one hand, as a pure mathematician, a geometer by trade, and, on the other, as a senior member of the university with an education-focused remit. It is true that pure mathematics in particular, and mathematics more generally, has the reputation for an old style of delivery – 'chalk and talk' – and one of the few places in the university where chalk boards can still be found is in the offices of mathematicians. However, I feel that this reputation is no longer accurate.

Mathematics (and other quantitative subjects, such as engineering or statistics) in fact lends itself to many different aspects of TEL, from the use of short recordings capturing the module lead, solving problems and talking through the solutions, to the use of mathematical software packages to generate questions for students and provide them with formative feedback; from embedding programming skills within taught modules, to developing the knowledge-searching and processing skills to explore unknown mathematical questions. However, when we consider the issue of the use of TEL more broadly, there are still definite issues to be addressed. The first is the issue of consistency. Much of the development of the use of TEL in its various guises is discipline dependent and is driven by the interests and needs of individuals. While this can be valuable from the point of view of students on an individual module, it does create the possibility of an inequity of experience of students across modules, depending on the interests and needs of the individual module leads.

This observation immediately leads to two others. The first of these concerns the availability of the hardware and software to make TEL possible. A good clue here is to consider the resources available to any member of staff in any lecture theatre on campus. There will almost certainly be a podium desktop computer linked to an overhead display projector and wireless access to the internet in the lecture theatre, but can the lecturer smoothly and easily screencast from their iPad to the projector? There may be lecture capture facilities available, but how well do they capture the use of white boards? More critical than the availability of hardware and software resources, is the training and support for members of academic staff to use these resources and to use them well.

In part, training needs are caught up in the transition of higher education from a focus on the delivery of facts to the development of skills for processing facts and communicating results. In the former case, the resource needs and the training needs are both relatively limited. If I can reach all the corners of the room with my voice, possibly assisted by a microphone, and my handwriting on the board can be read, I can transmit the information I intend to transmit. But once we shift the focus to the development of skills for processing and communicating, I need to now develop an entirely different set of skills, no longer viewing my audience as merely passive recipients.

This transition is underway but haltingly. My personal view is that a large reason for the uneven speed of this transition within individual universities and across the sector is the lack of clear institutional priorities for direction of travel and for the corresponding training and development needs of members of academic staff. Here, the institutional strategy becomes critical. The institution has a duty and responsibility to set the direction of travel for its members of academic staff, and to ensure that the training and support for these staff is in place. And this requires a significant shift in thinking from the institutions. Training is time-intensive and expensive. At research-intensive universities, most of the academic staff involved in teaching are part-time teachers. We are part-time researchers. We are part-time administrators, though most academic staff have relatively small administrative lives. And so creating the time and space to engage in this training and development takes effort and requires care.

From the bottom up – encouraging the use of technology-enhanced learning with students and staff through the use of Student Champions (iChamps)

In talking about how to engage students to use technology to enhance their learning, there needs to be some explanation here: we want to cover some misconceptions first. Firstly, there is no such thing as a 'digital native'. It is an over-hyped falsehood that has gone too far and needs to stop. Prensky (2001) coined the term to describe a generational divide: people of a certain age use technology naturally and have some kind of tacit skill set which they can adapt much more easily than the rest of us, those of us who were born in a time when PCs were not commonplace, and neither were mobile phones, social media and the web. Time and time again, 'digital natives' is how our students are referred to, those under 30 years old, who are assumed to know instinctively how to use within an academic setting the technologies that they use every day. This is, of course, a complete fallacy and should be disregarded. Students are no more adept at using the web than anyone else, however old, who is interested in its use and curious enough to see what various technologies can do – and they are the ones within our universities we need to make use of in the design of our programmes and as tools for engaging our students. The attitude makes all the difference, a point we will come back to later.

Secondly, the term 'technology-enhanced learning' (TEL) refers to the fact that we needed to find a better way of explaining the web-based learning that was dominating the higher education landscape. Although e-learning was commonly used, it probably related more often than not, to working with a stand-alone computer, something disconnected from the web and on which the user worked in isolation. As the web developed, so we turned our attention away from e-learning to TEL, purely because it meant more than a PC and a CD-ROM. 'Networked learning' is another term that could be applied, but we don't want to get too hung up on parlance. TEL in this case refers to any web-based technology that can be used to enhance educational practice – usually for engagement, but also as a tool to develop the skills that allow our students (and staff) to become effective users of the web and develop their digital literacies, knowledge and skills.

One exacerbating aspect of universities is that the members of academic staff are highly intelligent, highly motivated people. If an institution were to put into place a structure of standard tools, along with training opportunities and development programmes in how to use these tools and how to integrate them into their teaching, then we feel the take up among academic staff would be quite high. But there is a curious aspect of the academic mindset. We, and we are as guilty of this as many of our colleagues, tend to want to start from the beginning and find our own way. This is how we were taught as researchers and we sometimes seek to apply this framework, for lack of a better term, to everything we do. But this aspect is something that we think is peculiar to academia, and peculiar to pockets within academia. Given a clear path, academic staff will, we are convinced take the path of improvement and benefit to the students. If we make it straightforward for them to do so.

Digital literacies and why they are important to recognise

The term 'digital literacy' is another phrase bandied about, with very little thought about its meaning. When we use the term, we are referring to the set of skills that allow for a range of actions for effective use of the web: "*the capabilities required to thrive in and beyond education, in an age when digital forms of information and communication predominate*" (Littlejohn, Beetham and Mcgill, 2012) – not just how to use a computer or how to access and use the software. These skills are fundamental as we all work in a knowledge economy and are lifelong learners.

In terms of setting the scene for engagement with technology, these concepts – of who our students are, what we mean by the terms 'technology-enhanced learning' and 'digital literacies' – are vital to provide a foundation of 'value' for engagement. Providing value for the students is vital to engagement, regardless of our own motivations for using technology to enhance programmes. When purchasing new technologies, it is important to prioritise value to students, and be cautious of other considerations which often distract us such as meeting regulatory requirements, cost or other institutional objectives which may hinder engagement rather than inspire it.

The importance of digital literacy skills should never be underestimated. These are fundamental to any engagement with TEL as they provide the skills required to be effective and efficient learners, embracing the web to create, collaborate, communicate and be a true 'citizen of the web' (Ryberg and Georgsen, 2010). These skills are usually only paid lip service and projects come and go, rarely maintained once the funding goes. Such skills should be, by now, embedded into programmes and recognised as being as important as team working and communication in face-to-face settings. Our students know that they need to engage with people from around the world, that they need to be able to make the best use of technology, through informed practice, within the 'safe space' of their programme (before they launch themselves into their world of employment). Although they do not necessarily know how, so programmes or activities that allow these skills to be developed are essential (Li and Ranieri, 2010).

Linking this back to a point made above, one very helpful structure to put into place involves a framework. The lowest level of the framework contains those aspects of educational IT that all members of academic staff are expected to be able to use, and to use. This framework is more than a list of tools: it includes access information and training, as well as institutional expectations and best practice for the use of these tools. Higher levels of the framework contain tools that require some specialist training to use fluently, both on the part of academic staff and students, but since they live within this institutional framework, there are clear institutional expectations and champions who can assist those interested in using them. However, it is not enough to have such a framework sitting alongside the taught modules and programmes. The framework needs to be embedded within them, and there needs to be the institutional support on how best to use the educational IT for the module at hand. And it is here that the iChamps model becomes important, as part of this programme of institutional support.

The role of students as champions for engagement with digital literacies skills – Fiona Harvey, Education Development Manager, University College of Estate Management (UCEM) (UK)

My role had always been that of academic staff development, with a particular emphasis on technology. As an Education Development Manager, my role was to work with academic staff to support the implementation of technology to enhance their practice. This is not an easy task in a university where the focus is on research and not education. Nevertheless, I had established useful networks of people who were enthusiastic and engaged, willing to experiment and implement new ideas in their programmes, if the ideas satisfied their needs.

I had been introduced to the concept of digital literacies when I was a student at Edinburgh University on their MSc programme "*Digital Education*". In the very first module "*Introduction to Digital Environments for Learning*" we were encouraged to read about digital literacies skills and I realised then that this was exactly what was required to allow me to do my job more effectively. Being digitally literate is an ongoing goal, and requires continued engagement from staff and students, but it is also a life-long skill to be curious and explore the web through the lens of an informed individual and not blindly tripping and stumbling through the web, clueless as to how you got there or even what you have signed up for. So it was with this information that I took forward the ideas that I had as I could see that digital literacies were the bedrock for enabling staff and students to be able to make the best use of the web and associated tools. At the University of Southampton between 2013 and 2017 there was a successful drive to bring digital literacies to the attention of the university through a variety of activities and with the support of initial internal project funding. The Digital Literacies Project was designed to bring the term 'digital literacies' to the attention of the academic community, originally through a series of workshops, a new module and an final event. Within the project there was funding for one student to act as a champion for the project as we knew that we needed to get students involved as the whole point was to enhance their programmes. Without the buy-in from the students then none of the academic activities work. The ultimate aim, of course, was to bring digital literacies skills into programmes that would support students and staff to use technology effectively to enhance their programmes and it would then become the 'norm'. As it turned out, we didn't have just one student but we started with four. These students ran workshops and helped at the final event. The project was a success and the student champion model was carried over and funding was provided to maintain the Champions for the life of the learning and teaching unit.

The student champions model was known initially as 'DigiChamps' and evolved into the 'Innovation and Digital Literacies Champions' ('iChamps'). The basis of the model is that students should be involved in the development of skills, nothing else, and that they should be able to evidence all the work that they do. We were very clear that the role was not to replace a member of staff, but that they were there to support their academic member of staff and encourage other students to participate in whatever the project required. They served the function of support for academics to be able to try out the use of some form of TEL and they covered a range of projects from supporting students to write blog posts, using apps like Nearpod, and developing materials with the academic member of staff. The reason that the iChamps worked so well was that the students were able to build up their own confidence and the confidence of an academic member of staff, and that they kept track of their own contributions through the use of 'open badges' (explained below) and e-portfolios.

The key means of student engagement using this model was the shared working between the students and the staff. It was explicitly mentioned to both the academic lead and the iChamp that there was no hierarchy, that the student was as responsible for the success of their project as much as the academic. An outcome was to allow staff to explore new ideas around TEL, with the help of a nominated student within their programmes, in a supported environment. In addition, the students who took that particular module with the academic were not just thrown into the deep end and expected to pick up how the tools were used, but were supported by their peers and provided a supportive environment with very low levels of exposure to asking embarrassing questions. They were encouraged to engage and had the support to do it. Likewise, through this partnership approach, staff were able to bring in enhancements that otherwise they might not have done, held back by concerns such as lack of time and fear of failure in front of their students (a common concern); and, of course, they were able to develop their own digital skills.

One of the key indicators of engagement was through the use of 'open badges'. To become an iChamp required completion of a set of three badges. These were used, in this case, not as a motivator but to recognise the contributions that the students made. Each badge offered digital literacies skills and they served two purposes: for the institution, we could see what was being done and we had set these badges as a kind of standard to be achieved. For the students, they completed the activities and were awarded their badges as a result; once they had all three then they could claim the overall iChamp badge. All the badges required the students to provide evidence of their completed set tasks. The evidence for each formed the students' e-portfolio and, using Pathbrite (a Cengage reflection or e-portfolio tool), the students provided the URL for their specific e-portfolio in Pathbrite. All the badges required a contribution to the general iChamps blog which meant that students reflected on all their work as an iChamp. The engagement happened because there was value to the students as well as the staff involved. The projects were directed and specific to issues or ideas that directly related to the students and served a clear purpose for the staff who were involved.

There are challenges involved in implementing the iChamps model, as there are challenges in any significant programme of work. How, for instance, can the model be scaled up to allow for iChamps for all who are interested in using them? Ideally, and this is still work in progress, the iChamps model can be made relatively self-sustaining, perhaps having the experienced iChamps be part of the process for choosing both future iChamps and the members of academic staff for them to work with and the projects for them to work on. This would allow for the transmission of experience across generations, which would clearly be of benefit to all concerned.

Since the project began at the University of Southampton, I have now moved on to the University College of Estate Management (UCEM), and I am using the same model there for staff development. UCEM is a completely online university for the study of the Built Environment and heavily reliant on its staff and students to have digital literacies skills. I work with a team of Educational Technologists who are all in new roles working closely with academic staff and so the iChamps model is also useful for staff engagement. The use of e-portfolios and open badges for the students allows them to capture their work and show how it has been applied. Engaging students through the use of badges and e-portfolios within a face-to-face environment and within a very traditional university like the University of Southampton had its challenges, but within a completely online university, there are advantages and disadvantages. Not being together all the time is not that much of a barrier to staff engaging with each other – we communicate regularly through various online methods. However, the success of the iChamps model with exclusively online students depends on my team having the right skills as well as the confidence and vision to see the model through. This will be the next chapter of the iChamps model, within a vocational online setting.

The model, whether used for a campus-based or completely online university, is not just a chance for students to develop their digital literacies skills, but it also constitutes a strategic drive to support the institution to become digitally literate and use authentic student engagement. For programmes to be effective online and have the students at the centre of the process requires both staff and students to be able to use the web effectively. At UCEM, using the iChamps model to enhance student engagement, we are planning on selecting some of our online students to be part of the process and champion our projects over the next few years. This will build a community of practice for both staff and students, and in turn lead our digital literacies strategy. Within the University of Southampton, there has been a broad use of different types of strategy to engage with TEL through students and through various staff initiatives. Learning from our experiences of these initiatives will help us achieve our ambitions of supporting digital literacies across all our programmes, including research and engagement. Within both types of institution, there are challenges that need to be addressed, but fundamental to success in each case is the common application of reflective practice – on the part of members of the institution *and* the student body – in order to realise the mutual benefits to all. Working together through these partnerships in the ways that we have mentioned is essential to ensure that the interests of both students and the institutions of which they are part are given equal importance, and it is never that one holds precedence over the other.

References

Becker, S.A., Brown, M., Dahlstrom, E., Davis, A., DePaul, K., Diaz, V. and Pomerantz, J., 2018. *NMC Horizon Report 2018 Higher Education Edition*. Louisville, CO: EDUCAUSE. Retrieved from: https://library.educause.edu/~/media/files/library/2018/8/2018horizonreport.pdf (accessed 21 April 2019).

ECORYS, 2016. 'Digital skills for the UK economy', *Department for Business Innovation and Skills* (January), p.130. Retrieved from: https://assets.publishing.service.gov.uk/government/uploads/system/uploads/attachment_data/file/492889/DCMSDigitalSkillsReportJan2016.pdf

Fujitsu, 2018. *Research report: The road to digital learning*. London. Retrieved from: www.birmingham.ac.uk/Documents/HEFI/FUJ-Education-Report-UK.pdf (accessed 21 April 2019).

Gil-Jaurena, I. and Domínguez, D., 2018. 'Teachers' roles in light of massive open online courses (MOOCs): Evolution and challenges in higher distance education', *International Review of Education*, 64(2), pp.197–219. doi:10.1007/s11159-018-9715-0.

Harvey, F., 2018. 'Students as Digital Partners – empowering staff and students together', *Journal of Educational Innovation, Partnership and Change*, 4(1). Retrieved from: doi:http://dx.doi.org/10.21100/jeipc.v4i1.549.

Jaschik, S., 2015. 'Stanford president offers predictions on a more digital future for higher education', Inside Higher Ed. Retrieved from: www.insidehighered.com/ news/2015/03/16/stanford-president-offers-predictions-more-digital-future- higher-education (accessed 21 April 2019).

Kuh, G. D., 2009. 'What student affairs professionals need to know about student engagement', *Journal of College Student Development*, 50(6), pp.683–706. doi:10.1353/csd.0.0099.

Li, Y. and Ranieri, M., 2010. 'Are "digital natives" really digitally competent? – A study on Chinese teenagers', *British Journal of Educational Technology*, 41(6), pp.1029–1042.

Littlejohn, A., Beetham, H. and Mcgill, L., 2012 'Learning at the digital frontier: A review of digital literacies in theory and practice', *Journal of Computer Assisted Learning*, 28(6), pp.547–556. doi:10.1111/j.1365-2729.2011.00474.x.

Prensky, M., 2001. 'Digital Natives, Digital Immigrants.' *On the Horizon*, 9(5).

Ryberg, T. and Georgsen, M., 2010. 'Enabling Digital Literacy', *Nordic Journal of Digital Literacy*, 5(02), pp.88–100. Retrieved from: www.idunn.no/dk/2010/ 02/art03.

Salmon, G., 2000. *E-moderating: The Key to Teaching and Learning Online: EBSCOhost* (1st ed.). London: Taylor and Francis. Retrieved from: http://web.b.ebscohost. com.ezproxy.lancs.ac.uk/ehost/detail?sid=61499d32-f6d5-43c2-ab0f- dcb90af4c794@sessionmgr120andvid=0andformat=EBandrid=1#AN=56799andd b=nlebk (accessed 21 April 2019).

University College of Estate Management (UCEM), 2018. *About UCEM – University College of Estate Management*. Retrieved from: www.ucem.ac.uk/about-ucem/ (accessed 21 April 2018).

University of Southampton, 2016. *Reputation and rankings | University of Southampton*. Retrieved from: www.southampton.ac.uk/about/reputation.page (accessed 9 March 2018).

Chapter 16

Empowering students to enhance education at their university

Jenny Marie

Introduction

This chapter considers the contexts, philosophies and practical realities that lie behind schemes that aim to empower students to enhance education within a higher education (HE) setting. The context of a scheme is important for understanding what is possible and the difference it is trying to make; the philosophy speaks more to the beliefs that lie behind the schemes and the values that it exhibits; while the practicalities show the limits within which the work occurs.

I use my experience of leading a large institutional partnership scheme at University College London (UCL) (UK) for the past three years to explore these issues. UCL is a large research-intensive university, situated in the middle of London. It has approximately 40,000 students, just under half of whom are undergraduate, and approximately 80 departments. The scheme I lead has been highly successful; departments that received some form of support from it in 2015/16 had improvements in their National Student Survey (NSS) satisfaction rates that were statistically significantly higher than departments that did not engage with the scheme, both between 2015 and 2016 and from 2015 to 2017 and to 2018 (see also Marie and Azuma, 2018). The scheme has also supported the development of a whole range of resources and innovative practices. However, there have also been numerous challenges, which have led me to question the philosophical underpinnings of the scheme.

I discuss the limitations that I found with a 'students as change agents' model (Dunne, Zandstra, Brown, and Nurser, 2011) in terms of creating an environment conducive to the projects making a sustainable impact on education and as a mechanism for culture change across my university. As a result, I shifted the model behind the programme towards student/staff partnership (Healey, Flint and Harrington, 2014). However, the reality lags behind: students who initiate projects often fail to properly engage with staff, and students on staff projects are not always sufficiently empowered to contribute equally. Even where students appear to be, other commitments sometimes draw their attention away and staff have been frustrated by a lack of shared responsibility for seeing the project through. Partnership is not easy; it requires the negotiation of new roles in a context of participants simultaneously holding hierarchical ones (Cook-Sather, 2014).

At the same time, my institution is working towards an ideal of students being fully involved in all aspects of quality assurance and enhancement. As a result, we have invited students and departments with lower student satisfaction to work together to ensure there is sufficient student input on departmental enhancement plans and to implement parts of it in partnership. Despite a number of practical limitations (in particular time and money), these partnerships have been some of the most successful in terms of impact and conceptual changes amongst those taking part. This chapter explores how their impact has been ensured by their close link to departmental and institutional priorities and how students have overcome the institutional driver to make change that is meaningful for them.

Developing a partnership scheme for funding enhancement projects

The programme I lead, UCL ChangeMakers, was originally based on Exeter's 'students as change agents' scheme. The latter aims to give students the opportunity to make changes that are important to them: this may be to the environment, the local community or their educational experience. The changes are designed to make a lasting impact, through either making recommendations or having planned actions. For example, students persuaded the Business school to purchase 4,000 voting sets as a result of their project (Kay, Dunne, E. and Hutchinson, 2010).

Exeter's 'students as change agents' scheme originated in 2008, in a context of the UK government positioning students as customers of their education (Browne, 2010). This was fiercely contended (and still is) by the National Union of Students (NUS, 2012) and by many working in universities. The 'students as change agents' scheme was clearly positioned in opposition to student consumerism, with students and staff having collective responsibility for the university (Dunne et al., 2011). Though the concept of 'students as partners' already existed, in the UK context of the late 2000s it became positioned in opposition to the concept of 'students as consumers' (Neary and Winn, 2009). As I have argued elsewhere (Marie, 2018), this positioning is political rather than natural – partnership can serve the purposes of consumerism, as illustrated in the section 'Consumerism?' below.

When UCL ChangeMakers took the 'students as change agents' model up in 2014, there were many examples of such initiatives across the country – the most notable being at Birmingham City (UK) and Winchester (UK) (Nygaard, Brand, Bartholomew and Millard, 2013; Sims, King, Lowe and El Hakim, 2016) – and these influenced the form of the scheme. For example, we originally used the idea of bursaries from the University of Winchester (UK). The local context for our scheme also influenced its form. Based, as it is, in a department for academic development, it only funded projects that enhanced the student learning experience, rather than any aspect of the student experience as at Exeter. The Student Union recommended that we required the students to work with a staff partner from their department to give the projects legitimacy. The opportunity also existed for us to bring staff projects under the same scheme and to make it a condition that these were conducted in partnership with students. Philosophically, this came from a desire to create a single learning community at UCL; whereby any member of the community could apply for the funding.

Bringing the staff projects under the scheme allowed us to adopt the aim of encouraging a culture of student–staff partnership for educational enhancement work, based on the idea that partnership work should produce results that better meet student needs because while staff have subject and pedagogic expertise, students better understand the student learning experience (Cook-Sather, Bovill and Felten, 2014). In 2015/16, we drew the projects together under the scheme in a 'soft' way: we had funding ring-fenced for student-initiated projects and for staff-initiated projects, out of concern that the students would be out-competed for the funding by staff, who have more experience of writing grant bids. What we found was that (1) students wrote applications that were at least as good as those written by staff, particularly when we supported the application-writing process; and (2) that staff and students came together to write proposals and then did not know whether to submit their application as a student or staff project. The latter seemed to defeat our own purposes – we therefore abolished the distinction the following year and have found that the ratio of student and staff projects has been roughly equal in almost all funding rounds.

The challenges of student-led and staff-led projects

Despite our official abolition of the distinction between student and staff-initiated projects, it has remained far longer in our minds because there are significantly different challenges depending upon whether the project is student-led or staff-led, with truly collaborative projects being in the minority. An evaluation of the pilot year projects, which were all student-led revealed that students often did not work in partnership with their staff partners. Students thought that their staff partners were too busy; they found that they could run their projects alone; and communication between the students and staff was often difficult (Marie and McGowan, 2017). What we were finding at UCL, was that the 'students as change agents' model was not a model of partnership for enhancement projects: it was partnership at a higher, more conceptual level. This was recognised to some extent by the Exeter team, who wrote: "*the way in which the scheme is organised does not require huge time commitments for academic and professional staff: hence they are more likely to engage and to maintain that engagement*" (Kay et al., 2010).

At UCL, we found this was problematic for the projects making a lasting impact because students graduate, go on year abroad placements and so on. For the projects to make a lasting impact, they needed the buy-in of staff or the projects needed continuing support to enable a new set of students to take over and also gain recognition. At the end of 2015/16 matters came to a head; one of the projects we had funded that year was a highly successful project to organise a departmental conference in the geography department (Thorogood. Azuma, Collins, Plyushteva, and Marie, 2018). The project team approached us about gaining funding to run the project again the following year. My view, which was shared by the steering group, was that we could not fund such projects indefinitely or all our funding would eventually be used up supporting these projects. At the time we took a policy decision not to fund straight re-runs of projects; though we now offer continuation funding to support projects into their second year, with the explicit aims that they become embedded in (usually departmental) practice and they disseminate their work across the university. The decision led us to focus on the partnership element of the projects and to encourage students to see their project as aiming to change practice in the longer term, rather than to simply run a successful pilot or to make recommendations that are not taken up. The geography conference itself did run again the following year despite failing to collect participant feedback, because it gained the support of the head of department and because it opened participation to college students and school teachers, thus enabling it to access outreach funding (Thorogood et al., 2018). This served as a lesson to the ChangeMakers team that we needed to emphasise the importance of evaluation, stakeholder engagement and creative thinking about how to engage stakeholders with required resources. The outcome of doing so has been that 18% of all projects (student and staff-initiated) in 2017/ 18 embedded change in the year of the project, up from 10% in 2016/17 and a further 45% are estimated to have a good chance of embedding change within 2 years, up from 40% in 2016/17.

The staff-led projects have not yet been systematically evaluated in the same way. However, there is always a fear about to what extent students are being empowered to work in partnership with staff and to what extent are they are being directed by them. My colleagues, Sandra and Abbie, tell me that students on staff-led projects are more likely to refer to their staff partner as their supervisor, suggesting that staff and students are falling back on this more familiar model of a relationship. Grant (1999, as cited in Deuchar, 2008) has argued that the doctoral supervision relationship is profoundly unequal in terms of power. However, supervisory relationships are not all the same. Taylor (2005) identifies four styles: 'laissez-faire' whereby the student is seen as capable of managing both their doctoral work and themselves; 'pastoral', whereby the student is seen as requiring personal support; 'directorial' whereby the supervisor helps the student to manage their project but does not provide personal support; and 'contractual' whereby the support given in these two dimensions is negotiated. The staff partners will focus on supporting the student to undertake the project – thus being more 'directorial'. However, the level of support may be open to negotiation, as per the 'contractual' style.

My own experience of acting as a staff partner on enhancement projects bears out the idea that the staff partner role can vary, while remaining supervisory, even within the same project. On one project, I set the brief as being to create student guides to assessment and feedback but was open to the students' ideas about the format they should take and how they would go about creating them. The students opted to run focus groups to find out what students would gain from learning, what they wanted to know and to gain quotes about good practice that they could include within the guides. I would never have gone about the project in this way: but it has worked. Up to this stage, my role had been to encourage and to motivate the project through a series of meetings to discuss progress. Where my fellow staff partners became more directive was when the guides were at draft stage and we requested that they sought staff and student feedback and conducted student user-testing. At this stage, the students could have refused but the power lay with the staff: we were the ones that would arrange the production and distribution of the guides and we were unlikely to do that without them passing through some quality assurance process. Our role changed during the project from supervisor to a gate-keeper for the project's lasting impact.

As Alison Cook-Sather (2014) has argued, it is hard to adopt new roles while simultaneously holding onto our traditional hierarchical ones, as students or staff. One of the implicit assumptions in what has been written above is the support that we provide to the projects as a scheme. It has been fairly implicit because for us it has never been in question. Yet I have seen funding given to partnership projects with no support in place. Over the years we have developed this, such that all projects now have an opening meeting to ensure that they have a clear project plan, they have thought about how to embed this in practice and they have agreed how they will work together in partnership – in other words, they have started to form that contract.

Forwarding education in line with strategy

The 'students as change agents' model has one further difference from the one currently being pursued by UCL ChangeMakers. Dunne et al. (2011) explicitly position 'students as change agents' as going beyond partnership, which they state is usually institutionally driven, such that students make change meaningful and important to themselves.

In drawing the staff projects into UCL ChangeMakers, we also drew in some of the drivers behind these grants. Their purpose had been to forward UCL's research-based education strategy, the Connected Curriculum (Fung, 2017). Over time we realised that our decision-making about which projects to fund usually considered projects that would forward the Education strategy but not the Connected Curriculum as equally valid; we therefore changed the funding criteria to forwarding UCL's Education or Doctoral Education strategy.

The reasoning for adopting strategic criteria for the grants was pragmatic: if you want to take over staff grants in order to encourage a culture of partnership for educational enhancement work, you inherit the drivers for those grants. Yet, the philosophy of this is significantly different from that of students making the changes that they care about. The concept of partnership is founded upon the idea that students have situated knowledge about the student experience (Cook-Sather et al., 2014, Haraway, 1988) and it questions concepts of patronage, whereby institutions know what is best for their students (and staff). However, while it brings into question that institutions know best, it does not deny that they have some relevant expertise to bring to this question. As Cook-Sather et al. (2014) state, staff have pedagogic and subject expertise. This expertise will also be important in determining what educational changes will have the most impact. Institutional strategies go beyond this, considering the national and international context in which the institution sits, the institution's strengths, weaknesses and aims. Though some aspects are likely to be more pertinent to particular departments, the strategy adds another dimension of expertise.

Strategies exist to enable prioritisation of time, effort and funding. However, they need to exist outside of local contexts. For UCL ChangeMakers, students and staff put forward the projects that are important to them, based on their expertise in the student experience, the staff experience, subject-knowledge and/or pedagogic expertise. Our experience in running the projects (are they feasible, how likely are they to make a lasting impact, will they be run in partnership and so on) and strategy are layered over this to help us bring together all of this expertise to select projects that we believe are most likely to forward the student learning experience at UCL.

Institution-led change

The projects described above have originated at grass roots level, whether from students or staff, despite being judged, in part, on institutional priorities. In 2015/16, I started to design a package of partnership work, which originated with the institution. At that time, UCL changed its method of annual monitoring to an Annual Student Experience Review (ASER), whereby departments were given a data set and were asked to evaluate their provision and create a developmental plan for the coming year. Departments with low levels of student satisfaction, as measured by the National Student Survey (NSS), were given additional support in the form of meetings with senior managers and were asked to undertake a project in partnership with students in the area of Assessment and Feedback. Assessment and Feedback was chosen due to this being the area of the NSS for which UCL gets its lowest student satisfaction ratings and thus improvement in this area is an institutional priority.

The rationale behind the projects was that by increasing student engagement with their department, student satisfaction levels should also rise. This hypothesis was based on the finding of Zhao and Kuh (2004) that increased student participation in a learning community increases both student engagement and student satisfaction. Though Zhao and Kuh only included students within their definition of a learning community, broadening its definition to include departmental staff was not thought likely to change the benefits to student satisfaction. However, there was also a danger that if departments did not engage with the process they could send the message to their students that they did not care about them or their views. In other words, while the process was designed to provide a structure for improving the engagement of staff and students with each other; if staff failed to engage, this process risked highlighting that.

The project that was carried out in departments was informed, in the first year, by a mixture of the institutional framing described above, pedagogic input, student experiences and the departmental view. Having recruited students to conduct the projects, they were provided with some pedagogic training in assessment and feedback, designed to give them ideas about potential projects. Thus in the training they were introduced to ideas such as guided marking (see example 3a in Cook-Sather et al., 2014), marker's commentaries (QMUL, 2011), feedback pro formas and sheets for students to request a particular focus for the feedback they received (Bloxham and Campbell, 2010). The students then met with a departmental representative and I facilitated a meeting whereby they agreed a project between them. One of the things that surprised me (despite the example of the voting handsets at the University of Exeter (UK) described above) was how much more open staff were to ideas that came from their own students than they were to ideas from me as an academic developer. There is a concern that student partners should not be over-trained in pedagogy because it takes them away from their student perspective and positions them as having a deficit (Felten and Bauman, 2013). However, where students are allowed to judge pedagogic ideas from a student perspective, they can make the case for those they favour far more strongly than staff, even those whose expertise is in pedagogy.

Though this way of deciding the projects worked well, it was also very costly in terms of the support required from the UCL ChangeMakers team. There was also a further problem in that the students worked with their own department. While this meant that the students were completely familiar with the context of their work, it made it difficult for them to bring in good practice from elsewhere; the role was challenging for the students, who had to recommend enhancements to staff who taught and assessed them; and it created conflict with the role of student representatives, who were also expected to recommend educational changes. I therefore worked with the Student Union to devise a new role – that of the ASER facilitator, who is a student from a different department that meets with the department and student representatives to understand the departmental context before running a student focus group to better understand the student perspective. Coming from outside the department, they challenge the views of all parties and represent them back to each other, suggesting actions that can be taken to improve the student learning experience from their own experience in a different department. One of the things we are currently looking at is the possibility of the partnership project coming out of this work, whilst continuing to be conducted by staff and students from within the department.

Consumerism?

Partnership work, at a local level at least, does not need to be in opposition to consumerism. Through undertaking projects students gain important employability skills, such as project management, managing resources and change management (Thorogood et al., 2018). The latter is the third of UCL ChangeMakers aims, and this aim can be thought of as serving consumerism because research has shown that well-developed skills greatly enhance employability (Osmani Weerakkody, Hindi, Al-Esmail, Eldabi, Kapoor and Irani, 2015).

Beyond this, the outcomes of the projects can improve student satisfaction levels. The departments that had an assessment and feedback project in 2015/16 saw an average increase in their NSS scores in this area of 5.2%, compared to 0.9% for departments that had no such project (Marie and Azuma, 2018). When the normal UCL ChangeMakers projects are also taken into consideration, we see that departments with neither a ChangeMakers project at undergraduate level nor an Assessment and Feedback project saw a drop of 3.8% in their NSS overall satisfaction levels, compared to an increase of 3.5% for departments that had either (or both) a UCL ChangeMakers project at undergraduate level and/or an Assessment and Feedback project.

The aim of raising satisfaction levels can be critiqued – there is a difference between satisfaction and learning and the two sometimes conflict. The UK's National Student Survey (NSS), which is used to measure satisfaction levels, originated as part of the apparatus of students becoming consumers (Crawford, 2012). It was intended to be a tool for students to select their university based on student satisfaction levels, which are made public. The concept of student consumerism has been critiqued on many grounds: students cannot buy a degree; learning is an active process to which they must contribute – in other words they must be partners in their learning. Moreover, students are not sole experts in what is best for them: staff have the expertise in pedagogy and the subject, and standards are safe-guarded within the sector by external bodies such as the UK Quality Assurance Agency and professional bodies. Such arguments lie behind the rationale for partnership work. However, none of these arguments posit that it is a bad thing for students to get a good job on graduation or that students should not be satisfied with the education they receive, so long as satisfaction is seen within a broader context of learning.

There are many beneficiaries of higher education: the students themselves, the providers, employers and society. Students should have some rights and say, as per the consumerist model; so long as this is within a context of other stakeholders also having a say – in other words the consumerist model is okay so long as it represents the student voice as just one of the voices within a bigger frame of partnership.

Conclusion

Partnership schemes are products of their contexts. Each has its own aims and underlying philosophy, which will differ slightly from each other. What partnership work has in common is an underlying belief in situated knowledge and a philosophy of abundance rather than deficit. Students know things that staff cannot because they are not in the same situation; and students have knowledge and ideas to offer now – they do not have to wait until some future point when they are considered sufficiently formed. As a result of the abundance model, I have been cautious about training students in pedagogy – worried about moving them from their student perspective. Yet if we take the idea of situated knowledge seriously, students will retain this while gaining pedagogic knowledge. The work of the students negotiating the assessment and feedback projects above suggested that they can look at pedagogic ideas through a student lens and more powerfully argue for those that suit students with departmental staff than an academic developer can.

Most partnership work focuses on the relationship between staff and students. In this chapter, I have flagged another important partner that tends to be less considered: the institution, which I argue has expertise to offer in the form of understanding the institution's context and its strengths and weaknesses. 'Students as change agents' was in part a reaction against the institution setting the agenda. I believe that, practitioners in the UK at least, have over-compensated for this. The context is such that the importance of allowing students to help shape the agenda is now sufficiently recognised that we can consider not only the role and expertise that staff bring to this, but also the institution.

Partnership work may be entirely collaborative, but in the majority of situations it is likely to be led by either students, staff or the institution. Each approach offers its own challenges – which in the case of UCL included sustaining impact, empowering students, and institutional politics respectively. Further investigation is required to fully understand the different challenges that each faces. The staff-led projects at UCL suggest that, in a context of a lack of clarity about the relationship between staff and students, partners may be falling back onto a model that they are familiar with: that of supervision. More work is required to explore this fully, but if this is the case, we need to think about how to encourage the more contractual type of supervisory relationship that seems to be more in keeping with partnership work.

Partnership has been framed as being in opposition to consumerism. Yet consumerism has many facets to it. Partnership is in opposition to the idea that by paying fees students have no further responsibility for their own education. Yet, this can be interpreted in different ways. If partnership is considered at a macro level, whereby the student body and the university are both seen as responsible for enhancing the student learning environment, then students could be considered to fulfil their responsibility via student representation, the giving of feedback and/or students as change agents. The first two are still considered in line with consumerism – as they could be done by giving customer feedback and leaving it to the institution to respond. At a micro level, partnership occurs when staff and students have joint responsibility for an aspect of education. Yet the outcomes of this are likely to be those sought within a consumerist model – better employment statistics and improved student satisfaction. If the debate over whether we want/ work within a partnership or consumerist model is to move on, both partnership and consumerism need to be further unpicked.

References

Bloxham, S. and Campbell, L., 2010. Generating dialogue in assessment feedback: exploring the use of interactive cover sheets. *Assessment and Evaluation in Higher Education*, 35, 291–300. Retrieved from: https://doi.org/10.1080/02602931003650045

Browne, J., 2010. Securing a sustainable future for higher education: an independent review of higher education funding and student finance. Retrieved from: www.gov.uk/government/publications/the-browne-report-higher-education-funding-and-student-finance

Cook-Sather, A., 2014. Student–faculty partnership in explorations of pedagogical practice: a threshold concept in academic development. *International Journal for Academic Development*, 19, 186–198. Retrieved from: https://doi.org/10.1080/1360144x.2013.805694

Cook-Sather, A., Bovill, C. and Felten, P., 2014. *Engaging students as partners in learning and teaching: A guide for faculty*, John Wiley and Sons.

Crawford, K., 2012. Rethinking the student/teacher nexus: students as consultants on teaching in higher education. *In:* Neary, M., Stevenson, H. and Bell, L. (eds.) *Towards teaching in public: Reshaping the modern university.* Bloomsbury Publishing.

Deuchar, R., 2008. Facilitator, director or critical friend? Contradiction and congruence in doctoral supervision styles. *Teaching in Higher Education*, 13, 489–500. Retrieved from: https://doi.org/10.1080/13562510802193905

Dunne, E., Zandstra, R., Brown, T. and Nurser, T., 2011. Students as change agents: New ways of engaging with learning and teaching in Higher Education. Retrieved from: https://dera.ioe.ac.uk/14767/

Felten, P. and Bauman, H.-D., 2013. Reframing diversity and student engagement: Lessons from deaf-gain. *In:* Dunne, E. and Owen, D. (eds.) *Student engagement handbook: Practice in higher education.* Bingley: Emerald Group Publishing.

Fung, D., 2017. *A connected curriculum for higher education*, UCL Press.

Grant, B., 1999. 'Walking on a rackety bridge: Mapping supervision'. Paper presented at HERDSA Annual International Conference, July 12–15, Melbourne, Australia.

Haraway, D., 1988. Situated knowledges: The science question in feminism and the privilege of partial perspective. *Feminist Studies*, 14, 575–599. Retrieved from: https://doi.org/10.2307/3178066

Healey, M., Flint, A. and Harrington, K., 2014. Engagement through partnership: Students as partners in learning and teaching in higher education. York: HEA.

Kay, J., Dunne, E. and Hutchinson, J., 2010. Rethinking the values of higher education-students as change agents? Retrieved from: https://dera.ioe.ac.uk/1193/

Marie, J., 2018. The relationship between research-based education and student–staff partnerships. *In:* Tong, V. C., Standen, A. and Sotiriou, M. (eds.) *Shaping Higher Education with Students: Ways to Connect Research and Teaching.* UCL Press.

Marie, J. and Azuma, F., 2018. Partnership support for departments with low student satisfaction. *Student Engagement in Higher Education Journal*, 2 (1), 70–77.

Marie, J. and McGowan, S., 2017. Moving towards sustainable outcomes in student partnerships: Partnership values in the pilot year. *International Journal for Students as Partners*, 1 (2). Retrieved from: https://doi.org/10.15173/ijsap.v1i2.3081

Neary, M. and Winn, J., 2009. The student as producer: reinventing the student experience in higher education. *In:* Bell, L., Stevenson, H. and Neary, M. (eds.) *The Future of Higher Education: Policy, Pedagogy and the Student Experience.* London: Continuum.

Nygaard, C., Brand, S., Bartholomew, P. and Millard, L., 2013. *Student Engagement: Identity, Motivation and Community*, Farringdon, Libri Publishing.

Osmani, M., Weerakkody, V., Hindi, N. M., Al-Esmail, R., Eldabi, T., Kapoor, K. and Irani, Z., 2015. Identifying the trends and impact of graduate attributes on employability: a literature review. *Tertiary Education Management*, 21, 367–379. Retrieved from: https://doi.org/10.1080/13583883.2015.1114139

Queen Mary University London (QMUL), 2011. *Writing in Schools, Higher Education and Employment Settings.* Retrieved from: www.thinkingwriting.qmul. ac.uk/wishees/collections/quinnipiac/microbiologyundergraduatereport/ 55529.html (accessed 5 October 2018).

Sims, S., King, S., Lowe, T. and El Hakim, Y., 2016. Evaluating partnership and impact in the first year of the Winchester Student Fellows Scheme. *Journal of Educational Innovation, Partnership and Change*, 2 (1).

Taylor, S., 2005. *A handbook for doctoral supervisors,* London: Routledge Falmer.

Thorogood, J., Azuma, F., Collins, C., Plyushteva, A. and Marie, J., 2018. Changemakers and change agents: encouraging students as researchers through Changemaker's programmes. *Journal of Geography in Higher Education*, 42 (4), pp.540–556. Retrieved from: https://doi.org/10.1080/03098265.2018.1460804

National Union of Students (NUS) (2012) A manifesto for partnership, p.8. Retrieved from: www.nusconnect.org.uk/resources/a-manifesto-for-partnership/ (accessed 28 July 2019).

Zhao, C.-M. and Kuh, G. D., 2004. Adding value: Learning communities and student engagement. *Research in Higher Education*, 45, 115–138. Retrieved from: https://doi.org/10.1023/b:rihe.0000015692.88534.de

Chapter 17

Students as partners and peer coaches in student engagement

Themes from PASS scheme biographies

Digby Warren and Wilko Luebsen

Introduction

'Student engagement' is both a broad, variously defined concept and a collection of practices that are context-anchored. Certain definitions focus on students' level of engagement in educational activities, inside and outside the classroom, which contribute towards desired learning outcomes (Kuh, Kinzie, Buckley, Bridges, and Hayek, 2007; Krause and Coates, 2008); others emphasise that engagement involves emotional, cognitive and behavioural participation (Trowler, 2010, pp.5–6) that is affected by students' relationships and connections with others, and their autonomy, agency, identity and self-efficacy (Wimpenny and Savin-Baden, 2013). Student engagement can cover a range of processes, including learning and teaching, quality assurance and enhancement, curriculum development, peer-mentoring and collaborative learning, representational structures and institutional governance, and extra-curricular and community programmes (Webb, Russell, and Jarnecki, 2014; Harrington, Sinfield, Burns, 2016). Critical perspectives highlight issues of control, surveillance and genuine student-centredness associated with student engagement practices (Christie, 2014; Macfarlane and Tomlinson, 2017). Positive observed effects of student engagement include enhanced learning and development; improved grades, critical thinking and transferable skills; increased motivation, persistence and sense of connectedness, confidence and self-esteem (Trowler, 2010, pp.33–35).

Fostering student engagement in that richest sense is a core rationale of the PASS (Peer-Assisted Student Success) scheme introduced at London Metropolitan University (UK) since 2014–15. Aimed at assisting first-year students to achieve academic success and social integration, the scheme entails an institutional partnership with trained and paid peer mentors from the second/third-years (Success Coaches) who provide course-embedded and individual support, as role models themselves for student engagement in academic study and the life and opportunities of university. Using a coaching style, the Success Coaches (SCs) facilitate small-group sessions and one-to-one support which seek to help first-years in the same subject area with their learning needs, to succeed on their course, deal with personal issues and develop as more confident, independent learners (see Warren and Luebsen, 2017).

The PASS scheme is centrally coordinated by the university's Centre for Professional and Educational Development (CPED) and locally by staff leads in each of the six academic schools. PASS sessions are offered in almost all undergraduate courses, via one of the core first-year modules, where SCs meet with students in scheduled seminars, workshops, practicals, studios or laboratories, or lunchtime drop-ins. The scheme potentially reaches over 3,000 undergraduates, supported by around 160 active SCs who self-allocate to required slots and submit regular online reports together with their timesheets – for ongoing monitoring of operations and feedback to scheme organisers and course and module leaders.

In terms of the theoretical model on "*integrating students into educational change*" developed by Dunne and Zandstra (2011, p.17), the PASS scheme primarily straddles the axes identified as 'emphasis on the university as driver' and 'emphasis on student action' (not just 'student voice'), which would characterise it as the approach defined by Dunne and Zandstra as incorporating "*students as partners, co-creators and experts*". In our context, the university-wide scheme was initiated from the top by the institution, with the SCs as formally selected and trained partners in curriculum-based provision of student support, with potential scope to be 'co-creators' with teaching staff in designing and/or facilitating PASS sessions. Additionally, the SCs may be considered as 'experts' concerning their own accrued experience as successful, more senior students, which they can usefully draw on to advise first-year learners. Some proactive SCs even emerge as 'drivers' or 'agents for change' (Dunne and Zandstra, 2011.); and the partnership with SCs also extends to employing a small team of the most dynamic, able and experienced to assist with training new cohorts of SCs.

These themes are illuminated with reference to the personal biographies of a selection of SCs representing our diverse profile of students. Their stories illustrate why they became agents, their contributions to student engagement and the benefits that they have, in turn, gained. Data was collected during 2017 through a set of in-depth, semi-structured interviews with a purposive sample of 12 highly committed SCs from different subject areas, and mixed in terms of gender, age, race/ethnicity, and socio-cultural background. The transcribed interviews were analysed to identify common categories from which the following account arises, using quotations from the SCs to reflect their actual perceptions and experiences – typically reflecting the views of at least several interviewees.

Becoming engaged as Success Coaches

In their interviews, SCs revealed a variety of reasons for wishing to become engaged in the PASS scheme (see Figure 17.1). Some were directly inspired by their prior experience of the scheme. Usually this was a positive one, having themselves been helped and encouraged by their SCs: "*because my SC last year was… very useful for my academic path… Having someone next to you, available to help you and to make you feel okay is very helpful.*" However, a less satisfying encounter (for instance, in a few courses where the scheme was still taking shape) could also awaken a sense of service. One SC who, when a first-year student, felt their SC had not been very involved, became determined to help students "*get used to university life… and give the best advice from my own experience*" – as she would have liked to have received herself.

This desire of SCs to share their own experiences with new students was widely held: "*You are transferring the lessons from your mistakes and successes to help someone else and better their education or future.*" It connected with a genuine altruism, a desire to "*help people*", that was a strong motivator for many SCs: "*I was [previously] involved with charity work, and… I was trying to be helpful.*" The chance to earn "*extra money*" through paid work was obviously also a factor, but was never mentioned as a prime driver. Sometimes it was inspiration from their peers that prompted them: "*It was a classmate of mine who was doing SC… He was always talking about SC enthusiastically. He told me about the benefits and that it benefits both ways.*" Furthermore, this prospect of wider benefits and avenues of experience – to use "*for potential further study or employment*", for their personal development and CVs – was also attractive to some SCs: "*I thought that it would make more involved in university issues… It was an excellent opportunity for us to get to experience different people and to put it on our CV and university transcript.*"

Promoting student engagement in learning

In fulfilling their role, the SCs were deeply conscious of their part, and often pro-active, in facilitating first-year students' engagement in learning. They expressed a sense of passion about sharing their knowledge and responding to the different ways people learn: "*What I really enjoy is passing my knowledge to other people, explaining different things, seeing how people learn in different ways.*" Recognising that freshers (first-year students) can feel uncertain about approaching staff – "*A lot of students don't want to ask questions to the lecturer*" – and find it easier to talk to "*someone on their level*" or "*their own age*", SCs described how they sought to build trust, participation and confidence, through use of questioning and feedback (one SC called it "*a Socratic way of learning*"), consistent with the coaching philosophy espoused by the PASS scheme:

> *I'd rather go there and say, okay, so let's say we have this essay question. How would we go about it? What would be a good strategy to deal with this?… I think it worked well because people were more engaged, it wasn't really about listening to somebody teach or preach to them, but rather, "okay I need to do something",* as a student.

At the same time, SCs understood the importance of being "*kind but firm*", offering guidance but pushing first-years to take responsibility for their own learning:

> *If they see that you are firm,* [they realise] *that your help is linked to showing and leading them the right way, but not doing their work.;*
>   *So it was important for us to… make them understand that we are going to give you feedback and help you through, but you need to also build yourself up* [and] *be more confident. I would always push them more.*

SCs also spoke of the thought and preparation they invested to be effective in assisting students:

> *Every session is different. I have to revise for myself on the topic the students are working with;*
>   *In the first year of* [being a] *SC I just went to classes and tried to support the lecturer. This year I am trying to prepare myself more for each session so I can explain things easily, organise notes for that session.*

Some SCs went even further, organising, in liaison with tutors, extra sessions (for example, IT support session, workshop on critical thinking, meeting for foreign students on a foundation course) to address perceived needs – "*we were working from the weakness of students*" – or developing learning resources: "*I made some tutorial Q and A videos together with a lecturer and the media department… aimed at the first coursework, which was difficult for many students. I got feedback from students that it was really helpful.*"

Collaborative working also occurred among SCs, with some forming peer networks so they could support students as a team: "*In the drop-in sessions there would be other SCs present, and we would sometimes help students together or in groups.*" Another commented: "*If you are not strong in something, you can rely on other SCs. If a mentee needs help with Chemistry, an SC can send a message to the WhatsApp group and… we make sure the students get help*" and a third, "*My colleague B, we are friends and always in contact. We use our knowledge to reflect on what we are doing now, we consult each other… Both of us SCs have different skill sets and approaches to students.*" Hence, the diversity among the SCs is an asset in itself, for being able to work with diverse learners in different ways.

Building a learning community

Most students at London Metropolitan University (UK) are commuter students, many with work and family commitments, who fit their studies around their busy lives and attend only sporadically. As with other universities with significant numbers of these 'learn and go' commuter students (see Thomas and Jones, 2017; term cited on p.24), this presents a considerable challenge for developing a 'campus community', compared to more traditional campus-based universities where the academic, social, cultural and sporting life of students is combined. As Pokorny et al. (2017, p.555) have recommended, in the current HE environment where "*increasingly students stay at home to study*", universities need to focus on

"I" and "*promoting extra- and co-curricular activities congruent with commuting and creating social spaces for 'stayeducation' students to 'relax together'*".

In their UK study of commuter student engagement, Thomas and Jones (2017, p.7) found that students

> *tended to undervalue and under-participate in enhancement and social activities. It should be noted, however, that a significant number participated in ambassadorial and/or mentor type roles within their academic department. Such roles may appeal to commuter students because they have links within the academic sphere, and the activities tend to take place during the day.*

Hence it is encouraging that the PASS scheme, focused on the academic space and organised around such roles, has contributed towards building a learning community, as is apparent from the interviews with SCs, and also other data obtained via focus groups with first-year students and SCs respectively (see Warren and Luebsen, 2017).

This has been manifested in three particular respects. Firstly, it has afforded opportunities for co-learning among SCs and first-year students. As one SC put it: "*It's great to see younger people with fresher eyes on stuff. I am learning myself, and they are learning from me, it's a back and forth.*" Another SC ended up working on a project together with a student she had been mentoring. Secondly, it has generated feelings of friendship and connection: "*the PASS scheme helps a lot with making friends... It has expanded my social circle incredibly.*" Several SCs mentioned they had developed good friendships with individuals they had been assisting. Thirdly, it has helped to create a sense of community and belonging. This aspect was powerfully articulated in the focus group with SCs:

> *We not only facilitate, but we ourselves kind of get connected to different opportunities. You feel that you belong, that you are a part of university and you know each other.*

In their interviews too, SCs reflected on how they help to engender that sense of bonding among new students: "*I remember myself as a first-year student, I was quite frightened of what was going on, where to go and how to use different services. I believe that if they have us* [SCs], *seeing us around, having a chat, there is bonding created between us.*" Above all, the PASS scheme is fostering a self-renewing learning culture: "*Students can now fully experience both having a SC and being a SC. It builds this fundamental thing.*"

Challenges and agency

Another key dimension of SCs' engagement is their liaison with lecturers and student advocacy – areas where they can exercise agency. Certainly, some of the challenges they have faced tap into the qualities of initiative and commitment that the best SCs exemplify. Sometimes there were local logistical delays in finalising times and venues (*"How can I support in that module if I don't know where to go, where to be?"*), or some staff members who were not *"really invested"* in providing guidance or interacting with SCs or ensuring that SCs were properly introduced to the class – although, as one SC recalled from her first-year experience, students nevertheless soon discovered that SCs *"helped us a lot"*. So the onus was often on the SCs to contact module leaders and develop a rapport with them, even though staff as well as SCs had been supplied checklists of essential steps for meeting their responsibilities.

Where a positive relationship developed between staff and SCs, so did mutual understanding and influence. On the one hand, *"You get treated seriously because you are a SC and you can have an impact"*, which left some SCs feeling *"proud to be included and trusted"*. On the other, SCs could acquire a better appreciation of their lecturers: *"It's like a new level of respect for lecturers. They do a lot more than you assume they do."* As a channel of communication between teachers and students, SCs could find themselves in the role of *"mediator"*, facilitating clarity on both sides: *"Some students weren't confident enough to ask questions, [so SC was] acting like a link between student and lecturer. Sometimes lecturers [wrongly] assume that [students] know what they are talking about. It also helps the lecturer out as well."*

SCs could also facilitate finding solutions to student issues: *"I got involved by speaking to the course leader... [and] gathered students to discuss it first, and we pointed out what were the issues, but we also came up with solutions to the problems."*

Feedback from SCs could prompt changes in teaching, to aid student learning, such as taking a slower pace, adjusting to the students' level of understanding, allowing more time for coursework in class. Moreover, some SCs fervently embraced the role of student advocate: *"I noticed that a lot of students don't get their voice heard... I want to be that person that people come to when they have issues. I hope that more students feel stronger and empowered."*

These were the ones who become active as student representatives and in other ways.

Catalyst for further student engagement

Active participation in the PASS scheme has thus frequently been a catalyst for further engagement by the SCs, as summed up by one of the interviewees: *"I'm really involved in the university life and I love to help to improve the scheme"*. Additional areas of engagement have included:

- serving as student academic representatives (StARs) on their courses – for which their role as SC furnished both stimulus and confidence: *"you get to know about the problems going around, and you want to become more actively involved. So I became a student representative"*, *"I couldn't have done my role as a class representative as well as I do, if I wasn't a SC"*;

- involvement with the Students' Union (SU), which itself could trigger increased engagement: "*I went to the SU meetings. I felt that I had a lot to say. It made me more active*";
- one of the SCs interviewed became a Student Hub 'support worker' giving advice to students facing allegations of plagiarism, while another became an enthusiastic broadcaster on the SU radio station;
- organising activities for student societies – one SC, for instance, was leader of a dance group;
- becoming Student Ambassadors, trained helpers who assist with schools outreach and higher education orientation activities: "*Success coaching helped me get the recommendation for being a senior Student Ambassador*";
- supporting student induction programmes;
- volunteering – for example, helping as a lab assistant, offering free massage therapy for university sports teams, working on a community project in Africa.

SCs have also provided input to enhance PASS scheme recruitment and training, through giving feedback in annual evaluations and/or becoming trained trainers (under staff supervision) for the next year's cohort of SCs. In this capacity, they are 'co-creators' whose ideas and suggestions help to refine both the content and process of training, and the operation of the scheme more generally. For example, SCs highlighted that more attention should be placed on what new SCs would need to do to prepare themselves for, and in the delivery of, initial PASS sessions with first-year groups. As a new training aid, the exemplary SCs who were selected as trainers helped to compile a list of top tips for new SCs about how to make a success of the role.

Benefits of engagement

SCs gained a number of benefits as a result of their engagement in the PASS scheme, including:

- consolidating their academic knowledge: "*Through coaching you are revising to make someone understand the material. It made me understand and apply it in a context, you become more wise*";
- enhancing their academic skills: "*Also [improved] my method of study*"; "*after I started as a SC people told me that my writing had improved*";
- developing communication, organisational and leaderships skills:
  - "*[Being a] SC developed my communication skills, I gained confidence, talking to more students... how to speak in front of big groups, how to adapt to different audiences*";
  - "*It improved... my organisational skills. I am a student and I have another job. To manage everything was difficult in the beginning. Also my leadership skills. When we organise workshops or sessions with groups, you have to be emphatic, understand the needs of students*";

- enhancing interpersonal skills: *"you improve your social skills, how to handle different people with different backgrounds"*;
- increasing their self-confidence: *"I was always confident, but you still gain a level of, you become more confident and more tactful in how you go out and address situations"*;
- developing values and qualities that were deepened through working with peers from diverse backgrounds, such as empathy – *"you learn to put yourself more in other's shoes and understand"*, tolerance – *"It's made me more tolerant to understand that everyone is not like me"*, and respecting difference – *"Everyone is different.. That is very important"*;
- enhanced employability: *"I work in an NGO now. They were very interested in the fact that I had been part of the project and been a trainer especially. Now I am a programme lead for a programme with 15 to 17 year olds... It was an advantage in my CV."*

For some interviewees, the SC experience was truly transformational. It has led to:

- a full embrace of university opportunities: *"I put in more work to my studies now. I am more interactive at university than before. Before I would go to university, go to lectures, and go home. Now I'm coming in five or four days a week. I'm enjoying it, I'm talking to everyone, I'm sharing ideas, get new ideas."*
- deeper understanding of others: *"the one thing that will stick with me [is] don't judge a book by its cover. This is the only scenario where I have dealt with so many people. It has prepared me for [that], if I have to do that in the future;*
- inspiration for future studies – *" Now I'm actively seeking out jobs, masters and PhDs"* – or career: *"For my future I will consider teaching. I will definitely use my skills for my future career."*

Conclusion

Inspired by prospective benefits, altruism and their own experiences as first-years to become peer mentors who can help empower others by sharing what they have learnt with new enrolments, SCs also provide a communication bridge between students and lecturers that can prompt improved teaching and learning. Many SCs become involved in other ways too: as course representatives, as active members of the Students' Union and student societies, in volunteering and student induction, and as Student Ambassadors engaged in schools outreach – a virtuous circle of student engagement that continually renews our university community.

Since its inception, the PASS scheme has not only been beneficial to SCs and first-years but also for the organisation as a whole. It is regarded as a cost-effective way to increase student retention and progression rates by providing crucial assistance for first-years to aid their transition into HE at entry level, while helping to create a friendly and engaging environment. Based on annual evaluation, the

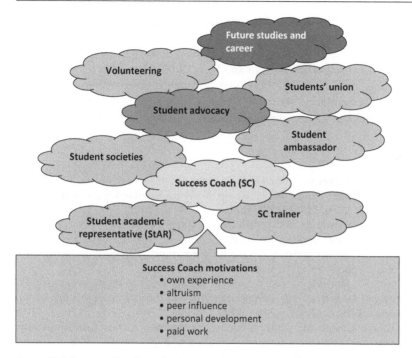

Figure 17.1 Success Coach motivations

initiative seems to have helped students to engage with their learning, in many cases fostering the creation of a local learning community at course and subject level. Promoting this sense of belonging is, as Pokorny et al. (2017) argue, particularly important in the case of commuting students. Year after year, the scheme has been gaining more popularity among staff and students and achieving increased staff buy-in to support the idea of embedding PASS sessions within their course contexts.

Given the university-wide scale of the PASS scheme, it relies on a cascaded training model: so, each year a small group SCs graduate to become trainers of the next cohort of mentors. Recruitment and training processes are annually improved, thanks to the input of SCs into the PASS scheme evaluation – another key aspect of this partnership.

As for their own progress, their histories testify to increased self-confidence and understanding of their subject, and development of interpersonal and other transferable skills valuable for future employment. These benefits may be analysed in the light of self-determination theory (Ryan and Deci, 2000; Niemiec and Ryan, 2009; Ryan and Deci, 2014), which posits that intrinsic motivation – associated with enhanced interest, effort, learning and satisfaction – is facilitated where conditions exist to meet three basic psychological needs for *autonomy, relatedness* and *competence*. By offering some scope for autonomy in how they support students (within their course framework), and opportunities for developing relatedness or connectedness with both their mentees and among the peer mentors themselves, their role as SCs has enabled them to grow in competence, conceptualised as self-efficacy (Ryan and Deci, 2000). As well as reinforcing the intrinsic motivation of SCs in these ways, through their contributions the SCs nurture engagement and a sense of belonging among the first-year students, for their own development of competence (see Warren and Luebsen, 2017).

References

Christie, H., 2014. Peer mentoring in higher education: issues of power and control. *Teaching in Higher Education*, 19(8), pp.955–965. Retrieved from: https://doi.org/10.1080/13562517.2014.934355

Dunne, E. and Zandstra, R., 2011. *Students as Change Agents. New ways of engaging with learning and teaching in Higher Education*. Bristol: ESCalate (Higher Education Academy's Subject Centre for Education). Retrieved from: http://escalate.ac.uk/downloads/8247.pdf

Harrington, K., Sinfield, S. and Burns, T., 2016. Student Engagement. In: H. Pokorny and D. Warren (eds.) *Enhancing Teaching Practice in Higher Education*. London: Sage Publications, pp.106–124.

Krause, K. and Coates, H., 2008. Students' Engagement in First-Year University. *Assessment and Evaluation in Higher Education*. 33(5), pp.493–505. Retrieved from: https://doi.org/10.1080/02602930701698892

Kuh, G.D., Kinzie, J., Buckley, J.A., Bridges, B.K. and Hayek, J.C., 2007. *Piecing Together the Student Success Puzzle: Research, Propositions, and Recommendations. ASHE Higher Education Report*, 32(5). San Francisco, CA: Jossey-Bass.

Macfarlane, B. and Tomlinson, M., 2017. Editorial: Critical and Alternative Perspectives on Student Engagement. *Higher Education Policy*, 30, pp.1–4. Retrieved from: https://doi.org/10.1057/s41307-016-0026-4

Niemiec, C. P., and Ryan, R. M., 2009. Autonomy, competence, and relatedness in the classroom: Applying self-determination to educational practice. *Theory and Research in Education*, 7, pp.133–144. Retrieved from: https://doi.org/10.1177/1477878509104318

Pokorny, H., Holley, D. and Kane, S., 2017. Commuting, transitions and belonging: The experiences of students living at home in their first year at university. *Higher Education*, 74, pp.543–558. Retrieved from: https://doi.org/10.1007/s10734-016-0063-3

Ryan, R. M., and Deci, E. L., 2000. Self-determination theory and the facilitation of intrinsic motivation, social development, and well-being. *American Psychologist*, 55, pp.68–78. Retrieved from: https://doi.org/10.1037//0003-066x.55.1.68

Ryan, R.M. and Deci, E., 2014. Self-determination theory. In: *Encyclopedia of quality of life and well-being research*, pp.5755–5760. Springer Netherlands.

Thomas, L. and Jones, R., 2017. *Student engagement in the context of commuter students*. London: Student Engagement Partnership.

Trowler, V., 2010. *Student engagement literature review*. York: Higher Education Academy. Retrieved from: www.heacademy.ac.uk/system/files/studentengagementliteraturereview_1.pdf

Warren, D. and Luebsen, W., 2017. 'Getting into the flow of university': a coaching approach to student peer support. *Journal of Educational Innovation, Partnership and Change*, 3 (1), pp.262–269.

Webb. T., Russell, E. and Jarnecki, L., 2014. *The principles of student engagement*. London: Student Engagement Partnership. Retrieved from: https://can.jiscinvolve.org/wp/files/2014/10/Student-Engagment-Conversation-Pamphlet-v11-ERussell.pdf

Wimpenny, K. and Savin-Baden, M., 2013. Alienation, agency and authenticity: A synthesis of the literature on student engagement. *Teaching in Higher Education*, 18(3), pp.311–26. Retrieved from: https://doi.org/10.1080/13562517.2012.725223

Chapter 18

Student partners as digital change agents

Clare Killen and Sarah Knight

Introduction: Digital student partnerships – an effective way of building a digitally capable and resilient workforce

The economic importance of developing a digitally capable workforce for the UK is acknowledged as 'enormous' (House of Lords Select Committee on Digital Skills, 2015) and technological innovation features heavily in the 2017 government white paper *The UK industrial strategy* (Gov.uk, 2017). The white paper recognises that we are part of a global economy that is changing rapidly, shaped by the emergence of new technologies. Numerous examples of technology-related industries identified as being of *'strategic value'* (Gov.uk, 2017, p.5) to the UK economy are cited within the white paper which also highlights how the businesses and citizens of the UK can *'benefit from the opportunity of technological change'* (Gov.uk, 2017, p.12). More generally, the use of digital technologies in our professional and personal lives is predicted to rise with government expectations that by 2037, 90% of all jobs will require some element of digital skills (Skills Funding Agency, 2016).

Emerging technologies can be disruptive in that they have the power to significantly alter the way we do things and the way businesses and society operate. For example, the increasing functionality of mobile phones means that we now communicate, access and share information and make transactions 'on the go'. The pace of change and the wide-ranging impact of new technologies means that the future workforce not only needs to be digitally capable but digitally curious. We need to be able to explore and adopt new technologies as part of our way of being and to absorb these into our lives without relying on formal training. We need to be digitally agile, responsive and resilient. Student–staff partnerships' model behaviours will help to establish digital agility and resilience and provide processes and protocols that can support future work, study and personal ambitions.

Partnership as a meaningful and active process

In *Engagement through partnership: students as partners in learning and teaching in higher education* (Healey, Flint and Harrington, 2014, p.7) partnership is described as a '*process and as a relationship in which all participants are actively engaged and stand to gain from the process of learning and working together*'.

Through the Jisc change agents' network (Change agents' network, 2015–16) we have seen evidence that the student–staff partnership approach is enabling universities to deliver effective student engagement activities. This approach also engages students in meaningful and active dialogue about the digital aspects of their learning experiences. Partnership approaches create opportunities to explore the role of technology in supporting students' studies and in preparing them for employment. They provide opportunities for all parties to bring varied skills, knowledge, expertise and enthusiasm to the table. They facilitate personal and collective growth, giving rise to new learning. Wider institutional benefits include the development of unique student-led approaches to obtain a goal, non-compartmentalised results, 'fresh-eyes' and, importantly, the benefit of working with people with the passion to make a difference.

Defining digital capability

Jisc defines digital capabilities as 'The capabilities which fit someone for living, learning and working in a digital society' (Jisc, 2015) and supports this with a digital capabilities framework for individuals (Jisc, 2017). The framework (see Figure 18.1) has six elements: ICT proficiency; information, data and media literacies; digital creation, problem solving and innovation; digital communication, collaboration and participation; digital learning and development; and digital identity and wellbeing.

The framework is not prescriptive and suggests broad areas of practice that individuals can explore relevant to their own needs and ambitions. It highlights the digital capabilities individuals may need to develop to support their education, employment and those needed to participate in an increasingly digital society. There is a clear and symbiotic relationship between efforts to improve digital capability and the wider foci of student engagement initiatives designed to enhance academic performance, improve the student experience, develop employability skills and address wellbeing issues. Student–staff partnerships offer a flexible and empowering model for change where participants bring individual strengths but meet as equal partners. As the case studies that follow illustrate, digital partnerships benefit individuals (students and staff), enhance professional practice and improve organisational efficiency.

Partnership models that support digital change

This section draws on some of the partnership implementation models developed by organisations participating in the Jisc change agents' network (Change agents' network, 2015–16), the Jisc digital capabilities community of practice (Change agents' network, 2017–current) in published case studies in the *Journal of Educational Innovation, Partnership and Change* (Walker, Knight and Kerrigan

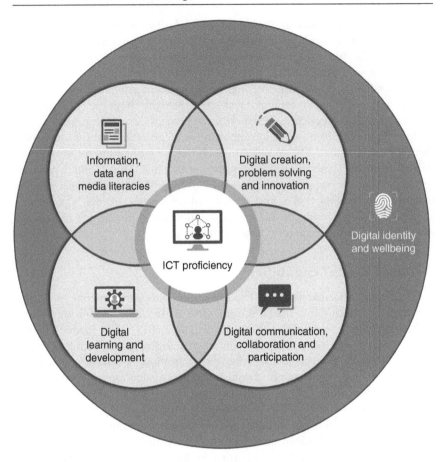

Figure 18.1 Jisc digital capability framework (individual model) – the six elements
Source: Jisc, 2019

2015–current) and Jisc's *Technology for Employability* reports (Chatterton and Rebbeck, 2015a, 2015b). The complex nature of many of the initiatives, and in some cases, the maturity of models developed over several years, means that all of the examples cited have benefits that are not confined to any one area of digital practice and have a broader conceptual basis beyond technological ambitions. For the purposes of this chapter, we have grouped them under the themes of:

- Digital partnership initiatives that support the development of employability skills;
- Partnership approaches designed to develop and embed digital practices within curricula;

- How student partnerships are supporting the development of both organisational digital capability as well as the digital capabilities of individuals.

Digital partnership initiatives that support the development of employability skills

Employers want students who are well prepared for work. Working in partnership helps students to develop digital skills to support their study as well as for their future careers. Partnership initiatives offer authentic experiences and opportunities to acquire skills and confidence over and above subject expertise. Skills such as technology-mediated teamworking, project and time management, problem-solving, communication and presentation techniques are valued by employers.

Case study

University of Southampton (UK): Mission Employable Project (Medland et al., 2015)

Students in the Faculty of Humanities at the University of Southampton led the creation of an employability strategy to address concerns. Internal research findings identified student misconceptions that graduates with humanities degrees were not as employable as more specialised or vocationally trained peers and revealed that students were not applying early enough for graduate employment schemes.

A team of four interns [student partners], supported by a faculty working group, established the 'Mission Employable' brand and launched a VIP alumni scheme and External Advisory Board to increase employer engagement. They collaborated with career destinations and faculty staff to develop content for a compulsory undergraduate first year employability module; designed a faculty-wide peer mentoring scheme; and developed an online tool to encourage students to reflect on their employability-related activities.

Students developed their digital confidence and capabilities throughout the project, using a range of technologies such as: a blog to support team collaboration and communication; Twitter and Facebook for publicity; LinkedIn to create a professional alumni network; iSurvey, an online application form to recruit mentors; an online quiz; and the virtual learning environment, which was used to develop blended learning content.

Case study

Birmingham City University (UK): OpportUNIty student jobs on campus (Jisc, 2014)

Supporting the development of practical and professional skills is an approach that is embedded throughout the various change agent and student partner initiatives in place at Birmingham City University (BCU).

The OpportUNIty student partner scheme was established within the university's human resources function and saw the creation of student jobs on campus as an outlet to offer students a first opportunity to fill many of the part-time positions available at the university.

OpportUNIty facilitates and supports students to apply for part-time jobs at BCU, to work while they study and to fit the job around their course requirements. The roles vary and include marketing roles, research assistants, mentoring, library assistants, student liaison officers, technicians and ambassadors. Around 1,000 jobs are made available each year to students across the university.

Students have reported that their wider involvement and employment has broken down barriers and made them feel included and more a part of the university as well as feeling able to approach staff members. It has also equipped them with valuable employability experience and helped to develop their skills.

> *A lot of employers are looking for what else you have done and these partnership projects are perfect for self-development. I can't tell you the transformational skills I have learned in public speaking, communicating and presenting, and those have all come from opportunities in working in partnership.*
>
> (Former student and student engagement officer at BCU)

These two models both support employability but are very different. One involves a small central team of student change agents working in a single faculty but contributing to cross-institutional initiatives. The student partners are engaged in action research and problem solving activities that will be of wider benefit to fellow students in their faculty. The second model has evolved over a ten-year period and is one of a suite of student partnership initiatives. The positive impact on the organisational culture is evident from the student comments. Running the scheme through the human resources function protects both individuals and the organisation and provides opportunities to formally record and recognise skills through performance appraisal mechanisms. Although not specifically digital in focus, these two examples do introduce opportunities for students to use technology to support their professional development and to record the development of digital capabilities. Both case studies also highlight the importance of developing the whole person and in providing opportunities for students to apply their wider learning over and above subject expertise. Subject specialist knowledge + employability skills + digital expertise amplifies employability.

Partnership approaches designed to develop and embed digital practices within curricula

Students learn best when they are actively involved in their learning and understand the learning processes. There is a natural expectation that the advantages of technology available to us in our everyday lives will also feature in our learning experiences. Working in partnership with students to create, use and evaluate digital learning experiences is beneficial for both staff and students. It facilitates effective learning design by combining pedagogic knowledge and subject expertise with curiosity, research and exploration as to how best digital interventions can enhance learning.

Case study

University of Leicester (UK): Digital Innovation Partnership (University of Leicester, n.d. and https://digitalcapability.jisc.ac.uk/case-studies/ university-of-leicester/)

Digital Innovation Partnership projects at the University of Leicester have been established to enhance and encourage the use of digital technology in learning and teaching and to support the development of digital capabilities for students and staff. Each partnership project includes the following roles:

- **Digital associates**: students with confidence and experience in a range of digital tools and approaches;
- **Digital innovators**: members of teaching staff seeking support and guidance to try out a digital practice in their teaching;
- **Digital advocates**: members of teaching staff who are confident early adopters of digital approaches able to offer insight and practical implementation advice.

Staff and students jointly identify areas within their learning and teaching environment where the use of digital technology could make a positive contribution and work together to design, implement and evaluate a digital practice within learning and teaching. Additional support is provided by the Leicester Learning Institute and IT Services.

Case study

Bath Spa University (UK): International virtual internship (Chatterton and Rebbeck, 2015)

The Learning Technology Group at Bath Spa University offers a form of student partnership through a virtual internship scheme. The scheme pairs postgraduate students in learning design at international universities with course teams at Bath Spa University to enhance curricula with blended and online approaches.

The internships involve a high degree of virtual collaboration and require the use of a broad range of technologies. The aim is to collaborate to jointly re-design course modules with the course team supplying the academic content. The learning design students support the academics in a formal learning design process and reconfigure the modules for blended/online (or distance) delivery. Typically, this includes production of artefacts such as video, podcasts and web materials. Each year the internships involve between ten and 15 postgraduate students from a range of institutions and last between eight to 12 weeks.

At the same time, the interns are mentored in developing and evidencing their professional knowledge and skills based around the Association for Educational Communications and Technology professional knowledge and skills framework.

The scheme supports cross-institutional collaboration and provides benefits to all those involved: the university benefits from the new and creative approaches, different cultural perspectives and new ways of working introduced by the newly qualified postgraduate students; academic staff experience professional development opportunities in formal learning design processes aligned with new technologies; and the interns benefit from work experience, mentoring and professional development. Formal follow up and feedback processes indicate that the interns find the experience highly valuable.

Again, these two models of student partnership are very different and yet both offer effective routes to curriculum enhancement, the development of digital capabilities and increased pedagogical awareness for students and staff. The professional and employability aspects are also well referenced with professional support and formal recognition through professional frameworks (University of Leicester and Bath Spa University).

How student partnerships are supporting the development of organisational digital capability as well as the digital capabilities of individuals

Formal funding for the Jisc change agents' network ended in 2016 but the work continues through the network – supported by Jisc but owned by the community; with the past four annual events hosted by network member institutions. The original ambition of the network was to drive change in technology enhanced learning. This is still highly relevant and is emerging as a notable feature in our work with institutions through the Jisc building digital capability service, feedback from organisations participating in the pilots of the digital discovery tool and student digital experience insights service (Jisc, 2015a–c; 2017a–e; 2018).

What is also clear from our work in supporting the development of digital capabilities and on enhancing the students' digital experience (Jisc, 2015a–c), is the critical need for leadership. It is vital to have approaches in place to support staff and students to develop their digital skills. An effective way of doing this is through partnership approaches that harness the skills, knowledge, expertise and enthusiasm of staff and students and expand reach and engagement. Working with students to champion or promote the importance of digital capabilities is a strategy actively used by approximately 70% of respondents who contributed to the *Ucisa* 2017 *Digital Capabilities Survey Report* (Ucisa, 2017).

Leadership is a central aspect of Jisc's *digital capabilities framework for organisations* (Jisc, 2017a–e) as detailed in our guidance on what makes a digitally capable organisation (Beetham and Killen, 2017). The concept of organisational digital capability looks beyond the capabilities of individuals and is concerned with the extent to which the identity, culture and infrastructure of an institution enables and motivates digital practices (see Figure 18.2).

While similar in appearance to the individual model (Figure 18.1), the organisational model serves a complementary but different purpose. It acknowledges that digital capabilities impact on, and are relevant to, all areas of university and college business, both academic and non-academic.

Universities taking a whole-institution approach typically address the development of digital capability from a strategic perspective, linked to other organisational priorities with a compelling vision and rationale supported by effective leadership. They are likely to engage in a number of coordinated activities, including student partnerships. They recognise that, in addition to preparing students for a digital world, educational organisations are digital businesses in their own right, using technology to manage the core activities of teaching, learning and assessment as well as in research activities and to support communication, administration and financial functions. Given the centrality of digital capabilities to wider organisational effectiveness, it stands to reason that in order to operate effectively, the organisation requires digitally capable staff and students.

The following case studies show how student partnership initiatives are contributing to the development of organisational digital capability.

Figure 18.2 Jisc developing digital capability: an organisational framework
Source: Jisc 2017

Case study

Lancaster University (UK): Digital ambassadors and student digital projects (Jisc, 2017d)

Lancaster University is addressing cultural, infrastructure and skills development needs through Digital Lancaster, their digital version of the overall strategic plan. Digital Lancaster sets out five goals: digital learning; digital design; digital expansion; digital communities and digital engagement. Digital fluency for staff and students is also recognised as one of four key digital capabilities the university needs to cultivate.

Digital Ambassadors are students who work on digital projects in partnership with their department, academic staff and learning technologists to develop digital use within teaching and learning. Initial assumptions were that the students who applied to take part in the projects would already have quite high levels of digital skills but, in reality, students were seeing it as an opportunity to develop and improve their skills. The ambassadors are leveraging wider support and participation by engaging their peers and staff are gaining additional insight and benefitting from student participation in co-design projects.

The digital student projects are varied. Examples include: teaching students at local schools about computer building and design; improving or extending use of specific technologies such as Panopto; developing the digital skills that students need for effective online research; improving the tracking of student involvement and performance in workshop exercises and fostering active participation and engagement in large lecture theatres.

Student and staff engagement in Digital Lancaster is an acknowledged achievement:

> *I think our proudest achievement is all the different things we have achieved but we have achieved them because we have listened to the students and the staff.*
>
> (Amanda Chetwynd, Provost for the student experience,
> Lancaster University)

Case study

University of Derby (UK): Student digital champions (Jisc, 2017e)

The University of Derby has a range of initiatives in place designed to enhance the digital experience for staff and students. These include a five-year technology enhanced learning strategy; a steering group focused on learning enhancement and developing the digital development of staff and students; support for programme teams to review and enhance their digital practice, a digital experience survey rolled out to all staff and participation in the pilots for Jisc's digital discovery tool and student digital experience tracker survey.

The commitment to developing digital capabilities and working in partnership with all stakeholders is clear:

> *I think, if I was giving advice to senior leaders on developing a digital vision for the institution, it would be to consult with academic staff and professional service staff, it would be to talk to key stakeholders which, of course, are our students and learners. It is only by understanding the motivations of all parties that you can really develop a strategy that will have purchase and buy-in across the whole institution.*

A network of student digital champions has been established to promote the use of digital resources and spaces across the university. The student digital champions are engaged in specific projects as well as in helping to train other students in how to use the various digital tools they are likely to encounter during their studies, such as e-portfolios and WordPress as a website creation tool. An interest in technology and the possibilities it can offer, the development of skills to enhance future employability prospects and an interest in contributing to the learning experience of others as well as to the university in general are just some of the reasons given by the student digital champions for getting involved.

(Professor Malcolm Todd, Pro vice-chancellor, academic and student experience, University of Derby)There are similarities in approach in both these case studies and yet the model is sufficiently flexible to accommodate a variety of digital aims, objectives and ambitions. Effective leadership and co-ordination will position student ambassadorial and championship initiatives carefully alongside other activities to ensure the potential benefits are realised and have cross-institutional reach and impact.

Conclusion

Feedback from participants shows that student partnership initiatives are effective and engaging. The impact is particularly powerful and empowering for those directly involved but when implemented in a holistic way can have a much wider reach and value. Such initiatives add to the student experience over and above study ambitions and offer valuable and authentic learning and developmental experiences. The reasons for engaging are usually intrinsic from both the student and staff perspectives – wanting to develop new skills, professional and curriculum practice, or seeking to make a difference to the student experience or the university generally. Reward and recognition for achievement and the contribution partnership work makes is important. This may be financial, via Higher Education Achievement Record transcripts and university awards, as a clearly mapped route to professional recognition, or through professional development review processes.

Student partnership models with a digital focus are perhaps an easy and non-threatening way into partnership working with an open acknowledgement that all parties bring different skill sets (but don't assume it is students who have all the digital skills). This can help to establish an equal partnership process and relationship as articulated by Healey et al. (2014, p.7). Different models are emerging of how students, staff and employers are working together: these may involve research, curriculum design, producing digital artefacts, providing consultancy, delivering and supporting training, mentorship and more. Many digital student partnership projects have a strong focus on developing the digital capabilities and employability skills of students but the potential outcomes are so much richer, as the case studies above reveal. Not all partnership models will have digital as an explicit focus but it is very likely that digital capabilities and their development will feature during implementation.

What is clear is that student partnership models are not just models for change, but models that facilitate lasting and meaningful change.

References

Beetham, H. and Killen, C., 2017. *Developing organisational approaches to digital capability.* Jisc. Retrieved from: www.jisc.ac.uk/guides/developing-organisational-approaches-to-digital-capability (accessed 3 April 2018).

Change agents' network, 2015–16. *Change Agents' Network: a network of staff and students working in partnership to support curriculum enhancement and innovation.* Jisc. Retrieved from: www.jisc.ac.uk/rd/projects/change-agents-network (accessed 1 March 2019).

Chatterton, P. and Rebbeck, G., 2015a. *Technology for Employability: study into the role of technology in developing student employability.* Jisc. Retrieved from: http://repository.jisc.ac.uk/6249/3/Technology_for_employability_-_full_report.PDF (accessed 2 April 2018).

Chatterton, P. and Rebbeck, G., 2015b. *Bath Spa University: International virtual internship in Technology for employability: HE case studies Study into the role of technology in developing student employability* (page 32). Jisc. Retrieved from: http://repository.jisc.ac.uk/6250/6/Technology_for_employability_-_HE_case_studies.PDF (accessed 1 March 2019).

Healey, M., Flint, A., Harrington, K., 2014. *Engagement through partnership: students as partners in learning and teaching in higher education.* Higher Education Academy. Retrieved from: www.heacademy.ac.uk/system/files/resources/engagement_through_partnership.pdf (accessed 3 April 2018).

GOV.UK, 2017. *The UK Industrial Strategy: building a Britain fit for the future.* GOV.UK. Retrieved from: www.gov.uk/government/topical-events/the-uks-industrial-strategy (accessed 28 February 2018).

House of Lords Select Committee on Digital Skills, 2015. *Make or break: The UK's digital future.* Parliament.uk. Retrieved from: https://publications.parliament.uk/pa/ld201415/ldselect/lddigital/111/111.pdf (accessed 28 February 2018).

Jisc, 2014. *Birmingham City University: OpportUNIty student jobs on campus.* Jisc. Retrieved from: https://can.jiscinvolve.org/wp/files/2014/10/CAN-BCUvFINAL.pdf (accessed 1 March 2019).

Jisc, 2015a. *Developing students' digital literacy.* Jisc. Retrieved from: www.jisc.ac.uk/guides/developing-students-digital-literacy (accessed 1 March 2019).

Jisc, 2015b. *Enhancing the student digital experience: a strategic approach.* Jisc. Retrieved from: www.jisc.ac.uk/guides/enhancing-the-digital-student-experience (accessed 6 April 2018).

Jisc, 2015c. *Building digital capability.* Jisc. Retrieved from: https://digitalcapability.jisc.ac.uk/ (accessed 2 March 2019).

Jisc, 2017a. *Building digital capabilities: The six elements defined.* Jisc. Retrieved from: http://repository.jisc.ac.uk/6611/1/JFL0066F_DIGIGAP_MOD_IND_FRAME.PDF (accessed 2 April 2018).

Jisc, 2017b. *Developing digital capability: an organisational framework*. Jisc. Retrieved from: http://repository.jisc.ac.uk/6610/1/JFL0066F_DIGICAP_MOD_ORG_FRAME.PDF (accessed 3 April 2019).

Jisc, 2017c. *Digital experience insights*. Jisc. Retrieved from: https://digitalinsights.jisc.ac.uk (accessed 2 March 2019).

Jisc, 2017d. *Lancaster University: Digital fluency for all*. Jisc. Retrieved from: https://digitalcapability.jisc.ac.uk/our-service/case-studies/lancaster-university/ (accessed 1 March 2019).

Jisc, 2017e. *University of Derby: Enhancing the digital experience for staff and students*. Jisc. Retrieved from: http://repository.jisc.ac.uk/6683/3/digital-capability-stories-derby-aug-2017.pdf (accessed 1 March 2019).

Jisc, 2018. *University of Leicester: Our digital campus: developing a digitally confident community of discovery*. Available at: Retrieved from: https://digitalcapability.jisc.ac.uk/our-service/case-studies/university-of-leicester/ (accessed 1 March 2019).

Medland, C., Tribe, J., Dudley, A., Smith, V. and Quince, E., 2015. 'Mission Employable': Creating a student-led employability strategy for the Faculty of Humanities, University of Southampton in *Journal of Education, Innovation, Partnership and Change*. Vol 1 (No 1). University of Greenwich. Retrieved from: https://journals.studentengagement.org.uk/index.php/studentchangeagents/article/view/207

Skills Funding Agency, 2016. *Review of publicly funded digital skills qualifications*. Retrieved from: www.gov.uk/government/publications/review-of-publicly-funded-digital-skills-qualifications (accessed 2 March 2019).

Ucisa, 2017. *2017 Digital Capabilities Survey Report*. Ucisa. Retrieved from: www.ucisa.ac.uk/bestpractice/surveys/digcaps/2017digcaps_report (accessed 2 March 2019).

University of Leicester (n.d.). *Digital Innovation Partnership*. University of Leicester. Retrieved from: www2.le.ac.uk/offices/lli/developing-learning-and-teaching/enhance/digital-innovation-partnership (accessed 1 March 2019).

Walker, S., Knight, S. and Kerrigan M. (eds.) 2015–present. *Journal of Educational Innovation, Partnership and Change*. University of Greenwich. Retrieved from: https://journals.gre.ac.uk/index.php/studentchangeagents/about (accessed 2 March 2019)

Chapter 19

Scholarship as student engagement in college higher education

John Lea, Rhonda Lobb, Jac Cattaneo and Jenny Lawrence

Introduction

This chapter looks at how a national three-year project in England has been exploring the issue of student engagement from the perspective of enhancing student scholarship skills. The Scholarship Project (Association of Colleges, 2018) involved a large group of English colleges who run Higher Education (HE) courses. We begin by briefly looking at the college HE context – its history, role, and some of its particular challenges. We then proceed to outline the scope of the national project and then, specifically, the role of scholarship in enhancing student engagement. The chapter finishes by looking at some specific examples of how student scholarship has been advanced in some of the colleges involved in the project.

College higher education in context

Higher education in colleges has a long history in the UK. Since the Second World War, UK colleges have consistently accounted for around 10% of the total of HE provision (Parry, 2009). Indeed, there are now more students studying on HE courses in UK further education colleges than there were in the whole UK HE sector at the time of the Robbins Report in 1963. The Robbins Report was a trigger for a number of reforms aimed at raising the participation rate in HE overall. In 2019 in England it reached for the first time the proposed 50% target set by Tony Blair's government in 1999, but it had been consistently above 40% for the period since that date. And these are remarkable figures, particularly given that the participation rate was well below 10% even into the 1970s. In this context it is perhaps a little surprising that the participation in college HE in the UK has not risen well above 10%.

There are a number of reasons, related to both policy and practice, why the college participation rate has not risen significantly. With regard to policy, both the Robbins Report and the 1992 incorporation legislation concentrated attention on increasing the number of universities. The Robbins Report led the way to the building of a number of new universities (affectionately known as 'plate glass', to distinguish them from the redbrick builds of the Victorian era), the conversion of some colleges of advanced technology (such as Brunel and Loughborough), and the expansion of polytechnics, which would concentrate on applied studies. And the 1992 legislation further cemented these developments by allowing institutions with polytechnic status to apply for university title, which the vast majority took advantage of almost immediately. Against this backdrop, it is perhaps not surprising that colleges began to be referred to as the Cinderella sector, with all the implications of being somewhat forgotten (Daley, Orr and Petrie, 2015).

In terms of practice, it is clear that the vast majority of colleges always saw themselves mainly as providers of further education. In this regard, government reforms simply heightened this sense. Even those colleges which combined further and HE found themselves having to increasingly carve out a mainly sub-degree HE niche. Indeed, the term sub-degree itself could be viewed as a somewhat (perhaps unintentionally) derogatory Cinderella label, but it was increasingly used in reform documents. Indeed, the major push towards the embedding of the foundation degree (from 1997 onwards) often referred to this new qualification as a sub-degree rather than a HE qualification in its own right (e.g. DfES, 2003).

All that said, it is also clear that many colleges have an avowed mission to ensure they serve their local communities. This is made manifest in wanting to serve local students – providing opportunities for those who cannot or do not want to access further and higher education away from their existing homes and families. In many cases these students will also be 'hard to reach' and are likely to be first generation entrants to HE (Simmons and Lea, 2013; Shaw, Humphrey, Atvars and Sims, 2017). Appropriate study support is likely to be essential in these cases. In addition, many colleges have long-standing relationships with local employers, and see themselves as fulfilling a local training need – providing technical and professional education courses in order to produce a highly skilled local workforce. These dual aspects of localism may provide the best explanation of why higher education in further education has not expanded significantly. Put simply, why would a college want to expand numbers and provision beyond and in excess of what the local community needs?

This story is complicated by the fact that local communities vary enormously throughout the country, as does the number of local institutions offering further and HE courses. In this context it is perhaps not surprising that a college like Blackpool and the Fylde – located geographically in a HE 'cold spot' – has thousands of students studying on its HE courses. But there are probably only a handful of colleges in the UK with these numbers, and many more with numbers below 500 and often below 100 students. But this also needs to be set against the backdrop of recent Area Reviews, and the resultant wave of current college mergers. Once the dust settles on this, it is highly likely that a much smaller number of larger colleges will be offering a suite of HE courses to around, and often over, 1,000 students each.

The Scholarship Project

The Scholarship Project was a Higher Education Funding Council for England (HEFCE) funded catalyst project, administered by the Association of Colleges (2018), aimed at raising the profile of college higher education in England by exploring the ways that forms of scholarship might be able to enhance student learning. This theme was identified due to the number of times that the need to develop a scholarly ethos had been mentioned in college reviews (Simmons and Lea, 2013), which endorsed the similar point made by HEFCE much earlier (HEFCE, 2001). The project ran from June 2015 to June 2018, and involved 46 further education colleges in England, all of whom ran some HE courses. Colleges bid to be involved in the project, but it was also important to ensure that the final number (which was not fixed) represented a spread of provision – from colleges who had a long track record of providing HE, to colleges which had only just begun providing HE courses; large general further education colleges and some specialist colleges; and the desire for a geographical spread of colleges.

The main output from the project was the production of a scholarship framework that would provide a range of resources which all colleges could adopt or adapt according to their specific needs. All the resultant resources were trialled and tested within the 46 colleges to confirm their robustness, and evaluated by a team of experts, drawn from the wider college HE community. The project was conceptually underpinned by the work of Ernest Boyer on the four scholarships – of discovery, of application, of integration and of teaching, and his later broader conceptualisation of an overarching scholarship of engagement (Boyer 1990; Boyer, 1996). The project was informed, not led, by Boyer's conceptualisations, and each college was able to interpret the word scholarship in its own way and tease out its implications in local context.

It became clear early on that the majority of the resources developed could be categorised under four broad headings or themes: curriculum development; quality enhancement; professorial development; and student engagement. The rest of this chapter concentrates on some of the work which emerged from the student engagement theme.

Student scholarship as student engagement

The Scholarship Project acknowledged that the term student engagement has a number of dimensions – including strategies aimed at heightening a sense of belongingness for students; extra-curricular out-reach activities; students as change agents within their institutions; as well as all the actions being taken by institutions to listen to the 'student voice'. These dimensions were not ignored, but the project's emphasis was much more on how the term scholarship could be favourably combined with engagement in order to enhance learning.

This combination was further conceptually underpinned by a reconsideration of the implications of von Humboldt's exhortation to place staff and students

236 John Lea et al.

Table 19.1 Examples of the ways in which learners may engage with Boyer's four scholarships

Types of scholarship	Illustrative example of ways of engaging learners
Scholarship of discovery	Engage in inquiry-based learning; undergraduate research and consultancy projects; co-research projects with staff.
Scholarship of integration	Engage in integrating material from different sources, including across disciplines; integrate life and work experience with academic studies; reflect on implications of studies for personal development.
Scholarship of application/ engagement	Engage with local, national, and international community service projects; volunteering; knowledge exchange projects; apply knowledge and skills in work-based placements.
Scholarship of teaching and learning	Engage in mentoring; peer support and assessment; collaborative group work; learners as explicit partners in educational development and inquiry.

Source: Healey, Jenkins and Lea, 2014: 57

in the service of scholarship (von Humboldt, 1810). By this he meant that staff were not there primarily to serve students (an early critique of student voice initiatives) but to ensure that students understood their role not just to receive knowledge but also to contribute to its furtherance. Today, these ideas can be found in the 'student as producer' movement (Neary and Winn, 2009) and the idea that students are not good learners because they have been taught well, but because they have actively taken part in the learning process itself. To this end von Humboldt was also clear that HE is not about imparting what we know, but exploring what we don't know. In essence, this is HEness, where a 'scholarly ethos' is not just a worthy pursuit in addition to other learning activities, it is in fact the core activity which defines a HE experience (Lea and Simmons, 2012).

In a forerunner project, funded by the then Higher Education Academy (now Advance HE), this active engagement of college HE students in forms of scholarship was explored and teased out by looking at how Boyer's four scholarships could be applied to student learning activities, as shown in Table 19.1.

This was then taken one step further by incorporating the localism of colleges mentioned earlier, by:

> *looking at ways in which, by evaluating their practice (thereby serving immediate client needs) they can also generate rich scholarly activities both for students and staff. Particularly, they can generate activities which invite staff to use their professional knowledge to engage students in work-related projects; staff and students carrying out enquiries that can benefit the local community; and become involved in the evaluation of pedagogic effectiveness.*
>
> (Healey, Jenkins and Lea, 2014: 54)

The Scholarship Project was keen to exploit this potential and began actively looking for examples of where this triangulation between staff, students and employers is being forged. However, this is not without its problems. Two such problems have loomed large throughout the project. First, a lot of staff in colleges clearly do not feel comfortable promoting student scholarship when their own scholarly profile is weak or underdeveloped and this was a recurring theme for a number of years in academic literature relating to college HE teachers (e.g. Young, 2002; Harwood and Harwood, 2004: Golding Lloyd and Griffiths, 2008; Feather, 2012). Indeed, some staff appeared annoyed that they were somehow being asked to become like university lecturers, particularly when they wished to remain college teachers (Simmons and Lea, 2013). And second, that the corporate and managerial structure of the majority of colleges has often resulted in scholarly activity and associated professional development being under recognised or undervalued (Lucas and Unwin, 2009; Lingfield, 2012; Creasy, 2013). In this context, time away from a traditional classroom setting might be viewed as dead time.

It was clear from the start that these issues could not be resolved within the confines of a three-year project. But it was also clear that significant headway could be made by utilising Boyer's notion of a scholarship of engagement particularly when explicitly related to the enhancement of learning. To this end, the project has been actively exploring how staff and students, working collaboratively in and out of the classroom, can significantly enhance forms of scholarly engagement (Boyer, 1996). And that Boyer's conceptualisation of – particularly – the scholarships of application, integration and teaching, explicitly do not require college teachers to become 'publish or perish' university academics. Indeed, it was this culture in elite universities in the US that Boyer was criticising and what prompted him to write his now seminal book (Boyer, 1990).

Developing student scholarship through the Scholarship Project

As the preceding paragraphs illustrate, developing scholarship in college HE settings has not been unproblematic. However, what the Scholarship Project was able to do well, was change perceptions of what scholarship might be and at the same time, shine a light on the linkages between lecturers' scholarly activity, student scholarship and learning gain, reinforcing the students as partners agenda at a pivotal time – and coinciding as it did with the launch of the Office for Students (OfS) (UK).

Engaging students in research from induction

Myerscough College (UK) and Bishop Burton College (UK) were two of the 46 colleges involved in the Scholarship Project and are two of the UK's leading land-based colleges. The provision at the two colleges includes foundation degrees and honours degrees in most subjects, with master's degrees also offered in a number of subjects. As part of the project, both colleges decided to alter their induction process for first year students in a bid to promote student retention and aid the transition for new students entering college HE.

The rationale for developing the induction process came from the 'What Works? Student Retention and Success' programme (Thomas, 2012), which asserts that well planned and thoughtful pre-entry and induction activities are significant factors in both engaging and retaining HE students. The report goes on to highlight how induction activities should allow students to make friends, get to know academic staff, understand the expectations of the institution, department and programme as well as develop crucial academic skills. While HE students in both colleges had previously undertaken an induction assessment, it was primarily used as a diagnostic tool which involved students conducting secondary research rather than primary research. When questioned about the pre-existing induction assessment, college lecturers agreed that the induction experience could be further exploited to develop research capacity in first year students.

The shift to becoming more self-directed in HE can cause considerable anxiety for first year students making this transition (Kandiko and Mawer, 2013). As students immerse themselves in their new surroundings, they bring with them current expectations which are shaped by a whole host of factors, including their past experiences, habits and beliefs in addition to the institutional discourse which they have been exposed to. Whilst this culture shift may be relatively seamless for some, it can be significantly challenging for others. This is where the opportunity to develop research skills during induction can be vital in shaping the new identity of HE students.

Several programmes across the two colleges had students work on projects which, whilst varied in scope and duration, involved students in collecting, analysing and disseminating primary data. The impact of being involved in research throughout the induction period was measured by a number of mechanisms, including pre and post assessment surveys where students were able to comment on a number of themes, including how the project had prepared them for HE. Responses to the surveys revealed that the induction activity was able to help them identify weaknesses early on in their studies and improve overall confidence. The majority of students also acknowledged how the project had introduced them to primary research and how they benefitted from receiving some personalised feedback so early on in their studies.

Whilst the students were able to obtain some early feedback which assisted their enculturation, their tutors were additionally able to gain some insight into the students' abilities. A year on from the first year induction project, second year students are then asked at the beginning of their programmes to reflect on their learning gain over the course of their first year. In the context of HE, learning gain is concerned with the distance travelled by students during their course in terms of increased knowledge, personal growth, acquisition and development of a wide range of skills. Having had the experience of doing research so early on in their studies and receiving pivotal feedback, the students thereby had a concrete experience to reflect back on.

Engaging students through peer-assisted study

The peer-assisted study sessions (PASS) model was pioneered in the United States and developed by Lund University in Sweden before reaching British HE. Studies of both UK-based (*Journal of Learning Development in Higher Education*, 2016) and international (*Journal of Peer Learning*, 2019) PASS schemes tend to locate them in universities rather than colleges. Under the auspices of the Scholarship Project, a PASS trial-and-test commenced in December 2016 at the Greater Brighton Metropolitan (UK) and Sussex Downs Colleges (UK). Its aim was to enhance college student engagement by adapting the university model to suit the professional, vocational and technical courses. PASS involves Level 5 volunteers (leaders) running group study sessions for the Level 4 students to revisit their course material. Leaders undergo thorough training on working with groups; they are not expected to teach, but to facilitate discussion about coursework. Level 5 students benefit from the acquisition of team-working and employability skills, while Level 4s have an opportunity to discuss elements of their courses which they find problematic with their peers. The scheme has been proven to enhance retention, achievement and progression at the University of Brighton (University of Brighton, 2019).

The trial-and-test proposed that PASS would be an excellent way for colleges' non-traditional and less confident HE students to develop the tools to reflect upon and share their own experience through working together. Boud defines peer learning as '*a two-way reciprocal learning activity... the sharing of knowledge, ideas and experience between participants*' (Boud, Cohen and Sampson, 2001, p.4). Acting as 'expert partners' (Mascolo, 2009, p.6), PASS leaders provide a confidential, approachable environment for peers to ask questions; they can also feed back to lecturers about student concerns or problem areas. In the process of developing the skills and knowledge to manage group situations, they are likely to acquire extra social and cultural capital (Bourdieu, 1992). Peer schemes also promote student agency and the co-construction of knowledge (Vygotsky, 1978; Jacoby and Ochs, 1995).

The PASS project followed an action research cycle (McNiff, 2013) with two iterations. The pilot involved students from six courses training along-side University of Brighton (UK) students. Once the colleges' Scholarship Development Manager had completed a PASS supervisor training, the scheme was rolled out to all HE courses in participating colleges. In the scheme's second iteration, the Scholarship Development Manager trained 60 students from 22 courses as PASS leaders. Data was gathered through questionnaires, focus groups and interviews at various points in the project, allowing continuous evaluation and reflection to feed back into the project.

As many PASS study techniques have been designed for academic courses (e.g. making meaningful lecture notes, exam revision, solving scientific or mathematical problems), our trial-and-test explored the development of additional strategies to engage college HE students in ways which are meaningful and relevant to their subject areas. Students were invited to be co-researchers in the creation and testing of strategies appropriate to their discipline's signature pedagogies. As a result, BA (Hons) Fine Art leaders ran a session on the construction of sketchbooks; FdA Musical Theatre leaders ran sessions on dance techniques; and FdA Business leaders worked with their first year group on presentation techniques.

The results of the trial-and-test demonstrated that the obstacles to involvement for all students were primarily workload, especially on FdA degrees, and the time-tabling of PASS sessions. However, the feedback demonstrated a clear development of an HE community of practice (Wenger, 2000), with a benefit to the scholarship of both mentors and mentees.

Engaging students through a scholarship intern programme (SchIP)

In 2014, North Lindsey College (UK) introduced a research stream to their Student Intern Programme as a response to their strategic plan to grow student partnership activity. A refined version of this research stream, the 'Scholarship Intern Programme' (SchIP), was trialled and tested with East Coast College (UK), in the 2016–17 academic year as part of the Scholarship Project. It is now firmly embedded in both colleges' strategies, policies and practice.

The rationale for introducing the internship was the recognised positive impact that post-graduate internships have on learning (Cook, Parker and Pettijohn, 2005) and employability (Sides and Mrvica, 2007). Programmes to support research in HE are normatively highly competitive, externally funded research projects frequently staffed by high achieving post-graduates (Nurse, 2015). In a college HE context, where staff rarely have research time written into workloads (Lea, 2014), and students often have competing demands on time and energies (Butcher, 2015), there may be little opportunity to engage in live research.

In contrast to externally funded projects, SchIP is shaped by the learning community to create a manageable, accessible and agile process for staff, students and the wider community (employers, community groups, charities, college partners) to collaborate in knowledge production (Lawrence, 2018a). Current students and recent graduates apply for a paid Scholarship Intern post, working on a staff-defined research project. Staff bid for project funding, and many do so with collaborative partners and alumni. Projects are often not focussed on academic outputs, but context specific outcomes: these could be identifying a meaningful solution to a challenge faced by a local charity; evaluating and refining with a student cohort on a learning and teaching innovation; or building a rich and unique portfolio of resources for future students in collaboration with college partners (see Lawrence, 2018b for more details).

This focus on outcomes has many benefits for students, who begin to understand scholarship and graduate skills as allied to employability whilst enjoying an authentic experience as researcher and staff member at a HE provider. There are, additionally, many benefits for staff, who grow research competencies and develop profiles which inform the delivery of research-based teaching and learning – further benefiting the student experience. Every attempt is taken to make the internships inclusive, and this has grown a sense of scholarly community: some projects may employ many interns so students may offer as much time to a project as they have available; interns also have the opportunity to work flexibly to agreed milestones and time scales which suits busy students who juggle many other commitments. In conclusion, the flexible and student-centred shape of the SchIP initiative has secured student engagement in scholarly partnerships.

Conclusion

Healey, Flint and Harrington (2014) remind us that, as a term, student engagement is ambiguous and contested. It is frequently depicted as a dichotomy in which the student is either engaged or disengaged, present or absent, but in fact it is far more complex, dynamic and nuanced. Indeed, even in the space of one hour, a student might experience spells of being engaged and disengaged, both within and outside the classroom. One thing we learnt earlier on in the Scholarship Project is that scholarship skills are an essential component in advancing a full and deep form of engagement. But engaged students do not come fully formed. They must be nurtured in a number of ways, to develop the skills and the confidence to problem-solve and increasingly take responsibility for learning. The examples we used above demonstrate some of the ways in which we have sought to advance this nurturing, and the project contains many more.

College HE is a fascinating context to explore the embedding of the widest forms of scholarship, including as it does many staff who are often not confident in their own research and scholarship skills, and where it may not be obvious to local employers what the relevance of scholarship is to employment. But rewrite this context into one where staff and students work collaboratively on college, community or work-based projects, and where the focus is on using research skills to find solutions to commercial and industrial problems. Here we soon find that forms of scholarly engagement can reach far beyond the traditional notion of the academic researcher, and allay fears that college teachers are slowly being turned into aloof academics, removed from class-based activities. And they also help to enact exactly what von Humboldt meant by putting oneself in the service of scholarship – where we look to explore what we don't know rather than what we do know. It is difficult to imagine how someone might do this is a disengaged manner. For von Humboldt it was also the essence of what a HE experience actually is, and in the contemporary context, it is also likely to make someone highly employable.

References

Association of Colleges, 2018. *The Scholarship Project*. Higher Education Funding Council for England/Association of Colleges. Retrieved from: www.aoc.co.uk/enhancing-scholarship-in-college-higher-education-the-scholarship-project (accessed 1 November 2018).

Boud, D, Cohen, R. and Sampson, J., 2001. *Peer Learning in Higher Education*. London: Kogan Page.

Bourdieu, P., 1992. *Language and Symbolic Power*. London: Polity Press.

Boyer, E.L., 1990. *Scholarship Reconsidered: Priorities for the Professoriate*. Princeton, NJ: Carnegie Foundation for the Advancement of Teaching.

Boyer, E.L., 1996. The scholarship of engagement, *Journal of Public Outreach*, 1(1), 11–20.

Butcher, J., 2015. *'Shoe-Horned and Sidelined'? Challenges for Part-Time Learners in the New HE Landscape*. York, HEA.

Cook, J. R., Parker, S. and Pettijohn, C. E., 2005. The perceptions of interns: A longitudinal case study, *Journal of Education for Business*, 79(3), 179.

Creasy, R., 2013. HE lite: exploring the problematic position of HE in FECs, *Journal of Further and Higher Education*, 37(1), 38–53. Retrieved from: https://doi.org/10.1080/0309877x.2011.644772

Daley, M., Orr, K. and Petrie, J. (eds.), 2015. *Further Education and the Twelve Dancing Princesses*. London: Institute of Education Press.

Department for Education and Skills (DfES), 2003. *The Future of Higher Education*, Cm5753, Norwich: Stationery Office.

Feather, D., 2012. Oh to be a scholar – a HE in FE perspective. *Journal of Further and Higher Education*, 36(2), 243–261. Retrieved from: https://doi.org/10.1080/0309877x.2011.614930

Golding Lloyd, M. and Griffiths, C., 2008. A review of the methods of delivering HE programmes in an FE college and an evaluation of the impact this will have on learning outcomes and student progression, *Journal of Further and Higher Education*, 32(1), 15–25. Retrieved from: https://doi.org/10.1080/03098770701765559

Great Britain, Committee on Higher Education, 1963. Higher education: report of the Committee appointed by the Prime Minister under the chairmanship of Lord Robbins 1961–63.

Harwood, J. and Harwood, D., 2004. Higher education in further education: delivering higher education in a further education context – a study of five South West colleges, *Journal of Further and Higher Education*, 28(2), 153–164. Retrieved from: https://doi.org/10.1080/0309877042000206723

Healey, M., Flint, A. and Harrington, K., 2014. *Engagement through Partnership: Students as Partners in Learning and Teaching in Higher Education*. York: HEA.

Healey, M., Jenkins, A. and Lea, J., 2014. *Developing Research-Based Curricula in College-Based Higher Education*. York: HEA.

HEFCE (Higher Education Funding Council for England), 2001. Supporting higher education in further education colleges: Review of colleges' strategy statements and support: A report to the HEFCE by the Further Education Development Agency. Report 01/07. Bristol: HEFCE.

Humboldt, W. von, 1810. [1970] On the spirit and organisational framework of intellectual institutions in Berlin. *Minerva* 8, 242–267.

Jacoby, S. and Ochs, E., 1995. Co-construction: an introduction, *Research on Language and Social Interaction*, 28(3), 171–183. Retrieved from: https://doi.org/10.1207/s15327973rlsi2803_1

Journal of Learning Development in Higher Education, 2016. Special Edition: Academic Peer Learning (Part II) Retrieved from: http://journal.aldinhe.ac.uk/index.php/jldhe/issue/view/21 (accessed 29 July 2019).

Journal of Peer Learning, 2019. Volumes 1 to 3 of the Journal of Peer Learning were published as Australasian Journal of Peer Learning. Retrieved from: https://ro.uow.edu.au/ajpl/ (accessed 29 July 2019).

Kandiko, C. B. and Mawer, M., 2013. *Student Expectations and Perceptions of Higher Education*. London: King's Learning Institute.

Lawrence, J., 2018a. Building scholarly cultures in partnership: University Centre, North Lindsey Scholarship Intern Programme, in Arnold, L. and Norton, L. (2018) *HEA Action Research: Sector Case Studies*. York: Higher Education Academy.

Lawrence, J., 2018b. The Scholarship Intern Programme Tool-kit. *The Scholarship Framework*. Retrieved from: www.thescholarshipframework.co.uk/resources/toolkit-intro (accessed 29 July 2019).

Lea, J., 2014. Capturing HE-ness in college HE, in Lea, J. (ed.) *Supporting Higher Education in College Settings*. SEDA Special No. 36. London: SEDA.

Lea, J. and Simmons, J., 2012. Higher education in further education: capturing and promoting HEness, *Research in Post-Compulsory Education*, 17(2), 179–193. Retrieved from: https://doi.org/10.1080/13596748.2012.673888

Lingfield, R., 2012. *Professionalism in Further Education: Final Report of the Independent Review Panel*. London: BIS.

Lucas, N. and Unwin, L., 2009. *Developing Teacher Expertise at Work: In-Service Trainee Teachers in Colleges of Further Education in England*. London: Institute of Education.

Mascolo, M. F., 2009. Beyond student-centred and teacher-centred Pedagogy: Teaching and learning as guided participation, *Pedagogy and the Human Sciences*, 1, 3–27.

McNiff, J., 2013. *Action Research, Principles and Practice*. Routledge.

Neary, M. and Winn, J., 2009. The student as producer: reinventing the student experience in higher education, in Bell L., Stevenson H. and Neary M. (eds.), *The Future of Higher Education: Policy, Pedagogy and the Student Experience*. London: Continuum, 192–210.

Nurse, P., 2015. *Ensuring a Successful UK Research Endeavour*. London: BIS.

Parry, G., 2009. Higher education, further education and the English experiment. *Higher Education Quarterly*, 63(4), 322–342. Retrieved from: https://doi.org/10.1111/j.1468-2273.2009.00443.x

Sides, C. H. and Mrvica, A., 2007. *Internships: Theory and practice*. Amityville, NY: Baywood Publishing.

Shaw, C., Humphrey, O., Atvars, T. and Sims, S., 2017. Who They Are and How to Engage Them: A Summary of the REACT Systematic Literature Review of the 'Hard to Reach' in Higher Education. *Journal of Educational Innovation, Partnership and Change*, 3(1), 51–64.

Simmons, J. and Lea, J., 2013. *Capturing an HE Ethos in College Higher Education*. Gloucester: QAA.

Thomas, L., 2012. *Building Student Engagement and Belonging in Higher Education at a Time of Change: Final Report from the What Works? Student Retention and Success Programme*. London: Paul Hamlyn Foundation.

University of Brighton, 2019. Peer Assisted Study Sessions at the University of Brighton. Retrieved from: https://blogs.brighton.ac.uk/pass/research-by-the-team/ (accessed 29 July 2019).

Vygotsky, L.S. (trans. Cole, Michael), 1978. *Mind in Society: Development of Higher Psychological Processes*. Cambridge, MA: Harvard University Press.

Wenger, E., 2000. *Communities of Practice: Learning, Meaning, and Identity*. Cambridge: Cambridge University Press.

Young, P., 2002. Scholarship is the word that dare not speak its name: Lecturers' experiences of teaching on a higher education programme in a further education college, *Journal of Further and Higher Education*, 26(3), 273–86. Retrieved from: https://doi.org/10.1080/03098770220149620a

Part IV

The future of student engagement

Chapter 20

Who defines success in higher education?

A student perspective on the future of student engagement

Madeleine Pownall

Student engagement has historically been discussed within academic literature as a term almost synonymous with student satisfaction, retention, engagement in educational developments, representation and general involvement in an academic community. In parallel to these conversations surrounding engagement and satisfaction, higher education (HE) has recently turned its attention to the notion of student success. Defining student success is challenging as the term is relatively contested and ambiguous within educational literature. Indeed, a critical student perspective is also notably absent from this conversation. In this chapter, I will draw upon my own experiences as a student to critically appraise the concept of success in the context of HE. I will examine how this term may be located within wider pedagogic issues that may not capture the nuanced and often diverse experiences of today's students. I will end by exploring how the future of student engagement must acknowledge the multifaceted nature of success in HE, whilst remaining sensitive to the complexities of the student experience.

My perspective

I finished my degree exactly twelve months ago. Throughout my studies as an undergraduate student I felt, by and large, 'Super Engaged'. I approached my lecturers for extra reading, I went to pedagogic and academic conferences, I worked as a research assistant, and I read beyond the scope of the reading lists. I discovered a genuine love for learning and found the academic environment stimulating, challenging, and exciting.

However, despite my enthusiasm for my subject, I was often late or absent from morning lectures because I had been working a night shift (in my part-time zero-hour contract job to support myself financially). I quickly became more interested in data analysis for my research assistant job than I was for my academic assignments. I found a niche area of psychology that fascinated me and found it difficult to put down these books in favour of mandatory reading lists. I failed modules. I chose family time over revision. Towards the end of my degree, I spent my evenings working on job applications instead of my dissertation. I never engaged with the student union. I did not join societies, including the psychology society, and generally avoided any group-based interaction. But I felt passionate and stimulated by the world of education. And I *loved* my degree.

So, with our theories and practice of student education, engagement, satisfaction in mind, what kind of student would I have looked like on paper? With decent (albeit relatively mixed) grades and mediocre attendance, would my university have considered me to be engaged? Would I have been considered a success?

What is success?

Before we can explore how and why I may or may not have been considered a successful student in the context of pedagogic theory and understanding, it is first important to set the scene for this complicated and nuanced term. The definition of success, as with most concepts in pedagogy, has been heavily contested (York, Gibson, and Rankin, 2015). Indeed, it can be interpreted in a multitude of different ways, depending on the institutional context and the agenda in which it is situated. Perhaps the most common thought is that success is a term in HE synonymous with 'student achievement' and is related almost exclusively to academic outcomes. For example, in the pedagogic literature, success is thought of as being related to academic attainment, student retention, and successful progression throughout the degree (Bean and Eaton, 2001; Choi, 2005). However, these definitions should be explored critically, considering whether this way of measuring success captures the full picture.

Indeed, the way in which we define success matters because it conveys to both educators and learners a set of principles against which both parties are measured. It also, crucially, sends an implicit message about what is valued in HE. We know that in universities metrics matter. They guide our pedagogic agenda, they determine funding and allocation of resources, and, perhaps most importantly, they contribute to our understanding of success and failure. I should note here that I am not necessarily concerned with the educational ethics or *value* of metric-based measurements of success. In psychology, the divisions between qualitative and quantitative methodologies run deep, despite emerging mixed-methods approaches to research. I am, rather, interested in critically exploring *what* these metrics contribute in the context of what we understand success to look like in HE. How does both what and how we measure influence what we understand success to mean?

Being successful means different things to different people, as is the case with most concepts in education. Here, I would like to share a student perspective of how the way we define, measure, and recognise success can contribute to wider pedagogic issues. For example, Lockhart, Wuetherick and Joorisity (2018) understand student success to mean a combination of student characteristics (e.g. personality, preparedness, locus of control), experiences (e.g. teaching and learning, belongingness, accountability), and outcomes (knowledge, perception, grades). The focus on belongingness (as per Yorke, 2016) is particularly interesting in the context of my own experiences within HE of *feeling* engaged, despite this not being reflected in the administrative metric data attributed to me. In this sense, and in relation to my own experiences, context is of upmost importance. If my engagement with my studies was reduced entirely to traditional metric measures of student success, I doubt I would have been considered 'engaged'. Yet, on almost every other dimension within HE – satisfaction, wellbeing, feeling part of a community of learners, feeling safe and happy within the context of university – I would have rated highly.

This introduces the concept that there are richer and more nuanced methods of understanding success, rather than academic attainment alone. Using grades as indicators of the success of an educational journey is simplistic and does not capture the multi-faceted, deeply subjective nature of the student experience. In my opinion, the fundamental problem with relying solely on these kind of administrative data collection to assess success is that they fail to acknowledge diversity of experience. Indeed, this diversity occurs both before, within, and after time shared in the classroom. For example, student nationality (Gebhard, 2012), gender (Kessels, Heyder, Latsch, and Hannover, 2014), academic preparedness (Lockhart, Wuetherick and Joorisity, 2018), sociodemographic background (Yorke, and Thomas, 2003) all contribute to the profile of a student (Hu and Wolniak, 2013). Therefore, we should acknowledge that students may enter university with a set of success parameters that may not necessarily map onto the values that are measured and celebrated in the institution.

Case study 1

To illustrate how metrics may not account for the multifaceted student experience and complexities of subjective understanding of success, meet Student A – we'll call her Annie.

Annie is a first-generation undergraduate student studying for a degree in psychology. She commutes from her home town into university by the train. She plays hockey every Thursday. To subsidise the gap between her student loan and her rent, she works part-time at a corner shop. She achieves an average of 62% in her university assignments but finds the university context quite stressful and prefers working at home rather than in the libraries. One day, Annie finally braved it and entered the library for the first time. She considered it to be one of the biggest successes so far in her degree. She does not have many friends on her course so prefers to socialise with friends from home.

Let's first consider Annie's case in the context of what we know from the pedagogic literature. Annie is a commuter student, a subgroup that is often reported to have lower student engagement (Jacoby, 2000), although this concept itself is contested (see Kuh, Gonyea, and Palmer, 2001). Annie may experience some university-related stress due to lack of a strong peer network, which is also associated broadly with academic outcomes (Saklofske, Austin, Mastoras, Beaton and Osborne, 2012). She is doing relatively well in her grades although does not fully engage in the 'learning community' (e.g. Zhao and Kuh, 2004) of her institution, which can make it challenging to connect with peers (Tinto, 2000). She is also a first-generation student, a group who benefit largely from peer support as a means to adjust to HE (Dennis, Phinney, and Chuateco, 2005). Due to Annie's potential feelings of imposter syndrome (Parkman, 2016), her one-time library visit was considered a personal milestone. This was her subjective measure of success, although this may not be in line with the measures attributed to her.

Therefore, if Annie's overall success at university was measured purely by metric measures, would she be considered to be currently engaged in her studies? Would metric measures of student engagement recognise her? Should the university be doing more to engage Annie?

Case study 2

With the same questions in mind, consider Student B, Henry.

Henry is a first-year undergraduate student. He's studying part-time following a career change after having his second child. He loves studying and has always wanted to return to university after his first degree. Most of his academic work is done on evenings and weekends due to childcare. His primary goal is a specific career path that requires a specialist undergraduate qualification; therefore, in his mind, as long as he passes the modules necessary to progress in the degree, he has succeeded.

Like all students, Henry will come to university with a set of knowledge, values, and experiences that will support and contextualise his learning. As a mature student, this may been even more relevant in his experiences (Toynton, 2005). He may not participate in 'student engagement' incentives and he may be satisfied with achieving the minimum grades which will enable him to progress to his chosen career path. Echoing the questions asked of Annie's profile as an (un)successful student, would Henry's approach to his education be considered a success? Has his institution done enough to engage him fully with his studies? Should they?

According to traditional metric measures of student success, the students described in these case studies may not be considered 'engaged' on paper. They do not engage in extra-curricular academic activities, they do not volunteer within their institution, they do not mentor or take advantage of mentoring schemes, and their attendance and grades are below average. In response to this, York,

Gibson, and Rankin (2015) offer a more nuanced and complex picture of student success, arguing that success is formed broadly of six main tenets: academic achievement, satisfaction, acquisition of skills and competences, persistence, learning outcomes and career success. They also note that students have both intrinsic and extrinsic measures of success; personal satisfaction is intrinsic, academic outcomes are more extrinsic. Annie's trip to the library or Henry's completion of his degree, therefore, may offer a satisfying levels of intrinsic success. However, they may now score as highly on more extrinsic, quantifiable measures of success.

Who gets to decide?

Some theories of student success have also focused on the students' relationship with their educational environment (e.g. Kuh et al., 2001), suggesting that success occurs when learning culture and personal development respond to one another. This brings up an interesting question of accountability and responsibility for student success. Ultimately, who gets to decide what success looks like in HE? Rendón, Jalomo and Nora (2000) posit that students and educators both share some responsibility for ensuring that culture, norms and personal goals are mapped onto one another effectively. I agree, and would like to continue the conversation surrounding the picture of success.

The process of defining success is entrenched within rigid and hierarchical power dynamics. In line with feminist pedagogic ways of thinking, critically exploring *who* defines success is as, if not more, insightful than looking at *how* it is defined. In this sense, it is important that conversations surrounding student engagement involve some level of student voice. This is often the missing link in HE conversations. Whilst there are well-documented and well-executed initiatives targeted at engaging students within educational curricula, and feedback, there is often a crucial link missing – a distinct lack of student involvement in the conversations surrounding student engagement and pedagogic practice itself. Without a sense of student voice, conceptualisation of success in the context of teaching and learning becomes challenging and unrepresentative. It does not capture the true experiences of what it is like to study at HE institutions.

More problematically, without a clear and critical student voice in these conversations, the concept of success is in danger of becoming paternalistic. In this sense, language really matters. The words we choose to frame concepts in the context of HE communicate ideas about how we value and understand the student experience. An ongoing dialogue between staff and student is the only way to challenge our reliance on metrics.

As with many others contested within HE, the definition, conceptualisation, and measurement of success should not be something that is *done* to students. It should be done with students, as per the 'students as partners' approach (Mercer-Mapstone et al., 2017). 'Students as partners' is a way of thinking about education that situates the learner and the teacher as equal agents. It dismantles power between the two and creates equity, and a space for collaboration and co-working. Importantly, it rejects the idea that learning is something that is done *to* a student, and instead celebrates the unique positions and perspectives that both parties have in the dialogue of education. Indeed, some measures of success appear to be in direct contrast to this approach. Success is individualistic and personal. It is, or rather it should be, self-defined. In the same way that 'students as partners' approaches attempt to use partnership to empower students to take more control over their own learning, our understanding of success would also benefit from a more nuanced and empowered perspective.

When we think about success we should also consider the wider context. Due to tuition fees and a culture of 'student as customer', this context is by its very nature political. Therefore, it is not enough to regard success as a score on metric individualist measures at the student level. We need to shift our focus and consider students in their own unique contexts. Student education does not happen in a vacuum.

Redefining success

In response to my thoughts about how success can be redefined to reflect these issues, I recently ran a day-long workshop on feminist approaches to teaching and learning in HE. We shared our frustrations and concerns with some of the traditional methods of measuring students at various points throughout their journey to and through education. One particularly engaging conversation was centred on the metric-based admission process. We discussed how reliance on purely metric-based admissions (i.e. through UCAS points alone) may not be suitable for non-normative student experiences. I was interested in this, and posed to the group how we may translate these issues to the context of student success throughout their degree. The room grew lively with shared frustrations and difficulty in defining the malleable, subjective, slippery nature of success in HE.

We decided together that we all understand the importance of contextualising entrance into university; we listen to students' experiences through their personal statements, and we are relying less on grades alone as indicators of students' suitability for HE. Yet, this approach is not entirely evident once students get through the door. We lose a sense of context, positionality, subjectivity.

In light of this, student engagement remains a prominent term and area of activity in HE. Within an outcomes-focused, neoliberal HE, student engagement now comes with a new partner, student success. Those who adhere to metric measurements need to remember that definitions of success are meaningless if they do not reflect a student voice. Institutions should remain mindful that the student community's engagements and successes do not always fit into rigid, quantifiable outcomes. It is important to remember the key pillars of student engagement – inclusivity, transformation and partnership – to ensure we are creating a HE where all students can thrive in their own individual way. Therefore, we should question, is student success, to use Tinto and Pusser's (2006, p 8) words, merely '*successful learning in the classroom*? Or does it, and should it, reflect a richer picture of students in their own unique context?

References

Bean, J., and Eaton, S. B. 2001. The psychology underlying successful retention practices. *Journal of College Student Retention: Research, Theory and Practice*, 3(1), 73–89. Retrieved from: https://doi.org/10.2190/6r55-4b30-28xg-l8u0

Choi, N. 2005. Self-efficacy and self-concept as predictors of college students' academic performance. *Psychology in the Schools*, 42(2), 197–205. Retrieved from: https://doi.org/10.1002/pits.20048

Dennis, J. M., Phinney, J. S. and Chuateco, L. I. 2005. The role of motivation, parental support, and peer support in the academic success of ethnic minority first-generation college students. *Journal of college student development*, 46(3), 223–236. Retrieved from: https://doi.org/10.1353/csd.2005.0023

Gebhard, J. 2012. International students' adjustment problems and behaviors. *Journal of International Students*, 2(2), 184–193. Retrieved from: https://jistudents.files.wordpress.com/2011/12/10-international-student-adjustment-problems.pdf

Hu, S. and Wolniak, G. C. 2013. College student engagement and early career earnings: Differences by gender, race/ethnicity, and academic preparation. *Review of Higher Education*, 36(2), 211–233. Retrieved from: https://doi.org/10.1353/rhe.2013.0002

Jacoby, B. 2000. Involving commuter students in learning: Moving from rhetoric to reality. In Kramer, M. (Series Ed.) and Jacoby, B. (Vol. Ed.). *New directions for higher education: Number 109. Involving commuter students in learning* (pp.81–87). San Francisco, CA: Jossey-Bass. Retrieved from: https://doi.org/10.1002/he.10909

Kessels, U., Heyder, A., Latsch, M. and Hannover, B. 2014. How gender differences in academic engagement relate to students' gender identity. *Educational Research*, 56(2), 220 229. Retrieved from: https://doi.org/10.1080/00131881.2014.898916

Kuh, G. D., Gonyea, R. M. and Palmer, M. 2001. The disengaged commuter student: Fact or fiction. *Commuter Perspectives*, 27(1), 2–5. Retrieved from: www.nsse.indiana.edu/pdf/commuter.pdf

Lockhart, W., Wuetherick, B. and Joorisity, N. 2018. Exploring the Foundations for Student Success: A SoTL Journey. *Collected Essays on Learning and Teaching*, 11. Retrieved from: https://doi.org/10.22329/celt.v11i0.4981

Mercer-Mapstone, L., Dvorakova, S. L., Matthews, K. E., Abbot, S., Cheng, B., Felten, P. and Swaim, K. 2017. A systematic literature review of students as partners in higher education. *International Journal for Students as Partners*, 1(1). Retrieved from: https://doi.org/10.15173/ijsap.v1i1.3119

Parkman, A. 2016. The imposter phenomenon in higher education: Incidence and impact. *Journal of Higher Education Theory and Practice*, 16(1), 51. Retrieved from: www.na-businesspress.com/JHETP/ParkmanA_Web16_1_.pdf

Rendón, L. I., Jalomo, R. E., and Nora, A. 2000. Theoretical considerations in the study of minority student retention in higher education. *Reworking the student departure puzzle*, 1, 127–156.

Saklofske, D. H., Austin, E. J., Mastoras, S. M., Beaton, L. and Osborne, S. E. 2012. Relationships of personality, affect, emotional intelligence and coping with student stress and academic success: Different patterns of association for stress and success. *Learning and Individual Differences*, 22(2), 251–257. Retrieved from: https://doi.org/10.1016/j.lindif.2011.02.010

Tinto, V. 2000. What we have learned about the impact of learning communities on students? *Assessment Update*, 12(2), 1–2, 12.

Tinto, V. and Pusser, B. 2006. Moving from theory to action: Building a model of institutional action for student success. National Postsecondary Education Cooperative, pp.1–51.

Toynton, R. 2005. Degrees of disciplinarity in equipping mature students in higher education for engagement and success in lifelong learning. *Active Learning in Higher Education*, 6(2), 106–117. Retrieved from: https://doi.org/10.1177/1469787405054236

York, T. T., Gibson, C. and Rankin, S. 2015. Defining and Measuring Academic Success. *Practical Assessment, Research and Evaluation*, 20.

Yorke, M. 2016. The development and initial use of a survey of student 'belongingness', engagement and self-confidence in UK higher education. *Assessment and Evaluation in Higher Education*, 41(1), 154–166. Retrieved from: https://doi.org/10.1080/02602938.2014.990415

Yorke, M. and Thomas, L. 2003. Improving the retention of students from lower socio-economic groups. *Journal of Higher Education Policy and Management*, 25(1), 63–74. Retrieved from: https://doi.org/10.1080/13600800305737

Zhao, C. M., and Kuh, G. D. 2004. Adding value: Learning communities and student engagement. *Research in Higher Education*, 45(2), 115–138. Retrieved from: https://doi.org/10.1023/b:rihe.0000015692.88534.de

Chapter 21

From then to now in student engagement

An academic's perspective

Colin Bryson

As one of the pioneers of the notion of student engagement, in this essay I want to reflect on my journey of the last fifteen years from the perspective of a lecturer (and head of an academic department) and consider the state of student engagement now, with a little bit of speculation about where it might be going. I can only claim to be a pioneer in the UK setting, as student engagement emerged as a big idea in the US forty years before and in Australia, twenty years before it did in the UK. However, its emergence in other systems of HE similar to the UK, such as South Africa (led by Jenni Case) and New Zealand (led by Nick Zepke and Linda Leach), occurred at the same time as in the UK. These colleagues, like me, were academics at the coalface of undergraduate teaching and we 'discovered' student engagement through talking to our students.

My own student engagement journey began when I had already spent twenty-five years working in a range of UK universities. I had just been promoted to Principal Lecturer in a large Business School on the basis of responsibilities I held, but then was given, slightly to my dismay, another big responsibility. I was asked to promote independent learning across a school with 5,000 students. I suspect the real reason that senior managers wanted this to happen was to free up my colleagues from large teaching loads so they could boost the research profile of the school. I enlisted the support of Len Hand, who had a rather longer pedigree than I had in the scholarship of learning and teaching. As neither of us knew much about independent learning in a scholarly or practical way, we decided to ask the students. Eventually we gathered evidence from ten focus groups across the range of degrees offered by the school. We were deliberately vague in our themes to avoid leading the discussion. The student evidence was a shock. Most of the students felt anonymous in a giant business school, knew no staff in any meaningful way and found the curriculum a *"joyless slog"*. Independent learning meant *"pushing us away"*. So the key issue was a lack of engagement due to how everything was organised and run in a 'teaching factory', the big numbers and low morale of both staff and students. Had I already read Dubet's (1994) work I would have noted that students had weak personal projects in terms of why they were doing a business degree, and for many it was a means to an end: to gain a 'good job'. Another strong feature that emerged was the emotional or affective element to engagement perceived by the students (something previously unrecognised in student engagement research in HE, although not in the schools sector, cf. Fredricks, Blumenfeld and Paris, 2004). Len and I wrote this up into one of the first articles about student engagement in the UK. Our theme was that by fostering stronger engagement we could inspire stronger and deeper learning. (Bryson and Hand, 2007).

Len and I felt that student engagement was so crucial that it must be prioritised and right at the heart of our practice. We found allies in colleagues such as Christine Hardy, Ed Foster and Ian Solomonides (who subsequently went to Australia and made a very major contribution to student engagement there). Influential players included the Staff Educational Development Association (SEDA), who encouraged us to publish collected work (Bryson and Hand, 2008) and subsequently a book (Bryson, 2014a), and the Higher Education Academy, who invited us to present at national events. We were very inspired by the insightful scholarly analysis of the educational sociologist, Mann (2001), who contended that there were powerful forces in HE that worked to alienate both students and staff: performativity, exclusion and 'othering', and the disempowering impact of assessment. We agreed that a constructive and positive influence on engagement is to build trust relationships between all parties leading to a meaningful discourse. However, staff acting as judge and jury in assessment really undermines this trust and presented us with a real conundrum to resolve. Assessment 'for learning' rather than 'of learning' offers some mitigation but not total alleviation of this difficult issue (Sambell, McDowell and Montgomery, 2013). At this stage nearly all of us working in the field were focussed on academic engagement, i.e. engagement in the curriculum and classroom, perhaps in large part because we were academic teachers. Len, Christine and I embarked on an in-depth, longitudinal study following twenty-four students across the three or four years of their degree in a range of subjects across the university. The powerful evidence from that gave us a much more nuanced understanding of student engagement and a recognition that influences on engagement for students included their whole lives rather than just the academic domain, and needed to include a sense of empowerment, belonging and identity (Bryson and Hardy, 2014). It also showed us there were dimensions of engagement that we, as staff, could influence only very indirectly. I read widely, in part because there was not much literature directly about student engagement available at the time. I assimilated what I read in an attempt to develop a conceptual model of student engagement. That was a five-year project (Bryson, 2014b) which ultimately led to the conclusion that student engagement was a complex multi-construct for which it was impossible to develop a single unified theory. Kahu's (2013) effort is probably the best attempt to do so, but as she acknowledges in a subsequent work (Kahu and Nelson, 2017) a student's sense of engagement is elusive, dynamic and inaccessible to the researcher, and certainly impossible to measure. I wholeheartedly agree: we can never pin down something that is located in sense of being of an individual.

There were now a wider group of people who felt that student engagement really mattered and, together with Julie Wintrup who worked with students in innovative ways at Southampton, Christine Hardy and I founded RAISE (Researching, Advancing and Inspiring Student Engagement) (RAISE, 2019). Our goal was, as embodied in that acronym proposed by my daughter, to advance awareness of student engagement. We marshalled all the arguments we could to persuade colleagues to embrace this within practice and policy. Although we realised that there were problematic issues, we confined these to discussions within the group of supporters, and sought to be more evangelical to those who less convinced. I recall making the business case to managers that if investing in practices which fostered student engagement allowed even one student to persist in HE who otherwise would have withdrawn, then it was worth their while. Given the fee regime in the UK then and subsequent tripling of fees in 2012, these arguments carried a lot of weight. Of course, our real agenda was much more about enhancing the student experience and, causally linked to that, their learning. Though the surface argument may have been retention (which of course matters in other ways, too) we were also deeply focussed on reconsidering the purpose of HE in the first place. I want to note though, in the face of later criticism that we were naïve in allowing student engagement to be linked to the transactional, market-driven model of HE that had been growing stronger and stronger through public policy in this period, that 'allowing' is hardly the right term as we had no control over that. Academics have not run universities, far less the HE sector, for a long time, and not in my lifetime. The proponents of student engagement that I knew and know all have benevolent intentions – we want to foster engagement so that students truly benefit from HE. That is much less about accumulation of human capital and rather more about transformative learning (Mezirow, 2000). Barnett (1997) describes that as developing criticality although I rather prefer Baxter Magolda's (2007) notion of self-authorship with the graduate being in control of their life and future through the capability they have gained – enhancing their 'ways of knowing'.

In my day job, however, it was not so easy to change policy and practice in my own academic school. Although I was now Head of Teaching and Learning, cultures at my institution changed with managers prioritising efficiency and 'lean engineering' models of education. This demoralised my colleagues and made them even less receptive at that time to embrace a student engagement approach. An irony of being promoted to this middle management role was that I no longer taught or interacted with students. In despair, I left. I nearly left the sector altogether, but in 2008 was offered the post of Director of the Combined Honours Centre in Newcastle. This was a very unusual department as it was just myself and two administrative colleagues supporting a degree of 400 students. A wonderful *tabla rasa* on which to practise student engagement, and in some need of that too. My Dean described the degree as a 'basket case' (after rather than before I started) as the National Student Survey (NSS) scores were very low due to students feeling no sense of identity or feeling part of anything. As a 'part-time' student in each of their two or three disciplines they felt excluded and had weak or no relationships with staff or each other. Although I had little influence over the curriculum I had considerable authority in other ways. So I invited the students to tell me what the problems were and what solutions they might suggest. And they did, and together we co-developed a holistic student engagement strategy. We went on a fantastic journey together, introducing no less than five types of peer support schemes and a host of extra-curricular initiatives. These were refreshed by new ideas as the students involved changed. The point that students can only be involved for three or four years is both frustrating and energising. In due course, we did introduce course components that the students felt were missing or desirable and we began to co-design the modules upfront together and then the students undertaking them, in a pedagogy of partnership, co-determine how the module unfolds and is assessed. Driving this have been the elected student representatives, the legitimate voice of the students. These approaches and their outcomes are recounted much more eloquently by the students than by me, in both publications (Furlonger, Johnson and Parker, 2014: Furlonger, Garner, Callaghan, Foreman and Bryson, forthcoming; Callaghan, 2016) and at conferences, where I always try to co-present with students. So from the start this was a partnership between students and staff – a theme I will return to.

Concurrent with these developments in my locality, student engagement as a policy and practice was exploding across the UK HE sector. The rise and rise of student engagement has already been covered thoroughly in this book. As far as academics are concerned – many of whom are rather far removed from policy making – I would contend that it has had less impact. Although every university may have a student engagement strategy (and senior managers have that within their remit), that does not always penetrate down into the academic departments, particularly if all the initiatives are led by central units. Of course, there are now many 'champions' of student engagement, official or unofficial, and some of these are in academic roles. But I do note that when colleagues come to present at the RAISE Annual Conference or write up an initiative as a case study for publication it is a solo effort or small group rather than a large collective who are practising student engagement in academic departments. So the rhetoric may be more than the reality. Having said that, student engagement is now a prominent component of the teaching qualifications that new academic staff undertake. There is also a growing cadre of staff in research-intensive universities, whose primary focus is learning and teaching. As yet, they are a bit of an underclass, and promotion and reward systems lag far behind in recognising an educator route over a researcher route. The metrics for 'excellent teaching' are not so simple as 'excellent research' (counting the papers and the grants)! The silver lining of tuition fee income becoming such a big contributor to university finance, is that recruitment of students and reputation now really matter to those who make the policy decisions. That comes at the steep price of repositioning the students and the staff, as I shall discuss.

The rise and rise of student engagement has brought some issues to the fore. Some of the academic heavyweights and commentators within research about HE have started to give the concept attention. There have been some scathing critiques although I am not so sure that these writers have actually read much of the student engagement literature. I recall the annoyance expressed by a student co-researcher who was reviewing these critical articles as part of a joint project. Her annoyance stemmed from the fact that student voices were entirely absent from most of this work and that the authors has decided arbitrarily what was 'good for students', dismissing employment aspirations, for example. There is a snobbish element too, where smaller single institutional studies are dismissed as less rigorous. For example, many of the studies covered in Trowler's literature review (2010) were based on data from the National Survey of Student Engagement (NSSE, 2019) in the USA. The problems with such data, purportedly rigorous, are critiqued elsewhere (e.g. Bryson, 2014b). The main problem with the paradigm of measurement of student engagement (using the NSSE and its variants) is that it is mistakenly based on the notion of the *ideal student* who engages behaviourally in a particular way. There is no such thing as an ideal student – what an arrogant and exclusive notion! Kelly, Fair and Evans (2017) made a strong case why this ideal student notion is flawed. It is galling that all scholars of student engagement are lumped together to be critiqued for something that many of us do not promote or believe in.

One form of critique of student engagement is to argue that it is vague, ambiguous and covers too much, to the extent that it has become all things to all people (Vuori, 2014). I do not agree that the way to remedy this is to define student engagement much more narrowly (Duzevic, 2015). I would contend that seeing student engagement as a broad multi-construct is absolutely fine, but then when applying the concept of student engagement in a research study it is essential to define what aspects of engagement are under investigation.

The most damning critique links student engagement to neoliberalism in HE. Zepke (2014, 2015a, 2015b) in a series of articles argues that student engagement has become so prominent because it aligns with neoliberalism. I do think he is being rather mischievous. It is indubitable that some policy makers at a senior level, steeped in the ideology of the market and positioning the student as customer, distort student engagement to fit this model in their policy development. But to argue that this is 'mainstream' overstates matters considerably.

Macfarlane and Tomlinson (2017) present six area of critique: student engagement as performativity; marketing; infantilisation; surveillance; gamification and opposition. However, they should note that practitioners of student engagement, and those who participate in RAISE for example, are as opposed as they are to notions of engagement as compliance. The application of attendance policies and other such coercive means of making students conform is entirely antithetical to our principles in fostering engagement.

Gourlay (2015) argues that there is far too much focus on the superiority of active learning and collaborative learning over more traditional teacher-led approaches, and that the advocates of student engagement privilege the former over the latter. The problem for me is that the weight of the evidence does show that being active and collaborative in learning is much more likely to transform thinking and position – to move towards contextual knowing (Baxter Magolda, 1992). The tension created here is not to force such learning approaches on students but to create an environment of respect where students willingly challenge themselves to enter the liminal space of troublesome knowledge (Land, Rattray and Vivian, 2014).

So is there validity to these critiques of student engagement? I would observe that there has been some appropriation of the term student engagement when it comes to policy and practice claimed 'in its name':

- There are overstatements in statements and strategies made which claim grandly that the particular institution believes in student engagement and working with students as partners whereas in fact a tiny minority of students and staff could actually validate that. This links to a performativity culture, exemplified by the Teaching Excellence Framework (Office for Students, 2019), where claims become evidence. Those who write such statements are not malign, if not very ethical, but trying to justify their existence in such a neoliberal world.
- There have been too many attendance policies introduced, although usually set up by well-meaning people who want to avoid students 'falling through the cracks' and reach out to those who do not attend. But these are easily abused by others who advocate narrow models of normative behaviour and invoke them to bully students. Linked to this are approaches which over-emphasise transactional behaviour – giving marks for turning up, for example.
- Policies and practices which are based on a 'one size fits all' model fail to accommodate the diversity of students or their aspirations.
- Some student engagement practitioners offer activities they believe students will benefit from and then accuse those who do not participate of being 'disengaged'. Choosing not to take part in something is not proof of being alienated (Fulford, 2017). I call this 'doing student engagement to students' and there is too much emphasis on 'what works' for some without consider-ations of why it works and who might be excluded.
- In a world where government and media ascribe much more status to 'having' rather than 'becoming' (Fromm, 1977) and degrees are valorised, participating in 'SE activities' can become another tick to add to the CV. Evaluation strategies for such activities can be based on this, too. I respect that students might be attracted to participate in the first place by such rewards but it is imperative that they gain more than that by taking part – the sort of gains that contribute to their 'graduateness'.

Therefore I do agree that are dangers of appropriation of the student engage-ment agenda. But the emergence and prominence of student engagement in

HE has given rather more constructive improvements and outcomes than if it had never happened and we had remained in the status quo that preceded. The principles underpinning it, the practices, and in the main, the policies have been highly beneficial. It is no coincidence that in parallel with student engagement and the wide range of initiatives to foster engagement the following changes have taken place.

- Access, persistence and student outcomes have improved significantly (although we must be careful in 'measuring' these outcomes).
- Student support is so much better and a much more important facet of the university.
- Curriculum and assessment have moved much more towards a student-centred model of engaged learning and the models now are much more inclusive of all students.
- Professional development of staff as supporters and facilitators of student learning is now a serious affair and much more systematic.
- Many staff have been recruited who focus on student engagement and who care about the student experience and actively promote student engagement.
- There are so many great practices that have been introduced and shared across the sector.
- It just makes the lives of those who study and work in HE so much better. It is a challenging environment with many pressures and an improved sense of engagement for all parties offers relief, motivation and fulfilment.
- In the main, student engagement provides an alternative positioning of students and staff to the neoliberal hegemony, and counters and alleviates the alienating neoliberal forces.

Reflecting on my own role in my department I can say with confidence that we have really embedded student engagement into all our local practice and culture. We now have a few more students (600 plus) but also eight staff with direct involvement in fostering engagement in our students. Some of them are graduates of the degree which seems to encourage even more enthusiasm about maintaining this agenda. The element of working in partnership has really grown and matured. Partnership has a set of further challenges and risks to both staff and students. We have some lively disagreements about how what working as partners entails and where its limits lie. As part of the maturing, we have sought to move from a model of a small number of super-engaged students (who achieved so much) to a much larger number in roles and activities, with the aim of being rather more equitable and inclusive. If we include the students undertaking the Combined modules with their pedagogies of partnership we have about a quarter of students participating directly in these activities. We also work with some of them on scholarly projects (and rather more on practice-based projects) that explore partnership and engagement. We try to practice a universal model of partnership rather than a selective model (Bryson, Brooke, Foreman, Graham

and Brayshaw, 2018). It takes time and experience for most of our student partners to genuinely feel empowered (Bryson and Callaghan, 2018, Furlonger et al.,
forthcoming. That pre-requisite is frustrating as we struggle to draw them into
such practices before second year at the earliest and they graduate all too soon.
But it seems the right thing to do to sow the seeds with many rather than develop
a privileged few much more.

If I cast my eye further afield, I note profound changes in the university in the
eleven years I have been here. Outside my own department I can advocate and
try to influence but have no real power to introduce change. The students are
more influential as change agents and the nature of a Combined degree together
with invitations (and awards) from the university has allowed them to spread the
agenda of student engagement and partnership. Our model of peer mentoring
has been adopted across the university, for example. But other initiatives have
foundered. Influenced by the wonderful example of the Learning and Teaching
Academy in Western Washington University (Werder and Otis, 2010) I tried
to introduce something similar at Newcastle where students and staff solved
problems together. It was an idea in advance of its time in this culture and did
not take off (Bryson, 2017). Across the university though, there is much more
evidence of student engagement practices in both academic departments and
opportunities offered by services such as Careers and the Library. There is much
more support for students, in general.

Although the pace of change has perhaps slowed across the sector, the student engagement agenda is spreading into parts it had not reached before.
The early adopters (such as Birmingham City (UK), Lincoln (UK) and
Winchester (UK)) have now been caught up with to some extent and there
is now more movement in the research-intensive Russell Group who were
generally slowest at the beginning. I suspect this is not a very reliable guide,
but a crude method to measure sectoral interest in student engagement is
the number of keynotes I get asked to do at institutional conferences, thus
having student engagement/students as partners as their theme. There was
a flurry of these events between 2008 and 2013, then the invitations slowed
down a bit. But they have really picked again in the last two years as more universities take these ideas up. It is notable that the TEF does not incorporate
student engagement directly into its assessment metrics. I am sort of relieved
about that as the measure they might have adopted would probably have been
deeply inappropriate (not that the metrics they do use have much to do with
good educational outcomes).

So what about the future? I do not want to speculate too much into the
future as the curtain starts to fall on my long career in HE. The future is in the
hands of others. There is some evidence though, that student engagement is
continuing to spread as a practice and spread further into subject departments
and academic practices. The focus on professional development has spread further than new staff as more experienced staff seek recognition. Recognition and
reward are becoming more accessible, and demonstrating practices which foster

student engagement assist individuals to evidence and gain individual recognition. RAISE and similar organisations are increasing membership and participation at events. As the previous generation of senior staff, brought up in a world before student engagement, start to retire, they are being replaced by those much more familiar with it. Thus we can expect student engagement to embed further. Neoliberal forces remain as strong as ever as the UK government moves even further to the right. Educational as well as research income to universities is under threat. That could cause a retrenchment and squeeze on resources for central initiatives. It should not stop academic staff drawing on student engagement principles in their practices. Why would we want to revert to previous practice? I recall colleagues arguing that students' attitudes would change as the fees ramped up. I do see more comments from students now about value for money, I cannot criticise that. The great majority of students did have and continue to have multiple motivations to study in HE, acquiring a degree alongside the learning and social dimensions. I have never had any complaints from students because we seek to engage them – that adds rather than detracts. All it requires is some conviction and maybe a bit of courage and a spirit of adventure, but not too many other resources. Student engagement is here to stay.

I do have some final words of advice to all those who practise student engagement in the future. I would advocate:

- the need to maintain the principles of student engagement (the ones proposed by RAISE[1] are not bad but any similar ones are fine);
- the need to problematise and not gloss over tricky issues and tensions that practising engagement might give rise to;
- the importance, whatever your role, to be take a scholarly approach in terms of informing yourself about what is already known and taking advice, in order to mitigate risk and foresee unintended consequences of actions;
- the need to find space to be critically reflective;
- not to forget the distinction between *students engaging* and *engaging students*;
- to actively oppose appropriation of student engagement.

Doing that will go far to ensure student engagement stays true to its origins and development as an authentic approach to improving learning for students and staff. I might suggest that working in partnership between all parties, and adhering to the principles of mutuality, respect and shared responsibility (Cook-Sather, Bovill and Felten, 2014) would ensure even better that student engagement practices and policy are most likely to deliver the most beneficial outcomes.

Note

1 RAISE, 2019. Our Definitions of SE: 10 Principles for Student Engagement. Available at: www.raise-network.com/about/principles/

References

Barnett, R., 1997. *Higher Education: A Critical Business.* Buckingham: Society for Research into Higher Education and Open University Press.

Baxter Magolda, M., 1992. *Knowing and Reasoning in College: Gender Related Patterns in Students' Intellectual Development.* San Francisco, CA: Jossey Bass.

Baxter Magolda, M., 2007. Self-authorship: The foundation for twenty-first century education. *New Directions for Teaching and Learning,* 109, pp.69–83. Retrieved from: https://doi.org/10.1002/tl.266

Bryson, C., 2014a. *Understanding and Developing Student Engagement.* London: Routledge.

Bryson, C., 2014b. Clarifying the concept of student engagement. In: *Understanding and Developing Student Engagement* (pp.1–22). London: Routledge.

Bryson, C., 2017. A cross-university initiative to enhance SOTL through a students-as-partners approach. *Journal of Educational Innovation, Partnership and Change,* 5(1), pp.216–228. Retrieved from: http://dx.doi.org/10.21100/jeipc.v3i1.578

Bryson, C., Brooke, J., Foreman, S., Graham, S. and Brayshaw, G., 2018. Modes of Partnership- Universal, Selective, Representational and Pseudo Partnership. *Student Engagement in Higher Education Journal,* 2(1).

Bryson, C., and Callaghan, L., 2018. Repositioning Higher Education to counter neoliberalism. A critical study of the outcomes of working in partnership between students and staff. Proceeding of the HECU9 Conference, Cape Town, South Africa, 17–18 November.

Bryson, C. and Hand, L., 2007. The role of engagement in inspiring teaching and learning. *Innovations in Teaching and Education International,* 44(4), pp.349–362. Retrieved from: https://doi.org/10.1080/14703290701602748

Bryson, C. and Hand, L., 2008. An introduction to student engagement. SEDA special, 22, pp.5–13.

Bryson, C. and Hardy, C., 2014. Nottingham tales; diverse student journeys through their undergraduate degrees, In: *Understanding and developing student engagement* (pp.25–46). London: Routledge.

Callaghan, L., 2016. From disengaged to super engaged: my student journey. *Student Engagement in Higher Education Journal,* 1(1).

Cook-Sather, A., Bovill, C., and Felten, P., 2014. *Engaging Students as Partners in Learning and Teaching: A Guide for Faculty.* San Francisco, CA: Jossey-Bass.

Dubet, F., 1994. Dimensions et figures de l'expérience étudiante dans l'université de masse. *Revue Française de Sociologie,* 35(4), 511–32.

Duzevic, I., 2015. A conceptual framework for analysing the impact of influences on student engagement and learning, *Tertiary Education and Management,* 21(1), pp.66–79. Retrieved from: https://doi.org/10.1080/13583883.2014.1000368

Fromm, E., 1977. *To have or to be?* New York: Harper and Row.

Fredricks, J., Blumenfeld, P. and Paris, A., 2004. School engagement; potential of the concept, state of the evidence. *Educational Review,* 74(1), pp 59–109. Retrieved from: https://doi.org/10.3102/00346543074001059

Fulford, A., 2017. Refusal and disowning knowledge: rethinking disengagement in higher education. *Ethics and Education,* 12(1), pp.105–115. Retrieved from: https://doi.org/10.1080/17449642.2016.1271578

Furlonger, R., Garner, N., Callaghan, L., Foreman, S. and Bryson, C., forthcoming. Empowering students through partnership in the curriculum. In Mukadam, A. and Mawani, S. (eds.), *Student Empowerment: Reflections of Teachers and Students in Higher Education.*

Furlonger, R., Johnson, S. and Parker, B., 2014. Experiences of engagement: The successes and issues from a student perspective. In Bryson C. (ed.) *Understanding and developing student engagement* (pp.79–90). London: Routledge.

Gourlay, L., 2015. Student engagement and the tyranny of participation. *Teaching in Higher Education*, 20(4), pp.402–411. Retrieved from: https://doi.org/10.1080/13562517.2015.1020784

Kahu, E., 2013. Framing student engagement in Higher Education. *Studies in Higher Education*, 35(5), pp.758–773. Retrieved from: https://doi.org/10.1080/03075079.2011.598505

Kahu, E. and Nelson, K., 2018. Student engagement in the educational interface: understanding the mechanisms of student success. *Higher Education Research and Development*, 37(1), pp.58–71. Retrieved from: https://doi.org/10.1080/07294360.2017.1344197

Kelly, P., Fair, N. and Evans, C., 2017. The engaged student ideal in UK higher education policy, *Higher Education Policy*, 30(1), pp.105–122. Retrieved from: https://doi.org/10.1057/s41307-016-0033-5

Land, R., Rattray, J. and Vivian, P., 2014. Learning in the liminal space: a semiotic approach to threshold concepts. *Higher Education*, 67(2), pp 199–217. Retrieved from: https://doi.org/10.1007/s10734-013-9705-x

Macfarlane, B., and Tomlinson, M., 2017. Critiques of student engagement. *Higher Education Policy*, 30(1), pp.5–21. Retrieved from: https://doi.org/10.1057/s41307-016-0027-3

Mann, S., 2001. Alternative perspectives on the student experience: alienation and engagement. *Studies in Higher Education*, 26(1), pp.7–19. Retrieved from: https://doi.org/10.1080/03075070123178

Mezirow, J., 2000. Learning to think like an adult. Core concepts of transformation theory. In J. Mezirow, and Associates (eds.), *Learning as Transformation. Critical Perspectives on a Theory in Progress.* San Francisco, CA: Jossey-Bass.

National Student Survey (NSS), The National Student Survey. Retrieved from: www.thestudentsurvey.com/ (accessed 21 August 2019).

National Survey of Student Engagement (NSSE), 2019. University of Indiana. Retrieved from: http://nsse.indiana.edu/ (accessed 30 July 2019).

Office for Students, 2019. Teaching Excellence and Student Outcomes Framework, 2019. Retrieved from: www.officeforstudents.org.uk/advice-and-guidance/teaching/what-is-the-tef/ (accessed 19 July 2019).

Researching, Advancing and Inspiring Student Engagement (RAISE), 2019. Retrieved from: www.raise-network.com/home/ (accessed 31 July 2019).

Sambell, K., McDowell, L. and Montgomery, C., 2013. *Assessment for learning in Higher Education*, London: Routledge.

Trowler, V., 2010. Student engagement literature review. Higher Education Academy. Retrieved from: www.heacademy.ac.uk/system/files/studentengagementliteraturereview_1.pdf

Vuori, J., 2013. Student Engagement: Buzzword or fuzzword? *Journal of Higher Education Policy and Management*, 36(5) pp.509–519. Retrieved from: https://doi.org/10.1080/1360080x.2014.936094

Werder, C., and Otis, M. (eds.), 2010. *Engaging student voices in the study of teaching and learning*, Virginia: Stylus.

Zepke, N., 2014. Student engagement research in higher education: questioning an academic orthodoxy. *Teaching in Higher Education*, 19(6), pp.697–708. Retrieved from: https://doi.org/10.1080/13562517.2014.901956

Zepke, N., 2015a. What future for student engagement in neoliberal times? *Higher Education*, 69(4) pp.693–704. Retrieved from: https://doi.org/10.1007/s10734-014-9797-y

Zepke, N., 2015b. Student engagement and neoliberalism: mapping an elective affinity. *International Journal of Lifelong Education*, 34(6), pp.696–709. Retrieved from: https://doi.org/10.1080/02601370.2015.1096312

Chapter 22

Higher education institutions and policy makers

The future of student engagement

Tom Lowe and Alex Bols

Introduction

Student engagement in England is at a crossroads. The competing pressures on student engagement activities, research and strategies in relation to whether students are customers or partners have for many years constituted a creative tension, but, as market forces become ever stronger, they risk ripping this tension at the seams. Such marketisation pressure is leading to divergence in the direction of travel, both within the United Kingdom (UK) higher education (HE) sector and between the wider UK and other nations across the globe. Previous chapters in this book have reflected on contrasting elements and practices of student engagement, both within the wider UK and internationally. This chapter seeks to draw together some of these themes and to reflect on changes over the past ten years, as a basis for suggesting how student engagement might develop in the future. Without aiming to predict, we do suggest a number of possible scenarios that could develop, according to (a) whether student engagement inclines more towards a collective approach or an individual one and (b) whether the policy agenda is more influenced by the consumer ethos or the partnership model.

We hope that these scenarios will provide a framework for students, institutions and policy makers, allowing them to consider which features of student engagement they might wish to retain and therefore how they might take active steps towards protecting these features. This chapter will focus, for the most part, on the English HE context in relation to student engagement, yet also draw on those practices adopted in various worldwide contexts. The global trends outlined in this chapter have relevance to the English HE sector, nationally or regionally, in the face of increasing marketisation and greater emphasis upon success criteria, outcomes and the scrutiny of students' experiences of their education. Since these forces may act as a carrot or a stick in terms of their influence upon discussions and activities related to student engagement, this chapter will weigh up, respectively, the consumer and the partnership agendas in HE.

Where was the English HE sector in 2009?

There have been many policy interventions and initiatives in England over the past ten years, as described by Bols in Chapter 3 (Bols, 2019). His research into the perceptions of representatives of students' unions in England and of English HE institutions with degree-awarding power generated a 46% response rate from the unions and 47% from the institutions. This survey repeated one conducted by the Centre for Higher Education Research and Information (CHERI) for the Higher Education Funding Council for England (HEFCE) into student representation, published in 2009 (Little, Locke, Scesa and Williams, 2009).

Bols' research compares the perceptions over the ten-year period and provides some interesting – and mixed – results in terms of the extent to which respondents believe that student representation has become more effective over this period (see Table 22.1). For example, in a comparison of data from 2009 and from 2018, perceptions about student representation on faculty/department committees are broadly similar: 13.6% of respondents in higher education institutions (HEIs) believed it was '*very effective*' in 2018, compared to 16% in 2009; amongst students' unions, it was 15.5% in 2018, compared to 13% in 2009. Amongst HEIs, there is a perception that student representation has become less effective, with 59.3% describing it as "*reasonably effective*" in 2018, compared to 71% in 2009; a perception that it is 'not very effective' reached 20.3% in 2018, compared to 9% in 2009. However, amongst students' union responses, the perceptions had moved in the other direction. By 2018, 56.9% of students' union responses believed student representation to be "*reasonably effective*" compared to 39% in 2009, with 19% thinking it "*not very effective*" compared to 37% in 2009. There are also differences when considering the effectiveness of student representation on institution-wide committees (see Table 22.2). The overall

Table 22.1 Effectiveness of student representation on faculty/departmental committees

	Very effective (%)	Reasonably effective (%)	Not very effective (%)	Not applicable (%)	Don't know (%)
HEI 2018	13.6	59.3	20.3	1.7	5.1
Students' union 2018	15.5	56.9	19	0	8.6

Source: Online survey – HEIs, n = 60; students' unions, n = 58

	Very effective (%)	Reasonably effective (%)	Not very effective (%)	Not applicable (%)	Don't know (%)
HEI 2009	16	71	9	4	0
Students' union 2009	13	39	37	0	11

Source: Online survey – HEIs, n = 80; students' unions, n = 39

Table 22.2 Effectiveness of student representation on institution-wide committees

	Very effective (%)	Reasonably effective (%)	Not very effective (%)	Not applicable (%)	Don't know (%)
HEI 2018	20	73.3	6.7	0	0
Students' union 2018	15.5	74.1	6.9	0	3.4
Combined 2018	17.8	73.7	6.8	0	1.7

Source: Online survey – HEIs, n = 60; students' unions, n = 58

	Very effective (%)	Reasonably effective (%)	Not very effective (%)	Not applicable (%)	Don't know (%)
HEI 2009	37	53	8	0	0
Students' union 2009	37	52	10	0	0

Source: Online survey – HEIs, n = 80; students' unions, n = 39

levels of effectiveness combining '*very effective*' and '*reasonably effective*' show broadly comparable results, with 90% amongst HEI responses in 2009 compared to the 93.3% in the 2018 research and 89% in 2009 amongst students' unions compared to 89.6% in 2018. However, amongst the responses there has been a shift from "*very effective*" and "*reasonably effective*". In 2009, 37% of both HEI and students' union responses rated student representation on institution-wide committees as '*very effective*' compared to the 20% amongst HEI responses and 15.5% from students' union respondents. However, whilst there were interesting differences in the views of HEIs and students' unions between 2009 and 2018, it would be worth exploring the extent to which there has been real change or whether there is now more of a shared understanding of the roles of student representation amongst HEIs and students' unions.

What has happened in the years 2009–2019 in UK higher education?

Writing this chapter in 2019, the authors are able to reflect on ten years of turbulent change for the English HE sector, now shifted from largely publicly funded to competitive and marketised: each HEI, both in England and the UK more widely, is scrutinised publicly against a variety of metrics and is consequently subject to directives and interventions. Between the years 2009 and 2019, HEIs have been shaped, year on year, by some welcome and some – arguably – unwelcome operational additions, which have had both push and pull influences upon the student engagement practices and discourses disseminated in this book. Two notable developments have been the increased attainment of young people – counteracting the demographic decline of 18-year-olds and so resulting in increasing numbers entering HE (UCAS, 2018; Giannakis, and Bullivant, 2016) – and, in England, a simultaneous removal of the student number limit for recruitment, making HEIs increasingly competitive for student intake and creating greater income volatility compared to fixed numbers previously.

This underpinning move towards marketisation resulting from the removal of student number caps was accelerated by the increase in student tuition fees (from £3,250 in 2009 to £9,250 in 2019), and has resulted in increased media and government concern that HE should provide 'value for money'. Policy developments include better information for students, accountability tools such as the development of a Teaching Excellence Framework and other regulatory changes have also had knock-on implications for the other parts of the UK and created an environment in which universities and colleges must be quick to view – and treat – their students as valued customers or partners in their learning.

Other nations (and notably the United States from the 1960s onwards) have experienced a similar pattern of change, with such similar features as an increased emphasis on metrics that drive league tables, student recruitment and retention and, finally, reputation, with the intention of creating employable graduates and delivering a high standard of student experience. In the digital, big-data market of education, student engagement as a movement, discourse and area of practice has been given a burst of energy, perhaps as a necessity but also as a demonstrated set of steps and conversations to enhance and protect HEIs as communities, rather than create places of commodity.

Where could the UK HE sector be in the next ten years, 2019–2029?

The HE sector is changing rapidly and is likely to continue to do so for some time, as the market becomes further embedded within it and providers decide to position themselves in particular ways or make rapid adjustments to their offer on the basis of market trends. If the pressure on HEIs continues in this direction, then students will become increasingly interested in their educational experience and their perceived investment, as will other interested parties: government, parents, tax payers and the media.

The remainder of this chapter will consider different factors that might have impact upon student engagement. The 2018 Quality Code described both *"individual and collective"* student engagement approaches and the wider policy implications of a more consumer or partnership approach to education. These different scenarios are represented in Figures 22.1 and 22.2 below and reflect the extensive range of student engagement practice, debates and tensions discussed throughout this edited collection. Looking into the future is always a difficult balance between considering existing trends and influences and recognising that

Representative partnership — *Partnership* — *Cooperative partnerships*

Representative partnership

Pros	Cons
Students and academics feeling part of a shared academic community	Resource-intensive for the institution to gather representative views; requiring much time and effort of students
Joint ownership of the student academic experience	This approach can provide particular challenges for less traditional modes of study or students
Engaged students will feel greater ownership of the own learning	Not all students want ownership of their education; those more instrumentally-minded might want merely to get a qualification

Cooperative partnerships

Pros	Cons
HEI-wide cooperative partnership schemes can, on the basis of numerous projects, create a culture of student–staff partnership	Resource-intensive for HE staff members (time and funding)
Cooperative partnerships supported by a broader scheme across a HEI, enabling partnership between students and staff more widely	The selection of the students can be open to bias and the students could be the super-engaged
HEI-wide co-operative partnership schemes can create a culture of partnership between students and staff, rather than customer (student) and service provider (educator)	Students are not always democratically elected or accountable, so their enhancement projects may not reflect or represent the wider student body/cohort

Student representation → ← Individual engagement

Consumer rights champions

Pros	Cons
Students are able to demand change, rebalancing power differentials	Students are less involved in developing solutions
Ability to hold the institution to account if things go wrong	Creates a more adversarial approach between students and institution
Getting recourse – including financial – when things go wrong	Lose a valuable learning opportunity to help fix problems

Individual agents

Pros	Cons
Surveys and open engagement opportunities are open to all students to engage	Such research methods as Likert scales, often used in surveys, frequently lack environmental controls and offer crude data
Complaint systems offer process and procedures for students to feedback on personal situations relating to their education in a formal approach	Because of the power structures involved, complaint systems and procedures demand great student confidence; also, the policies are often couched in challenging HE language
As learners, students are in the powerful position of feeding back about the HEI easily and publicly via social media	A 'student as customer' mind set can begin with sporadic uncontrolled social media posts which can damage the reputation of the HEI, staff members or students

Consumer rights champions — *Consumer-driven* — *Individual agents*

Figure 22.1 Future scenarios of student engagement paradigm

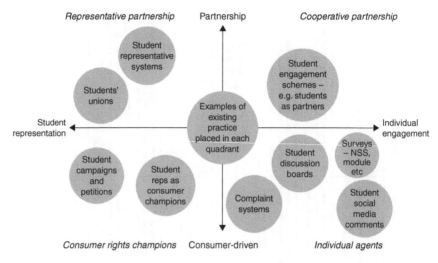

Figure 22.2 Example student engagement practices on paradigm

unexpected events or developments can make predictions look quickly out of date. Indeed, other factors and developments may end up disrupting student engagement and could result in radically different modes of study, whether via technology, work-based learning, accelerated or decelerated qualifications or something that we haven't even thought of yet.

Scenarios

Rather, therefore, than trying to look into a crystal ball and attempting to iden-tify where we think student engagement may go in the future, we are looking at different possible scenarios based on some of the major trends affecting HE. To develop the scenarios, we considered the two major considerations with impact upon student engagement: the extent to which student engage-ment will be based on a more consumer-driven/market-driven approach; or whether the student engagement/partnership approach will win out in the end. The vertical axis on the Figures 22.1 and 22.2 outlines the choice of direction introduced in Lowe and El Hakim's introductory chapter, showing two options for institutions in a marketised HE, where students are viewed as customers on one extreme and partners on the other. In Figure 22.2, the horizontal axis depicts what Bols outlines in Chapter 3, namely the tension between students engaging in their own education as an individual and large, democratic stu-dent representation schemes offering elected student engagement opportunities based on structures, accountability and processes. For this axis we therefore considered the extent to which student engagement will be on a more individual or a collective basis. By using these two axes we created four possible scenarios which we have labelled as:

- *Representative partnership*
- *Cooperative partnerships*
- *Consumer rights champions*
- *Individual agents*

We, the authors of this chapter, believe that different forms of student engagement practice can be placed on this model. It is likely that, over the next ten years, student engagement practices, students and the universities they learn within will be pulled in all four directions, collectively or individually, and we suggest that readers might wish to consider reflecting on the potential impact of this within their own institutions. As ever, with future-gazing, it is doubtful that any of these scenarios will be realised in their entirety, but, by considering the different options and drivers, we might be able to consider some of the possible different futures and how we might move to a preferred future or counter some of the worst features of options that we might wish to avoid.

I. Representative partnership

The scenario in the top-left-hand corner of Figure 22.2 is based on the possible future where the partnership approach has won out against the consumer model and is looking at the collective rather than individual end of the engagement spectrum. Many who are engaged in the student engagement space would consider this approach to student engagement as utopia. In this scenario, students can feed in their collective perspectives in relation to identification of the issues, analysis of the problem and then development of the solution. In this scenario, students are engaged in a community of learning and are respected as full equal partners within this community. For example, in this scenario, student views about their modules or units would be gathered. However, rather than waiting till the end of the course and saying what went wrong, as in an autopsy, students would be engaged the whole way through the course and making clear their views through dialogue. In addition, whilst there would still be an end-of-module survey, it would be developed jointly by students and academics – they would all share in

Table 22.3 Representative partnership pros and cons

Pros	Cons
Students and academics feel part of a shared academic community.	Gathering representative views is resource-intensive, for the institution and for the students.
Joint ownership of the student academic experience.	This approach can provide particular challenges for less traditional modes of study or students.
Engaged students will feel greater ownership of their own learning.	Not all students want ownership of their education; some, more instrumentally minded students, might just want to get a qualification.

the analysis of results and the development of an action plan and all would have shared ownership of the survey process.

It should, however, be recognised that this future is not without its difficulties, not least the resource implications for both the institution and the students' union as well as the students themselves (see Table 22.3). This approach is incredibly resource-intensive. HE has become increasingly diverse in recent years, both in terms of the backgrounds of the students and also the way in which they are studying (Craft, 2018; Lea, 2015). Even taking account of just those on full-time undergraduate degrees, the population has become more diverse; gathering a collective view would therefore require either large numbers of involved students or large-scale research to identify the issues that are both widely and deeply felt across the whole student cohort. For those students engaged in collective engagement activities, it would probably be necessary to speak to a large number of the students or run research or other approaches to gather a representative view, all of which would cost money and/or time. Furthermore, the ways in which students are studying have changed as well: more accelerated degrees, work-based learning, technology-enhanced delivery and apprenticeships and other modes of study all are likely to require different ways of engaging those students who are time-poor.

There may also be unforeseen problems, such as unintended tyranny over genuine minority need by a majority opinion. In one institution, for example, where a course was due to start at 08.30, the tutor concerned felt it appropriate – and responsive to the likely wishes of most participants – to offer the later start time of 09.00. Most, indeed, were grateful, but the two students with children had already booked a whole term's childcare on the basis of the published earlier time; these two students, feeling uncomfortable about upsetting their peers, chose not to voice their concerns and ended up paying for a daily additional half hour of childcare. Thus, responding to majority views may – and in this case, did – have unintended and unfair consequences, regardless of the best of intentions.

Recommendations and considerations

Whilst the scenario is unlikely to be realised completely, it will be possible to ensure that some of the positive features of the approach are taken on board. These include:

- ensuring that students feel that they are able to voice their concerns and that they will be listened to should be a key feature of any HE model in the future;
- students should be able to engage with shaping their educational experience as much or as little as they want, rather than the institution having unrealistic expectations about their engagement;
- a consideration of how technology might be used to facilitate better engagement from wider groups of students.

2. Cooperative partnerships

The next scenario considers what a partnership approach might look like if focused on individual engagement. Differing forms of these types of student–staff partnerships are outlined throughout this edited collection: 'students as partners', 'students as change agents' or 'student academic partners' schemes. Cooperative partnerships can differ from the representative ones discussed above, as they operate throughout institutions and have varying purposes, roles and responsibilities, from course level to management, yet often these 'students as partners' projects seek to engage individual students to run a change project or research an issue. However, the students involved in these schemes are often not democratically elected and therefore not necessarily representative of the wider student cohort (see Table 22.4).

Reflecting on these institutional practices, the outcome of the student engagement scheme often varies, according to: whether the student is elected or not; whether a student is partnered with an academic staff member for a research project, a student panel member on a quality assurance board or sitting on a university management committee. Because of the growth of types, commitments and forums of student engagement activities as outlined in this collection, the practicalities of democratically electing for every post is a challenge, as noted above. However, these opportunities do form a valuable part of the student engagement practice movement, discourse and study area.

Selective or cooperative student–staff partnerships are positive, in that they can perform set tasks: for example, a student might work with a course leader

Table 22.4 Cooperative partnership pros and cons

Pros	Cons
HEI-wide cooperative partnership schemes can create a culture of partnership between staff and students based on numerous projects.	Resource-intensive for HE staff member (time and funding).
Cooperative partnerships supported by a wider scheme across a HEI, making partnership possible for a wider range of students and staff.	Opportunities may not be accessible to students with other commitments (e.g. paid work, caring responsibilities, additional study requirements, travel).
Schemes offer opportunities for students to become deeply engaged with educational developers as project partners, above mere student voice or representations.	Students are not always democratically elected or accountable, so their enhancement projects may not reflect or represent the wider student body/ cohort.
Large HEI-wide cooperative partnership schemes can create a culture of partnership between staff and students, rather than customer (student) and service provider (educator).	The selection of the students can be open to bias and the students could be the super-engaged.

during the spring vacation to enhance their programme. The student who has availability during the spring vacation is able to commit a high number of hours and thus a great deal of work to the project; the staff member, whose role it is to take a lead on course enhancements, has the time in their work contract and, no doubt, a significant desire to take part in the project. This example may represent the ideal, but readers might justifiably think: "*But what if student or staff member have other commitments?*" This is where all student engagement approaches hit the question of accessibility for those involved and it is important to cover both parties in this discussion.

Student engagement partnership projects, which often require a considerable time commitment, instantly create accessibility barriers to any students who have constraints on their time, such as: commuting students (Maguire and Morris, 2019; Thomas and Jones, 2017); parents or those with caring responsibilities; those in part-time/full-time work; those following a demanding course with high contact time; or, simply, those engaged in too many other campus activities, such as sport or societies, to undertake a student–staff partnership project. These are very physical barriers to student engagement opportunities, but there are less tangible barriers relating to students' perception of student–staff partnership projects: not deeming themselves smart enough to take part in educational development; the characteristics of previous student partners creating aspects of bias (race, disability/ability, age, class, academic achievement); a low sense of belonging to the programme due to previous alienation, leading to poor accessibility to the staff, making the project seem unattractive. In the past, these students have been wrongly referred to as 'hard to reach', but, often, these factors are present, preventing students from engaging in student–staff partnership projects: alienation, favouritism and barriers to participation (Cook-Sather and Porte, 2017; Goddard, 2017; Shaw, Humphrey, Atvars and Sims, 2017). Many of the above factors may also affect staff, who often have been excluded from discussions relating to the accessibility of student engagement approaches discourse and who increasingly find themselves on the front line of HE reforms With ever-increasing accountability and ever-decreasing time; this means that many staff simply do not have the time to commit to student engagement partnership spaces, as they are often dealing with high workloads, research commitments and contracts which limit their ability to engage in creative spaces (Flint and Millard, 2018).

Although there are significant barriers, as outlined above, time-intensive student engagement projects – which have often taken the form via large 'students as partners' schemes (see Marquis, Guitman, Black, Healey, Matthews and Dvorakova, 2018; Lowe, Shaw, Sims, King, and Paddison, 2017; Marie, Arif and Joshi, 2016) – have positive potential and offer mutually beneficial educational development from which all parties gain. This collection illustrates clearly that students engaged in these opportunities do derive from them rewarding, transformational and empowering experiences. Researched benefits include an increased sense of belonging (Thomas, 2012), employability skills (Moore and Morton, 2017), greater criticality and becoming (Bryson, 2014) and statistical benefits, such as academic achievement and retention (Sims, Luebsen, and Guggiari-Peel, 2017). The staff member tasked with educational development demonstrates increased momentum, owing to fresh energy from outside the academy, additional hours of support and valuable student perspectives; the students do not just feed into the projects, but co-construct, design and build initiatives in which students are partners from origin to fruition. For the strategic leaders of the HEI, or the department tasked with educational developments, 'students as partners' initiatives offer a positive means of doubling capacity, by matching students with staff, creating meaningful relationships in cohorts, possibly increasing student satisfaction and generating an enhanced employability experience for the students involved.

Recommendations and considerations

- Ask cooperative partnership projects to research the wider student experience of the wider student body/cohort;
- Annually review the accessibility and diversity of 'students as partners' opportunities;
- Ensure there is an open and accessible selection process which engages a wider range of students democratically.

3. Consumer rights champions

In a future where the market is dominant and students have fully embraced the power of being a consumer, the role of student engagement could take the form of student rights champion (see Table 22.5 for a list of the pros and cons). In this scenario, you could expect to hear students and their students' unions, who are embracing the fact that they are paying for their education, make increasingly vocal demands on the basis of value for their money, complain when things go wrong and expect that the institution will fix any issue quickly. In this scenario, you could expect student champions to challenge a partnership model of a university by saying "*I'm paying you to fix this; I will not waste my valuable time helping you fix it,*" as well as mass student complaints, demands for enhancements and students' unions organising campaigns and protests for

Table 22.5 Consumer rights champion pros and cons

Pros	Cons
Students are able to demand change, rebalancing power differentials.	Students are less involved in developing solutions.
Ability to hold the institution to account if things go wrong.	Creates a more adversarial approach between students and institution.
Getting recourse – including financial – when things go wrong.	Loss of a valuable learning opportunity to help fix problems.

their education to develop. The student representative becomes a powerful part of the feedback process, with representatives able to identify the problems and to hold the institution to account to fix them (Freeman, 2016; Brooks, Byford, and Sela, 2015). Where student representatives often claim that there are power imbalances between themselves and the academics and institution, this would firmly give them a more powerful position to demand real change (Fletcher, 2017).

There could be a perceived disadvantage of students not being involved in developing the solution to the problem that they have identified, but they will also have strengthened power to evaluate any solution that the institution develops. However, in a market where students are not easily able to retake their education or move to another institution, this could result in an unnecessarily adversarial approach rather than a joint collaboration to respond to problems and, in the process, further their own learning and development.

Recommendations and considerations

Whilst the scenario is unlikely to be realised completely, it will be possible to ensure that some of the positive features of the approach are taken up. These include:

- re-balancing any power differentials between students, academics and the institution;
- creating shared goals between faculty teams and students, or institutions and their students' union;
- considering how student representatives can be empowered to articulate the concerns of students and how they can critique potential solutions.

4. Individual agents

The final quarter of the quadrant in Figure 22.2 refers to the means by which students may become engaged in their educational experience as individuals, not supported by a wider initiative with other students or as part of a formal committee. This scenario might become more likely in the future, as technological developments allow more direct engagement of students to feed back their views in real time rather than just through surveys. The scenario refers to an increased marketised emphasis on HE, where students become potential consumers of their studies (Bunce, Baird and Jones, 2017), separate from the wider university and far away from any ethos of membership or partnership. This quadrant also refers to individual engagements away from a 'wider representations' structure such as students' unions and representatives discussed above, and also from initiatives where staff and students work together in partnership or engage in discussion on university committees. When these mechanisms are not available, students who wish to engage for positive or negative reasons in this quadrant will resort to their own agency, open feedback opportunities and university organisation processes to engage with their university concerning educational developments. Examples of 'individual agent' student engagement mechanisms are:

- institutional and nationwide surveys, such as the National Student Survey (NSS), National Survey of Student Engagement (NSSE), or course-level evaluation forms;
- one-off feedback opportunities on campus noticeboards, social media etc.;
- HEI and students' union mechanisms for student complaints, academic appeals and other written means of feedback;
- individual relationships and informal conversations with academic and professional services staff;
- individual student social media posts in the public domain.

Table 22.6 summarises the pros and cons of the different approaches. The initial methods of engaging students rely wholly on either the HEI or the governing body enacting these pathways for students to engage in their education's development. Institutional surveys, whether run locally or nationally, are certainly often cited as the most efficient means of gathering students' views of their education, offering opportunities for the staff facilitator to distil students down by student demographic, academic discipline or even by each institution on a national level. These surveys, of course, are already – and increasingly on a local level – used for university-ranking league tables and for trouble-spotting; they carry a growing amount of influence over institutional reputation. The majority of these surveys are neither conducted in a controlled environment nor as methods of research; any readers who have taken even one seminar in the use of surveys for large populations will know that such methods as Likert scales are riddled with limitations (Senior, Moores and Burgess, 2017; Porter, Whitcomb and Weitzer, 2004). What is easy for HEIs in using module evaluation forms, first-year surveys or the National Student Survey, is their ability to gather a large amount of student data, though how representative and meaningful some of these forms of student engagement are is questionable. As an alternative to them, which have produced inevitable survey fatigue (Senior et al., 2017), many HEIs have begun to use other means of gaining students' views. These take the most traditional shape of feedback boards, online polls and idea submissions and even public polls for students to complete via apps to rate a programme.

The latter three types of student engagement occurrences or pathways rely a great deal on the individual student and their social agency, or capital, which allows them to take advantage of non-supported mechanisms for engagement. The first of these is the means of student engagement most known to all working in a front-line role in HE: the individual conversations that occur alongside, before or after a delivered lecture, development session or one-to-one advice. This feedback is valuable to the educator who is able to gain useful information to gauge 'how it is going' and what issues the student/s is/are facing. The second means for individual students to raise their views outside schemes are any formal

Table 22.6 Individual agent pros and cons

Pros	Cons
Surveys and open engagement opportunities are open to all students to engage.	Surveys can be used too often as a means of engaging students, causing survey fatigue, and they often focus on majority responses, ignoring the minority.
Surveys offer an efficient means of engaging with large cohorts of students and a means of analysis by demographic, year of study or discipline.	Research methods like Likert scales, used in these surveys, often have no environmental controls and offer crude data.
Complaint systems offer process and procedures for students formally to feed back on personal situations relating to their education.	Complaint procedures and systems take a considerable amount of confidence, given the power structures involved, and the policies are often written in inaccessible HE language.
Students, as the learner, are in a powerful position where they can easily and publicly feedback on the HEI via social media.	A 'student as customer' mindset can begin with sporadic uncontrolled social media posts which can damage the reputation of the HEI, staff members or students.

channels they have open to them, where they can – usually – complain, or appeal a grade. These systems often rely on the HEI's values when they are setting the channels up to ensure that they are accessible to students for raising issues, that they are not too time-consuming and that they are transparent. Unfortunately, these processes are often indeed quite a strain on the student who usually is in an uncomfortable position already because of the inherent power imbalances between staff and students.

As stated, these opportunities may not be accessible, relying on a high amount of confidence, personal relationships, agency and knowledge for a student to be able either to approach HE academics or professionals informally or use the mysterious HE systems to raise their views to make a formal complaint/ appeal. If one reflects at this point on Sarah Mann's seminal work on alienation in HE, portraying universities as foreign lands, one begins to understand how complicated it can be to follow university complaints procedures (Mann, 2001). Finally, one further route that students have today, which students of the past did not have, is the ability to use social media like Facebook, Twitter and online forums to announce their feedback on the HEI publicly. This is a powerful form of student engagement and can be incredibly valuable to the HEI if positive stories are shared by students, but, if they are negative, it can be harmful to the reputations of both the HEI and its staff. Many people already operate this approach when dissatisfied with their electricity provider, telephone contract or a restaurant's service, but do we facilitate students to do this with regard to their education? This is marketised student engagement at its most extreme and is one outcome for a university that does not prioritise accessible student engagement methods, schemes, mechanisms and support so that students may raise their views, whether positive or negative, in a constructive setting.

Recommendations and considerations

- Follow up HEI-wide surveys with further investigation and engagements with students via meaningful conversations with student representatives;
- Review the accessibility and clarity of student complaint and appeals procedures to ensure they place the student in as little discomfort as possible;
- Ensure that student engagement pathways (e.g. student representatives, feedback forums and other methods) are available, are effective and are known to students so that they can use those, rather than social media, to feed back on their education.

Conclusion

The future of student engagement and how it will feature in associated projects, policy, strategies and even language is a question often posed, yet difficult to answer, even over a relatively short time period of ten years. What is clear to many is that the focus is increasingly on HE outcomes, centred upon the student (or consumer), whether in relation to student learning, graduate employability or value for money (Office for Students, 2018). The authors of this paper are both advocates of student engagement discussions, priorities and exploration as a means of protecting the continuous development of education in HE.

Student engagement activities and approaches can be placed anywhere on the paradigm in the four scenarios above, with regard to their representativeness versus the individual or partnership versus the customer. As we bring together this collection, 'student engagement' can be defined in a multitude of ways and the chapters within this book reflect these, which is both a strength and also a weakness. The buzzwords 'student engagement' and their purpose have created a banner for activity and scholarship, but the term can be dismissed derogatively as a 'fuzzword' (Vuori, 2014, p.509). It is therefore up to researchers, practitioners, students and leaders to ensure we so define 'student engagement' that it does reflect our commitment to such principles as inclusivity, meaningfulness and reciprocity for all parties and avoid the agenda of 'student as customer' (Fletcher, 2017; Healey, Flint and Harrington, 2014; Bryson 2014; Zepke, 2013, p.1). As Buckley cautions the sector, the "*lack of conceptual clarity carries a number of risks. If we are not clear about what student engagement is, then our ability to improve, increase, support and encourage it through well-designed interventions will be severely diminished*" (Buckley, 2014, p.2).

Student engagement is core to the protection and survival of community, partnership, collaboration and development in HE and, if we abandon these principles or even appropriate the term into a customer-focused role, the very nature of our HE sector can change to one that is marketised, user-focused and service-driven. In 2009, the CHERI report came out at a time of change in UK HE; in 2019, many of the same drivers for change exist and some have become even more acutely relevant. Student engagement was important then, in 2009, as it is now, ten years later, to create meaningful conversations, research and projects between staff and students, in order to develop education in our communities and beyond.

References

Bols, A., 2019. The changing nature and importance of Student Representation. In: Lowe, T. and El Hakim, Y. (eds.), 2019, *A Handbook for Student Engagement in Higher Education*. London: Routledge.

Brooks, R., Byford, K. and Sela, K., 2015. The changing role of students' unions within contemporary higher education. *Journal of Education Policy*, 30(2), pp.165–181. Retrieved from: https://doi.org/10.1080/02680939.2014.924562

Bryson, C., 2014. *Understanding and Developing Student Engagement* (SEDA Series). London: Routledge.

Buckley, A., 2014. How radical is student engagement? (And what is it for?). *Student Engagement and Experience Journal*, 3(2), pp.1–23. https://doi.org/10.7190/seej.v3i2.95

Bunce, L., Baird, A. and Jones, S.E., 2017. The student-as-consumer approach in higher education and its effects on academic performance. *Studies in Higher Education*, 42(11), pp.1958–1978. Retrieved from: https://doi.org/10.1080/03075079.2015.1127908

Craft, A. (ed.), 2018. *International developments in assuring quality in higher education* (Vol. 6). London: Routledge.

Cook-Sather, A. and Porte, O., 2017. Reviving humanity: Grasping within and beyond our reach. *Journal of Educational Innovation, Partnership and Change*, 3(1), pp.299–302. Retrieved from: https://doi.org/10.21100/jeipc.v3i1.638

Fletcher, A.F., 2017. *Student voice revolution: The meaningful student involvement handbook*. CommonAction Publishing.

Flint, A. and Millard, L., 2018. 'Interactions with purpose': Exploring staff understandings of student engagement in a university with an ethos of staff–student partnership. *International Journal for Students as Partners*, 2(2), pp.21–38. Retrieved from: https://doi.org/10.15173/ijsap.v2i2.3410

Freeman, R., 2016. Is student voice necessarily empowering? Problematising student voice as a form of higher education governance. *Higher Education Research and Development*, 35(4), pp.859–862. Retrieved from: https://doi.org/10.1080/07294360.2016.1172764

Giannakis, M. and Bullivant, N., 2016. The massification of higher education in the UK: Aspects of service quality. *Journal of Further and Higher Education*, 40(5), pp.630–648. Retrieved from: https://doi.org/10.1080/0309877x.2014.1000280

Goddard, H., 2017. Reframing 'Hard to Reach' Student Engagement. *Journal of Educational Innovation, Partnership and Change*, 3(1), pp.68–70. Retrieved from: http://dx.doi.org/10.21100/jeipc.v3i1.628

Healey, M., Flint, A. and Harrington, K., 2014. *Engagement through partnership: students as partners in learning and teaching in higher education*. York: Higher

Education Academy. Retrieved from: www.heacademy.ac.uk/system/files/ resources/engagement_through_partnership.pdf

Lea, J. (ed.), 2015. *Enhancing learning and teaching in higher education: Engaging with the dimensions of practice.* Milton Keynes: Open University Press.

Little, B., Locke, W. Scesa, A. and Williams, R., 2009. *Report to HEFCE on student engagement.* HEFCE, Bristol, UK. Retrieved from: http://oro.open.ac.uk/ 15281/

Lowe, T., Shaw, C., Sims, S., King, S. and Paddison, A., 2017. The development of contemporary student engagement practices at the University of Winchester and Winchester Student Union, UK. *International Journal for Students as Partners,* 1(1). Retrieved from: https://doi.org/10.15173/ijsap.v1i1.3082

Maguire, D. and Morris, D., 2019. Homeward Bound: Defining, understanding and aiding 'commuter students'. Higher Education Policy Institute, Report 114. Retrieved from: www.hepi.ac.uk/wp-content/uploads/2018/12/HEPI-Homeward-Bound-Defining-understanding-and-aiding-%E2%80%98commuter-students%E2%80%99-Report-11429_11_18Web.pdf

Marquis, E., Guitman, R., Black, C., Healey, M., Matthews, K.E. and Dvorakova, L.S., 2018. Growing partnership communities: What experiences of an international institute suggest about developing student–staff partnership in higher education. *Innovations in Education and Teaching International,* pp.1–11. Retrieved from: https://doi.org/10.1080/14703297.2018.1424012

Moore, T. and Morton, J., 2017. The myth of job readiness? Written communication, employability, and the 'skills gap' in higher education. *Studies in Higher Education,* 42(3), pp.591–609. Retrieved from: https://doi.org/10.1080/ 03075079.2015.1067602

Mann, S.J., 2001. Alternative perspectives on the student experience: alienation and engagement. *Studies in Higher Education,* 26(1), pp.7–19. Retrieved from: https://doi.org/10.1080/03075070123178

Marie, J., Arif, M. and Joshi, T., 2016. UCL ChangeMakers projects: supporting staff/ student partnership on educational enhancement projects. *Student Engagement in Higher Education Journal,* 1(1).

National Student Survey (NSS), 2019. Retrieved from: www.thestudentsurvey.com/ about.php (accessed 1 February 2019).

National Survey of Student Engagement (NSSE), 2019. Retrieved from: http:// nsse.indiana.edu/html/about.cfm (accessed 1 February 2019).

Office for Students, 2018. *Securing student success: Regulatory framework for higher education in England.* Retrieved from: www.officeforstudents.org. uk/publications/securing-student-success-regulatory-framework-for-higher-education-in-england/v

Porter, S.R., Whitcomb, M.E. and Weitzer, W.H., 2004. Multiple surveys of students and survey fatigue. *New Directions for Institutional Research,* 2004(121), pp.63–73. Retrieved from: https://doi.org/10.1002/ir.101

Senior, C., Moores, E. and Burgess, A.P., 2017. "I can't get no satisfaction": measuring student satisfaction in the age of a consumerist higher education. *Frontiers in psychology,* 8, p.980. Retrieved from: https://doi.org/10.3389/fpsyg.2017.00980

Sims, S., Luebsen, W. and Guggiari-Peel, C., 2017. Exploring the role of co-curricular student engagement in relation to student retention, attainment and improving inclusivity. *Journal of Educational Innovation, Partnership and Change,* 3(1), pp.93–109. Retrieved from: http://dx.doi.org/10.21100/jeipc.v3i1.605

Shaw, C., Humphrey, O., Atvars, T. and Sims, S., 2017. Who they are and how to engage them: a summary of the REACT systematic literature review of the 'hard to reach 'in higher education. *Journal of Educational Innovation, Partnership and Change*, 3(1), pp.51–64. Retrieved from: http://dx.doi.org/10.21100/jeipc. v3i1.685

Thomas, L., 2012. *Building student engagement and belonging in higher education at a time of change: a summary of findings and recommendations from the What Works? Student Retention and Success programme.* London: Paul Hamlyn Foundation. Retrieved from: http://lizthomasassociates.co.uk/commuter_students.html

Thomas, L. and Jones, R., 2017. *Student engagement in the context of commuter students.* London: Student Engagement Partnership. Retrieved from: www. lizthomasassociates.co.uk/projects/2018/Commuter%20student%20engagement.pdf

UCAS, 2018. A record percentage of young people are off to university, 16 August. Retrieved from: www.ucas.com/corporate/news-and-key-documents/news/ record-percentage-young-people-are-university (accessed 1 February 2019).

UKSCQA and QAA, 2018. Student Engagement Advice and Guidance Theme, *UK Quality Code for Higher Education.* United Kingdom Standing Committee for Quality Assessment and Quality Assurance Agency for Higher Education. Retrieved from: www.qaa.ac.uk/quality-code (accessed 8 August 2019).

Vuori, J., 2013. Student Engagement: Buzzword of Fuzzword?, *Journal of Higher Education Policy and Management*, 36(5), pp.509–519. Retrieved from: https:// doi.org/10.1080/1360080x.2014.936094

Zepke, N., 2013. Student engagement: A complex business supporting the first year experience in tertiary education. *International Journal of the First Year in Higher Education*, 4(2). Retrieved from: https://doi.org/10.5204/intjfyhe.v4i2.183

Chapter 23

Student engagement for educational developments (SEED)

Yassein El Hakim and Allan Goody

Context and scalability of students engaged in educational development

It is clear from the chapters in this book that a key potential in our educational systems is not being fully actualised (Maslow, 1943). This potential could be tapped more deeply and with more impact if we include our fellow learners, or students as they are described all over the world, in educational developments. This occurs in pockets but is growing where the benefits to all involved are observed and celebrated. It is largely the higher education context that has empowered this movement of students being engaged in educational development, in particular: increasing student fees, a need for greater research outputs and a student desire to have close contact with staff (Chickering and Gamson, 1987; Gibbs, 2011). These have led to a macro trend of students being more actively involved in research across an institution, both for Educational Development and across all subject areas. For example, at University College London, its 'Connected Curriculum' brilliantly demonstrates the power of research and the research process, which are explicitly embedded within the curriculum, to the benefit of the student learning experience (Fung, 2017).

Looking at the growth of student engagement globally, students engaged in educational development could generate one of the largest research subject areas. As more schemes grow in each institution, more outputs will be created and disseminated at events, such as the BCUR (British Conference of Undergraduate Research)[1] or national conferences that celebrate student research outputs and contributions. Additionally, recent reports by UNESCO (e.g. 2017) state that from 2010 to 2014, the number of students in higher education institutions has doubled from 100 million to 207 million. In the same period the gross enrolment ratio increased from 19% to 34%, which is the percentage of the population within a five-year age group immediately following secondary school graduation (typically, ages 19 to 23). If many schemes are interested in student engagement as an antecedent to positive learning experiences and outcomes, then such a focus could create the largest global community of staff and students researching and publishing together, focusing on student or learner engagement.

It is also becoming clear that demand for higher education globally is growing disproportionately to the number of lecturers who can teach at the required levels. Macro trends have begun to demonstrate that in some subject areas, particularly software development or coding, sites like Github.com[2] are creating independent and autonomous learning communities, which are growing rapidly. They are established outside of university structures and revered as the leading space for subject knowledge alongside peer-to-peer development and learning. In these communities the transparent evidence of your work and your ability to learn new skills and knowledge quickly, with the ability to apply these practically, is more valuable than anything else. One's 'learnability', if you will, is soon to be the currency of choice for employers and entrepreneurs. Universities need to take heed and be positioned at the centre of these international communities of learners, going beyond the academy, where even research findings and the anonymised raw data associated with research can be engaged.

Collaboration, inclusion and equity

There are several chapters in this book that draw on evidence outlining the positive impact that students engaged in educational development create. Felten (Chapter 11) encourages us to be focused on human relationships in student engagement, citing Matthews' (2016) case for "*more collaborative forms of engagement between students and academics*" (p.2). Felten further suggests that engagement be viewed through the lens of students as partners, subsequently creating or "*offering new or reframed theory and constructs*" (Matthews, Cook-Sather, Acai, Dvorakova, Felten, Marquis and Mercer-Mapstone, 2019), "*practices*" (Cook-Sather, Bovill, and Felten 2014) and "*evidence of outcomes*" (Mercer-Mapstone, Dvorakova, Matthews, Abbot, Cheng, Felten, Knorr, Marquis, Shammas, and Swaim 2017, p.4).

Cook-Sather et al. (2014) defined pedagogical partnership as "*a collaborative, reciprocal process through which all participants have the opportunity to contribute equally, although not necessarily in the same ways, to curricular or pedagogical conceptualization, decision making, implementation, investigation, or analysis*" (p.6–7). Citing research from the United States, Australia, Canada, Malaysia, Sweden, and the United Kingdom, the authors stated that the benefits far outweigh the challenges (Cook-Sather, this volume, Chapter 7) and concluded that pedagogic partnerships provide an intersection for student engagement and academic development where belonging can be fostered for all students and staff.

Bovill and Woolmer (Chapter 6) state the importance of student evaluation and of increasing the opportunities to evaluate learning and teaching and student engagement initiatives as the whole learning community benefits from students' perspectives. This importance was clearly observed through the TESTA methodology and process (Jessop, El Hakim and Gibbs, 2014). By students feeding back their diverse perspectives, reflections and ideas on the programmatic assessment experience, the teaching teams could triangulate the data to provide a larger range of ideas for enhancing programmatic assessment. The best results were seen most quickly when the programme teams spoke directly and collaboratively with the students about the results of the process and the ways in which things may change. Bovill and Woolmer (Chapter 6) go on to cite that, "*increased dialogue between staff and students benefits not just evaluation, but student belonging, the building of academic community, teaching quality and learning outcomes*" (Gibbs, 2012; Lamport, 2003; Mårtensson, Roxå and Stensaker, 2014).

Leadership, empowerment and collective capability

The roles that students will occupy through their learning will vary in the future but their co-leadership of their learning experiences and environments will continue to strengthen. Whether this is through involvement (through selected working groups, projects, committees or fellowships) or crowdsourced feedback aligned with agile-style improvements to each learning experience or pathway, their role as leaders in the improvement of an institution's ability to deliver world-class learning experiences, will only grow (Cook-Sather, Chapter 7).

Peter Cook (2000, cited in Gill, 2006, p.6) described six implications for leadership:

1. *the ability to learn and adapt to change through signposts which are understood by the whole organisation;*
2. *using both logic and intuition to guide the organisation's direction;*
3. *balancing structure and chaos according to stakeholders' needs;*
4. *risk-taking within a safe environment;*
5. *personality differences overshadowed by a consuming mania with a shared purpose;*
6. *emergent strategy arising from the synthesis of **collective capability**.*

His last point of "collective capability" is a crucial one. It suggests that *all of an organisation's members* could share the responsibility for leadership and when differences/disagreements and debates arise, use them as points of creativity. This is an attribute actively developed in some of the world's most successful businesses such as Google, IBM and Apple. Such companies are regularly quoted on the topic of creativity and innovation and actively provide staff space for reflection, collaboration and playing/experimenting. It was reported that Google employees are given at least one day a week to pursue their own interests (*The Independent*, 13 January 2011). Higher education providers have similar attributes to these organisations. Both have high percentages of highly educated staff, their core work builds on and progresses previous knowledge, collegiality is both emphasised and essential, the workforce is often very passionate about their work, and the connection between the company and the users is central to success and growth. However, there appear to be two distinct differences:

1. Technology companies have been hyper-focused on the user experience as a core part of their business models: removing clicks, creating intuitive flows and user interfaces to improve the user experience, whereas academic institutions have often been hyper-focused on research income and esteem, whilst change has been restricted as a result of ageing technology infrastructure, and academic tradition.

2. Academic staff in universities have also been given a relatively high level of academic autonomy, so that leading them in any one particular direction is endearingly described by Mick Healey (2009) as "*herding cats*"; whereas this may also be interpreted as 'distributed leadership'.

In leading change, students engaged in educational developments could benefit from staff and institutional leaders having more autonomy to create change together, as opposed to making changes *for* the students. This collaboration often leverages open and honest dialogue between multiple stakeholders where communication breakdowns can be avoided. If the culture too can be influenced, helping align motivations of the individuals involved, then autonomy-supportive and intrinsically motivating environments can result in individuals persisting longer, exerting more effort and performing better (Mageau and Vallerand, 2003). Academic autonomy, empowerment of fellow learners, and a desire to increase our collective capability could therefore create phenomenal contexts for change and co-ownership of learning experiences, environments and organisations.

Spillane, Halverson and Diamond (2004) articulate eloquently the many ways in which leadership occurs and its interaction with culture by stating:

> *Rather than seeing leadership practice as solely a function of an individual's ability, skill, charisma, and/or cognition, we argue that it is best understood as a practice distributed over leaders, followers, and their situation. Attending to the situation as something more than a backdrop or container for leaders' practices, we consider sociocultural context as a constitutive element of leadership practice, an integral defining element of that activity.*

(p.11)

This view of leadership supports a culture of academic autonomy and speaks to the need for distributed leadership across multiple stakeholders and further supports students occupying trusted and empowered positions within the leadership teams in their specific contexts (Jones, 2017).

Empowering self-determined student engagement

The literature and content written across many chapters speaks to an immovable and significant power and a potential encapsulated in student voices, perspectives, feedback, satisfaction and engagement. We should note that honest and open feedback, even 'uncomfortable conversations', are also cited as a key element within the vulnerability research by Brown (2012). This single element can have significant impacts on an institution's national and world league table standings. In fact, when students' unions across the UK wanted to oppose the marketisation of higher education, some boycotted the National Student Survey (NSS), whose results they saw as a key part of the marketisation process (CUSU, 2019). This created a fantastic example of self-determined learning and student engagement where CUSU (2019) cited concisely:

> *The results of the NSS are used to pit universities against each other in rankings and create a competitive market in higher education, which turns students into passive consumers and damages the quality of education we receive by forcing universities to pour money into marketing and superficial or misguided changes that drive up 'satisfaction' statistics without tackling real structural issues. These changes have already been hugely damaging to students and also put several universities at financial risk, and students shouldn't let their voice be a part of it.*

The students' unions in this example are demonstrating courage, proactivity, self-determination and scholarship. They objectively reflect on the evidence describing research showing the effect of 'unconscious bias' from NSS respondents depending on the ethnicity of their lecturers. This has been shown to be one of the most significant influencers on the overall satisfaction of UK undergraduates (Bell and Brooks, 2016). There were also some successes of the NSS which were not alluded to. The NSS and similar surveys have focused university management teams on students' learning experiences at a time when institutional funding, outputs, staff promotions and leadership roles were heavily aligned to research. Not to undermine the importance that research plays in our higher education institutions globally, but unfortunately prolific and/or eminent researchers do not *always* make the best line managers, administrators or especially teachers. One wishes for a prolific researcher, pragmatic manager or administrator and *passionate* teachers, be they lecturers, tutors or supervisors.

Many have questioned whether such surveys or metrics should feed into league tables given the perverse effects or the 'unintended consequences' league tables can create, such as gaming of the metrics. This was evidenced in the Dimensions of Quality Report (Gibbs, 2011) where contact hours being included in league tables caused universities to reflect and address any areas where the contact time was 'too low'. Gibbs (2011) goes on to state that class contact hours alone have "*very little to do with educational quality*" (p.21). Instead, it is more important to consider the effect of contact hours on students' out-of-class efforts. Combining Chickering and Gamson's (1987) first principle of encouraging student–faculty contact with research by Gardiner (1997) and Trigwell and Ashwin (2004), students have been found to make greater overall weekly effort in some institutions over others despite having comparatively fewer class contact hours (HEPI, 2006, 2007). Pascarella, Seifert and Blaich (2008) also list studies that demonstrate that if you act on the 'seven principles of good practice' (Chickering and Gamson, 1987) then this improves student outcomes. Additionally, where the National Survey for Student Engagement (NSSE) is collected, it is often used by institutions in many countries to learn from, instead of to form league tables.

By empowering students to be self-determined and creating partnerships between them and academic partners or an international community of peers (e.g. Researching, Advancing and Inspiring Student Engagement – RAISE),[3] students and staff gain empathy for each others' contexts and can identify and create optimised ideas, practices, solutions and policies. Within educational development, institutions that create ownership, belonging and courage in their students will likely gain benefits and outputs reiterated throughout this book. There are challenges, issues and uncomfortable conversations (Brown, 2012), but the impacts and positive changes that have occurred are often cited as being disproportionately powerful, time after time (Cook-Sather, Chapter 7). Ultimately, with the personal development of students we see the unachieved potential of higher education slowly become more realised. When every student is engaged in pedagogic partnerships (Cook-Sather, Chapter 7), evaluation (Bovill and Woolmer, Chapter 6), educational developments (El Hakim and Lowe, Chapter 5) and enhanced governance structures (Lowe and Bols, Chapter 22), we will see the potential increasingly actualised.

Challenges and future opportunities for educational developer

Educational development (also known as academic development and faculty development) has a universal mission and while the approach and role of educational development in higher education is evolving, the end goal remains the enhancement of the student learning experience. This is reflected in the definition adopted by the International Consortium for Educational Development (ICED)[4] from the work of Brenda Leibowitz (2014).

> *'Academic Development' is about the creation of conditions supportive of teaching and learning, in the broadest sense. This would include the provision of the support, as well as the generation of conditions that are supportive. For me, 'teaching and learning' itself would also include the teaching and learning of academics as well as students.*

Educational developers need to think strategically about how to align our collective ambition to improve learning with those of our universities, organisations and future employers, as our roles as learning designers, academic and educational developers and learning scientists will be in high demand soon.

The demand for the work of academic developers will also require a shift in our conceptualisation of academic development. While Leibowitz's "*the creation of conditions supportive of teaching and learning, in the broadest sense*" is all-encompassing, we can easily, and generally unintentionally, view teaching and learning in a very narrow sense, that is, back to the tips and tricks of teaching and curriculum. What we need to do, as Kathryn Sutherland (2018) suggests, is to take a more holistic view of academic development. We cannot see our work in isolation or restricted to one aspect of academic work.

Sutherland asserts that we should consider all the aspects of an academic's work including research, administration and leadership as well as teaching and take an institution-wide approach, not just a focus on academic staff. And that includes students. Often support of and engagement with students outside the teacher – student (classroom) relationship has been left to professional staff. These professional staff might know our students and their needs and ambitions better than academic staff know them. Academic development needs to embrace all the players, not just in our traditional higher education institutions but those providers emerging and already incorporating education as an integral part of their business.

With the advent and growth of MOOCs and SPOCs (massive, open online courses and small, private online courses, respectively), universities will not be the only ones building expertise in learning science and educational development. For example, private companies Futurelearn and Coursera recently gained investment of £50m and $103M, respectively (O'Grady, 2019; Lunden, 2019). The investment in the development of 'learning pathways' that allow students to learn against set outcomes and concept thresholds, without the cost or commuting times to on-campus experiences, are significant. As soon as these are more acknowledged by employers as key skill development methods, their growth could be exponential given the demand globally for specific skill development. The teams that will build such learning experiences will be highly paid and highly skilled in the science of learning and educational developers should be well-positioned to inform and scale similar learning experiences within and without universities.

In the future following the likes of the University of London accrediting learning pathways from Google, institutions will create the ability for learners to learn from an array of providers and institutions. The University of London currently recognises five courses of the Google IT Support Professional Certificate as constituting prior learning for its BSc degree programmes:

- Technical support fundamentals;
- The bits and bytes of computer networking;
- Operating systems and you: Becoming a power user;
- System administration and IT infrastructure services;
- IT Security: Defence against the digital dark arts.

This is a trend being witnessed globally with many institutions and companies creating learning pathways for such platforms. RMIT University and Deakin University have also created micro-credentials for learners once they have completed pathways. These developments have seen growing popularity globally as the user experience is prioritised and the learning pathways have been gamified to varying extents. The use of learning pathway providers having a radical focus on the learning experience will become a central tenet of educational development within institutions, too. Whether the experience is optimised for the learning process, positive sentiment and/or outcomes, the 'learning experience' will be of paramount importance in a more globally competitive and accessible world, particularly online.

Growing SEEDs (student engagement for educational developments) internationally

The universality of educational development is best evidenced by the professional societies and networks that belong to ICED as member networks. The current 26 member networks represent most regions of the world. More societies and networks exist or are in formative stages with a view to joining ICED and they have the same end goal. The member networks of ICED can be found at www. icedonline.net.

ICED aims:

1. *to help partner organisations develop their capacity for educational development in higher education through the sharing of good practice, problems and solutions;*
2. *to increase the number of partner organisations of ICED;*
3. *to help educational developers in countries where no national network exists to form such a network;*
4. *to support educational development in higher education in developing countries;*
5. *to link with other national and international organisations.*

(ICED, 2019)

These professional societies and networks are passionate, open, engaged, developmental, but most importantly, collegiate communities that promote educational development and the improvement of learning.

Student Engaged Educational Developments (SEEDs) have taken varying forms as demonstrated throughout this book and many international examples have been drawn on as good practice. Students in different universities engaging in different ways and sharing those experiences across a national or an international network of students and staff working together on educational development could: spread good practice more quickly, refine and iterate schemes together and enhance the powerful outputs and impacts even further. An example of this is the Matariki Undergraduate Research Network (MURN)[5] which connected undergraduate researchers investigating learning and teaching from four universities based in four countries – University of Western Australia,

Australia; University of Otago, New Zealand; Durham University, UK; and Queen's University, Canada.

The Staff and Educational Development Association (SEDA)[6] is the UK network for those passionate about improving learning. The examples of SEDA's engagement with students in educational development include: awarding funded places for students to present at conferences, publishing student submissions in *Educational Developments* (SEDA's quarterly magazine), and working in partnership with students as a key stakeholder for national higher education priorities. The Higher Education Research and Development Society of Australasia (HERDSA)[7] similarly supports students to participate in HERDSA conferences both as presenters and panellists. The Hong Kong branch of HERDSA has been very proactive in engaging students in educational development though its Redesigning Student Learning Experience in Higher Education Project.[8] In this project, student teams under the mentorship of academic developers redesigned the learning experiences in their courses in ways that they determined best supported their learning.

As ICED is an international network it could be seen as a fantastic channel to communicate and disseminate students engaging in educational development activities to the other networks, contributing to the achievement of the first and fifth objectives of the international body.

Conclusion

Throughout this book there are a number of key elements of student engagement for educational developments:

1. We learn more from our differences (and different perspectives) than we do from our similarities. The more diverse our communities of practice are, the more we are challenged to empathise with the experiences of others. This can only make our communities stronger and our society more accepting, inclusive and reflective. In so doing, we benefit from the growth of our collective intelligence and productivity. This is re-iterated in the United Nations' Sustainable Development Goals 2030,[9] in particular Goal 4: 'Ensure inclusive and equitable quality education and promote lifelong learning opportunities for all' – which now seeks to increase participation, engagement, progression and success of marginalised and disadvantaged communities.
2. Even the most empowering of student engagement schemes will still struggle with inherent power relations within their structures. The need for student empowerment among students engaged in educational developments (SEEDs) is illustrated and discussed given the benefits of creating openness, trust and transparency through such schemes.
3. Students engaged in educational development could have a substantial impact on the educational system of the future, beyond today's relatively

limited impact, as cited by Bryson (Chapter 21). If certain principles are successfully applied (El Hakim and Lowe, Chapter 5), the impact that SEEDs could have globally could be enhanced further and sustained indefinitely, whilst empowering the growth of the educational institutions that engage in this way through facilitation of online communities and learners.

4. Relationships are central to student engagement and peer engagement, like peer-assisted learning schemes, may be essential for widespread scalability and for creating a strong community of practice.
5. Actualising student potential to impact and improve the learning experiences and environments of other students through partnership creates clear benefits for all.

The concept of student engagement is nothing new. Ideas often become topical for a short while but fall away due to inertia and resistance to change within the academy at all levels, including students.

The teacher is no longer merely the-one-who teaches, but one who is himself taught in dialogue with students, who in turn while being taught also teach. They become jointly responsible for a process in which all grow.

(Freire, 1981:67)

Let us continue as an academic community, with a passionate movement taking root and growing, so that we can ensure students are empowered and engaged in educational developments to continue to broaden our community and the dialogue. Let us persist through any resistance presented and embrace the need for transparency, diversity, ownership, trust and collaboration in our society, within higher education and beyond.

Notes

1 BCUR (British Conference of Undergraduate Research) Available at: www.bcur.org/ (accessed 31 August 2019).
2 Github ONLINE Available at: https://github.com/ (accessed 31 August 2019).
3 RAISE (Researching, Advancing and Inspiring Student Engagement) Available at: www.raise-network.com/home/ (accessed 31 August 2019).
4 ICED (The International Consortium for Educational Development) Available at: https://icedonline.net/ (accessed 31 August 2019).
5 MURN (Matariki Undergraduate Research Network) ONLINE: www.matarikinetwork.org/education/matariki-undergraduate-research-network/ Available at: (accessed 31 August 2019).
6 SEDA (Staff Educational Development Association) Available at: www.seda.ac.uk/ (accessed 31 August 2019).

7 HERDSA (Higher Education Research and Development Society of Australasia) Available at: www.herdsa.org.au/ (accessed 31 August 2019).

8 HERDSA (Higher Education Research and Development Society of Australasia) *Redesigning Student Learning Experience in Higher Education – HERDSA HK Student Project Report 2017*. Available at: http://herdsahk. edublogs.org/2019/06/05/redesigning-student-learning-experience-in-higher-education-herdsa-hk-student-project-report-2017/ (accessed 31 August 2019).

9 United Nations Sustainable Development Goals 2030. Available at: https:// sustainabledevelopment.un.org/?menu=1300 (accessed 31 August 2019).

References

Bell, A.R. and Brooks, C., 2016. Is There a Magic Link between Research Activity, Professional Teaching Qualifications and Student Satisfaction? Retrieved from: https://ssrn.com/abstract=2712412 (accessed 27 August 2019)

Chickering, A. W. and Gamson, Z. F., 1987. Seven Principles for Good Practice in Undergraduate Education. *Wingspread Journal*, 9, 1–10. Retrieved from: https:// doi.org/10.1016/0307-4412(89)90094-0

Cook-Sather, A. and Felten, P., 2017. Ethics of academic leadership: guiding learning and teaching. In Frank Wu and Margaret Wood (eds.), *Cosmopolitan Perspectives on Becoming an Academic Leader in Higher Education* (pp.175–191). London: Bloomsbury Academic.

Cook-Sather, A., Bovill, C. and Felten, P., 2014. *Engaging students as partners in learning and teaching: a guide for faculty*. San Francisco, CA: Jossey-Bass.

CUSU, 2019. Boycott the NSS. Retrieved from: www.cusu.co.uk/takeaction/boycott-the-nss/ (accessed 28 August 2019).

Fung, D., 2017. A Connected Curriculum for Higher Education. London, UCL Press.

Gardiner, L. F., 1997. Redesigning higher education: producing dramatic gains in student learning. ASHE-ERIC Higher Education Report 7. Washington, DC: Association for the Study of Higher Education.

Gibbs, G., 2011. *Dimensions of Quality*. Higher Education Academy. Retrieved from: www.heacademy.ac.uk/system/files/dimensions_of_quality.pdf (accessed 20 August 2019).

Healey, M., 2009. Research Informed Teaching. Conference presentation at the University of Winchester

Higher Education Policy Institute (HEPI), 2006. *The Academic Experience of Students in English Universities*. Oxford: Higher Education Policy Institute.

Higher Education Policy Institute (HEPI), 2007. *The Academic Experience of Students in English Universities*. Oxford: Higher Education Policy Institute.

Jessop, J., El Hakim, Y. and Gibbs, G., 2014. The whole is greater than the sum of its parts: a large-scale study of students' learning in response to different programme assessment patterns. *Assessment and Evaluation in Higher Education*, 39(1), 73–88. Retrieved from: https://doi.org/10.1080/02602938.2013.792108

Jones, S., 2017. *Leading the Academy: Distributed Leadership in Higher Education*. Australia: Higher Education Research and Development Society of Australasia.

Leibowitz, B., 2014. Reflections on academic development: what is in a name? *International Journal for Academic Development*, 19(4), 357–360. Retrieved from: https://doi.org/10.1080/1360144x.2014.969978

Lunden, I., 2019. Online learning startup Coursera picks up $103M, now valued at $1B+. TechCrunch. Retrieved from: https://techcrunch.com/2019/04/25/online-learning-startup-coursera-picks-up-103m-now-valued-at-1b/?guccounter=1andguce_referrer_us=aHR0cHM6Ly93d3d3cuZ29vZ2xlLmNvbS8a ndguce_referrer_cs=mUyBcZHjr7GzJam8ovQNHQ (accessed 20 August 2019).

Mageau, G.A. and Vallerand, R.J., 2003. The coach–athlete relationship: a motivational model. *Journal of Sport Sciences*, 21, 883–904.

Maslow, A. H., 1943. A Theory of Human Motivation. *Psychological Review*, 50(4), 370–96.

Matthews, K., Cook-Sather, A., Acai, A., Dvorakova, S., Felten, P., Marquis, E. and Mercer-Mapstone, L., 2019. Toward theories of partnership praxis: an analysis of interpretative framing in literature on students as partners in teaching and learning. *Higher Education Research and Development*, 38(2), 280–293. Retrieved from: https://doi.org/10.1080/07294360.2018.1530199

Matthews, K., 2016. Students as partners as the future of student engagement. *Student Engagement in Higher Education Journal*, 1(1), 1–5. Retrieved from: https://espace.library.uq.edu.au/view/UQ:404147/UQ404147_OA.pdf

Mercer-Mapstone, L., Dvorakova, S.L, Matthews, K.E., Abbot, S., Cheng, B., Felten, P., Knorr, K, Marquis, E., Shammas, R. and Swaim, K., 2017. A systematic literature review of students as partners in higher education. *International Journal for Students as Partners*, 1 (1), 1–23. Retrieved from: https://doi.org/10.15173/ijsap.v1i1.3119

Northouse, P.G., 2010. *Leadership: Theory and Practice*. London: Sage Publications.

O'Grady, N., 2019. The Open University secures £50M investment in social learning platform FutureLearn. Retrieved from: https://about.futurelearn.com/press-releases/the-open-university-secures-50m-investment-in-social-learning-platform-futurelearn (accessed 20 August 2019).

Pascarella, E.T., Seifert, T.A. and Blaich, C., 2008. Validation of the NSSE benchmarks and deep approaches to learning against liberal arts outcomes. Paper presented at the annual meeting of the Association for the Study of Higher Education, Jacksonville, FL. Retrieved from: www.researchgate.net/profile/Tricia_Seifert/publication/228381194_Validation_of_the_NSSE_Benchmarks_and_deep_approaches_to_learning_against_liberal_arts_outcomes/links/00b7d531e5cf13887b000000.pdf

Spillane, J. P., Halverson, R. and Diamond, J. B., 2004. Towards a theory of leadership practice: A distributed perspective. *Journal of Curriculum Studies*, 36, 3–34.

Sutherland, K. A., 2018. Holistic academic development: Is it time to think more broadly about the academic development project? *International Journal for Academic Development*, 23(4), 261–273. Retrieved from: https://doi.org/10.1080/1360144x.2018.1524571

The Independent, 2011, *Google searches for young Einstein's*. Retrieved from: www.independent.co.uk/life-style/gadgets-and-tech/news/google-offers-50000-prize-in-search-for-young-einsteins-2183193.html (accessed 20 August 2019).

Trigwell, K. and Ashwin, P., 2004. Undergraduate students' experience at the University of Oxford. Oxford: Oxford Learning Institute. In Gibbs, G. (ed.),

2011. *Dimensions of Quality*. Higher Education Academy. Retrieved from: www.heacademy.ac.uk/system/files/dimensions_of_quality.pdf (accessed 20 August 2019).

UNESCO, 2017. Six ways to ensure higher education leaves no one behind. Retrieved from: www.ungei.org/6_ways_to_ensure.pdf (accessed 20 August 2019).

Index